GOVERNING THE ENVIRONMENT

The Transformation of Environmental Regulation

Marc Allen Eisner

LYNNE
RIENNER
PUBLISHERS

BOULDER
LONDON

Published in the United States of America in 2007 by
Lynne Rienner Publishers, Inc.
1800 30th Street, Boulder, Colorado 80301
www.rienner.com

and in the United Kingdom by
Lynne Rienner Publishers, Inc.
3 Henrietta Street, Covent Garden, London WC2E 8LU

Library of Congress Cataloging-in-Publication Data
Eisner, Marc Allen.
  Governing the environment : the transformation of environmental regulation /
Marc Allen Eisner.
       p. cm.
  Includes bibliographical references and index.
  ISBN-13: 978-1-58826-460-2 (hardcover : alk. paper)
  ISBN-10: 1-58826-460-2 (hardcover : alk. paper)
  ISBN-13: 978-1-58826-485-5 (pbk. : alk. paper)
  ISBN-10: 1-58826-485-8 (pbk. : alk. paper)
  1. Environmental policy—United States. 2. United States—Politics and government—
2001– 3. Environmentalism—Political aspects—United States. I. Title.
GE180.E47 2006
363.7'05610973—dc22

                                                          2006024722

British Cataloguing in Publication Data
A Cataloguing in Publication record for this book
is available from the British Library.

Printed and bound in the United States of America

 The paper used in this publication meets the requirements
of the American National Standard for Permanence of
Paper for Printed Library Materials Z39.48-1992.

    5   4   3   2   1

GOVERNING THE
ENVIRONMENT

For Patricia

Contents

Figures and Tables

■ Figures

■ Tables

Preface

The arguments and research reflected in this book were presented at various meetings and conferences, and the book has benefited greatly from the comments of discussants and colleagues at those venues. As I offered my work for professional consumption, I was simultaneously "field testing" the book. For the past several years, I have taught a course at Wesleyan University organized around the central arguments in the book. I lectured through this material, assigned draft chapters and supporting documents, and invited my students to offer their critiques. Thankfully, because Wesleyan students are a rather contentious lot, they have been delighted to comply. While some students reflexively rejected discussions of markets, property rights, and corporate environmentalism, most were willing to consider the evidence and entertain the argument that future gains in environmental quality may in fact require the integration of public regulation and private sector initiatives in a larger system of environmental governance.

I began this project in 2000, and it has never been far from my mind, whether while scaling the mountains of New England with my wife, Patricia, and our sons, Benjamin and Jonathan, walking the windswept shores of Lake Michigan with my parents, searching for woodcocks in the Connecticut dawn with Jack Perruccio and Sadie, tracking deer through the forests of western Wisconsin with Barry Rumpel and my brother Naben, or discussing rural homesteading and the "good life" with my brother Joel in the hills of North Carolina. They have weathered my lengthy descriptions of the project and deepened my love of nature. They have taught me the meaning of stewardship through the examples they have set with their lives. Although I assume responsibility for all errors of omission and commission in this volume, much of the motivation for this work must be attributed to the friends, students, and colleagues who have shaped my understanding of the environment and our place in it.

Environmental Protection and Governance: An Introduction

The commitment to economic growth grounded in private property, free enterprise, and market exchange created unprecedented employment opportunities, incomes, and consumption choices in the United States; it also produced growing environmental degradation that became the source of growing public concern in the late 1960s. In 1970, President Richard Nixon and Congress responded to the wave of environmental concern by creating the Environmental Protection Agency (EPA) and passing landmark legislation that set the legal and institutional foundations for the contemporary environmental era. Subsequent decades would be punctuated by sharp political conflicts and hyperbolic rhetoric linking the EPA to a long list of maladies, including inflation, unemployment, and a loss of international competitiveness. Today, after nearly four decades, environmental protection policy is the most heavily funded regulatory responsibility in the United States—and, many would suggest, the most important. Although the EPA's budget is the largest of all federal regulatory agencies ($7.6 billion in 2006), it pales in comparison to the costs borne by state and local regulatory governments, by corporations, and ultimately by consumers and taxpayers.

The EPA has never had a shortage of critics. Yet there is clear empirical evidence that its regulatory efforts have contributed to significant gains in environmental quality. There have been considerable achievements in the control of air and water pollution and solid and toxic wastes since the first Earth Day in 1970. This success is remarkable for several reasons. First, one must acknowledge the sheer complexity of the tasks involved. The EPA is responsible for regulating the generation and disposal of air, water, and solid wastes by virtually all companies in the United States. For this to occur, it must develop the scientific data to understand how various pollutants interact and pose threats to the health of human beings and a variety of ecosystems. It must translate the scientific determinations into policies managing the behavior of a diverse universe of public and private organizations. To accomplish these tasks, the EPA must work at the intersection of multiple scientific and social scientific disciplines and evolving research programs.

Second, the EPA has been responsible for enforcing regulatory statutes that are both highly complex and at times difficult to reconcile. Cognizant that the new environmental initiatives could be undermined by changes in the party composition of the presidency or future Congresses buffeted by mobilized interest groups, legislators wrote exhaustive regulatory statutes that defined the EPA's responsibilities with extraordinary detail. Congress severely constrained the agency's discretionary authority to set its own regulatory agenda, redeploy budgetary resources, and explore various means of managing pollution. It also sought to protect the new policies by providing environmental interest groups with the right to sue the EPA to force it to execute its nondiscretionary functions. Thus the technical complexity inherent in policy was mirrored by a procedural and administrative complexity unparalleled in other regulatory agencies.

Third, the nature and distribution of costs and benefits have created a remarkably difficult political climate. The costs of environmental policy are both significant and concentrated. They create strong incentives for businesses to mobilize in opposition to policy and in opposition to the EPA more generally. The political impact of these costs is only amplified by sharp partisan divisions and congressional localism. At the same time, benefits are often diffuse, probabilistic, and located in a distant future. By imposing regulatory controls, the EPA can reduce the magnitude of environmental risk, but the risks as experienced by individual citizens may not be great enough to create incentives to mobilize in support of policy. One should not be surprised that the EPA has been embroiled in controversies throughout its history. Although these controversies have not resulted in regulatory retrenchment, they have foreclosed any expansion of the EPA's mandate (e.g., the last significant changes to US air pollution laws occurred in 1990). Moreover, the EPA's budget has failed to keep pace with the growth of the economy and, when adjusted for inflation, has not grown since the mid-1970s.

Although the EPA's achievements to date are rather impressive, there is reason for concern. Many fear that this record of achievement may not extend into the future unless significant changes are made in the design of the US system of environmental protection. Further progress will require a shift from end-of-the-pipe controls to pollution prevention. This, in turn, requires changes in product and process design that are simply beyond the reach of public policy. A central goal of this book is to explore the potential for a significant reformation of the system of environmental protection. The core argument, to be developed throughout the following chapters, is simply stated: Over the course of the past several decades, there have been a number of important innovations in the private sector, including advances in corporate environmental management, the development of environmental codes by trade associations, and the global dissemination of international environmental standards. These innovations have come in response to a complex set of factors, including regulatory requirements and the desire to preempt new regulations, corporate concerns over liability, and pressures from consumer markets, financial markets, and corporate supply chains. These innovations may not be a substitute for public regulation. However, if they are integrated into public regulation in a meaningful fashion, they can provide a means of getting at precisely the set of issues that are central to pollution prevention. This integration would involve transforming traditional environmental regulation into a system of environmental governance wherein regulators, standard-setting organizations, associations, and corporations act with greater coordination to address a commonly recognized set of problems. The core elements of this system are currently in place. The question is whether they will be integrated or whether they will exist as systems that sometimes reinforce, and sometimes conflict with, one another.

■ Overview of the Book

This volume is designed to expansively and critically analyze the potential for transitioning to a system of environmental governance without simultaneously sacrificing the significant advances in environmental quality realized over the course of the past several decades. In Part 1, by necessity, we begin with an overview of environmental policy and politics. Chapter 2 provides a primer on environmental regulation, exploring the justification for environmental regulation, the array of policy instruments available to regulators, and the core regulatory statutes enforced by the EPA. Chapter 3 turns to the environmental policy subsystem (e.g., the EPA, Congress, the presidency, the bureaucracy, the courts, and the interest group universe). This examination provides an overview of the complex set of political-institutional actors involved in the definition and implementation of environmental policy.

The chapters that constitute Part 2 of the volume explore the original regulatory design decisions and subsequent efforts to manage some of the negative consequences of these decisions. Chapter 4 examines regulatory design and performance. When Congress passed the major environmental protection statutes of the 1970s, it made an explicit decision to employ command-and-control regulatory instruments. That is, regulations dictated pollution control technologies for broad classes of companies and imposed ambitious compliance timetables backed with significant penalties. It would have been impossible to tailor regulatory requirements to meet the specific technologies and processes in each regulated firm. The decision to apply a "one size fits all" approach (or, more accurately, a "one size fits many" approach) allowed for greater certainty of results under conditions of information scarcity. However, it resulted in the imposition of extraordinary compliance costs. Some firms were overregulated, others were underregulated; few would suggest that the solutions prescribed by policy constituted the most cost-effective means of controlling pollutants. But this was a trade-off that Congress was willing to make. Even though regulatory design has resulted in unnecessary costs and rigidities, the EPA has been a qualified success. Yet as will be argued, advocates' efforts to keep environmental protection on the agenda by portraying an environment in crisis undercut public recognition of the EPA's performance record, thereby creating the political space for ongoing reform efforts.

During the 1970s, poor macroeconomic performance combined with heightened business mobilization to create ongoing pressure for reform. Each president responded by imposing elaborate review processes that forced regulators to take costs into account, thereby challenging the original regulatory design decisions and adding another level of complexity to environmental policy. These efforts are explored in Chapter 5. By the 1990s, many recognized that environmental policies had generated positive results; the largest corporations were now in compliance (or "beyond compliance" in many cases). Yet there were concerns that further advances would be limited as long as environmental policy was constrained by original regulatory design decisions. Thus the Clinton administration worked to "reinvent" regulation and make the EPA more responsive, flexible, and results-oriented, and to create new partnerships to reinforce policy. Reinvention was hamstrung, however, by original regulatory design decisions; it was difficult to integrate the new partnerships into a regulatory system premised on command-and-control instruments and adversarial relationships with business, as explored in Chapter 6. During the George W. Bush presidency, voluntary partnerships have continued to flourish. Yet given the slow rate of regulatory rule making and the dearth of well-developed regulatory initiatives, partnerships have been embraced as a substitute for policy rather than a means of improving regulation, as explored in Chapter 7.

When thinking of environmental protection, it is common to imagine regulating factories with bellowing smokestacks and mills pouring endless streams of sludge into nearby waterways. Yet seldom considered are the myriad decisions made by corporations on a daily basis regarding product design, the selection of inputs, and the disposition of multiple waste streams—decisions that have enormous environmental ramifications even if they are largely invisible to external observers. Pollution prevention requires many changes in product and process design at the level of the firm. These changes cannot be imposed from above using traditional regulatory instruments. Rather it may be necessary to delegate greater authority to corporations, which possess the greatest knowledge about their technologies, products, and markets, and to create incentives for innovations in pollution control and prevention. This, in turn, raises important questions regarding the monitoring of corporate compliance and the maintenance of some semblance of public accountability. Without some means of forcing accountability, "reform" may be little more than an abdication of regulatory responsibility.

As noted above, the past two decades have witnessed some rather remarkable innovations in the private sector. These innovations are the subject of Part 3 of the book. Corporations are increasingly integrating environmental concerns and business strategies, designing products with the goal of minimizing waste flows, and implementing environmental management systems to systematically reduce pollution. This trend in corporate environmentalism is the subject of Chapter 8. Trade associations have also embarked upon some interesting self-regulatory efforts, in many cases requiring their members to abide by ambitious environmental codes subject to third-party certification. Moreover, the International Organization for Standardization has promulgated a set of standards for environmental management systems requiring third-party certification. These code- and standard-based systems of self-regulation are examined in Chapter 9. The question remains: How can one integrate such initiatives with policy? Chapter 10 offers an initial response to this question by examining hybrid forms of regulation, including the Dutch covenants and the EPA's National Environmental Performance Track.

Global environmental protection is the topic of Part 4 of the volume. At present, there are few credible international environmental regulatory institutions. For international regulatory institutions to be effective, they must be able to impose regulations on nation-states, monitor compliance, and impose credible sanctions for noncompliance. A number of factors militate against the creation of such institutions, as discussed in Chapter 11. Yet the lack of such institutions need not be definitive in foreclosing a search for cooperative solutions. The Montreal Protocol, which addresses substances that deplete the ozone layer, provides an example of successful international cooperation in banning chlorofluorocarbons. The success of the Montreal Protocol gave hope to many that such agreements could provide a means of managing other global environmental problems, such as biodiversity and climate change. Yet one must question whether the protocol's success was the product of a unique set of factors (e.g., a strong scientific consensus, supportive public opinion, preexisting domestic commitments backed by domestic regulatory agencies) that are absent in the area of climate change. Chapter 12 compares the Montreal Protocol to the Kyoto Protocol, which addresses global climate change.

The Montreal and Kyoto Protocols seek to address discrete environmental problems. But these problems pale in complexity compared to the larger issue of sustainable development. Beginning in the early 1990s, many environmental analysts and the United Nations called on countries to take seriously the need for sustainable development, and to change the trajectory of economic development, in order to prevent further degradation and to ensure that future generations have opportunities comparable to those available today. Chapter 13 examines the sustainable development debates in detail. Pursuant to Agenda 21, countries formed national councils on sustainable development to explore how domestic policies and practices might be tailored to promote sustainability. In the United States, the President's Council on Sustainable Development recommended a number of changes that would involve heavy reliance on some of the innovations examined in Chapters 8–10. Whether the concept of "sustainable development" is a useful focus for policy, the council envisioned a system in which cooperation would replace adversarialism, leading ideally to a politically sustainable system of governance.

To what extent can any of the alternative approaches to environmental protection offer a solution to domestic and global challenges? In the absence of such institutions, can sufficient gains be made by reconfiguring policy to promote pollution prevention efforts on the part of corporations, and to harness market forces to reinforce regulatory goals? In concluding the volume, Chapter 14 develops a broad proposal for genuine regulatory reinvention in the United States. The core argument is that the current system of environmental regulation must be transformed into a system of environmental governance, one that seeks the integration of standard public policy tools, market forces, and association and standard-based self-regulation. Before this argument can be developed with sufficient care, we must examine in greater detail the EPA and the larger policy subsystem responsible for making and implementing policy.

Part 1

Environmental Policy and Politics

A Primer on
Environmental Protection

The term "regulation" describes public policies that are explicitly designed to manage economic activity and its consequences at the level of the economy, the industry, or corporation (or, where appropriate, bank, labor union, or farm). Environmental protection policies are regulatory policies designed to manage pollution and its negative consequences for human health and environmental quality more generally. Since environmental protection is a form of regulatory policy, this chapter begins with a discussion of regulation. Second, it explores the key regulatory instruments that are used to manage the environment. Finally, it provides an overview of the key legislative foundations for the regulation of air pollution, water pollution, and hazardous and toxic wastes. A discussion of the environmental policy subsystem is reserved for Chapter 3.

■ Understanding Regulation

Policy analysts often draw a distinction between economic and social regulations. Economic regulations are public policies that govern the conditions under which firms may enter and exist in the market, their competitive practices, the permissible size of economic units, the flow to market, and the prices that they can charge. Agencies like the Securities and Exchange Commission, the Federal Communications Commission, and the US Department of Agriculture are examples of economic regulatory agencies. As these examples suggest, economic regulatory agencies commonly regulate on an industry-specific basis and convey benefits to regulated parties (e.g., protection from competition, price-fixing authority, and direct subsidies). There are exceptions, of course. Antitrust policy regulates competitive conditions on an economywide basis; the agencies that enforce the antitrust statutes have economywide jurisdiction.

Social regulations, in contrast, are public policies that force firms to exercise greater responsibility for the health and safety of workers and consumers and the negative byproducts of the production process. Major social regulatory agencies include the Occupational Safety and Health Administration, the Consumer Product Safety Commission, and the Environmental Protection Agency. Social regulatory agencies tend to have economywide regulatory authority and impose concentrated costs on regulated parties (e.g., by mandating pollution control technologies) and diffuse benefits for the population as a whole (e.g., a reduced prevalence of pollution-related illnesses or product-related injuries). Most economic regulatory agencies were created during the Progressive Era and the New Deal, whereas the major social regulatory agencies were created during the 1970s to force higher levels of corporate accountability.

Theories of Regulation

There are many competing theories of why we regulate. The most elemental and least developed is the public interest theory of regulation. One hesitates to label this as a "theory" at all. Rather it is, more correctly, a broad normative assumption that government as a public trust acts to keep private interests in check (see, e.g., Redford 1954). Although appeals to "the public interest" make good political rhetoric, public interest theory does little to define what constitutes the public interest, nor does it offer much to explain why and how we actually regulate. Nonetheless, many early regulatory statutes delegated tremendous authority to regulatory agencies and directed them to regulate "in the public interest." This act of delegation reflected a great optimism regarding the capabilities of agencies like the Interstate Commerce Commission and the Federal Trade Commission to execute their duties with political neutrality and professional expertise (see Eisner 1991). Unfortunately, their optimism was often unjustified.

Many economic regulatory agencies became subject to regulatory capture. That is, rather than regulating to protect the public, they began to act on behalf of the regulated industries. Some analysts suggest that capture occurred because the original constituencies supporting the agencies in question declined over time, forcing regulators to seek political support from the industries themselves (Bernstein 1955; Huntington 1952). The economic theory of regulation, in contrast, explains capture as the inevitable product of a political exchange. A regulated industry provides political support to key legislators, who in turn direct agencies to act in such a way as to benefit the industries in question (e.g., by creating barriers to entry, and price supports). Citizen-consumers often fail to oppose these policies because they are unaware of their existence, or because the costs are so broadly diffused that they are easily exceeded by the costs of mobilization (Stigler 1971). One response to this state of affairs was a wave of deregulation in the 1970s, which culminated in the elimination of many regulatory policies and agencies.

Of course, capture should be highly improbable in social regulatory agencies due to their imposition of concentrated costs and diffuse benefits. Nonetheless, there are ample opportunities for rent- or transfer-seeking wherein organized interests exchange political support for policies that produce benefits for group members while imposing the costs on the unorganized or poorly organized (see Buchanan, Tollison, and Tullock 1980; Rauch 1999). This rent-seeking is often difficult to detect, because the policies may be the product of underlying "Bootlegger-Baptist" coalitions, a term introduced by Bruce Yandle (1983) in reference to the coalitions that supported local laws banning the sale of liquor on Sundays. Thus, Congress may design legislation that meets the demands of environmentalists (the Baptists) by promoting more stringent air pollution regulations, while simultaneously catering to select economic actors (the bootleggers) by fashioning requirements that impose higher standards on new entrants in order to restrict competition. In the end, the creation of Bootlegger-Baptist coalitions may guarantee passage while sacrificing effectiveness (see Yandle 2000). Regional political-economic coalitions have often played the bootlegger role in environmental policy, using regulations to impede the relocation of industries to other regions (see Bensel 1984; Sanders 1987).

To be fair, many who use the phrase "public interest" equate it with the use of policy to prevent or compensate for various forms of market failure. Markets fail for numerous reasons. For example, there may be externalities when costs and benefits are not captured by prices. Pollution is the classic example of a negative externality. When society (rather than the consumer) bears the costs of pollution, it subsidizes the products in question, leading to higher levels of consumption than would exist under normal circumstances. The existence of public goods provides a second source of market failure. Such goods, like national defense, can only be enjoyed collectively; one's consumption of the public good does not detract from others' consumption (the condition of "nonrivalry in consumption"). Moreover, those who do not contribute to the provision of the good cannot be effectively excluded from its consumption (the condition of "nonexcludability"). Free-riding becomes endemic and the public good is provided at inadequate levels—if at all—by the market. Information scarcity provides a third source of market failure, insofar as information is necessary for rational actors to make decisions about how to further their own self-interest. Transaction costs (i.e., the costs of searching for information, negotiating contracts, and enforcing contracts after they have been executed) constitute a fourth source of market failure. If transaction costs become sufficiently large, they can prevent parties from executing mutually beneficial exchanges. Finally, perfect markets require that all actors function as price takers rather than price makers—the situation that prevails when firms conspire to fix prices.

Governments can impose policies to prevent or compensate for various forms of market failure. Negative externalities like pollution can be managed through regulatory policies mandating the use of specific control technologies, the costs of which are incorporated into prices. With respect to public goods, government can impose taxes to force all beneficiaries to contribute. Alternatively, in some cases government can establish private property rights over what was once a public good, thereby creating greater incentives for stewardship. Information scarcities can be managed through regulations that force mandatory information disclosure. For example, regulations require that banks disclose all of the costs associated with loans so that consumers can make an informed decision. However, to say that policies can address one or another source of market failure is not to say that market failure provides a sufficient justification for policy. Indeed, many regulatory policies nominally address sources of market failure while furthering interests that are distinctly private. Since this point may appear counterintuitive, let us explore it in greater detail.

Legislation requiring pollution control technologies or new protective technologies on the shop floor may be crafted artfully to impose greater costs on new facilities, thereby creating regulatory barriers to entry that benefit established companies. Insofar as this new investment may have embodied better technologies, the ultimate victim may be the environment, workers, or the public more generally. Mobilized interests have become quite adept, through the use of regulations that appear to further the public interest, at securing advantages that would not be available through normal market competition. In so doing, the good that could be accomplished via policy may be grossly compromised. Costs may be imposed on consumers in the name of the public interest despite the fact that they are designed, in large part, to allow a given industry or set of firms to claim pecuniary gains. The key point is not that all regulations serve as a Trojan horse for private interests. Rather it is that blanket generalizations regarding the public interest component of regulation are difficult to sustain.

Although there are clearly some public goods dimensions to environmental quality (particularly with respect to nonexcludability), when the theory of market failure is used to make the case for environmental protection regulation, it is usually through reference to the existence of negative externalities. Pollution is correctly understood as a negative externality, a cost of production that is not incorporated into the price of the resulting goods and services. To control these externalities, governments can force corporations to "internalize" these costs. The key question is one of means: How will regulators force regulated parties to meet their obligations? This is a question best addressed by turning to the issue of regulatory instruments.

■ Regulatory Instruments and Environmental Protection

Regulators have a wealth of different kinds of policy instruments to choose from. The regulatory model adopted in the United States has placed a great reliance on command-and-control instruments. Government essentially *commands* businesses to adopt specific standards and *controls* their behavior through the imposition of negative sanctions (Sinclair 1997: 534). Technology-based standards mandate the use of a particular technology and are usually presented in broad terms that reference the state-of-the-art at the time. The EPA, for example, employs several technology-based standards, ranging from "best practicable control technology currently available," which is sensitive to current industry practices and the interplay of costs and benefits, to "best available control technology," which requires the most stringent technology available without reference to cost. Of course, there are various intermediate categories (e.g., "best demonstrated control technology"). The movement from one end of the spectrum to the other is usually phased in over a multiyear period, and different standards are often applied to existing facilities and new construction.

In contrast, regulators may apply performance-based standards, which establish maximum levels of pollution compatible with regulatory goals. In environmental protection, two kinds of performance standards are prevalent. Ambient standards address the concentration of key pollutants in a given area, whereas emission standards regulate the amount of pollution that can be discharged from a specific source. The two are often related, insofar as regulators may seek to meet ambient standards through the imposition of emission standards. Although regulators may provide regulated parties with the flexibility to choose among an array of pollution control methods, performance-based standards are frequently combined with technology-based standards. For example, under the 1970 amendments to the Clean Air Act, the EPA established national ambient air quality standards for a list of six pollutants. State regulators, in turn, compiled implementation plans that detailed how air quality regions would be brought into attainment. This usually involved prescribing specific technology standards for pollution sources. The combination of performance- and technology-based standards makes great sense: the latter can be embodied in permits to facilitate monitoring and enforcement.

In contrast to command-and-control regulation, policymakers may adopt market-based instruments (see Tietenberg 1990). "Market-based instruments . . . encourage behavior through market signals rather than through explicit directives regarding pollution control levels or methods." They "are often described as 'harnessing market forces' because if they are well designed and implemented, they encourage firms (and/or individuals) to undertake pollution control efforts that are in their own interest and that collectively meet policy goals" (Stavins 2000: 1). There are a variety of market-based instruments. Pollution taxes, for example, can be charged to a firm based on the amount of pollution it generates. In theory, firms will reduce their level of pollution to the point where the tax is equal to the marginal cost of abatement. However, regulators may lack information on abatement costs, which may vary dramatically across firms and over time. As a result, while pollution taxes make great theoretical sense, regulators may not be able to predict in advance the impact that a given rate of taxation will have on aggregate levels of pollution (see Cropper and Oates 1992).

In response to these shortcomings, there has been considerable interest in cap-and-trade systems. Regulators can determine in advance an acceptable level of pollution (the cap) and issue credits allowing for pollution up to the prescribed level. Credits can be purchased, sold, or saved for future use (something that is referred to as "pollution banking"). On a periodic basis, firms are required to provide regulators with credits covering their emissions, and incur fines for any excess pollution. If the fines are sufficiently onerous, companies will have strong incentives to possess sufficient pollution credits. Cap-and-trade systems carry a number of advantages. First, regulators can specify in advance a desired level of pollution, thereby eliminating the uncertainties inherent in pollution taxes. Second, because credits are tradable, there can be greater incentives for firms with a comparative advantage in abatement to go beyond regulatory standards. Because firms with a comparative disadvantage in abatement can purchase credits, the system should generate greater efficiencies, thereby allowing society to achieve a given level of pollution reduction at the lowest possible cost.

Despite these advantages, proposals for tradable permits are often embroiled in controversy. Critics may shudder at the thought of purchasing the right to pollute, assuming (incorrectly) that pollution is a completely avoidable act. The normative concerns may not be assuaged by verifiable claims of effectiveness and efficiency. Moreover, critics often fear that trading may not be appropriate in some cases, because it could result in higher levels of pollution in certain areas, creating "hot spots." Businesses are often concerned that decisions regarding the allocation of permits (e.g., should they be auctioned or grandfathered) could prove disadvantageous for some firms. These objections have often created great opposition to pollution trading (Hahn and Hester 1989; Keohane, Revesz, and Stavins 1998). Where trading has been introduced on a voluntary basis, regulators have often imposed a host of costs (e.g., expensive pollution modeling, taxes on banked credits), thereby creating disincentives for participation (see EPA 2001d).

Regulators, moreover, may use mandatory information disclosure as a regulatory instrument. For example, under the Toxic Release Inventory, companies are legally required to disclose their use of various toxic chemicals. This information is made available to the public, in part, on the assumption that disclosure will create incentives for firms to reduce their use of toxic chemicals. Similarly, the Securities and Exchange Commission requires firms to disclose significant environmental liabilities (e.g., Superfund sites) on the belief that such information may prove important for investors. Information disclosure on things such as fuel efficiency and recycled content may create incentives for higher levels of environmental stewardship. Although mandatory disclosure does not dictate outcomes, "if designed properly, information disclosure should cause firms to engage in a process of 'critical self-assessment' that will induce them to make steady improvements in environmental performance" (Fiorino 2004: 410).

Property rights and legal liability may serve as important policy tools as well. Under the common-law theories of negligence or nuisance, parties may be held liable for environmental damages. If there are well-defined property rights, one can assume that parties will have an incentive to monitor behavior that might compromise the value of their property and to defend their rights via the court system. Unfortunately, information scarcity and transaction costs may limit the efficacy of liability under common-law doctrines (see Coase 1960). In contrast, Congress can establish statutory liability, as it did through the Comprehensive Environmental Response, Compensation, and Liability Act (CERCLA) of 1980, which created a mechanism for evaluating abandoned hazardous waste sites and assessing liability for cleanup costs (Friedman, Downing, and Gunn 2000: 327). Unlike standard liability, under CERCLA the EPA bears much of the costs of collecting information on pollution and pursuing potentially responsible parties.

Our discussion of regulatory policy instruments must be refined with an important caveat. It is common to view regulatory instruments as mutually exclusive—one must select command-and-control instruments or market-based instruments, for example. This characterization may obscure the importance of various instrument mixes (Sinclair 1997). Indeed, policy instruments are less fruitfully viewed as mutually exclusive alternatives than as tools that may be used in conjunction. Consider a simple example: Several state regulators and the EPA have experimented with regulatory green tracks since the 1990s. Green tracks provide special benefits (e.g., reduced inspection priority and streamlined reporting) for firms with a documented history of strong environmental performance and quality environmental management systems. Such experiments may prove successful, in part, because regulators have successfully combined multiple policy instruments. Although authority is delegated to regulated parties, traditional command-and-control regulatory instruments remain in force to create incentives for meetings one's obligations.

Instrument Choice

The choice of policy instruments is shaped by a host of criteria, including certainty of results, cost (e.g., economic efficiency), administrative feasibility (e.g., demands of enforcement, compatibility with existing laws), robustness (i.e., effectiveness under a variety of circumstances), corrigibility (i.e., flexibility and reversibility), timeliness (i.e., the capacity to provide rapid results), dynamic efficiency (i.e., impact on incentives to innovate), public acceptance, and compatibility with normative values. Certainly, trade-offs must be made among competing values. Instruments that are robust may not fare well with respect to efficiency. Instruments that are efficient may run afoul of a normative commitments (see Averch 1990: chap. 2; Richards 2000).

It is useful to view the decision over instrument choice as being shaped by three factors: informational constraints, the priority attached to certainty of results, and compatibility with existing regulatory statutes. In an ideal world, regulators would have exhaustive data on the full universe of pollutants, and the scientific knowledge necessary to set specific pollution thresholds. Moreover, they would have a sufficiently detailed technical knowledge of products and processes to be able to assign specific pollution control technologies on a firm-by-firm basis. Regulation could constitute a synthesis of scientific research and engineering; scientific findings could be translated seamlessly into comprehensive changes in corporate practices. In reality, regulators work under conditions of profound information scarcity. Information on the health implications of pollution is often fragmentary, based on epidemiological studies on vastly different populations and exposure levels. Moreover, knowledge on abatement may be widely diffused, even within the confines of regulated firms. Regulators do not have the budgetary, administrative, and legal resources to access this information. Managing the knowledge problem is one of the core challenges of instrument choice.

As a result, policymakers are confronted with a choice between two second-best alternatives. First, they can translate pollution thresholds into mandatory technological standards for regulated firms, albeit at a higher level of aggregation (e.g., the industry, or sector) due to the lack of firm-level knowledge of production processes, inputs, and available abatement technologies. If standards are backed with credible sanctions, they can achieve certainty of results. Alternatively, regulators can attempt to manage the knowledge problem by setting performance standards and delegating authority to regulated parties, essentially allowing firms to exercise great discretion in decisions regarding the means by which they will achieve the prescribed levels of performance. These alternate paths involve important trade-offs.

Regulations that rely heavily on command-and-control instruments can guarantee certainty of results. But because the standards are overly broad, many firms may be either overregulated or underregulated. Corporations are not granted the discretionary authority to select pollution control strategies that best reflect their mix of products, processes, technologies, and internal management systems. Certainty of results can be achieved only through the imposition of high compliance costs. At the same time, this strategy engenders high opportunity costs in two senses. First, as compliance costs mount, firms have a strong incentive to delay and litigate, thereby postponing mandated pollution reductions. Second, this strategy can obviate incentives to go beyond standards, thereby creating a performance ceiling and settling for "compliance" when more is possible.

Regulatory delegation economizes on compliance costs by assigning far greater discretionary authority to those with the most intimate knowledge of products, processes, and technologies. To the extent that market mechanisms are employed, regulatory deregulation may create incentives for firms with lower marginal abatement costs to go beyond compliance in the hope of trading credits with their higher-cost counterparts. However, regulatory delegation sacrifices the certainty of results that has been a hallmark of public regulation. Regulators may not be able to predict in advance how regulated parties will respond to the incentives created by policy. Equally important, regulatory delegation does not fully resolve the knowledge problem, but transforms it into an agency problem. When one actor delegates authority to another, a principal-agent relationship is established. Principals must be wary that their agents will abuse the grant of authority (see Eisner, Worsham, and Ringquist 1996). Given that corporations are profit-seeking enterprises and that managers have a fiduciary responsibility to maximize shareholder wealth, there may be clear incentives for shirking or opportunistic behavior. These incentives may be reinforced by informational asymmetries. Indeed, the same factors that necessitate delegation subsequently limit the capacity of regulators to monitor the behavior of the regulated.

Thus, information scarcity forces regulators to embrace one of two alternatives: command-and-control regulation that guarantees certainty of results at a high cost, or regulatory delegation that economizes on costs but creates new sources of uncertainty. Although regulators might make a reasoned argument on behalf of either option, compatibility with existing regulatory statutes can limit choice. Congress rarely allows regulators much latitude in instrument choice. As will be developed in greater detail in Chapter 4, Congress has consistently favored certainty of results over competing values, thereby providing limited opportunities for regulatory delegation. Indeed, despite the diverse set of instruments available to regulators, the United States remains heavily dependent on command-and-control instruments.

■ Core Environmental Protection Policies

The statutory foundations for environmental regulations in the United States were established largely in the 1970s. Although there were some important amendments in subsequent years, they were relatively rare. In 1970, President Nixon created the Environmental Protection Agency and Congress passed the landmark amendments to the Clean Air Act (see Chapters 3 and 4). For now, it is sufficient to note that the EPA was created through a bureaucratic reorganization that consolidated environmental offices from throughout the executive branch. To facilitate consolidation, the EPA adopted a media-specific organization; separate offices were created for regulating air pollution, water pollution, and solid and hazardous wastes. This organization was reinforced by subsequent environmental statutes that established EPA authority over a media-specific organization. Although the EPA quickly became the largest regulatory agency in the nation, it was nonetheless dependent on a rather decentralized implementation structure. Regional offices executed much of the agency's duties, and regulatory legislation assigned vital duties to state regulatory agencies. Given the organization of the EPA and the focus of environmental legislation, the following examination of policies will, quite naturally, assume a media-specific focus.

Regulating Air Pollution

In the 1960s, Congress passed a series of acts hoping to encourage state regulation, including the Air Quality Act of 1960, the Clean Air Act of 1963, and the Air Quality Act of 1967. Although a few states assumed responsibilities for air pollution, there was little progress due to the lack of resources and statutory requirements (Ringquist 1993: 45–46). As the salience of the environment crested in the wake of the first Earth Day in 1970, Senator Edmund Muskie (D-ME) drew on the outpouring of popular support to sponsor new legislation that would overcome the limitations of the earlier efforts. The result was the landmark 1970 amendments to the Clean Air Act.

The Clean Air Act amendments of 1970. The Clean Air Act amendments of 1970 directed the EPA to create national ambient air quality standards. establishing thresholds for so-called criteria pollutants. These pollutants included carbon monoxide, hydrocarbons, lead, nitrogen dioxide, photochemical oxidants (later changed to ozone), sulfur dioxide, and total suspended particulates. For each substance, the EPA set primary air quality standards to protect public health (including particularly sensitive populations like children and the elderly) and secondary air quality standards to protect public welfare (including animals, crops, vegetation, and buildings).

Because the scientific study of air pollution was relatively underdeveloped, Congress directed the EPA to revisit its standards every five years. While the EPA had great discretion in setting the standards, it had little discretion in the application of economic analysis. Congress mandated that primary air quality standards be based solely on human health effects, without consideration of welfare benefits, costs, or economic impacts (EPA 1987).

The EPA exercised authority for mandating specific reductions for automobile emissions. It also set new source performance standards for new stationary sources (e.g., factories), specifying in detail the kinds of pollution control technologies that could be employed on an industry-specific basis. The Clean Air Act amendments divided the nation into 247 air quality control regions. For each of the criteria pollutants, the regions were designated as being in "attainment" or "nonattainment." Responsibility for meeting the national ambient air quality standards fell to the states. The states were required to submit to the EPA implementation plans that provided a detailed discussion of state performance standards for existing stationary sources, plans for enforcing federal requirements, and how these and additional state actions would result in meeting the air quality standards. The Clean Air Act amendments required that states submit their implementation plans by 1972, with EPA approval by 1977. The air quality standards had to be met by 1979. If states failed to comply, the EPA was authorized to impose its own implementation plans. States that failed to meet the statutory deadlines could also face a loss of federal highway and federal pollution control funds.

The Clean Air Act amendments of 1977. The Clean Air Act amendments of 1977 reflected a dose of reality combined with a complicated set of compromises between environmentalists and industry advocates. By the mid-1970s, it was clear that the Clean Air Act had been overly ambitious. The submission and approval of state implementation plans and progress in achieving primary national ambient air quality standards were behind schedule. Thus, Congress extended the deadline for the approval of state implementation plans to 1982 and the deadline for achieving primary air quality standards to 1987. Automobile producers received a two-year extension on mobile source regulations. While these delays concerned environmentalists, they were bolstered by the decision to resolve a controversy over the ability of factories to relocate to pristine regions to avoid the costs of pollution control in nonattainment areas. The Sierra Club had sued the EPA to force it to prevent such responses. In *Sierra Club v. Ruckelshaus* (344 F. Supp. 253 [D.D.C. 1972]), the district court required that implementation plans include provisions to prevent significant deterioration of areas that met or exceeded the national ambient air quality standards. Subsequent agency regulations that created a more complex set of classifications for attainment areas were formalized by the 1977 amendments. The changes in policy were supported by organized labor and members of Congress from Rust Belt states who clearly understood that the policy provisions to prevent significant deterioration would impede the movement of industry to the nonunion Sun Belt (Hays 1978; Morriss 2000).

The clearest compromise came in the treatment of coal-fired utilities. To achieve required pollution reductions, utilities were beginning to use low-sulfur coal from mines in the western United States (or "compliance coal") rather than the high-sulfur coal from eastern mines. Although this strategy had the effect of reducing pollution (and thus furthering the goals of the Clean Air Act) it raised concerns of eastern mining interests who were fearful of losing market share and of environmentalists who felt that utilities were exploiting a regulatory loophole rather than installing pollution control technology. There may be no better example of Bootlegger-Baptist coalitions than the provisions of the 1977 amendments that required that all new coal-fired utilities meet a new source performance standard that mandated expensive scrubbers and allowed state and federal officials to require the use of regionally available coal if the use of coal from other regions would result in a loss of jobs (Ackerman and Hassler 1981; Adler 2000). As Jonathan Adler explains, the amendments extended "the life of older, otherwise obsolete, coal-fired plants. By imposing scrubber requirements on all new coal plants, Congress made older plants more cost-effective . . . some regions of the country actually saw an increase in sulfur dioxide emissions as a result of the new law, and the amount of scrubber sludge requiring disposal increased substantially" (2000: 8).

Although the technology requirement for coal-fired plants is a classic example of command-and-control regulation combined with transfer-seeking, the 1977 amendments also provided a statutory opening for the use of market-based instruments. Three years earlier, the EPA began to experiment with "netting." In 1974 it allowed companies in nonattainment areas to create new sources of emissions only if they achieved equal reductions in emissions elsewhere in their plants and installed control equipment that met lowest-achievable emission rate standards. The net impact of the new emission source would be zero. Two years later, the EPA began to experiment with limited emissions trading. New facilities could now be built in nonattainment areas if they could purchase offsetting reductions from other firms in the area. The "offset policy" was authorized by the Clean Air Act amendments of 1977. With new statutory foundations in place, the agency continued to experiment. In 1980 the EPA allowed firms to place an imaginary bubble over a plant, treating it as a single emission source and pursuing reductions where they could be achieved cost-effectively. They could bank emission reduction credits to offset future emissions or to sell to other firms (Rosenbaum 1998: 172–173).

While the trading policy was formalized in 1986, participation rates were lower than anticipated, because the policy was hard to reconcile with a system premised on command-and-control instruments. For example, bubbles had to be approved through a revision of state implementation plans, "a factor that has discouraged their use." As the EPA explained:

> Emission trading has not lived up to expectations; trades have been fewer and offset prices lower than many had expected. . . . In order to assure that air quality did not deteriorate, state environmental administrators often required expensive air quality modeling prior to accepting proposed trades between geographically separated parties. Deposits to emission banks typically were "taxed" by the air quality management authority to meet SIP [state implementation plan] requirements or to generate a surplus that the area could offer to attract new firms. Offset ratios greater than unity further depressed the value of ERCs [emission reduction credits]. In many areas, it appears that ERCs had an economic value less than the transaction costs of completing a sale to another party. (EPA 2001d: 75)

The effort to create pollution markets as a means of reconciling economic growth and environmental protection was an important experiment, albeit one that was difficult to harmonize with the existing regulatory design.

The Clean Air Act amendments of 1990. The Reagan administration's antiregulatory posture forestalled new Clean Air Act amendments for much of the 1980s. In 1988, George H. W. Bush promised that, if elected, he would bring a "kinder, gentler" form of conservatism to the White House and would be, among other things, an "environmental president." Although many environmental activists were skeptical of the presidential candidate's claims, in 1989 the Bush administration promoted the long-awaited amendments to the Clean Air Act. The amendments focused on three major issues: urban air pollution, toxic air emissions, and acid rain. Urban air pollution is largely a product of automobile emissions and persistent ozone problems. The 1990 act shored up the regulations regarding automobile pollution reduction. Gasoline refiners were required to reformulate the gasoline used in areas with persistent smog problems. Cars were required to be equipped with warning systems to monitor pollution control devices; these devices were required to work for 100,000 miles, doubling the earlier requirement. Moreover, the emission inspection program requirements were strengthened and extended to forty metropolitan areas.

The Clean Air Act amendments of 1970 directed the EPA to identify and regulate air toxics. Yet by 1990 it had only listed and regulated seven chemicals. The 1990 amendments addressed this problem by including a list of 189 hazardous air pollutants, with the goal of achieving overall reductions of some 75 percent. The EPA was directed to regulate the listed toxics and add additional chemicals to the list when deemed necessary. The EPA was directed to identify and categorize sources of pollution for the listed chemicals, and make regulating major sources a priority. In a departure from past regulations, the EPA was instructed to give regulated entities maximum flexibility in compliance. Although they were expected to employ maximum available control technology, they were given great discretion in meeting these requirements. Moreover, they were allowed to offset pollution in one facility with reductions in other facilities. Companies that made reductions of 90 percent before the introduction of EPA regulations would be given additional time to achieve the remaining 10 percent.

The acid rain program (Title IV) was the most innovative portion of the 1990 amendments to the Clean Air Act. The program emerged through complicated negotiations involving the Bush administration, Congress, industry, and environmental groups. Earlier regulatory decisions permitted coal-fired power plants to disperse pollutants through the construction of tall smokestacks. The resulting atmospheric concentrations of sulfur dioxide and nitrogen oxides produced acid rain. The costs and benefits of regulation would fall on different regions of the country, thereby creating regional coalitions that were not easily captured by standard partisan politics. High-sulfur coal producers, the United Mine Workers, and utilities in the midwestern states had the most to lose from regulations. Low-sulfur coal producers (largely in the western United States), western utilities, and northeastern states that had been most severely impacted by acid deposition would claim the greatest benefits (Layzer 2002: 264–288; EPA 2001d: 274–275). During the 1980s, these regional disputes prevented the development of viable acid rain regulations.

The Bush administration promoted a cap-and-trade approach that had been developed by the Environmental Defense Fund. Under the 1990 amendments to the Clean Air Act, reductions in sulfur dioxide were to be realized by setting a cap on emissions that would reach approximately half the 1980 level. Utilities were given allowances (2.5 pounds of sulfur dioxide per million British thermal units, multiplied by average consumption of British thermal units for 1985–1987), with additional allowances to help offset compliance costs and secure congressional coalitions. This allowance rate would be reduced in a secondary phase. Allowances that were not used could be banked or sold through bilateral transactions or auctions. New sources were required to purchase allowances and meet the new source performance standards (EPA 2001d: 75–85). Under the cap-and-trade system, market instruments were combined with the requirement that all facilities install continuous emissions monitoring systems (a demand of environmental groups). Emissions and allowances were reconciled on an annual basis. If utilities exceeded their allowances, they were penalized at a rate originally set at $2,000 per ton (and indexed for inflation).

Regulating Water Pollution

Although the federal government's regulation of water quality originated with the River and Harbor Act of 1886, attention to water pollution waned until the decades following World War II. The Federal Water Pollution Control Act was passed in 1948 and amended in 1956. Legislative efforts accelerated after 1965, with the passage of the Water Quality Act (1965), the Clean Water Restoration Act (1966), and the Water Quality Improvement Act (1970). With each statute, the federal role increased. However, the water pollution laws were characterized by a lack of coordination and effective implementation, and a heavy reliance on pork barrel projects. Riding the wave of public opinion, Senator Muskie once again worked to expand and rationalize the nation's environmental laws. The resulting Federal Water Pollution Control Act amendments of 1972 (hereafter, the Clean Water Act) consolidated and expanded on existing efforts, establishing an ambitious goal: zero discharges into the nation's waters by 1985.

The Clean Water Act of 1972. The Clean Water Act of 1972 established the goal of zero discharge—possibly the most challenging regulatory goal ever—combined with the interim goal of making all waters "fishable and swimable" by July 1, 1983 (i.e., within a decade of the passage of the act). The new law focused on effluent limitations, the "quantities, rates, and concentrations of chemical, physical, biological, and other constituents amount of pollutants" discharged from a given source. The EPA, in turn, was directed to establish industry-specific technological standards. Because the zero-discharge goal was technically unachievable, the Clean Water Act is often cited as the paradigmatic example of technology forcing regulation. Concerns over regulatory costs led Nixon to veto the act. However, strong bipartisan support in Congress, the political salience of the environment, and the impending presidential election combined to guarantee an override.

Under the Clean Water Act, industrial sources of water pollution were required to implement the best practicable control technology by 1977 and the best available technology by 1983. Under the former standard, the EPA identified the appropriate pollution control technologies by industrial category, considering a host of factors, including costs, facility age, and production processes. The latter standard went beyond reduction to achieve the complete elimination of discharges. The Clean Water Act provided a different set of standards for new facilities. The EPA standards for new industrial point sources varied across some twenty-seven industrial categories. If the EPA determined that zero discharge was achievable, it could be required for new sources. As one might expect, the differential treatment of new and existing sources created support, particularly among Rust Belt legislators anxious to stem the relocation of industry to the southern United States.

Standards were incorporated into the National Pollutant Discharge Elimination System (NPDES). under which industrial sources were required to acquire permits specifying the mandated pollution control technology and submit to rigorous reporting requirements. Under the Municipal Wastewater Treatment Grant Program, which provided a counterpart for sewage treatment facilities, municipal facilities were required to employ secondary treatment by 1977, and employ best practicable control technology by 1983 to achieve 80–90 percent reductions in organic wastes. The federal government assumed 75 percent of the construction costs for new sewage treatment plants, and was authorized to spend $18 billion between 1973 and 1977, thereby reducing state compliance costs and guaranteeing congressional support (Eisner, Worsham, and Ringquist 2000: 140).

As with air pollution regulation, the states had a vital role to play in implementation of the Clean Water Act. They were required to establish water quality standards for all of their waters based on use (e.g., recreation, fish and wildlife propagation, public water supplies, industrial and agricultural uses). The EPA had the power to reject state standards, in part or in whole, and ultimately, to impose its own standards. Beginning in 1975, the states were also required to submit annual reports containing an inventory of all point sources, an assessment of water quality and goals, and a description of programs for managing nonpoint sources of pollution. Finally, state environmental regulators played an important role in the NPDES permit process, insofar as any entity that discharged pollutants into a waterway had to possess federal and state permits. These permits had to be consistent with the technology-based effluent limitations and were valid for no more than five years. Given the regulatory demands, obtaining permits became an ongoing activity for many firms.

By the mid-1970s, it became clear that the Clean Water Act's ambitious timetables would prove impossible to meet. Accordingly, Congress entered a protracted process of amending the legislation. The final result, the act's 1977 amendments, provided extensions on the compliance deadlines and granted the EPA the authority to make extensions on a case-by-case basis for facilities that made a "good faith" attempt to meet the original deadline (although all facilities were required to achieve full compliance by January 1, 1979). Similarly, the EPA was given the authority to grant an extension of up to six years for a municipal treatment plant's installation of secondary treatment facilities if the failure in compliance resulted from a lack of federal funding or from delays in ongoing construction. In addition, the 1977 amendments changed the requirements for the implementation of best available technology. Industrial facilities were given a one-year blanket extension on the discharges of conventional pollutants, and the EPA was authorized to provide permanent waivers, on a case-by-case basis, if the costs of additional reductions were deemed unreasonable when compared with the benefits.

These and subsequent extensions were both necessary and predictable. The determination of best available technology ran well behind schedule. Between 1979 and 1987, only twenty-nine such technology regulations were developed and, reflecting the litigiousness of US regulatory culture, almost every new regulation was met by court challenges (Ringquist 1993: 56). As Walter A. Rosenbaum notes, these delays were anticipated. Yet advocates were "convinced that only by pressing technology relentlessly for rapid compliance with regulations could they sustain the sense of urgency and bring sufficient weight of federal authority to bear on polluters to obtain their long-term objectives" (1998: 208). Policy created an inherently conflictive relationship between the regulated and the regulators, thereby preventing capture. It forced massive, long-term investments that would be impossible to reverse in the future. Moreover, the provision of tens of billions of dollars in sewage grants under the Municipal Wastewater Treatment Grant Program created a massive pork barrel that would guarantee the ongoing support of members of Congress anxious to provide benefits for their districts.

The Water Quality Act of 1987.   The Clean Water Act emphasized point sources such as industrial plants and sewage facilities. Nonpoint source pollution (e.g., farms, feedlots, and stormwater runoffs) received little attention. Yet by the late 1980s, there was a consensus that these nonpoint sources were a major contributor to water pollution. The Water Quality Act passed with near unanimity over a presidential veto, and focused attention on nonpoint sources. Within eighteen months of passage of the legislation, each state was required to conduct a nonpoint source pollution assessment. The states were also required to compile implementation plans and timetables to detail how best management practices would be used "to reduce, to the maximum extent practicable," the pollution from each source. A mechanism was created for making federal grants to states to assist in funding up to 60 percent of the costs of executing the implementation plans.

In addition to nonpoint sources of pollution, the Water Quality Act increased the regulations of toxic pollutants in water. Earlier legislation was primarily concerned with traditional water pollutants. Yet many toxic chemicals were unaffected by standard treatment methods; waters remained polluted by toxins event after the effluents had been subjected to best available cleanup technologies. Under the Water Quality Act, states were required to identify and implement pollution control strategies for toxic chemicals. New control requirements were imposed on sources of toxic pollutants and embodied in new NPDES permits. Industrial polluters were now required to pretreat their effluents to eliminate toxins before their introduction into public treatment facilities or waterways. Finally, the Water Quality Act made some significant changes in funding of municipal treatment plants. Rather than continuing the endless stream of public funding, the new system provided onetime grants on a state-by-state basis to create state revolving loan funds. The Clean Water State Revolving Fund Program, capitalized at over $20 billion, funded $28.9 billion in wastewater treatment projects between 1988 and 2001 (EPA 2001b: 9).

Hazardous and Toxic Wastes

Although air and water pollution provide regulators with some difficult challenges, they pale in comparison to hazardous and toxic wastes in terms of the complexity of regulation. Industry develops new chemicals at a rate that simply outpaces the capacity of regulators to assess the environmental ramifications. The EPA's Chemical Substance Inventory, part of the Toxic Substances Control Act, listed some 75,000 chemical substances in 2006. Yet information on many of these chemicals is, at best, woefully incomplete. The EPA's regulatory role can be fruitfully viewed as focusing on two related issues: the regulation of the use, transportation, and disposal of substances that are deemed to be hazardous or toxic, and the remediation of polluted sites.

Regulating the generation, use, and disposal of hazardous wastes.

In 1976, Congress passed the Resource Conservation and Recovery Act (RCRA), an amendment to the Solid Waste Disposal Act of 1965, to regulate hazardous wastes. The hazardous waste management program created under the RCRA (40 CFR 261, Subpart C) designated wastes as hazardous if they had one or more hazardous characteristics (i.e., ignitable, corrosive, reactive or explosive, toxic), if they appeared on one of several preexisting lists of approximately 900 hazardous wastes, or if they had hazardous constituents. Although the RCRA addressed solid wastes, it defined them as including "sludge . . . and other discarded material, including solid, liquid, semi-solid, or contained gaseous material." It was fully anticipated that the set of hazardous chemicals would not be limited to those previously listed; as noted above, new chemicals are created on a regular basis, many of which could be designated as hazardous.

The RCRA created a cradle-to-grave system of regulation. Facilities generating more than 1,000 kilograms of hazardous waster per month (a threshold that was subsequently reduced to 100 kilograms per month) had to comply with regulations regarding storage containers and labeling, and with stringent record-keeping and reporting requirements documenting the generation, use, transfer, and disposition of wastes. The information was stored in a manifest system that was also maintained by companies transporting hazardous materials. Finally, treatment, storage, and disposal facilities had to meet rigid construction and performance standards, abide by EPA permit requirements, and, once again, comply with detailed record-keeping and reporting requirements. Unfortunately, because the generation of new chemicals greatly outpaces regulatory resources, and because the majority of hazardous wastes are disposed of on-site rather than transferred, one might question the efficacy of the system created under the RCRA.

The system of cradle-to-grave regulation was enhanced with the passage of the Emergency Planning and Community Right-to-Know Act in 1986. Under the act, businesses are required to report the amounts and locations of toxic chemicals to state and local governments as a means of facilitating responses to chemical emergencies. The EPA and states are required to collect data on the release or transfer of toxic chemicals on a facility-specific basis; this information is subsequently made available in the Toxics Release Inventory, a public database. This inventory was subsequently expanded, under the Pollution Prevention Act of 1990, to include waste management and source reductions. Although there were no quantitative restrictions on the use of Toxic Release Inventory chemicals, there is clear evidence that the inventory has stimulated source reduction. It may not matter whether this results from efforts to prevent negative investor reactions (Hamilton 1995) or efforts to minimize future liabilities, or is an example of the old adage "what gets measured gets managed." It is clear that the use of Toxic Release Inventory chemicals has fallen precipitously since the creation of the reporting requirements (Karkkainen 2001; Konar and Cohen 1997).

In 1984, Congress reauthorized and amended the RCRA with the Hazardous and Solid Waste Amendments (HSWA). The relationship between Congress and the Reagan administration had been full of conflicts, many of which focused on mismanagement and the hostility of administration appointees toward the agency's mission and Congress, and found their ultimate expression in the resignation of administrator Anne M. Burford and Rita Lavelle, the assistant administrator for solid waste and emergency response (Davis 1984a). With the HSWA, Congress responded to the EPA's glacial progress in issuing RCRA regulations and permits by legislating detailed regulatory standards that would take effect if the EPA failed to meet the twenty-nine different deadlines for specific activities (Rosenbaum 1998: 243–244). Some of these "hammer clauses" could have had stunning implications. For example, the HSWA required that the EPA publish, within sixty-six months, its decisions regarding the banning of land disposal for hazardous wastes listed under the RCRA. A failure to issue a decision by that date would result in an automatic ban on land disposal (Davis 1984b). Fortunately, the EPA responded to most of the deadlines in the HSWA, thereby leading to the full implementation of the RCRA.

Superfund and the regulation of toxic waste dumps. In 1980, Congress passed the Comprehensive Environmental Response, Compensation, and Liability Act (CERCLA). Congressional action was a response to the events at Love Canal, in Niagara Falls, New York. The health threats associated with the concentration of toxins forced the permanent relocation of 239 families and thrust the issue onto the policy agenda, setting the stage for the passage of CERCLA in 1980. Under the act, sites that *may* constitute a threat and require cleanup are initially placed into the Comprehensive Environmental Response, Compensation, and Liability Information System (CERCLIS). Once the EPA conducts a preliminary investigation, a site may be placed on the National Priorities List if it poses the highest potential threat to human health and the environment as determined by its score under a complex hazard-ranking system. Sites on the national list are given priority for cleanup. With CERCLA, Congress adopted the "polluter pays" principle. Rather than paying for the remediation out of general revenues, some mechanism had to be created to assess and assign liability. Under CERCLA, potentially responsible parties include anyone historically connected to the site, including the firms that generated or transported the waste and the former or current owners or operators (but not financiers). Congress created the most stringent liability standards possible, making the liability strict, joint, and retroactive. Strict liability means that the government does not have to prove negligence; parties are liable even if they were in compliance with all of the laws that existed at the point in question. Under joint and several liability, many parties may be held liable, but even a single party can be forced to bear the entire burden regardless of the amount of waste it contributed. Finally, retroactive liability conveys the notion that parties are liable for actions taken before the passage of CERCLA (Reisch and Bearden 1997).

As one might imagine, efforts to assess and assign liability generate large litigation and legal costs. According to a 1994 report by the General Accounting Office (GAO 1994: 4–8), de minimis parties responsible for minor contamination spent, on average, $31,800 on legal costs, whereas major players with three or more sites spent an average of $3.5 million on legal costs. Depending on the level of liability, the proportion of total legal costs ranged from 46 percent (for de minimis parties) to 28 percent (for major players with three or more sites). While some of these legal costs were incurred through interactions with the EPA, 35 percent of surveyed firms had brought legal actions against their insurance carriers, and fully 71 percent had been involved in third-party suits, typically with other potentially responsible parties hoping to minimize their share of overall cleanup costs.

Because it may prove impossible to identify responsible parties or recover costs on so-called orphan sites, CERCLA created the Superfund

Trust Fund. It was financed through general revenues and an excise tax paid by the petroleum and chemical industries. In 1986, Congress passed the Superfund Amendments and Reauthorization Act (SARA), which added an additional $8.5 billion to the Superfund and prohibited corporations from declaring bankruptcy in response to cleanup liabilities. It also increased the discretionary authority of the EPA to use out-of-court settlements to accelerate the assignment and collection of cleanup costs. The authorization for the Superfund tax expired at the end of 1995. As a result, the cleanup of orphan sites now occurs at a pace that is determined by budgetary allocations. In recent years, declining levels of budgetary support have created significant barriers to site remediation (EPA 2004b).

■ Conclusion

Environmental protection regulations are often justified as a means of compensating for market failure, forcing corporations to internalize the costs of pollution that might otherwise be thrust onto society as an externality. When designing the regulatory system, Congress could have chosen from a large repertoire of policy instruments. The demand for certainty of results found expression in a heavy reliance on command-and-control instruments. Although Congress has adopted alternative instruments—ranging from trading to mandatory information disclosure—they have been superimposed upon a system premised on the primacy of command-and-control instruments. As Richard B. Stewart notes: "Despite the vigorous and often telling criticisms of the regulatory status quo, and despite some successful or promising use of alternative regulatory strategies, we remain stuck in the same basic regulatory system that was established in the 1970s, when all of the major federal regulatory statutes that we currently have were enacted. . . . During the entire thirty-year period from 1970 to 2000, there have been only two instances in which Congress has adopted legislation that has made significant use of alternatives to the command system" (2001: 22–24). In essence, environmental protection regulation in the United States comprises a largely uncoordinated set of regulatory statutes premised on the use of command-and-control instruments. With a few notable exceptions (e.g., the 1990 Clean Air Act's cap-and-trade program for acid rain), the use of alternative instruments has largely occurred on the margins or in an experimental fashion. The ongoing reliance on command-and-control instruments reflects the primacy assigned to certainty of results in comparison with competing values. Before exploring the decision to emphasize certainty over competing values and its implications for the evolution of environmental policy and politics, we must explore the policy subsystem in greater detail.

3

The Environmental
Policy Subsystem

The Environmental Protection Agency is the central actor responsible for environmental policy. Yet no examination of environmental policy would be complete without going beyond the bounds of the agency. The EPA is situated in a larger policy subsystem. It competes and cooperates with other agencies that share environmental responsibilities, some of which exercise their mandates in ways that contribute to the very problems the EPA is directed to remedy. It has no budgetary resources other than those that are granted to it by Congress and the president. Its legal authority is grounded in statutes passed by Congress and often shaped by subsequent court decisions. All of these actors remain subject to the ongoing demands of environmental interest groups and business associations seeking to shape policy outcomes. This chapter begins with a brief discussion of policy subsystems, and then examines the EPA and the larger subsystem in which it functions. What emerges is a portrait of a complex political-institutional structure that, when combined with the complexity of the statutes examined in Chapter 2, has profound impacts on environmental policy and politics.

■ Policy Subsystems

Policy subsystems comprise interest groups and governmental actors from congressional committees and bureaucratic agencies who have a stake in a given policy (see Eisner, Worsham, and Ringquist 2006: 22–24). They can be relatively open to entry, or they can be tightly constructed policy monopolies that create significant institutional and intellectual barriers to entry. Subsystems are characterized by great stability compared to the raucous interest group competition that occurs in the larger political system. Subsystem actors often have a shared understanding of problem definition, credible solutions, and preferable distribution of costs and benefits. They build alliances around mutually beneficial policies and thus have a stake in preventing the introduction of interests or issues that would disrupt the equilibrium. Reflecting the fragmentation of the US system, many policy areas have multiple competing subsystems with overlapping sets of actors (Thurber 1991; Worsham 1997).

"Stability" is a relative term. Pressures for change may emerge from internal subsystem dynamics. Key participants from interest groups, congressional committees, and administrative agencies change over time; policy debates evolve, changing the relative status of different groups of subsystem actors. Pressures may result from macropolitical changes (e.g., the election of a new president, changes in partisan control of Congress). Moreover, exogenous shocks such as war or recession may also impact on subsystem politics, increasing the pressure to address new problems and thereby upsetting existing alliances. The prolonged period of stagflation of the 1970s, for example, created pressures in multiple regulatory subsystems. Presidents introduced new regulatory review processes; demands for deregulation swept across multiple subsystems. Political entrepreneurs successfully expanded the scope of conflict, breaking down the barriers to what were at one time impermeable policy monopolies (Baumgartner and Jones 1993; Krehbiel 1991; Riker 1990; Sabatier and Jenkins-Smith 1993; Schattschneider 1960).

In reality, the environmental policy subsystem is a collection of policy-specific subsystems, reflecting the media-specific nature of US environmental policy. There is some variation between the actors surrounding air pollution policy and water pollution policy, for example. Because a detailed examination of each of the subsystems is beyond the scope of this chapter, the discussion here is restricted to environmental policy more broadly, and identifies the key governmental actors and interest groups.

■ The Environmental Protection Agency

The EPA, the central agency responsible for implementing environmental policy, is the largest of all federal regulatory agencies, with a 2005 fiscal year budget of approximately $7.8 billion, supporting approximately 18,000 full-time employees. Although the EPA's budget has grown dramatically in nominal terms, this growth has been illusory when controlled for inflation. The dearth of real budgetary growth (see Figure 3.1) is particularly striking when one recognizes the dramatic growth in the size of the economy (and the number of regulated entities) and the expansion of the EPA's regulatory duties. The agency's budget is far greater than that of other regulatory agencies. In fact, its budget is almost twice the combined budgets of the

Figure 3.1 Environmental Protection Agency Budgets, 1971–2005

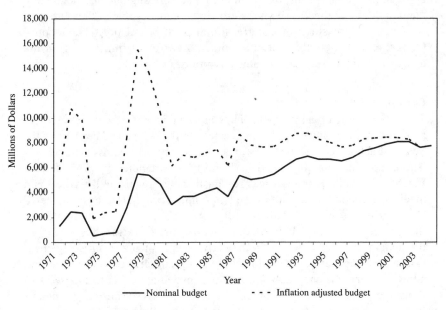

Data source: EPA budget summaries, various years.

Consumer Product Safety Commission, the Federal Trade Commission, the Nuclear Regulatory Commission, the Federal Communications Commission, the Securities and Exchange Commission, the Federal Energy Regulatory Commission, the Commodity Futures Trading Commission, the Federal Deposit Insurance Corporation, the Equal Employment Opportunity Commission, and the Occupational Safety and Health Administration.

The EPA's budget provides a good indication of the agency's regulatory priorities. Its largest commitment comes in the area of clean and safe water, a goal that claimed $2.94 billion, approximately 39 percent of the EPA's budget, in fiscal year 2005. Land preservation and restoration, funded at $1.8 billion, constituted 23 percent of the budget. Clean air and global climate change claimed $1 billion, some 13 percent of the budget (EPA 2005b: app. D). Two points are critical when understanding the agency's budget. First, a sizable portion of the EPA's budget, approximately $1.25 billion, or 15 percent, is passed on to state, local, and tribal governments in the form of categorical grants. For example, in 2005 the agency's budget included $248 million in grants for air and radiation regulation, $509 million for water pollution regulation, $121 million for regulations affecting drinking water, $204 million for hazardous waste regulations, $52 million for pesticides and toxics, and $119 million for multimedia regulations (EPA 2005b: app. A). In nominal terms, the funding for categorical grants has doubled in the past decade, reflecting both the growing regulatory role of the states and the ongoing pressures of congressional pork barrel politics. Second, Congress and regulatory statutes place significant limitations on the agency's ability to set its own budgetary priorities.

Organizational Structure

The EPA is formally an independent agency and is under the direction of an administrator appointed by the president with the advice and consent of the Senate. Each office also operates under the direction of an assistant administrator appointed by the president. The EPA is structured by program (see Figure 3.2), with separate offices responsible for organizing activities on a media-specific basis (e.g., all of the air pollution programs are administered by the Office of Air and Radiation; the water programs are coordinated by the Office of Water). This media-specific organization has persisted throughout the EPA's history. In the early days, a media-specific organization made implicit sense. It facilitated bureaucratic consolidation and allowed the new agency to begin its work immediately. Yet it imposed significant costs, as regulatory compliance often involves "shifting" pollutants (e.g., converting airborne pollutants into solid pollutants) rather than preventing them in the first instance. Moreover, the existence of several parallel regulatory processes also increases costs for regulated parties. Rather than applying for a single permit, for example, companies must work simultaneously through permit processes in different offices, thereby creating significant delays and compliance costs. Despite ongoing critiques of the EPA's organizational structure, efforts to create an integrated system have been unsuccessful. As long as congressional committees divide jurisdiction on a media-specific basis, the structure will remain secure.

Implementation Structure

Although the key decisions regarding environmental protection are made by the EPA's office in Washington, D.C., responsibility for implementation is far more decentralized. The EPA has ten regional offices, which are assigned responsibility for the implementation of policy within their states (Region 1, for example, is headquartered in Boston and has responsibility for the New England states). Some two-thirds of EPA personnel are assigned to the regional offices, each of which operates with a certain amount of autonomy and has a unique organization. Thus Region 1 is organized into several offices, many of which combine responsibilities for regulating across media, whereas Region 9 (responsible for California, Nevada, and Arizona) has a more traditional structure, with air, water, waste

Figure 3.2 The Environmental Protection Agency

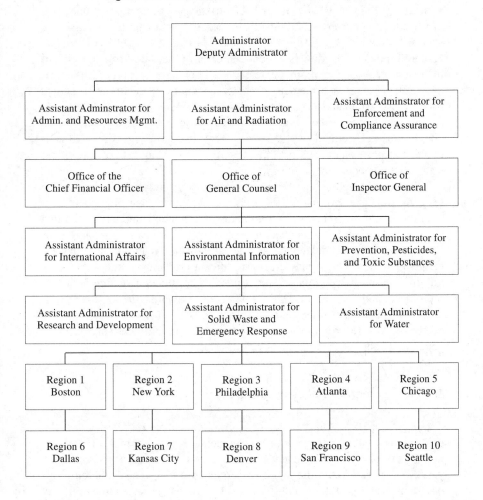

management, and Superfund divisions. Mirroring the organizational diversity, there are variations in the regulatory rigor across regions (see Hunter and Waterman 1992).

The regional offices work closely with state regulators, which are primarily responsible for implementation. Most environmental statutes delegate significant responsibilities to the states, whose role has grown dramatically, in part, as a product of President Ronald Reagan's New Federalism and the belief that decentralization would promote higher levels of responsiveness, accountability, and innovation (Ringquist 1993). The importance of states in environmental protection is clearly exhibited by the fact that they spent $15.1 billion on environmental protection in 2003, compared with $8.7 billion in 1996 (adjusted for inflation). Approximately one-third of the 2003 funds were from federal sources. On a per capita basis, average state spending increased from $36.22 in 1986 to $51.80 in 2003 (Brown and Kiefer 2003). Yet spending is but one indicator of the states' role in environmental protection. Far more impressive are the states' responsibilities for data collection and enforcement. Over 94 percent of the environmental data used by EPA databanks is collected by the states. Moreover, over 90 percent of the combined enforcement actions are conducted by the states (Environmental Council of the States 2001). It is no exaggeration to conclude that policy depends on the capacity and willingness of individual states to implement federal policy.

State performance and regulatory capacities have been quite uneven (Siy, Koziol, and Rollins 2001). Many states have gone beyond federal requirements in some areas of environmental protection, and have exhibited a great deal of innovation. Others have consistently failed to discharge their obligations. Whereas delegation and decentralization may produce superior results in some states, it may create significant problems in states that have not invested in their regulatory structures. Rather than delegating authority indiscriminately, greater care might be taken to identify the kinds of problems that require a stronger federal role. Similarly, greater efforts might be taken to promote professionalization, cooperation, and data-sharing more generally (Rabe 2003).

■ Environmental Policy in Congress

Although the EPA was created through an executive reorganization, the growing national commitment to environmental regulation in the 1970s was largely the product of a strong consensus in Congress. In a span of six years, Congress created the legislative foundations for the regulation of air pollution, water pollution, and toxic and hazardous wastes, actions initially driven by strong public support. As the nation began to experience stagflation, and as the high costs imposed by the new regulatory initiatives were publicized, critics charged that escalating regulatory costs were undermining economic performance (see Chapter 5). Moreover, businesses began to mobilize with far greater vigor, effectively countering environmental interest groups that had been so successful in shaping the agenda of the early 1970s (Vogel 1989). The 1980 elections brought a sea change in Washington. Ronald Reagan was elected president based, in part, on a commitment to scaling back the role of the federal government and providing regulatory relief. Moreover, a Republican majority was elected to the Senate for the first time since 1955. Increasingly, partisan conflicts undermined the possibility of new environmental statutes or an expansion of EPA resources; gridlock became the norm (Kraft 2003). The prospects for new environmental laws disappeared with the 1994 elections, when Republican majorities assumed unified control of both chambers of Congress. The House Republicans, armed with the Contract with America, explicitly sought to restrict the role of the regulatory state. Although progress on the Contract with America essentially ended by the late 1990s, sharp partisan divisions and narrow majorities created gridlock, forestalling new legislation.

In reality, many factors militate against environmental policymaking in Congress. To understand why, one only need consider three factors: congressional incentives, the inherent features of environmental policy, and the organization of Congress. In congressional studies, it is axiomatic that members of Congress have the proximate goal of reelection. They may seek to gain influence or make good public policy, but this is impossible unless they retain their positions and rise through the ranks (Fenno 1973; Mayhew 1974). The goal of reelection impacts on behavior in many ways. There is a strong tendency toward localism. Senators and representatives must be cognizant of how a given piece of legislation will impact on their states and districts. In addition, because reelection is impossible without campaign funds, members must be concerned with how political action committees and donors will react to new policies. The existing system of campaign finance is heavily skewed toward moneyed interests, creating a strong bias in support of corporate interests.

Second, one must consider the inherent features of environmental policy, which is characterized by concentrated costs and diffuse benefits. Corporations subject to regulation will be forced to bear costs immediately. These costs are concrete and easily calculated, creating a strong incentive for mobilization. In contrast, the benefits of environmental protection are diffuse and, when viewed at the perspective of the individual, may be insufficient to justify the costs of political mobilization. Perhaps new legislation strengthening hazardous waste regulation could reduce one's risk of developing cancer in twenty years. But if the risks are already low, slight changes in the probability of an adverse outcome may not provide incentives to support policy. Finally, environmental policy is characterized by its complexity. A full appreciation of policy would require more than a passing familiarity with natural and social science. As a result, policy is often portrayed in overly simplistic terms, and those who may be affected by policy may be incapable of determining its ultimate impacts and identifying the myriad compromises and costs inherent in the legislation.

Third, one must consider the organization of Congress as an institution. Congress is highly fragmented, consisting of two chambers, thirty-five standing committees, and over 150 subcommittees, with additional select and joint committees. Responsibility for environmental policy is spread over twelve committees and twenty-five subcommittees. It is difficult to build consensus and coordinate initiatives within this highly fragmented system. Members of Congress often seek committee positions, because they have some connection to the interests of key constituents. Coordination across committees and subcommittees may require that members of Congress sacrifice constituent interests in the name of coherent public policy. While this may occur under special circumstances, it is far more likely that policies will come to reflect complicated compromises designed to meet the needs of multiple parties in fragile coalitions, and to safeguard or promote local constituents or mobilized interests.

There is much to suggest that the sharp partisan divide within Congress has partially overcome this general fragmentation. The League of Conservation Voters issues its National Environmental Scorecard for each Congress, assigning each representative and senator a score on a 100-point scale based on his or her votes on key environmental issues. Figure 3.3, which presents the mean congressional voting scores, clearly reveals a growing partisan divide on the issue of the environment. Thus, during the 1980s, the difference between the mean scores of the two parties in the House and Senate were 31.4 and 27.8 points, respectively. By the period

Figure 3.3 Environmental Voting Records, 1981–2003

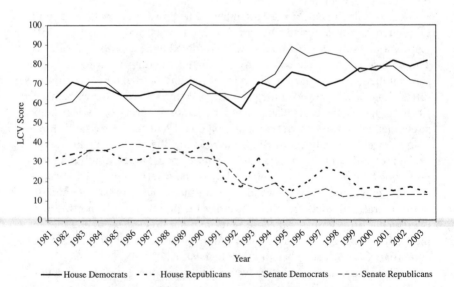

Data Source: League of Conservation Voters, National Environmental Scorecard, various years, http://www.lcv.rg/scorecard.

2000–2003, this divide had grown to 64.3 points in the House and 62.3 points in the Senate. One should not be surprised, given these sharp divisions, that development of new regulatory statutes has been frozen (for an examination of the factors shaping the growing partisan divide, see Shipan and Lowry 2001).

■ Environmental Policy and the Presidency

The president is usually viewed as being the center of the political universe, holding enormous powers over public policy. These powers are exercised in several ways. First, the president can shape the policy agenda both through efforts to influence public opinion and through the submission of legislation to Congress. Second, the president is responsible for negotiating international treaties and agreements—an increasingly important power given the prominence of global environmental issues. Third, the president has important powers over the bureaucracy, including the constitutional authority to appoint top administrators who can shape policy through implementation. Budget requests for each agency, moreover, are initiated by the president after negotiations between the agencies and the Office of Management and Budget (OMB). Finally, the president can use executive orders to impose regulatory review procedures that force agencies to justify significant new regulations.

Although presidents are usually viewed as being the most important actors in the development of public policy, this has rarely been the case in environmental protection. As Dennis L. Soden and Brent S. Steel note: "the president's long-term political goals have not included the environment as a driving force in any administration in the modern era." They explain that the environment often assumes "second-tier status, falling in the agenda-building process to more politically practical issues such as the economy, crime, and national defense. For the president, the economic dog has wagged the environmental political tail in most cases" (1999: 344). Despite the inherent importance of environmental protection, its claim on federal government resources is modest. In decades since its creation in 1970, the EPA's share of federal outlays has only exceeded 1 percent on one occasion (1977). During the presidency of Ronald Reagan, the EPA's share of outlays fell from 0.9 percent to 0.5 percent, and it has remained relatively stable at 0.4 percent of federal outlays since 1989. Other governmental obligations, ranging from defense spending to old-age pensions, dwarf the EPA's budget (Soden and Steel 1999: 321). Moreover, because the environmental policy subsystem is highly fragmented, with power exercised by multiple agencies, congressional committees, courts, and state regulators, opportunities for presidential control are quite limited. Presidents may make the reasonable determination that their limited political capital is better invested where it can yield unambiguous results.

Although the environment is usually seen as a Democratic issue, the two Democratic presidents since 1970 have had limited opportunities to promote an active environmental agenda. President Jimmy Carter was forced to govern in an era defined by stagflation and a fuel crisis; when the environment moved onto the agenda, it usually took the form of demands for regulatory reform or deregulation. In the 1990s, opportunities were constrained by President Bill Clinton's centrist policy positions, the overriding goal of deficit reduction, and a new Republican majority in Congress. Surprisingly, the major environmental statutes were passed during Republican presidencies, often over the threat or exercise of the presidential veto. Yet Republican presidents have had some success using their appointment powers, budget requests, and executive orders to shape policy implementation. Every Republican president since Richard Nixon has used these powers to promote regulatory reforms designed to reduce compliance costs and force agencies to subject regulations to economic analysis. Of course, the president is but one of multiple, competing principals placing demands on the EPA. The signals sent by the president and Congress can create a "whiplash" effect as agencies accelerate and decelerate their regulatory activities and as actors initiate new efforts to counteract competing strategies of political control (see Whitford 2005).

The president manages environmental policy through two executive offices: the Council on Environmental Quality (CEQ) and the OMB's Office of Information and Regulatory Affairs (OIRA). In June 1969, President Nixon issued an executive order to create the cabinet-level Environmental Quality Council. With the passage of the National Environmental Policy Act of 1969, Congress renamed the council, placed it within the Executive Office of the President, and expanded its duties. The chair of the CEQ, a presidential appointee requiring Senate confirmation, is the president's primary environmental adviser. The chair provides an annual report to the president, oversees environmental policy, and coordinates federal environmental efforts, at times resolving policy disagreements among agencies. Although the CEQ's creation was met with great fanfare, its power is minimal. Positions on the council have frequently remained vacant. Even President Clinton left positions empty and, in 1993, sought its elimination, albeit unsuccessfully.

If the CEQ has had minimal influence and power since its inception, the same cannot be said of the OMB-OIRA. It has played a central role in administering the regulatory review requirements established under a series of executive orders. These regulatory review systems, explored in Chapter 5, were created to force regulatory agencies to analyze the economic impacts of significant policies before their promulgation. Although the OMB had been used to impose regulatory review requirements since the early 1970s, during the Reagan presidency the OMB-OIRA began to enforce regulatory review by preventing agencies that failed to conduct the necessary analysis from publishing announcements of rule making in the *Federal Register,* thereby stopping the regulatory process through administrative means. Subsequent presidents have altered the regulatory review requirements, but the OMB-OIRA remains one of the more effective instruments of presidential influence over regulation (Vig 2003).

While the CEQ and the OMB-OIRA provide the president with some important management tools, presidents have had their greatest impact on environmental policy through the power of appointment. Presidential appointments to the top positions at the EPA have generally signaled the president's orientation toward environmental protection. Thus, when Reagan appointed Anne Gorsuch in 1981, his selection of a corporate lawyer and state legislator with minimal environmental credentials provided clear evidence of the low priority assigned to the EPA. Gorsuch resigned her position, leaving behind her a record of battles with the EPA bureaucracy and Congress (see Burford and Greenya 1986). Reagan sought to manage the conflicts by appointing William D. Ruckelshaus, the first EPA administrator (1970–1973) with credentials that would placate congressional critics (Landy, Roberts, and Thomas 1994: 246–251). When George H. W. Bush was elected on promises of a "kinder, gentler" form of conservatism, the shift in governing philosophies was symbolized through the appointment of William K. Reilly, former president of the World Wildlife Fund and the Conservation Foundation.

Clinton also selected a high-profile appointee for the EPA, Carol M. Browner. From 1991 to 1993, Browner had served as the secretary of Florida's Department of Environmental Regulation, and previously in Washington as legislative director for Senator Al Gore, Clinton's vice president. George W. Bush's first appointment to the EPA symbolized a shift in emphasis. Christine Todd Whitman, former governor of New Jersey, was a high-profile nominee from a state that had experimented with an innovative regulatory green track that became one of the models for subsequent experiments at the EPA (see Chapter 7). But however strong her reputation as governor, she lacked the environmental experience and credentials of her immediate predecessors. When she resigned in 2003, she was replaced by Mike Leavitt, a former governor of Utah who had a strong reputation for collaborative environmental management (i.e., efforts to regulate through creative public-private partnerships). When Leavitt moved to head the Department of Health and Human Services, he was replaced by Stephen L. Johnson, the first career EPA scientist to hold the position.

■ **Environmental Policy and the Bureaucracy**

Although the EPA is the epicenter of environmental policymaking, there is nothing to suggest that it has been successful in controlling the activities of other agencies with environmentally relevant mandates. Most executive departments have some environmentally relevant duties (see Table 3.1 for a partial list of these departments). In some cases, like the Department of Energy or the Department of Interior, these duties are central to an agency's overall mandate. In other cases, like the Department of Defense (which is responsible for the Army Corps of Engineers and the Oceanographer of the Navy) and the Department of Commerce (which houses the National Oceanic and Atmospheric Administration), the duties are more peripheral. The fragmentation of the bureaucracy is far greater than that which exists within Congress. The challenge of coordinating and integrating their activities is simply too great.

Many agencies' environmental responsibilities are shaped (if not vitiated) by the duties to service the needs of special constituencies with strong congressional support. Consider the US Department of Agriculture (USDA). Some of its components—the US Forest Service and the Natural Resources Conservation Service—have explicit environmental responsibilities. Their

Table 3.1   Agencies with Environmental Responsibilities

Defense Nuclear Facilities Safety Board
Department of Agriculture: Forest Service; Natural Resources Conservation Service
Department of Commerce: National Oceanic and Atmospheric Administration; National Marine Fisheries Service; National Ocean Service; Office of Ocean and Atmospheric Research; National Environmental Satellite, Data, and Information Service
Department of Defense: Army Corps of Engineers; Oceanographer of the Navy
Department of Energy: Entire agency
Department of Interior: Bureau of Land Management; Bureau of Reclamation; Minerals Management Service; National Park Service; Office of Surface Mining Reclamation and Enforcement; US Fish and Wildlife Service; US Geological Survey
Department of Justice: Environment and Natural Resources Division
Department of Labor: Mine Safety and Health Administration; Occupational Safety and Health Administration
Department of State: Undersecretary for Global Affairs; Assistant Secretary for Oceans and International Environmental and Scientific Affairs
Department of Transportation: Federal Aviation Administration, Office of Environment and Energy; Federal Highway Administration, Office of Planning, Environment, and Reality; Surface Trasportation Environment and Planning Cooperative Research Program
Federal Trade Commission: Bureau of Consumer Protection
Nuclear Regulatory Commission
Tennessee Valley Authority

significance for the environment, however, is dwarfed by the role of the USDA in promoting agribusiness and advocating the use of pesticides and fertilizers, which are of growing environmental concern. A similar story could be told about other agencies. The Department of Energy, created in 1977 to consolidate energy-related offices and allow for integrated management of energy across fuel sources, quickly assumed the role of a constituent agency. After a number of reorganizations, it became structured by fuel source and assumed the mission of protecting industry actors, thereby frustrating integrated management and any effort to coordinate agency policies to meet larger environmental goals (see Eisner, Worsham, and Ringquist 2006: chap. 10). Energy policy must be a cornerstone of an effective environmental policy; alternative fuels and conservation are central to issues like air pollution and global climate change. Given the close connections between the Department of Energy and industry, it is highly unlikely that environmental protection will ever be given priority over industry concerns.

There are regulatory agencies outside of the executive departments that execute mandates with environmental implications. The Nuclear Regulatory Commission, for example, is responsible for regulating the safety of the nuclear energy industry. The Federal Trade Commission enforces consumer protection regulations that govern the kinds of claims that can be made by manufacturers. This has become increasingly important as corporations engage in "green-washing," seeking to create an image of environmental responsibility by making unverifiable claims or advertising their products as being "organic," "natural," or "environmentally friendly" (see Greer and Bruno 1996).

In conclusion, although the EPA is the central actor in the environmental policy subsystem, a plethora of bureaucratic actors have a direct impact on the environment. More important, many of their policies—from the promotion of pesticides by the USDA and the leasing of grazing lands at below-market prices by the Department of Interior, to the promotion of fossil fuel exploration by the Department of Energy—may well contribute to the very problems that the EPA is forced to regulate. One might presume that the president would have the capacity to coordinate policies through some of the mechanisms described above, but these efforts are frustrated by several factors, including the sheer magnitude of the task and the fact that agencies often have little discretion over whether to execute policies mandated and funded by Congress.

■ Environmental Policy and the Courts

The courts have played a greater role in environmental protection than in most regulatory policy areas. In part, this reflects the fact that the environmental statutes are among the most complex laws ever written. As Dan

Tarlock notes, Congress assigned the EPA "impossible tasks such as balancing health protection with economic efficiency, and resolving difficult scientific and technical questions to promulgate fair, effective, timely and legal regulations" (2002: 610). The existence of multiple, competing, and potentially irreconcilable duties opened the door to controversies that would have to be resolved by the courts. But more important, the rise of environmental protection occurred in tandem with the so-called new administrative law (Stewart 1975). Increasingly, courts advocated expanded standing, allowing a broader range of actors to access the judicial process and challenge the results of administrative decisionmaking. Congress facilitated this expansion by explicitly granting citizen groups the opportunity to sue the EPA. Expanded standing was understood as being a means of furthering democratization and creating mechanisms to hold administration agencies accountable. This role became ever more important after the election of 1980: "In 1981, the Reagan administration took office determined to roll back environmental regulation. Congress did not comply and, instead, the EPA and the federal land management agencies tried to reinterpret the strong protection mandates adopted in the 1970s to lessen protection duties." Under these conditions, "litigation proved to be quite effective in stopping administrative 'lawlessness'" (Tarlock 2002: 585).

The issue of standing was an important one. Under traditional doctrines of standing, economic injury was a prerequisite for parties hoping to access the courts. This began to change in a series of federal court decisions, following *Scenic Hudson Preservation Conference v. Federal Power Commission* (354 F. 2d 608 [2d Cir. 1965]). The expansion of standing found its clearest legislative expression in the Clean Air Act of 1970, the first environmental statute to authorize citizen suits. Under the act, "any person may commence a civil action" in federal district court in response to violations of standards, permits, or enforcement orders, or to force the EPA to execute its nondiscretionary duties. The act authorized parties to recover legal expenses, thereby providing greater incentives for citizen groups to challenge moneyed corporations and government agencies (Weinberg 2003: 37). Citizen suits provided a key means of subjecting the EPA's actions to judicial review (Andreen 2003).

As a result of these and comparable provisions, citizen suits (or, more correctly, suits filed by environmental interest groups) have been an important part of the larger history of environmental protection. They have been most important when they have been action-forcing, responding to the EPA's failure to execute its nondiscretionary duties. Action-forcing suits have had many results, as explained by Robert L. Glicksman (2004). First, they have forced the creation of new regulatory programs (e.g., the Prevention of Significant Deterioration Program). Action-forcing suits have also forced changes in the focus of regulatory programs. For example, under the Clean Water Act of 1972, the EPA could regulate toxic water pollutants through two different means: health-based standards and technology-based standards. When it decided to adopt the former approach, the scientific complexity and limited data delayed the issuance of standards. A series of citizen suits were consolidated and heard before the federal district court for the District of Columbia. In the resulting consent decree, the EPA agreed to adopt technology-based standards as a means of imposing industrywide regulations.

Action-forcing suits have also forced expansion of existing regulatory programs. For example, in *Natural Resources Defense Council Inc. v. Train* (411 F. Supp. 864 [S.D.N.Y. 1976]), the EPA was sued for its failure to list lead as a criteria pollutant to be regulated under the Clean Air Act. Although the EPA argued that such decisions fell within its discretionary authority, the court disagreed. Citizen suits can also prove instrumental in accelerating implementation. Consider the example of Clean Water Act implementation. Under the act, states are required to develop water quality standards identifying the use of the specific body of water and the relevant quality criteria. Where technology-based standards are insufficient to meet the quality criteria, states must calculate a total maximum daily load (i.e., the amount of a given pollutant that can be assimilated by a body of water without exceeding permissible concentrations). The maximum load is used to set limits for specific pollution sources. The EPA had been slow in setting water quality standards; states were failing to execute their duties. From the 1980s onward, environmental groups began filing suit at the state level. As a generalization, the courts have found that the prolonged failure of states to submit maximum-load calculations is tantamount to a "constructive submission" of no such calculations, which in turn creates an obligation to approve or disapprove of the resulting submission. Since disapproval would be the only rational response, the EPA would then be required to impose its own maximum load, thereby accelerating the implementation process (Glicksman 2004: 375).

Despite these examples, judicial action in the environment has created clear problems. As R. Shep Melnick notes: "the consequences of court action under the Clean Air Act are neither random nor beneficial." By expanding some programs, they have depleted scarce budgetary resources. Moreover, "court action has encouraged legislators and administrators to establish goals without considering how they can be achieved, exacerbating the tendency of these institutions to promise far more than they can deliver," thereby contributing to the "frustration and cynicism among participants of all stripes" (1983: 344). In recent years, there appears to be something of a reversal in the trend toward judicial activism; courts are increasingly restrictive in their interpretation of standing. This is a source of grave concern for advocates. As Philip Weinberg notes: "Limiting standing in environmental litigation gives government agencies and industry carte blanche to violate laws enacted to safeguard public health and protect natural resources." The courts can only "curb abuses by the other two branches . . . if litigants are free, within reasonable and historic limits, to enter the courthouse" (2003: 52).

■ **The Interest Group Universe**

Popular portrayals of environmental politics often invoke powerful images of threadbare activists and small grassroots organizations battling colossal corporations. While this portrayal may have been accurate at one time, it no longer is. As Christopher J. Bosso documents in *Environment, Inc.*, major groups have been remarkably successful in attracting donations and using these funds to develop professionalized organizations. Between 1994 and 2002, for example, the annual revenues for the largest environmental groups increased from $640.7 million to $2.124 billion. Between 1997 and 2002, the net assets of these same groups more than doubled, from $2.039 billion to $4.257 billion, although the Nature Conservancy's land acquisitions accounted for some $2.9 billion of this total. As Bosso notes, environmental groups have successfully made a transition to become "mass-based professional advocacy organizations," with professional staffs, diversified revenues, and "the kind of management procedures one expects to find in any well-run nonprofit organization—or any corporation, for that matter" (2005: 98, 104, 148).

Not surprisingly, the largest environmental groups are the older organizations that were founded to focus primarily on conservation issues. These groups include the Sierra Club, the National Audubon Society, the Izaak Walton League, the Wilderness Society, the National Wildlife Federation, the Defenders of Wildlife, the Nature Conservancy, and the World Wildlife Fund. The combined annual budgets of these groups approaches $500 million. The newer generation of environmental groups emerged in the period 1967–1971, leveraging the growing salience of the environment and support from activists involved in the antiwar and civil rights movements. These groups include Environmental Defense (formerly the Environmental Defense Fund), Friends of the Earth, Environmental Action, the League of Conservation Voters, the Natural Resources Defense Council, and Greenpeace USA. Whereas some of these groups have successfully maintained their membership roles and budgets (Environmental Defense and the Natural Resources Defense Council have annual budgets in excess of $30 million), others have been far less successful. Friends of the Earth has lost more that half of its members since 1980, and has an annual budget of some

$4.3 million. Environmental Action, partially responsible for organizing the first Earth Day in 1970, had over 20,000 members in the 1980s but formally closed its doors in 1996 (Bosso and Guber 2003).

Environmental groups use a number of methods to shape environmental regulations, policies, and practices. Most mainstream organizations focus on traditional lobbying. Others, like Environmental Defense and the Natural Resources Defense Fund, have used litigation quite effectively. As Jacqueline Vaughn Switzer and Gary Bryner note, these groups "made environmental litigation an art form, moving group strategy from the legislative to the judicial arena" (1998: 22). The League of Conservation Voters has published its National Environmental Scorecard since 1970, reporting the percentage of votes on key environmental issues that were cast in favor of the environment. One of the more interesting old-guard environmental groups, the Nature Conservancy, focuses on the acquisition and preservation of natural resources. It has acquired or otherwise protected through conservation easements some 116 million acres of land.

New and old groups alike have embraced the Internet as a means of providing a much larger audience with information on key environmental issues and campaigns. In the past two decades, a small number of radical environmental groups have rejected the tactics embraced by mainline environmental groups like the Sierra Club. For example, Earth First! draws on a unique strategic repertoire including civil disobedience and industrial sabotage. While groups like Earth First! have attracted much media attention, they are by no means representative. Their greatest impact may be in providing convenient illustrations for opponents of environmental protection anxious to portray environmentalism as part of the radical fringe.

Business associations have increasingly mobilized to shape environmental policymaking. Following the regulatory defeats of the early 1970s, business organizations quickly recognized the need for a greater organizational presence in Washington. Trade and peak associations claimed larger budgets and professionalized, creating large staffs of scientists to conduct research (Vogel 1989; Wilson 1990). These investments, unmatched by environmental and consumer advocacy groups, provided business associations with a comparative advantage in the framing of regulatory legislation and public policy more generally.

A number of business associations and corporations have also joined together in recent years to form larger umbrella organizations. The US Business Council for Sustainable Development, for example, was created in 2002, and represents major trade associations (e.g., the American Forest and Paper Association) and corporations (Dow Chemical Company, DuPont, Shell Oil) in working to frame policy debates over the issue of sustainable development. Similarly, the Global Climate Coalition was founded in 1989 to represent a business perspective on climate change policy. The coalition was a staunch opponent of the Kyoto Protocol and a strong advocate of corporate voluntarism and market-based regulatory instruments. Many groups strategically adopt politically ambiguous names (e.g., the National Wetlands Coalition, the Evergreen Foundation, the National Endangered Species Act Reform Coalition, and the Council on Water Quality) that appear to suggest, at first glance, an independent environmental focus free of business ties. When taken together, they play a major role in raising questions about the adequacy of regulatory science and shaping the legislative and regulatory agenda.

As E. E. Schattschneider noted more than four decades ago, "the flaw in the pluralist heaven is that the heavenly chorus sings with a strong upper-class accent" (1960: 34–35). Since the passage of the Federal Election Campaign Act amendments of 1974, political action committees have become major players in campaign funding, and businesses have greatly outpaced environmental groups in their contributions. In the 2004 election cycle, for example, environmental groups contributed $1.6 million, 87 percent of which went to Democratic candidates (see http://www.opensecrets. org). These figures pale in comparison to donations from corporate political action committees. Once again, drawing on the 2004 election cycle, candidates were funded heavily by a number of sectors with a strong stake in environmental policy, including the energy and natural resources sector ($52 million, 75 percent of which went to Republicans), agribusiness ($53 million, 71 percent of which went to Republicans), transportation ($51 million, 74 percent of which went to Republicans), and construction ($71 million, 72 percent of which went to Republicans).

Outside the traditional categories of business lobbying and campaign funding, an additional trend can be easily identified. In response to environmental policy debates and well-publicized environmental disasters, trade associations began to devote greater resources to self-regulation. Many associations developed environmental codes and management programs. The Responsible Care Program, for example, was introduced in the wake of the Union Carbide disaster in Bhopal to enhance the use, transportation, and disposal of chemicals. Following the *Exxon Valdez* oil spill, the American Petroleum Institute introduced its Strategies for Today's Environmental Partnership to manage environmental, health, and safety issues in the extraction and transportation of petroleum products. Similarly, the American Forest and Paper Association developed its Sustainable Forestry Initiative to manage forests as ecosystems. In these and in other cases, the goals have been to manage public perceptions about the industry, reduce the likelihood of future problems, and limit the demand for new regulations. Association-based self-regulation is explored in greater detail in Chapter 9.

■ Conclusion

It is easy to attribute policy outcomes to the decisions of a single actor—a president who embraces (or rejects) environmental protection, for example, or an EPA administrator who is committed (or uncommitted) to protecting the public. Yet policy outcomes are the product of a complex set of political-institutional forces. Actors within a policy subsystem struggle over the control and direction of policy. They may empower regulatory agencies to pursue certain objectives, but often under significant legal and resource constraints reflecting compromises among multiple interests or the demands of preserving fragile coalitions. Agencies addressing a common policy area may represent very different constituencies; the policies of one agency may contribute to the very problems that other agencies are required to manage. In the end, one encounters a great deal of disorganization and uncertainty, particularly in an area like environmental policy, which involves such a plethora of actors. How does one manage such uncertainty?

Part 2

The Evolution of Regulatory Design and Reform

Regulatory Design and Performance

On April 17, 2000, EPA administrator Carol M. Browner delivered a speech marking the thirtieth anniversary of Earth Day. She noted that one of the foundations for the success in environmental protection was a fundamental shift in national commitments: "the nation committed itself to the task of eliminating pollution, to restoring our lands and waters to their uses, and to protecting public health without regard to cost. Let me repeat those last four words—'without regard to cost.' This represented a sea change in our nation's approach to environmental protection." She went on to observe that "the historic commitment that was the foundation for our success in conquering environmental degradation was based on a simple premise—protect public health first, and then figure out how to deal with the costs. Set the necessary protective health standards, and then work out a strict time frame for industries to innovate and devise ways to meet those standards" (Browner 2000). Strict standards, technology-forcing mandates, a general disregard for costs—these were the core components of regulatory design as exhibited in the initiatives following Earth Day 1970.

This chapter begins with a general discussion of regulatory design. The central observation is that regulatory design is driven not by a quest for efficiency or effectiveness but by the goals of achieving certainty of results and preserving today's victories. Next it examines the shifting political climate surrounding Earth Day 1970 and the ways in which the growing salience of the environment forced environmental protection onto the policy agenda and shaped decisions regarding regulatory design. After reviewing the positive environmental gains of the past several decades, the chapter concludes with a discussion of how support for environmental protection has fared since the first Earth Day, and the seeming disjunction between popular assessments of the environment and the empirical record.

■ The Politics of Regulatory Design

Institutions matter. This has been a consistent message from researchers in political science and related disciplines over the past two decades. Rules, roles, and formal structures are of critical importance when understanding politics and policy (March and Olsen 1989; Weaver and Rockman 1993b). They shape the organization of interests and structure elite and interest group access to sites of policymaking. They determine the extent to which administrative agencies and executives are insulated from elective institutions and how—or whether—mobilized groups are integrated into the policy process. The way agencies are organized and staffed will also affect whether policymakers have access to certain bodies of expertise (e.g., through professionalization or external advisory structures), and the extent to which this expertise is integrated into decisions regarding resource flows, policy design, instrument choice, and evaluation. Similarly, institutional design will determine the ways in which other governmental and nongovernmental actors are integrated into policymaking and implementation. These factors will affect the focus, coherence, and performance of policy.

Although original choices regarding institutional and policy design shape ensuing events, they are neither permanent nor determinative. As a result of successive contests over policy, new designs are often superimposed upon the old and combined with new policy initiatives. In the worst situations, agencies may be forced to function within a complex environment characterized by irreconcilable missions and a disjunction among mandates, policy instruments, and resource flows. They may be denied the authority to set priorities and bring order to the chaos. At the same time, policy-learning continues to occur within agencies. Actors usually deal with uncertainty and ambiguity "by trying to clarify the rules, make distinctions, determine what the situation is and what definition 'fits'" (March and Olsen 1989: 161). The changes they make are usually incremental; officials seek to adjust existing institutional capacities to meet new contingencies. Yet new challenges may force a departure from existing routines and stimulate the development of new capabilities. In short, agencies continually evolve within the parameters established by initial decisions regarding regulatory design, albeit seldom in accordance with some overarching logic or plan.

Many social scientists portray legislation as the product of a political exchange between self-interested parties. Interest groups demand policies that further their interests and offer political support to vote-maximizing politicians. The design of institutional structures (e.g., legislative committees and decision rules) can shape coalition formation and the manner in which group demands are translated into policy. Much of what composes public policy is simple rent- or transfer-seeking. Organized interests exchange political support for policies that produce benefits for group members while imposing the costs on the unorganized or poorly organized (Buchanan, Tollison, and Tullock 1980; Rauch 1999). Because these costs are usually diffuse and hidden, those who bear them rarely have the incentives to mobilize. The results may contribute to the welfare of society; in contrast, they may force taxpayers to subsidize organized interests. There is little to suggest that a dispassionate calculation of social costs and social benefits regularly informs or constrains the decisions of key participants. In any event, as coalitions are formed and reinforced with benefits, attention turns to institutional design. How can one design institutions to preserve today's gains in an uncertain future?

The history of regulation is replete with examples of this dynamic. Historically, economic regulatory policies provided classic examples of rent-seeking behavior. Policies erected competitive barriers, replaced the price mechanism with administrative rate-setting, and allowed regulated industries to function as de facto cartels. These outcomes were secured, in part, through institutional design. Legislators delegated enormous discretionary authority to regulators, who in turn made decisions in close consultation with the regulated industry. Social regulations, although less vulnerable to capture due to their inherent features (e.g., imposition of costs on an economywide basis), have not been immune to rent-seeking behavior. The legislative victories realized in environmental protection and other social regulatory arenas have been preserved through core decisions in regulatory design. This accomplishment has come at a relatively high cost, however, insofar as it has compromised the dynamism and adaptability of the regulatory system.

At first glance, this may seem counterintuitive, particularly for those who believe that there is a clear distinction between the rough-and-tumble world of politics and the more sober, technocratic world of administration. The dichotomy between politics and administration—an intellectual inheritance from the Progressive Era—is premised on a belief that the passage of legislation marks the end of politics and the beginning of the technical task of implementation (see Goodnow 1900; Wilson 1887). Yet political struggles infuse the design of institutions and the resulting administrative process. Groups that prevail in political struggles face immediate uncertainty about what the future may hold. Will public opinion follow the classic Downsian model of the issue attention cycle (see Downs 1972), wherein alarmed discovery and euphoric enthusiasm are followed by a gradual decline of public interest as the costs of significant gains become clear? Will supportive legislative majorities evaporate? Will hostile executives impose their own agendas? In response to these questions, the winners in political struggles often seek to manage uncertainty through what Terry M. Moe describes as "the politics of structural choice." Winners design structures and processes to preserve their victories, even if they compromise the ability of the agency to achieve its purposes:

> The driving force of political uncertainty . . . causes the winning group to favor structural designs it would never favor on technical grounds alone: designs that place detailed formal restrictions on bureaucratic discretion, impose complex procedures for agency decisionmaking, minimize opportunities for oversight, and otherwise insulate the agency from politics. The group has to protect itself and its agency from the dangers of democracy, and it does so by imposing structures that appear strange and incongruous indeed when judged by almost any reasonable standards of what an effective organization ought to look like. (1989: 275)

Legislative coalition building requires compromise among potentially opposing groups. The same is true in the politics of structural choice. The minority may seek to "impose structures that subvert effective performance and politicize agency decisions" (Moe 1989: 277). In the end, this process may generate structures that are designed to fail or that, at the very least, prove incapable of achieving their purposes effectively.

When groups emerge victorious in legislative battles, they may seek to insulate today's successes against future assaults or changes in the political landscape. This is accomplished through core decisions regarding regulatory design—decisions that structure future politics and the capacity of various groups (including the bureaucrats themselves) to shape policy outputs. Decisions must be made about whether an agency will be placed in an executive department or given greater independence, thereby increasing its vulnerability to legislative pressures. Decisions must be made about whether interest groups will have a formal role in policy development (e.g., through placement on advisory bodies). Decisions must be made about the specificity of statutory mandates. Congress can delegate the authority to define precise policy goals and the flexibility to employ a variety of analytical methods (e.g., cost-benefit analysis) and policy instruments. Alternatively, Congress can write exhaustive legislation that imposes detailed and mandatory directives and statutory timetables, essentially using legislation to program implementation. These decisions will go far in shaping regulatory politics, agency performance, and the relationship between regulators and regulated parties.

As should be clear, there is little reason to believe that regulatory design decisions will be driven by the quest for efficiency or effectiveness. These values would require a greater delegation of authority to administrators, thereby magnifying the very uncertainty that parties seek to reduce. Rather, they seek certainty and accountability, and design structures and policies that will further these values. Nothing is permanent in politics, however, and with each new political contest, winners will seek to preserve their victories by altering existing structures and processes or by imposing new structures and processes upon the old. The politics of regulatory design is never a one-stage game. Each stage may place new layers of rules, roles, and routines on top of those that already exist, resulting in greater incoherence than anyone would accept under normal circumstances.

■ Environmentalism and Regulatory Design

Contemporary environmental protection regulation emerged out of a long national commitment to conservation. Conservation finds its roots in the decades surrounding the beginning of the twentieth century, as the United States witnessed a growing interest in the preservation of public lands and the scientific management of natural resources. John Muir, founder of the Sierra Club, worked to protect wilderness areas from commercial development. Progressive intellectuals, like Gifford Pinchot, sought to reconcile development and conservation through wise management. Under the influence of Pinchot, the Department of Interior's Division of Forestry, which he headed, began to promote sustained yield forestry (Kraft 2002). Environmental protection, in contrast, emphasizes the mission of limiting the negative impact of pollution on the health of humans and the larger ecosystem. Moreover, environmental protection has been understood as an important tool in holding corporations accountable, making the policy area far more salient in the late 1960s as environmental activists increasingly portrayed environmental degradation as emblematic of government-sanctioned corporate cupidity.

The environment emerged as a salient issue in the late 1960s, and the rapidity of its emergence is well worth noting. If pollution was a significant problem in the mid-1960s, the public had not recognized it as such. In a national poll by the Gallup Organization in February 1968, only 1 percent of respondents cited water and air pollution as "the most important problem" facing the community today. In a national poll by Louis Harris and Associates in July 1967, only 38 percent of respondents believed that air pollution had become worse compared with a few years previous, whereas 57 percent believed that pollution had remained about the same. Things would change significantly in the next several years. By February 1970, public opinion on air pollution had literally flipped. In response to the same question, 53 percent of the population believed that air pollution had become worse, whereas 39 percent believed it had remained the same.

The growing salience of the environment was reflected in and reinforced by the events surrounding the first Earth Day, on April 22, 1970. Wisconsin senator Gaylord Nelson organized Earth Day in the hope of channeling the activism exhibited in the civil rights and antiwar movements into the cause of the environment. On Earth Day, demonstrations and teach-ins attracted massive turnouts; Congress adjourned so members could return to their districts to participate in the events. This level of congressional attention made great practical sense, given the opinion polls. In an April 1970 Gallup poll, 53 percent of respondents cited "trying to reduce pollution of air and water" as one of three national problems that they would "like to see the government devote most of its attention to in the next year or two." In an August 1970 Harris poll, 59 percent identified pollution control as an area that should receive additional funds, placing it ahead of all other domestic and foreign policy areas.

Heavy media coverage undoubtedly contributed to the heightened demand for a policy response. Although there is no perfect way to measure salience, one means commonly adopted is to compile data on the number of stories on a policy problem in a given year by conducting a keyword search of the *Reader's Guide to Periodical Literature* (see Baumgartner and Jones 1993; Eisner, Worsham, and Ringquist 2006). Although this methodology has obvious limitations, a story count can clearly illustrate the changing salience of water and air pollution in the period in question (see Figure 4.1). As is clearly evident, for the period in question, the number of stories on air

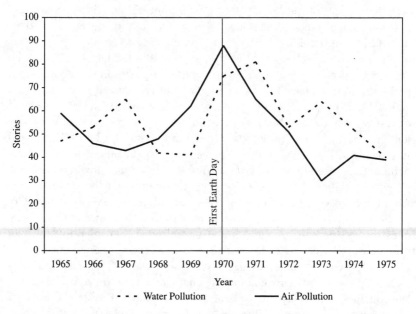

Figure 4.1 The Salience of Pollution, 1965–1975

Data source: Reader's Guide to Periodical Literature.

pollution peaked in 1970, corresponding to Earth Day. Given the trends in salience, environmental advocates and elected officials intent on capitalizing on public sentiment were wise to move when they did. Indeed, an October 1970 Gallup poll revealed that 58 percent of adults thought that the issue of pollution would be extremely important in making their decisions as to how to vote in the upcoming congressional elections (another 30 percent stated that the issue would be fairly important, with only 9 percent finding the issue unimportant). If the poll numbers were not enough, the newly founded League of Conservation Voters began to issue its National Environmental Scorecard, detailing the environmental voting records of legislators. In 1970, it targeted the "dirty dozen" members of Congress with the worst environmental records, seven of whom were defeated in the November elections.

From Salience to Public Policy
Elected officials responded rapidly to the growing salience of the environment. In May 1969, President Richard Nixon created the Environmental Quality Council, with cabinet-level status, and the Citizens Advisory Committee on Environmental Quality. In December he appointed a committee to consider the creation of an environmental agency as part of the Ash Council's efforts to reorganize the federal bureaucracy. As the year drew to a close, Congress passed the National Environmental Policy Act, which Nixon signed with great fanfare on New Year's Day 1970 (see Lewis 1985). The new act stated that it was the nation's policy "to encourage productive and enjoyable harmony between man and his environment; to promote efforts which will prevent or eliminate damage to the environment and biosphere and stimulate the health and welfare of man; to enrich the understanding of the ecological systems and natural resources important to the Nation" (42 USC § 4321). To that end, the act required that "every recommendation or report on proposals for legislation and other major Federal actions significantly affecting the quality of the human environment" be accompanied by an environmental impact statement (42 USC § 4332). It also directed the president to compile and submit to Congress an annual report on environmental quality, and gave the Council on Environmental Quality statutory foundations and the responsibility of preparing the report and evaluating the environmental impact statements (42 USC § 4343–4444).

Nixon maintained the momentum in his January 1970 State of the Union address. He declared: "The great question of the seventies is . . . shall we make our peace with nature and begin to make reparations for the damage we have done to our air, to our land, and to our water? Restoring nature to its natural state is a cause beyond party and beyond factions. It has become a common cause of all the people of this country. . . . Clean air, clean water, open spaces—these should once again be the birthright of every American. If we act now, they can be." Nixon went on to note that the commitment would require "comprehensive new regulations" and noted explicitly that this commitment would be costly: "We still think of air as free. But clean air is not free, and neither is clean water. The price tag on pollution control is high. Through our years of past carelessness we incurred a debt to nature, and now that debt is being called."

Senator Edmund Muskie (D-ME), chief environmentalist in Congress, had used his position on the Senate Public Works Committee to promote environmental legislation for several years. Although the Senate had been working on revisions to the Clean Air Act, the heightened salience of the environment created an opportunity for far greater changes than anyone might have expected. Moreover, Muskie was anxious to counter an air pollution report by the Ralph Nader Study Group (Esposito 1970) that had chastised him for the ineffective policies he had promoted in the past. When Muskie introduced the new Clean Air Act amendments, he noted that Congress's duty was not "to be limited by what is or appears to be technologically or economically feasible." Instead, it was "to establish what the public interest requires to protect the health of persons," even if this meant that "industries will be asked to do what seems to be impossible at the present time" (116 Cong. Rec. 32901–32902 [1970]). The Clean Air Act amendments of 1970 would mark a sea change in environmental regulation. Wary of Muskie's presidential aspirations, Nixon proceeded with his plans to create a new environmental agency. The Environmental Protection Agency was created with Reorganization Plan no. 3, on July 9, 1970. After consultation with Congress, the EPA opened for business on December 2, 1970. By all indications, Nixon's plans bore political fruit. By January 1971, one year after he had delivered his State of the Union address and two years after he had signed the National Environmental Policy Act, a Harris poll revealed that a larger percentage of the population believed that Nixon would "do the best job" addressing air and water pollution (36 percent) compared to Muskie (33 percent).

The EPA was established as part of a larger (and ultimately unsuccessful) presidential effort to rationalize the federal bureaucracy by reducing redundancy and fragmentation through agency consolidation. Rather than creating the EPA from the ground up, the reorganization combined offices and programs from fifteen agencies, placing 5,743 bureaucrats in what was, in essence, a holding company for regulators drawn from agencies with vastly different missions and cultures (Eisner 2000b: 139–140). The creation of a new agency was imbued with politics from the beginning. It was "popular with environmentalists and many members of Congress because they viewed the consolidation of the various federal programs dealing with pollution control as a way to increase regulatory power and visibility. The

White House staff, on the other hand, saw the more centralized approach as a way to give the executive branch more control" (Andreen 2003: 256). The EPA's authority was not derived from an organic act. The authority it exercised was created by the new regulatory statutes—in particular, the various amendments to the Clean Air Act and the Federal Water Pollution Control Act (or Clean Water Act) discussed in Chapter 2. Although Nixon favored an integrated agency, the EPA quickly assumed a media-specific organization, a decision that was reinforced by the media-specific responsibilities of congressional subcommittees and, ultimately, the media-specific focus of the new legislation.

When drafting the new environmental statutes, extraordinary care was taken to craft provisions that would shape regulatory politics well into the future. The advocacy groups that mobilized around environmental protection were gravely concerned with the power of big business in US society. The goal was to promote reforms that would force the government to hold business accountable (see Eisner 2000b; Harris and Milkis 1996). The dark history of regulatory capture raised important questions for environmental advocates and policy entrepreneurs. How could regulatory design prevent capture (or, more to the point, how could it foil capture by the *wrong* interests)? How could it thwart the erosion of governmental commitment over time, should the configuration of political forces change and environmentalism lose its political appeal? As Terry M. Moe explains: "by imposing strict requirements and deadlines on the agency" environmental interests "reduced the likelihood that resurgent business and state-local interests could someday turn agency discretion to their own advantage. Scientifically, this strategy was surely unwise. Politically, it made good sense" (1989: 313).

The environmental initiatives of the 1970s were the product of a new policy subsystem that linked environmental interest groups, key congressional subcommittees, and the EPA. Environmental groups worked closely with their congressional allies to secure their victories through regulatory design. They secured preferential access to sites of policymaking, thereby creating a relatively well-insulated policy monopoly. In his EPA oral history, William Ruckelshaus (1993), the first administrator of the EPA, recalled: "we accepted much of the initial agenda of the environmental movement. In fact, the new agency worked with environmentalists, whose demands helped create EPA in the first place. They were allies, at least in part." Ruckelshaus noted the durability of the "so-called 'iron triangle' relationship between the environmental movement, the EPA staff, and the Congressional committee staffs. Some of it has to do with job security; some of it has to do with a certain amount of zealotry inside EPA. . . . There has existed among them a symbiosis, in which the environmental movement used the agency as an antagonist to raise money and get more members; and the agency used the environmental groups to sue for objectives they were trying to accomplish, but could not otherwise gain. The same is true of the Congressional committees."

The goals of preventing regulatory capture and insulating the new environmental protection policies from future assaults were pursued in several ways. In contrast to the vague and skeletal regulatory mandates of the past, the new environmental legislation was exhaustively detailed to constrain bureaucratic discretion. Detailed and mandatory directives, statutory deadlines, and a strong reliance on command-and-control instruments and technological standards minimized the potential for industry influence and agency inaction. Indeed, in some cases, a consideration of costs was statutorily prohibited, thereby limiting business influence over policy formation. The mandates and instruments created an adversarial relationship between the regulated and the regulators, creating further barriers to industry influence. Extended rule making and intervener funding provided greater opportunities for environmental group participation in agency activities; expanded standing allowed environmental groups to use the courts to force agency action (see Eisner 2000b: 134–200; Landy and Cass 1997).

Certainty of results and accountability were the hallmarks of the new system, even if their pursuit imposed unnecessary costs and rigidities. Detailed regulatory mandates, technology- rather than performance-based standards, and a heavy reliance on command-and-control instruments dramatically limited flexibility in compliance and undermined the potential for innovations. There were no incentives for going beyond regulatory standards; policy created a regulatory ceiling rather than a floor. Because of the media-specific organizational structure, regulated parties had to comply with multiple parallel policy processes and incur unnecessary delays and costs. Resources were often devoted to media-shifting rather than pollution prevention. The high costs, long delays, and large penalties ensured that protracted litigation would become part of the policy process, exacerbating the culture of adversarial legalism (Kagan and Axelrad 2000; Vogel 1986). For many environmental groups that participated in regulatory design, the ability to insulate victories from future political assaults was well worth the costs.

■ Assessing the Performance Record

Public support for environmental protection remains strong more than three decades following the creation of the EPA. In part, this may be a product of performance. There is strong empirical evidence that the environment is far cleaner today than it was at the beginning of the environmental decade. Yet for reasons to be developed in greater detail below, it is questionable whether the public fully recognizes the magnitude of the EPA's accomplishments. Before developing this strand of the argument, the performance record of the EPA should be considered. This is a difficult judgment to make with precision. As with most public agencies, for the EPA the outputs that are of most relevance here are difficult to measure. One cannot directly measure units of environmental quality or develop a simple summary of change over time. However, if policy is examined at a lower level of aggregation, it is possible to identify some useful indicators.

Assessments will depend, in part, on the quality and availability of data. In the case of air pollution, there are excellent data on concentrations of criteria pollutants. With respect to other policy areas, however, data are not nearly as clear. A systematic assessment of the effects of the Clean Water Act is hampered by limited data and problems of aggregating data across bodies of water and pollutants (Harrington 2003: 21). A large proportion of the states have yet to develop water quality standards and assess the quality of their watersheds (GAO 2000). Comparable problems exist in the case of hazardous wastes. As the Superfund enters its third decade, there is little agreement about how best to evaluate its performance. A most prevalent indicator—"constructions completed"—reveals little about the magnitude of the underlying problems and the related health and environmental risks. The adoption of this indicator, moreover, may create perverse incentives for regulators. In the quest to generate large numbers, they may focus on the least-complex sites, backloading the most complicated and costly cleanups (see Probst and Sherman 2004).

Air Pollution Performance

Despite the magnitude and complexity of the tasks assigned to the EPA by the Clean Air Act, the performance record has been quite impressive. The six criteria pollutants covered by the Clean Air Act are ozone, particulate matter, carbon monoxide, nitrogen dioxide, sulfur dioxide, and lead. Between 1970 and 2001, these pollutants fell by some 25 percent. At first glance, this might appear to be a modest accomplishment. However, this 25 percent reduction did not occur in a steady state economy. During this same period, gross domestic product increased by 161 percent and vehicle miles traveled increased by 149 percent. Reflecting efficiency gains, fuel consumption during this period increased by 42 percent, a rate of growth that was only slightly ahead of the population growth rate, at 39 percent. Although it is difficult to project levels of pollution absent regulation, one can assume that they would have tracked fuel use or population growth. In this context, a 25 percent reduction is impressive (EPA 2002c: II-1).

The acid rain program created under Title IV of the Clean Air Act amendments of 1990 has been remarkably successful as well. In 1990, sulfur dioxide emissions stood at 15.9 million tons. Without policy, emissions were projected to increase to 18.7 million tons by 2010. In contrast, by 2001, emissions had fallen to 10.6 million tons, on track to a 2010 goal of 9 million tons (less than half the projected level absent Title IV). A similar story can be told with respect to nitrogen oxides, emissions of which stood at 6.7 million tons in 1990. Without Tile IV, these emissions were projected to increase to 8.8 million tons by 2010. Under Title IV, emissions fell by 2 million tons per year by 2001 (EPA 2002c: II-2). Parties could purchase pollution credits under the cap-and-trade system. Pollution beyond permitted levels was to be penalized at a rate of $2,000 per ton. Due to high levels of compliance and the rapidity of reductions, there has been a surplus of allowances, and penalties have been rare (Burtraw 2000). Thus, in 2002, parties could purchase pollution credits at $160.50 per ton, about one-tenth of original estimates (Burtraw and Mansur 1999). Although some question the adequacy of the targets, there is a consensus that the cap-and-trade system has provided the means of achieving rapid implementation at a fraction of the anticipated costs (see Environmental Defense 2000).

The EPA continues to refine and extend its regulations. Consider the treatment of particulate matter, the airborne solid particles and liquid droplets that are a product of combustion, dust, and chemical reactions. Although suspended particulates were covered by the Clean Air Act of 1970, regulations focused on coarser particles (e.g., an EPA standard that set levels for particulate matter of ten micrometers in diameter). Fine particles (e.g., less than 2.5 micrometers in diameter) pose a significant health threat, resulting in heart and lung disease, and in 1997 the EPA promulgated a new standard for these. In 1999 it created a monitoring network and began a three-year process of data collection on fine particulate concentrations to identify trends, areas not in attainment with the new standards, and regional and seasonal differences. The EPA is currently refining measurement methodologies and working with states in developing guidance for the implementation of the standard.

Water Pollution Performance

At first glance, the accomplishments in the area of water pollution appear to be substantial, particularly when viewed in light of what existed prior to the creation of the EPA. As the agency notes in its strategic plan for 2003–2008:

> Thirty years ago, about two-thirds of the surface waters assessed by states were not attaining basic water quality goals and were considered polluted. Some of the Nation's waters were open sewers posing health risks, and many water bodies were so polluted that traditional uses, such as swimming, fishing, and recreation, were impossible. Today, the number of polluted waters has been dramatically reduced, and many clean waters are

even healthier. A massive investment of federal, state, and local funds has resulted in a new generation of sewage treatment facilities able to provide "secondary" treatment or better. More than 50 categories of industry now comply with nationally consistent discharge regulations. In addition, sustained efforts to implement "best management practices" have helped reduce runoff of pollutants from diffuse, or "nonpoint," sources. (EPA 2003a: 31)

Yet progress on water pollution is difficult to measure. The United States has 2,262 watersheds and innumerable streams, rivers, ponds, and lakes. The rivers and streams alone run some 3.6 million miles. Although 92 percent of the Great Lakes shoreline has been assessed, other data are more limited: 6 percent of ocean shorelines, 19 percent of rivers and streams, 36 percent of estuaries, and 43 percent of lakes, ponds, and reservoirs. The EPA categorizes those water bodies that have been assessed as good (i.e., fully supports intended uses) or impaired. Of the waters assessed by the states, approximately 40 percent still do not meet basic quality standards (EPA 2004d: II-1). This ignores the massive gaps in the data, which may lead one to question whether this representation is valid.

As part of its planning process, the EPA sets a number of strategic objectives connected to its goal of ensuring clean and safe water. Two seem most closely related to the performance under the Clean Water Act. The first, and arguably the most important goal, is to increase the percentage of the population who have access to clean drinking water. In 1983, 83 percent of the population served by community water systems received water from systems for which there had been no violations of federally enforceable health standards during the year. By 1998, this figure had increased to 85 percent, with a further increase to 91 percent by 2003 (EPA 2002c, 2004d: II-22). The EPA has set a goal of 95 percent by 2006 (EPA 2005b: II-2). A second strategic objective by 2006 was to increase to 800 the number of watersheds where at least 80 percent of assessed waters meet state water quality standards (EPA 2005b: II-2). For 2002, the EPA set an interim goal of 600 watersheds. However, it fell substantially short of this goal—achieving a mere 453 watersheds—and subsequently revised its goal to 500 watersheds by 2005 (EPA 2004d: II-28). Performance problems reflect the heavy reliance on the states. As of 2002, only half the states had effective programs for water quality standards; data collection and reporting have yet to be standardized. Other indicators of performance connected to this objective (increasing the number of states and tribal governments with up-to-date water quality standards and restoration and protection of estuaries through the implementation of comprehensive conservation and management plans) are ahead of schedule.

Although the indicators of clean water performance are more difficult to interpret than those for air pollution regulation, two key points are clear.

First, there have been clear gains in water quality since the passage of the Clean Water Act in 1972, although more precise generalizations are hampered by the quality of the data and the difficulties inherent in aggregation. Second, where performance has lagged, a key source of the difficulties can be traced to regulatory capacity in the states. Differences in state performance reflect a number of factors, including budgetary commitments, levels of legislative professionalism, and the extent of the problems within the states in question, factors that are beyond the reach of the EPA (Teske 2004: 182–192). In 2003 the EPA introduced water quality trading, a market-based program that, in theory, might provide gains in water pollution regulation (see Chapter 7). The success of the program will depend, ultimately, on state-level regulatory capacity.

Hazardous and Toxic Waste Performance

What of hazardous wastes? By 2004 the Superfund had initiated some 7,900 "removal response actions." Of the 1,494 sites on the National Priorities List, it had controlled human exposure at 82 percent and controlled groundwater migration at 65 percent. Moreover, it had completed construction on 886 of the listed sites, some 58 percent of the total (EPA 2004d: III-2). Over the course of the past decade, annual completion numbers have ranged from a high of 88 (1997) to a low of 40 (2004). It is difficult to draw any conclusions from figures that do not reveal the "size, complexity and cost of the respective sites, rendering a half-million-dollar site cleanup indistinguishable from a half-billion-dollar site cleanup" (National Advisory Council for Environmental Policy and Technology 2004: 80). Moreover, without a clear indication of the universe of potential sites, it is difficult to draw any conclusions regarding whether the Superfund has addressed the problem it was created to resolve.

Cleanup costs are potentially immense, particularly at so-called megasites, where costs exceed $50 million. Performance depends heavily on success in identifying potentially responsible parties and forcing them to bare the costs. In 1998, some 70 percent of new remediation at nonfederal National Priorities List sites was initiated by private parties. By 2003, potentially responsible parties had been identified, and settlements had been reached or enforcement actions taken before remediation began, at 90 percent of Superfund sites (EPA 2004d: III-21). The EPA has been quite successful in recovering 100 percent of the costs from potentially responsible parties when it spends Superfund trust moneys (EPA 2004d: III-20). Yet with the expiration of the Superfund tax in 1995 and declining budgetary support, there remain profound concerns about the adequacy and pace of remediation at orphan sites.

While Superfund cleanups address remediation needs, the Resource

Conservation and Recovery Act addresses the practices at existing facilities with the ultimate goal of preventing environmental damages. The RCRA's Corrective Action Program evaluates hazardous waste treatment, storage, and disposal facilities. Based on the human health and environmental risks posed by actual or potential releases, the EPA designates facilities on the basis of priority. As of 2004, there were 1,714 RCRA corrective action high-priority facilities. Of this number, human exposure had been controlled at 73 percent (1,246), an increase from 61 percent (1,049) in 2002 and 47 percent (814) in 2001. Similarly, groundwater migration had been controlled at 61 percent of the facilities, an increase from 51 percent in 2002 (EPA 2004d: III-20).

In summary, by any measure, the environment has improved substantially since the creation of the EPA and the passage of key environmental regulatory statutes in the early 1970s. There have been great gains in the regulation of air pollution; the record on water and hazardous wastes is positive, but the quality of data prevents simple generalizations. Progress should not be surprising. The central regulatory statutes mandated command-and-control instruments and imposed ambitious implementation timetables backed with significant sanctions. Moreover, the United States invested hundreds of billions of dollars in environmental protection—a level of commitment that would have been impossible to imagine at the dawn of the modern environmental era.

■ Two Cheers for Environmental Protection?

In his classic study "Up and Down with Ecology," Anthony Downs (1972) argued that public opinion tends to follow a rather predictable pattern. Public opinion peaks following a focusing event such as Earth Day. As the costs of addressing the problem become clear, one should expect a rapid decline in levels of public interest. For policy advocates, the lessons of the issue attention cycle should be clear. First, strike while the iron is hot. Elected officials have the most to gain politically when issue salience is high. Second, lock in today's victories and insulate them from an uncertain future through institutional design. Both lessons were applied by environmental advocates and elected officials, who seemed to understand implicitly the Downsian dynamic. Yet even if there were short-term declines in issue salience after the 1970 Earth Day peak, the support for environmental protection has exhibited remarkable durability. A 1973 Roper poll revealed that 34 percent of respondents believed that environmental protection laws had not gone far enough, whereas 32 percent believed that the nation had "struck the right balance." When the same question was asked in 1983, 48 percent believed that environmental protection had not gone far enough, a percentage that would reach 63 percent by 1992. Polling results from 2005 confirm that the US population remains committed to environmental protection. In a 2005 Harris poll, respondents were asked: "Do you think there is too much, too little, or about the right amount of government regulation and involvement in the area of environmental protection?" To which 47 percent of respondents believed that there was too little government regulation, with another 32 percent claiming the right amount. Only 19 percent believed that there was too much regulation—a number that is largely consistent with what polls revealed for much of the 1970s. Similarly, the Harris poll asked: "Do you think of yourself as an active environmentalist, sympathetic to environmental concerns, neutral, or unsympathetic to environmental concerns?" While "active environmentalists" constituted 12 percent of the respondents, fully 58 percent claimed to be sympathetic to environmental concerns, with another 24 percent claiming to be neutral (and 4 percent unsympathetic). Indeed, when examining the salience of environmental protection using the methodology employed above, one discovers that levels of salience achieved in 1970 would seem miniscule compared with levels in subsequent decades (see Figure 4.2).

Given the EPA's positive (if qualified) performance record, one might assume that the public's support for environmental regulation is easily explained. The public demanded higher levels of environmental quality,

Figure 4.2 The Salience of Environmental Protection, 1965–2005

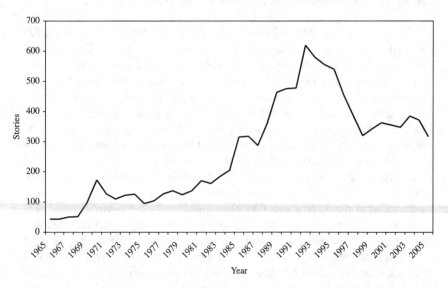

Data source: Reader's Guide to Periodical Literature.

elected officials created the necessary policies and allocated resources, and the EPA executed its mandates with relative success. Indeed, a solid majority of the public maintain a positive assessment of environmental quality as they experience it. In a Harris poll conducted in October 2004, respondents were asked: "Do you feel good about the quality of the air, water, and environment where you live and work, or not?" To which 71 percent reported feeling good; only 29 percent reported not feeling good. Yet there appears to be a troubling disjunction between how Americans view the environment as they experience it, and environmental gains more generally. According to a 2000 survey conducted by Princeton Research Associates, only 18 percent of the population believed that major progress had been made in solving environmental problems since Earth Day 1970. The majority (52 percent) believed that only minor progress had been made, whereas 23 percent believed that there had been no progress or things had actually become worse. Similarly, a poll sponsored by the League of Conservation Voters in 2001 asked respondents to opine on whether the environment had improved, become worse, or stayed the same in the previous five years. Only 20 percent of respondents saw an improvement in the environment, whereas 42 percent thought the environment had become somewhat worse or much worse (34 percent thought it had remained about the same). Similarly, an October 2004 Gallup poll asked respondents to state whether they worried a great deal, a fair amount, only a little, or not at all about various environmental problems, to which 48 percent claimed to worry a great deal about water pollution, with an additional 31 percent worrying a fair amount. With respect to air pollution, 39 percent claimed to worry a great deal, with an additional 30 percent worrying a fair amount. Paradoxically, a majority "feels good" about the environment where they work and live *and* a majority have a negative appraisal of environmental quality more generally.

How does one explain the negative appraisal of environmental gains over the past several decades? Perhaps performance is assessed in light of unrealistic expectations? How much pollution and environmental risk should be tolerated in the United States? Public opinion polls would seem to provide a simple answer: none! A telephone survey conducted in 1999 by Wirthlin Worldwide asked respondents to state their agreement or disagreement with the following statement: "When it comes to environmental pollution, any amount of potential health risk should not be tolerated." To which 60 percent strongly agreed, with an additional 17 percent agreeing somewhat. Less than a quarter of respondents disagreed somewhat or strongly. The belief that "any amount of potential health risk should not be tolerated" is simply incoherent, although not surprising given the difficulty the population has in conceptualizing risk (see Zeckhauser and Viscusi 1990). Reflecting this view of risk, a 2005 Harris poll found that 40 percent strongly agreed and 34 percent somewhat agreed with the statement: "Protecting the environment is so important that requirements and standards cannot be too high, and continuing environmental improvements must be made regardless of cost." When taken as a whole, it would appear that a majority of the population believe that there are no acceptable levels of environmental risk and no limits to what should be done to achieve zero risk. Given these expectations, could any performance record be sufficient?

There is a second, more compelling explanation. The first challenge for policy advocates is to get an issue onto the policy agenda; the second challenge is to keep it there (see Kingdon 1984). A steady flow of sensational news stories that portrays discrete events as emblematic of a much larger crisis is an important means of mobilizing citizens and convincing elected officials that there are electoral benefits to be claimed from addressing a given problem. As noted above, there is a clear disjunction between how citizens evaluate the environment as they experience it, and their judgments about environmental quality more generally. Citizens experience the environment in this second sense through media coverage and political rhetoric, both of which tend toward the sensational. In Figure 4.3, the salience data presented in Figure 4.2 are combined with a count of stories involving both environmental protection and environmental crisis. While there have been a large number of stories on environmental protection in any given year, they have been framed by crisis—an interesting portrayal given the performance data presented above. The media characterization of policy issues is more

Figure 4.3 The Salience of Environmental Protection and Crisis, 1994–2005

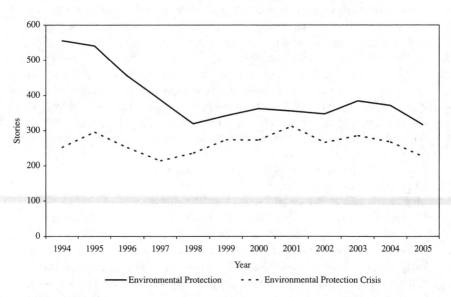

Data source: Reader's Guide to Periodical Literature.

than a trivial issue. If the environment is depicted as being in a perpetual state of crisis, policymakers, advocacy groups, and citizens may lack the discernment to identify areas that constitute a genuine source of concern and are deserving of additional resources. Moreover, public support for environmental protection has not created a secure climate for the EPA. There is an odd disjunction between public assessments of the gains in environmental protection, and the empirical record of EPA performance, which much more closely tracks the experiences with the environment. This gap places environmental policy and the EPA in a vulnerable position. Although there is little support for regulatory retrenchment, there is little opposition to ongoing calls for reform.

■ Conclusion

Almost four decades ago, the nation embarked on the most ambitious and expensive regulatory experiment in its history. The decisions to adopt command-and-control instruments backed with significant fines, to constrain the consideration of compliance costs, and to write exhaustive regulatory mandates that provided the newly created EPA with little discretionary authority, were made with two ends in mind. First, Congress sought to provide certainty of results, regardless of cost. Second, Congress sought to insulate the new policies from an uncertain future. As the performance review in this chapter suggests, the experiment has been largely successful. There have been significant and verifiable improvements in environmental quality regardless of medium. This is not to say that the data on environmental performance are universally positive or that the achievements have been sufficient. Although air pollution levels are some 25 percent below the 1970 threshold, for example, the growing prevalence of respiratory illnesses—a product, in part, of exposure to ozone and particulate pollution—suggests that there is much room for improvement. With respect to water, although a majority of rivers, streams, lakes, ponds, and reservoirs in the United States are categorized as "good" (i.e., not "impaired"), the universe of potential sites is limited to the relatively small proportion of the waters that have been assessed.

Where regulatory performance has fallen short of expectations, resource constraints have often been cited as the main culprit. Yet budgetary constraints are only part of the story. Environmental quality reflects the behavior of public and private actors; it is impossible to separate the effects of policy from changes in corporate practices, technology, and patterns of resource use that were not the direct product of policy. During the past several decades, corporations have responded to changing regulatory and legal circumstances and the heightened salience of the environment more generally. Regulation has been part of the story. But many firms have gone beyond regulation, implementing management systems that were not mandated by public policy, and reengineering products and processes to reduce environmental impacts. Others have remained woefully lax in their environmental practices.

Ideally, the EPA would have greater latitude to maximize the environmental returns from changing corporate practices. Ideally, it would create greater opportunities for experimentation and innovation. This would simultaneously create greater incentives for corporate environmental management and allow the EPA to better target its scarce resources to regulate firms that have proven unwilling or incapable of meeting their legal obligations. Unfortunately, the EPA has yet to discover a means of integrating private sector innovations into the larger regulatory framework. Arguably, the greatest barrier to such integration is the original regulatory design that reinforces adversarialism and provides minimal discretion to administrators and the regulated. As argued in Chapter 2, regulatory delegation may provide opportunities for cost savings. However, it magnifies uncertainty insofar as authority is delegated under conditions of information scarcity. The basic regulatory design adopted in the 1970s prioritized certainty of results over competing values, and this basic commitment has remained firmly in place.

The failure to depart from the original regulatory design carried additional consequences. The heavy reliance on command-and-control instruments and the disregard for compliance costs carried significant political consequences. The 1970s was remembered both as the decade of the environment and the decade of stagflation, a vexing combination of high inflation and sluggish growth. Critics of regulation were quick to make the argument that the new social regulations were imposing unprecedented costs on the economy that vanquished incentives to reinvest. Although correlation is not causation, in political discourse correlation is often sufficient.

While Senator Muskie may have genuinely believed that Congress should not be concerned with economic feasibility, presidents would not share this disregard for costs. From the early 1970s to the present, each president has introduced initiatives to enhance regulatory accountability. A long series of executive orders empowered the Office of Management and Budget to require the application of cost-benefit analysis in regulatory decisionmaking. Although these efforts were highly contentious, by the 1990s there appeared to be a broad consensus that cost-benefit analysis had a legitimate role to play in regulatory oversight. Attention turned to regulatory reinvention—the creation of public-private partnerships that could generate innovative solutions to regulatory problems and leverage private sector resources to partially compensate for the lack of budgetary growth at the EPA. To what extent have these reform and reinvention efforts been sufficient to compensate for the limitations imposed by the original regulatory design?

Regulatory Reform
or Reversal?

At the dawn of the modern environmental era, the system of environmental protection was, at best, anemic. Today, the largest firms are routinely in compliance and, despite significant economic expansion, the environment is in most respects far cleaner than it was a generation ago. The achievements in environmental protection are all the more remarkable given a regulatory design premised on command-and-control instruments and a general disregard for compliance costs. A dispassionate observer might arrive at two broad conclusions. First, one can justifiably count environmental regulation as a qualified success. Second, economic growth and environmental protection—while clearly at tension—may in fact be compatible. One would not arrive at these conclusions on the basis of the regulatory reform debates of the past three decades.

Deregulation and regulatory reform have been on the agenda of every presidential administration since 1970. Although the demands for reform have been the strongest during periods of economic stagnation, they have found an expression even during periods of growth. Over the course of the past several decades, critics have presented a strong and multifaceted case in support of reform. Some of the arguments have focused on the political economy of regulatory capture. Others have cited costly regulatory mandates that create strong inflationary pressures, undermine incentives for investment, and drive companies to outsource production to nations with less stringent regulatory requirements. These claims have led invariably to calls for remedies ranging from wholesale deregulation to the imposition of regulatory review based on cost-benefit analysis.

This chapter provides an overview of the arguments for deregulation and regulatory reform. Since the Nixon presidency, regulatory critiques have stimulated a series of regulatory reforms designed to force agencies to justify significant regulations through a consideration of costs or the formal application of cost-benefit analysis. Although Congress passed statutes that prohibited a consideration of costs as a means of shaping policy decisions and structuring regulatory politics, the imposition of cost-benefit-based regulatory review by successive presidents can be interpreted as a means of forcing agencies to consider costs explicitly as part of the regulatory process. Different policy venues attract different interests and further competing values, adding an additional level of complexity to regulatory policy.

■ Regulation, Rent-Seeking, and Reform

The critique of regulation that began to take shape in the 1950s focused initially on economic regulations. Early appraisals presented a capture theory of regulation built on the empirical observation that, historically, many regulations have done more to support regulated parties than the citizens they were nominally designed to protect. In *Regulating Business by Independent Commission,* Marver H. Bernstein (1955) provided a life-cycle theory of regulatory commissions. During the exhilarating days of gestation and youth, agencies have great energy; their missions are backed by strong public and congressional support and budgetary growth. However, as commissions enter maturity, their mandates lose political support (often as a result of earlier successes) and agencies must search for new political patrons. They often find this support in the industries they are charged with regulating (see also Huntington 1952). Others, including Gabriel Kolko (1963, 1965) and Grant McConnell (1966), suggested that regulatory capture was not the infelicitous product of an agency life cycle, but was intended from the beginning. Indeed, there is much evidence that representatives of regulated industries played a key role in regulatory design during the Progressive Era and the New Deal, often with the explicit goal of using policy to manage competition and circumvent state regulations.

This political critique of regulation was reaffirmed by the economic theory of regulation. According to George J. Stigler (1971), industry seeks a variety of policies, ranging from direct subsidies to regulations controlling prices, flow to market, and conditions of entry and exit. Regulations allow industries to function as cartels, free from competitive market pressures. Elected officials are willing to exchange regulations for political support, even if this transaction imposes costs on consumers. In essence, organized interests exchange political support for policies that produce benefits for group members, whereas the costs are forced onto the unorganized. At first glance, one would expect such an arrangement to stimulate a negative response from voters. But this was unlikely, because voters are often unaware of specific regulations, and the costs imposed on each individual citizen are smaller than the costs of mobilizing in opposition.

Politics makes for strange bedfellows. The political and economic critiques of regulation united consumer advocates from the left and free market advocates from the right. During the late 1960s and early 1970s, Ralph Nader and his colleagues investigated a number of regulatory agencies and produced a set of exposés (see Fellmeth 1970; Green 1972, 1973). These critiques, motivated by New Left concerns over the role of public policy in reinforcing the dominance of the corporation in the United States, demanded that regulatory agencies be transformed to fight for the interests of the citizens. If that proved impossible, captured agencies should be eliminated. These demands were quickly reinforced by the mobilization of free market advocates and business associations responding, in large part, to economic uncertainty. The stagflation of the 1970s seemed impervious to traditional macroeconomic policy tools. Analyses funded by business associations and a number of newly created conservative think tanks claimed that regulatory costs and rigidities could be causally linked to recession, inflation, a decline in corporate investments, and a general loss of US competitiveness in international markets. Although the empirical case for these connections was rarely made with care, elected officials were quite responsive. Competitive deregulation targeted agencies regulating railroads, trucking, civil aeronautics, communications, and finance. Reforms eliminated barriers to entry and increased the role of market forces in setting prices that had been formerly determined by regulatory bureaucracies working closely with regulated parties (Derthick and Quirk 1985; Eisner 2000b: 170–200).

Consumer advocates joined the assault on old-style economic regulations and captured agencies, yet their support for reform turned into opposition when the focus of critics shifted to the new social regulations. The policies implemented by the EPA, the Occupational Safety and Health Administration, and the Consumer Product Safety Commission—all products of the early 1970s—were created to regulate the negative impacts of corporate practices on workers, consumers, and the environment. They were counted as major victories among liberal policy advocates. Close alliances between environmental groups, congressional committees, and the EPA were sufficient to stem the tide of deregulation that began in the 1970s. While new environmental mandates would be rare, there would be no legislative assaults on the EPA. Reformers would have to use other strategies. Demands for reform, as a result, were typically aimed at the presidency. The vast majority of reforms were initiated through executive orders and implemented by the Office of Management and Budget. Whether the reform ideas were relatively modest or far more substantial, they were embroiled in controversy. When seen through the lens of the politics of regulatory design, one can understand why. If every major aspect of regulatory design reflects the outcomes of political struggles, even minor reform efforts can be interpreted as a grand political assault.

All of the key regulatory reform initiatives stemming from the presidency have involved the imposition of review processes. These review processes have usually assigned powers to the OMB and, after the passage of the Paperwork Reduction Act of 1980, to the OMB's Office of Information and Regulatory Affairs. The processes have required executive agencies to pay closer attention to costs, often through the application of cost-benefit or cost-effectiveness analysis. Before reviewing the reform initiatives of the past several decades, it is important to briefly review cost-benefit analysis and the reasons it has proven so controversial in the area of social regulation.

■ Costs, Benefits, and the Environment

Conceptually, cost-benefit analysis is quite simple. It is a methodology that converts streams of costs and benefits to present value, and generates a statistic summarizing the relationship between the two (e.g., net present value, or the benefit-cost ratio). The basic presumption is that, under conditions of scarce resources, one must strive to promote policies that provide the greatest benefits. Stated another way, if there are multiple ways of achieving a given benefit, one should employ the means that cost the least, thereby conserving resources for other uses. If there is a fixed budget for environmental protection—which is unquestionably the case—success in maximizing net benefits should have positive ramifications for the environment. Cost-benefit analysis provides a means of identifying those policies that will prove most efficient in realizing their goals. It can also be used in making decisions about the allocation of resources among competing policies. Moreover, it is argued by some that, to the extent that agencies use cost-benefit analysis as the basis for their decisions, these decisions should exhibit greater transparency and therefore allow for greater accountability.

At first blush, one might be hard-pressed to understand why the application of cost-benefit analysis would prove to be controversial. To arrive at a better understanding of the concerns, it is useful to consider the methodology. A standard equation for calculating net present value (NPV) is presented in Figure 5.1. The basic components of this model are easy to identify. One must calculate the net benefits (i.e., subtract costs from benefits) for each period and then discount the result to determine its present value. By adding the discounted net benefits from each period, one can arrive at a summary statistic—the NPV—that captures the present value over the life of the policy. Alternatively, one can divide the discounted benefits by the discounted costs to calculate the benefit-cost ratio, or the "return" for each dollar invested.

The need to discount arises from the fact that money loses value over time. Consider the following illustration: The present value of $10 million

Figure 5.1 Cost-Benefit Analysis and Net Present Value

$$NPV = (B_T - C_T) + \frac{B_{T+1} - C_{T+1}}{(1 + i)^1} + \frac{B_{T+2} - C_{T+2}}{(1 + i)^2} + \ldots + \frac{B_n - C_n}{(1 + i)^n}$$

enjoyed today is $10 million. Yet that same sum, if received in five years at a 5 percent discount rate, would be worth $7,835,262 today. Time has a comparable impact on costs. If one compares a policy that would require an immediate expenditure of $10 million, it would be less preferable, all else remaining equal, than a policy requiring an expenditure of $2 million today, and $8 million in the tenth year. The cost of the second policy in today's dollars, assuming a discount rate of 5 percent, would be $8,268,209, due to the impact of time. The lesson is simple: benefits and costs that occur in a distant future have a lower value today than benefits and costs that occur in the short term. As a generalization, the policies that perform the best with respect to cost-benefit analysis will have front-loaded benefits and back-loaded costs—a rare combination.

Environmental policies are at a distinct disadvantage when using cost-benefit analysis. Most environmental policies require large initial costs. Communities may be required to invest in expensive filtration systems today, for example, to reduce the concentrations of arsenic in public drinking water. The benefits for human health—in this case, a reduction in bladder cancer and other maladies—may not be realized for a decade or more, given the long latency period. If future benefits are expressed in today's dollars, the impact of time may severely compromise the justification for policy. Moreover, one must consider an additional fact: costs that are incurred today take the form of real, concrete expenditures. Corporations and communities can calculate these costs with relative precision, and they have a powerful incentive to mobilize in opposition. In contrast, estimates of future benefits are usually quite soft, due to their probabilistic nature and their sensitivity to underlying scientific assumptions.

There are several additional issues that have contributed to concerns about the use of cost-benefit analysis in environmental issues. First, to conduct a cost-benefit analysis, all costs and benefits must be expressed in dollar terms or monetized. Policy-related costs are automatically expressed in monetary terms. If a coal-fired plant has to install scrubbers, the costs will be expressed in dollar terms. In contrast, the benefits of policy may include a future reduction in illness, disability, and death, enhanced visibility, and less damage to fragile ecosystems, all of which are difficult to quantify and monetize. There are ongoing controversies, for example, about how one should go about determining the value of a human life for policy purposes. Certainly, lifetime earnings would provide one clear measure, albeit one that could create a bias in favor of policies protecting those with higher incomes. A more common approach is to determine the value of a statistical life (VSL) through revealed preferences. One can arrive at a rough estimate on the basis of the wage that premium workers demand for an incremental increase in the risk of death. If workers demand $600 per year of additional compensation for each additional 1-in-10,000 risk of a work-related fatality, the VSL would be $6 million. Realistic calculations of the value of life can prove politically divisive. For example, during the George W. Bush presidency, the OMB suggested—and then withdrew—a recommendation that the EPA discount the VSL based on the age of the individual. The suggestion that a person aged seventy was worth 37 percent less than his or her younger counterpart attracted the objections of the American Association of Retired Persons, which referred to it as the "senior death discount" (Skrzycki 2003).

When comparing the value of life as represented in the policy decisions and analyses of various agencies, one is struck by the different values assigned to human life. Since 1995 the Federal Aviation Administration has valued a life at $3 million, whereas the EPA has used a VSL of $6 million. When one looks at the costs per life saved in actual policies, the variation is great even within a given agency. W. Kip Viscusi and Ted Gayer (2002: 57–58) provide a striking example: The EPA's regulation of trihalomethane, a chemical byproduct of the interaction of water disinfectants and naturally occurring organic matter in drinking water, saves lives at a cost of $600,000 apiece. The EPA's regulation of the pesticide Atrazine/alachlor in drinking water, in contrast, would save one life at a cost of $274 billion. If one sets the VSL at $6 million, one could make a case for strengthening the regulation of trihalomethane until the cost per life saved approached this figure. One could also justify abandoning the regulation of Atrazine/alachlor and using scarce regulatory resources where they would yield greater returns in lives saved.

Second, there is no way to capture the manner in which the costs and benefits of policy are distributed in society. Cost-benefit analysis, like welfare economics more generally, assumes that policies that increase income should be preferred to those that reduce income, all things being equal. But all things are rarely equal. As has become increasingly clear in the debates over environmental justice, there are growing concerns that environmental problems are concentrated in poor neighborhoods in inner cities, which are already forced to bear enormous costs. A policy that requires the cleanup of industrial waste in inner-city brownfields might deliver great benefits to the residents even if the policy does not compete well with alternatives that generate a more favorable benefit-cost ratio. There may be strong justice-based claims for alleviating environmental problems. Yet cost-benefit analysis has no means of adding weight to the benefits received by specific populations. If equity is an important value to be furthered by policy, it may require a decision to go beyond a narrow calculus of costs and benefits.

A third issue automatically arises. Although one may celebrate the inherent value of a species or a particular ecological niche, cost-benefit analysis is concerned solely with the effects of policy that accrue to human beings. One might follow Christopher D. Stone (1974) and ask: "Should trees have standing?" For advocates of cost-benefit analysis, the answer is a resounding no. The methodology contains a strong anthropocentric bias that makes man the measure of all things. The analysis focuses on potential economic uses of a given resource, rather than its absolute value. The rich diversity of life may be reduced to its market value—a crude and grossly incomplete representation—or ignored altogether if there is no market value. Even if we accept the anthropocentric bias, one might question how to measure accurately the pleasure individuals receive from a day hiking in the mountains or knowing that a species has been preserved. There have been some efforts to arrive at rough estimates. Analysts may not be able to determine the dollar value of the enjoyment derived from hiking in the wilderness. However, one can calculate the costs incurred by those seeking to use the wilderness in this fashion (e.g., travel costs, other out-of-pocket expenses) and arrive at a rough estimate. As one recent study notes: "It would be wrong to think of economic values as dollar-denominated numbers in one's brain to be downloaded when a person is asked the worth of a beautiful ocean sunset; rather, such a value might be inferred from the things that one gives up to see the sunset (e.g., the cost of travel to the ocean)" (Kopp, Krupnick, and Toman 1997: 12). Similarly, analysts may use contingent valuation to help monetize a given benefit. This methodology entails the polling of a sample group as to how much they would be willing to pay for a certain environmental amenity (e.g., to prevent the extinction of a specific species). While this process may generate some concrete figures, one must ask whether the pleasure of seeing a bald eagle in flight or a porcupine caribou running free in the Arctic National Wildlife Refuge makes their preservation more significant than that of some less charismatic species (Gramlich 1998: 136–138).

One might stipulate that cost-benefit analysis has serious limitations and nonetheless conclude that it may still find a place in the analyst's toolkit. However, critics often argue that it has negative impacts on policy discourse more generally. The equations and numerical calculations may create a false sense of objectivity and certitude. Those who lack a familiarity with the methodology may find themselves excluded from the discussions of policy. As Lisa Heinzerling and Frank Ackerman observe:

> Cost-benefit analysis is a complex, resource-intensive, and expert-driven process. It requires a great deal of time and effort to attempt to unpack

even the simplest cost-benefit analysis. Few community groups, for example, have access to the kind of scientific and technical expertise that would allow them to evaluate whether, intentionally or unintentionally, the authors of a cost-benefit analysis have unfairly slighted the interest of the community or some of its members. Few members of the public can meaningfully participate in the debates about the use of particular regression analyses or discount rates which are central to the cost-benefit method. (2002: 26)

Cost-benefit analysis may obscure the enormous uncertainty inherent in analysis, while creating a dense technical discourse that excludes citizens from participating in debates that may have significant impacts on their health and the quality of the environment. In the end, many critics conclude, the real costs of cost-benefit analysis may be too great.

■ Cost-Benefit Analysis and Regulatory Reform

When groups are excluded from policy subsystems, they frequently try to capitalize on salient events to recast the debates, expand the scope of conflict, or force policy deliberations into a friendlier venue. Even if the old policy subsystem remains in place, parallel subsystems may emerge that will represent different visions of policy, models of the underlying problems, bodies of expertise, and interests (Baumgartner and Jones 1993). The environmental policy subsystem in Congress, as noted earlier, was dominated by environmental activists and interest groups. It failed to recognize a legitimate role for business participants and was skeptical of any role for economic analysis. The presidency provided an alternative venue, particularly once regulation was linked rhetorically to stagflation in the 1970s. One should not be surprised, therefore, that the OMB has been the central actor in the imposition of regulatory review processes.

Environmental advocates and their congressional patrons clearly understood the challenge posed by economic analysis. Congress placed statutory constraints on the ability of the EPA to consider costs and thus employ cost-benefit analysis at critical points in the regulatory process. In part, this reflected an understanding that a comprehensive consideration of compliance costs could elevate the influence of business in the policy process, thereby reducing the EPA's conformity to goals established by Congress and supported by environmental groups. Consider the Clean Air Act amendments of 1970. Congress explicitly directed the EPA to base primary national ambient air quality standards on air quality criteria, allowing a margin of safety to protect the public health, but statutorily prohibited the consideration of compliance costs. When setting secondary air quality standards, the EPA was allowed to consider a broader range of benefits, but costs were once again excluded. The national emission standards for hazardous air pollutants were also to be set on the basis of public health concerns without any consideration of costs or economic feasibility. The Clean Air Act was not exceptional. The Clean Water Act, the Safe Drinking Water Act, the Resource Conservation and Recovery Act, and the Comprehensive Environmental Response, Compensation, and Liability Act all placed some restrictions on the EPA's consideration of compliance costs, cost effectiveness, and economic impacts (see EPA 1987).

Although Congress played the central role in assigning duties to the EPA, the president was held responsible for economic performance. To the extent that the EPA and other regulatory agencies implemented policies that could impact on economic performance, presidents had a strong incentive to create new mechanisms of control (Moe 1989: 320). These incentives would only grow during the 1970s, as stagflation became the dominant economic problem (see Figure 5.2). Poor macroeconomic performance combined with heavy business mobilization to force the consideration of regulatory impacts into a new venue (Vogel 1989: 146). Beginning in the Nixon administration, presidents required by executive order (EO) that regulatory agencies conduct analyses of significant rules. In 1971 the Office of Management and Budget instituted a quality-of-life review process requiring agencies to accompany significant regulations with a summary description comparing the costs and benefits of the alternatives and a justification for the decision. During the Ford presidency, EO 11821 (39 Fed. Reg. 41501, November 29, 1974) created the "inflation impact statement," which was replaced in 1976 by the "economic impact statement" via EO 11949 (42 Fed. Reg. 1017, January 5, 1977). Ford also created the Council on Wage and Price Stability, which was chiefly responsible for monitoring private and public sector activities, including regulations, that were contributing to inflation. Under the Ford regulatory review processes, significant regulations were to be accompanied by an analysis of costs, benefits, and economic impacts. These efforts were continued during the Carter presidency, with EO 12044 (43 Fed. Reg. 12661, March 24, 1978), which mandated a "regulatory analysis" with consideration of costs and economic impacts, and required agencies to select the "least burdensome" alternative. Carter created a new interagency body, the Regulatory Analysis Review Group, to review the regulatory analyses, as well as the Regulatory Council, to coordinate regulatory agendas (Landy, Roberts, and Thomas 1994: 66–70). The impacts of the Ford and Carter review processes on the EPA were mixed. Some of the EPA's rules were statutorily exempt. Moreover, it is unclear whether decisions were grounded in analyses or simply justified after the fact (Miller 1977). Yet these initiatives unquestionably elevated the status of economic analysis within the EPA. Economic professionalization occurred in other agencies as well, creating

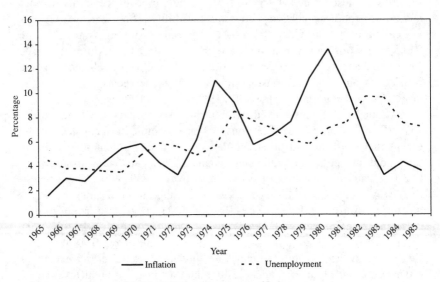

Figure 5.2 Inflation and Unemployment, 1965–1985

Data source: Bureau of Labor Statistics, Department of Labor.

powerful internal constituencies for reform (Derthick and Quirk 1985; Eisner 1991).

Regulatory Reform and Relief: The Reagan Presidency

Regulatory analysis was a centerpiece of the Reagan administration's regulatory strategy, and it provides the single best example of how economic analysis can enter into the politics of regulatory design. Reagan's reform strategy had several components. Loyalists were placed in key management positions. Where possible, functions were delegated to state-level regulators. Draconian budget cuts forced a reduction of regulatory staff. In the case of the EPA, the agency lost one-third of its operating budget and one-fifth of its staff, including a cadre of scientists who generated the scientific foundations of new rules and initiatives. The new Task Force on Regulatory Relief, under the direction of then–vice president George H. W. Bush, was touted as a place where businesses could appeal agency decisions if they felt that they had not been given a fair hearing within the agency (Vig 2003: 107–109). With respect to environmental protection, one could argue that the task force created new access points for business interests that had been systematically excluded under the original regulatory design (Eisner 2000b: 170–200).

Most important for present purposes, the administration built on earlier initiatives to introduce a system of centralized regulatory clearance. Under EO 12291 (46 Fed. Reg. 13193, February 19, 1981), all major proposed and final rules had to be accompanied by regulatory impact analyses (RIAs) that subjected the rule to cost-benefit analysis. Major rules, as in the past, were defined as regulations that would have an annual economic effect of $100 million or more (or that would have a major or significant impact on prices, costs, competition, employment, investment, productivity, or competitiveness). However, the OMB was given the discretion to determine that a rule was significant even if it did not reach this threshold; alternatively, it could waive the requirements altogether. EO 12291 was very explicit in what it expected from RIAs:

> Each preliminary and final Regulatory Impact Analysis shall contain the following information:
>
> (1) A description of the potential benefits of the rule, including any beneficial effects that cannot be quantified in monetary terms, and the identification of those likely to receive the benefits;
> (2) A description of the potential costs of the rule, including any adverse effects that cannot be quantified in monetary terms, and the identification of those likely to bear the costs;
> (3) A determination of the potential net benefits of the rule, including an evaluation of effects that cannot be quantified in monetary terms;
> (4) A description of alternative approaches that could substantially achieve the same regulatory goal at lower cost, together with an analysis of this potential benefit and costs and a brief explanation of the legal reasons why such alternatives, if proposed, could not be adopted; and
> (5) Unless covered by the description required under paragraph (4) of this subsection, an explanation of any legal reasons why the rule cannot be based on the requirements set forth in Section 2 of this Order. (§ 3, para. d)

Agencies subject to the executive order were required to submit a preliminary analysis to the OMB at least sixty days before the publication of a notice of proposed rule making, and a final RIA at least thirty days prior to the publication of the final rule. The RIAs were then reviewed by the OMB-OIRA. Noncompliance would result in the suspension of the rule-making process.

There were at least two significant differences between the role of the OMB under EO 12291 and the review systems put into place by prior administrations. As Thomas O. McGarity notes: "This marked a major institutional departure form the Carter Administration program under which the burden was on the [Council on Wage and Price Stability] or [Regulatory Analysis Review Group] to demonstrate that a regulation was *not* cost effective" (1991: 21). Under 12291, the presumption was reversed and agencies had to demonstrate to the OMB's satisfaction that they had conducted the appropriate analysis and could defend their decisions. Second and more important, the OMB could prevent publication in the *Federal Register* for agencies that failed to meet the requirements of the executive order. Agencies were required to "refrain from publishing its final Regulatory Impact Analysis or final rule until the agency has responded to the Director's views, and incorporated those views and the agency's response in the rulemaking file." In essence, the OMB was given the authority to stop the regulatory process when agencies failed to muster the necessary evidence and analyses.

In June 1981 the OMB issued its "Interim Regulatory Impact Analysis Guidance" to assist agencies in meeting the requirements of the executive order. The document instructed agencies to clearly justify the need for the regulation in terms that may have seemed alien to environmental regulators:

> The statement of the need for and consequences of the proposed regulatory change should address the following questions: (a) What precisely is the problem that needs to be corrected? (That is, what market imperfection(s) give(s) rise to the regulatory proposal? Causes, not just symptoms, should be identified.) (b) How would the regulatory proposal, if promulgated, improve the functioning of the market, or otherwise meet the regulatory objective(s)? Since regulatory failure may be a real possibility, is it clear that the proposed regulation would produce better results than no regulatory change? (Imperfectly functioning markets should not be compared with idealized, perfectly functioning regulatory programs.) (quoted in Kelly 1987: 285)

The OMB simultaneously informed agencies that they should be prepared to quantify and monetize costs and benefits, using a 10 percent discount rate. As noted earlier, the choice of discount rates can have a significant impact on the present value of future costs and benefits. Given that regulatory costs tend to be front-loaded and benefits occur in the future (often the distant future), the selection of a high discount rate created greater difficulties for agencies hoping to justify their policies in terms of cost-benefit analysis.

The regulatory review process created significant difficulties for the EPA. The RIAs were often incomplete and returned to the agency. The difficulties stemmed from many sources, including the inability of the agency to develop the necessary scientific and economic data, the difficulties of quantifying and monetizing benefits, various statutory and judicial deadlines, and resource constraints that prevented the agency from maintaining the needed corps of analysts. The last difficulty may have been the most profound. According to the EPA, during the period 1981–1986 the cost of preparing analyses for major rules ranged from $210,000 to $2,380,000, with an average cost of $675,000 (Congressional Research Service 1994; Eisner, Worsham, and Ringquist 2000: 158–159; EPA 1987: 5–6). Given these impacts, one should not be surprised that more than half the EPA's RIAs were rejected by the OMB-OIRA. During the Reagan presidency, when the new review requirements were combined with large budget cuts and a leadership who were openly hostile to an active agenda, the number of new environmental rules fell precipitously (West and Barrett 1996). Indeed, the number of pages in the *Federal Register*—a commonly used measure of the growth of the regulatory state—fell significantly during the 1980s, reflecting the impact of the Reagan administration's strategy (see Figure 5.3). OMB reviews of the EPA's activities set a high-water mark that subsequent administrations would never match (see Figure 5.4).

A Kinder, Gentler Regulatory Review?

George H. W. Bush did not exhibit the same resistance to environmental regulation as his predecessor, as exhibited by the appointment of World Wildlife Fund president William Reilly to the EPA and subsequent support from the Bush administration for growing regulatory budgets and, most importantly, the Clean Air Act amendments of 1990 (see Chapter 2). Yet despite this difference, Bush remained committed to centralized regulatory review. The process created by EO 12291 remained in place. Agencies

Figure 5.3 Annual *Federal Register* Pages, 1965–2005

Data source: General Services Administration.

Figure 5.4 OMB-OIRA Reviews of the EPA, 1981–2005

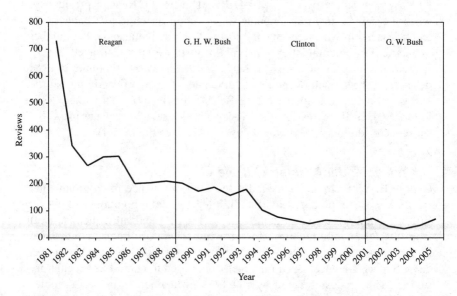

Data source: General Services Administration and Office of Management and Budget, http://reginfo.org.

were required to accompany new rules with RIAs, which depended, in turn, on the use of cost-benefit analysis. In addition, Bush created a new body for regulatory review, the Council on Competitiveness, under the direction of Vice President Dan Quayle. Whereas the Reagan task force reviewed existing regulations, the Quayle council struck a more proactive stance and sought to prevent the promulgation of new rules or, at the very least, to force changes that would reduce their economic impact (Rauch 1991).

The Council on Competitiveness played a relatively minor role in the early years of the Bush presidency. Things changed, however, with the publication of a number of articles comparing Bush's regulatory record to that of his predecessor. Whereas Reagan's first term witnessed significant reductions in new regulations (as revealed, in part, by a 22 percent reduction in the number of proposed and final rules published in the *Federal Register* from 1980 to 1981), this trend was reversed during the Bush presidency. For example, an article in the nonpartisan *National Journal* referred to Bush as "the regulatory president" (Rauch 1991) and claimed that the number of pages in the *Federal Register* in 1991 was the third highest in history, with regulatory spending some 22 percent higher than the final year of the Carter presidency (Furlong 1995). Bush responded by expanding the role of the

Quayle council and, more importantly, announcing a moratorium on new regulations in his 1992 State of the Union address.

In January 1992 the Bush White House issued a memorandum to executive agencies providing guidance for the ninety-day regulatory moratorium. The goals of the moratorium were to reduce the regulatory burden, promote economic growth, and eliminate obsolete regulations. Agency heads were directed to use the moratorium to evaluate regulations, identify those that created unnecessary burdens and undermined economic growth, and accelerate initiatives to eliminate them. A reduction in the flow of new regulations, it was hoped, would allow for a greater investment in regulatory review. On April 29, 1992, President Bush presented the moratorium as a success (Vice President Quayle claimed that it had already created annual savings of $10–20 billion), and extended the moratorium for four more months. Although the moratorium was scheduled to expire at the end of August 1992, it was retained until the end of the Bush presidency largely by the OMB, which claimed that it remained in effect unless officially rescinded by the president. Although the moratorium may have been a politically useful nod to the conservative base in an election year, there is little evidence that it forced a major reduction in the level of regulatory activity, in large part because regulations are often mandated by statute by a Congress that wants to limit the discretionary authority of agency executives and the presidents they serve (Duffy 1997).

President Clinton and Regulatory Review

After twelve years of Republican control of the White House and a year-long regulatory moratorium, environmental activists relished the 1992 victory of Bill Clinton and Al Gore. On the first day of the new Democratic administration, Vice President Gore sent a clear message that change had arrived, proclaiming: "Today we are sending a clear message to the special interests who used the Council on Competitiveness as a back door to avoid the law. That back door is closed. No longer will special interests receive special favors. No longer will our laws be ignored or undermined. No longer will decisions that should be made in public be made in private. In this administration, everyone will play by the rules and public decisions will be public information" (quoted in West and Barrett 1996: 71). In 1993, Clinton signed EO 12866 (58 Fed. Reg. 51735, October 4, 1993), formally revoking the Reagan-era executive orders.

Yet if supporters believed that the era of regulatory review had drawn to a close, they were in for an unpleasant surprise. EO 12866 noted the need for a regulatory system that "improves the performance of the economy without imposing unacceptable or unreasonable costs on society [and the need for] regulatory policies that recognize that the private sector and private markets are the best engine for economic growth." EO 12866, when combined with EO 12875 (58 Fed. Reg. 58093, October 28, 1993), created a new planning process that once again recognized an important role for cost-benefit analysis in regulatory decisionmaking. EO 12866 presented the new administration's regulatory philosophy in clear terms:

> Federal agencies should promulgate only such regulations as are required by law, are necessary to interpret the law, or are made necessary by compelling public need, such as material failures of private markets to protect or improve the health and safety of the public, the environment, or the well-being of the American people. In deciding whether and how to regulate, agencies should assess all costs and benefits of available regulatory alternatives, including the alternative of not regulating. Costs and benefits shall be understood to include both quantifiable measures (to the fullest extent that these can be usefully estimated) and qualitative measures of costs and benefits that are difficult to quantify, but nevertheless essential to consider. Further, in choosing among alternative regulatory approaches, agencies should select those approaches that maximize net benefits (including potential economic, environmental, public health and safety, and other advantages; distributive impacts; and equity), unless a statute requires another regulatory approach. (§ 1a)

The Clinton administration's procedure was similar to the procedures of its predecessors in many ways. Agencies had to identify "significant regulatory actions" (a category that was somewhat broader than that adopted under Reagan's EO 12291), and conduct cost-benefit analyses on these actions. As in the past, the OMB had the discretion to waive the requirements for some rules and determine that other rules were, in fact, of sufficient significance to warrant analysis. Moreover, agencies were required to respond to OIRA concerns and were prohibited from publishing in the *Federal Register* until the OIRA approved of the analysis or waived review requirements (§ 8). However, there were clear differences as well. The administration recognized that many of the benefits of regulation are difficult to quantify and thus would be less insistent on monetization. It also acknowledged the validity of a broader range of criteria beyond cost-effectiveness: "When an agency determines that a regulation is the best available method of achieving the regulatory objective, it shall design its regulations in the most cost-effective manner to achieve the regulatory objective. In doing so, each agency shall consider incentives for innovation, consistency, predictability, the costs of enforcement and compliance (to the government, regulated entities, and the public), flexibility, distributive impacts, and equity" (§ 1b[5]). Moreover, it elevated stakeholder engagement in the regulatory process, suggesting that regulatory analysis should engage a broad set of affected parties (§ 6a).

Many of the core features of the Reagan-Bush regulatory review process were maintained, albeit with some significant modifications. Yet the Clinton administration also reached back to the example of the Carter-era Regulatory Council to create a new body, the Regulatory Working Group, chaired by the OIRA director. Under EO 12866, agencies were required to submit an annual regulatory plan to the OMB that presented their future activities and a discussion of how they would reduce risks and how the risks in question compared to others being addressed. The plans were distributed among members of the Regulatory Working Group to promote coordination. In the event that an agency's plans conflicted with regulations from other agencies, a process was put into place to force harmonization. Moreover, the working group was to serve as a forum for discussing a host of issues, including innovative regulatory techniques, comparative risk assessment, and streamlining processes to reduce burdens on small businesses.

What is one to make of regulatory review under Clinton? Certainly, the hopes that a Democratic administration would bring an end to centralized regulatory review were quickly dashed. Yet there were distinct differences between the approach taken during the Clinton presidency and the approaches of its immediate predecessors. As one analysis suggests, the system created under EO 12899 provided agencies with far greater latitude in the development of regulations, while reversing the erosion of public accountability that seemed to be one of the negative consequences of earlier regulatory review processes. Given the creation of the Regulatory Working Group and the emphasis placed on collaboration and stakeholder engagement, it appeared "to have become more open, less confrontational, and somewhat less intrusive on the administrative process." At the same time, an additional key lesson of the transition from Reagan-Bush to Clinton was clear: "centralized review that is initially based on the criterion of economic efficiency is adaptable to the mainstream regulatory priorities of both political parties, and is likely to appeal to any president who will be elected in the foreseeable future" (Hahn 2000: 573).

■ **Conclusion**

For a generation, executive-branch agencies have been required to conduct cost-benefit analyses to justify their regulatory actions, and the OMB-OIRA has claimed responsibility for regulatory clearance. By preventing publication of rule making in the *Federal Register,* the OMB can stop the regulatory process until agencies comply with regulatory review procedures. When Reagan issued EO 12291 in 1981, many critics interpreted this as an administrative assault on democratic politics waged by Republicans beholden to corporate interests. While these critiques may have had some merit, it would be inaccurate to view regulatory review as a partisan matter.

Although Vice President Gore denounced regulatory review in grandiloquent terms, the Clinton-era regulatory review processes did not fully dismantle the system put into place during the Reagan presidency. If one doubts that regulatory review is no longer a strictly partisan issue, one only need consider the fact that following the victory of George W. Bush in 2000, the new administration retained the Clinton administration's review process.

In fact, it may be more useful to view regulatory review through the lens of the administrative presidency (see Nathan 1983). Students of the presidency have long noted the disjunction between the perceived and actual powers of the presidency (Neustadt 1991). Although the vast majority of regulation occurs within the executive branch, Congress has exercised the greatest control over agency activities by passing highly detailed statutes that provide minimal discretion for administrators. Presidents can exercise power over regulation through the appointment of key personnel and through budgetary decisions, but can do so only to the extent that their decisions receive the active or tacit consent of Congress. At the end of the day, the Senate must confirm presidential appointments; the president's budget is virtually rewritten by Congress. Moreover, appropriations riders have been used creatively to prohibit agencies from spending funds on specific regulatory duties. Regulatory review and clearance, centralized in the OMB, provide the president with an important tool in shaping regulation. Yet it is a blunt tool, and one can question its effects given the role of other actors.

In *Reviving Regulatory Reform,* Robert W. Hahn conducted a comprehensive survey of regulations with respect to their cost-benefit performance. He found that, for the period 1981–1996, regulations had a net present value of $1.8 trillion for final rules and $386 billion for proposed rules. Although the EPA was responsible for 66 percent of the final regulations, it accounted for one-quarter of the total net benefits. Moreover, its regulations, when taken as a whole, had a net benefit only because nineteen rules promulgated under the Clean Air Act yielded very high net benefits:

> All EPA rules promulgated under the Comprehensive Environmental Response, Compensation, and Liability Act, the Clean Water Act, the Toxic Substances Control Act, and the Federal Insecticide, Fungicide, and Rodenticide Act have negative net benefits. Since the Toxic Substances Control Act and the Federal Insecticide, Fungicide, and Rodenticide Act are regarded as "balancing" statutes, meaning that they contain statutory language that requires agencies to balance the benefits and costs of regulations, it is remarkable that all EPA rules authorized by those statutes have negative net benefits. A closer look at the two Federal Insecticide, Fungicide, and Rodenticide Act rules and the four Toxic Substances Control Act rules reveals that the EPA either identified benefits for those regulations and did not quantify the benefits or simply did not identify any benefits. . . . Only regulations based on the Clean Air Act and the Safe

> Drinking Water Act yield positive net benefits. In the case of the Safe
> Drinking Water Act, one regulation addressing lead and copper accounts
> for over 95 percent of the benefits of all the act's regulations. Without one
> rule that substantially reduces lead content in gasoline, net benefits for the
> Clean Air Act drop from about $590 billion to just over $200 billion.
> (2000: 41, 44)

Hahn's analysis strongly suggests that the impact of cost-benefit analysis
has been less than one might imagine. Costs and benefits are neither consistently calculated nor routinely used as the basis for decisionmaking. With
the exception of a few highly beneficial regulations, the larger track record
is one of costs that exceed benefits. Even if the EPA were committed to the
use of cost-benefit analysis, one would find that there were statutory barriers to making all regulatory actions cost-beneficial. Of course, one would
not expect to find such a commitment at the EPA.

In a speech celebrating the thirtieth anniversary of Earth Day, EPA
administrator Carol M. Browner (2000) decried "the ongoing attempts to
'poison the well,' so to speak, by infusing cost-benefit considerations into
the very definition of protectiveness." She went on to ask: "Would we have,
say, required the removal of lead from gasoline 25 years ago if the costs to
industry were weighed against the benefits? How would we have determined what the benefits would be? What is the value of a few IQ points for
a child? What is the value of a human life?" Such questions arise when
environmental regulators reflect on the role of cost-benefit analysis. There
remains great skepticism over the ability to quantify and monetize the benefits of social regulations. The professional norms of many regulatory
bureaucrats conflict with a prioritization of efficiency relative to other values. Nonetheless, cost-benefit analysis has become an important force in
shaping agency decisionmaking, even if it is not strictly determinate.

Reinventing Environmental Protection: Flexibility in an Iron Cage

The regulatory reforms of the 1970s and 1980s forced agencies to employ regulatory review based on cost-benefit analysis to improve performance, at least nominally. During the 1990s, regulatory review requirements were combined with a far more novel approach: regulatory reinvention. The central goal of the reinvention of government (REGO) was to apply lessons derived from the private sector to make government more responsive, effective, and efficient. Whereas regulatory review required hierarchical control and the application of economic analysis, REGO involved fostering collaborative and cooperative relationships between regulators and the regulated. This chapter begins with an examination of the core arguments in support of REGO and the political environment that shaped the Clinton administration's decision to embrace REGO, and then examines and assesses the REGO efforts of the EPA. In the end, these efforts, while novel, revealed the power of the original regulatory design decisions.

■ Reinventing Government

In 1992, David Osborne and Ted Gaebler (1992) published a book titled *Reinventing Government: How the Entrepreneurial Spirit Is Transforming the Public Sector.* The central argument of the book was quite simple: government can be made far more effective and responsive if reformers apply some of the core lessons derived from the private sector. Rather than remaining wed to outdated notions of hierarchy and centralized control, agencies should decentralize authority, empower communities, and adopt a customer orientation. The bureaucratic adherence to rules should be replaced by a dedication to mission and a focus on results. Rather than reacting to problems as they occur, agencies should adopt a preventative focus. The influence of *Reinventing Government* was magnified by its timing. Many policymakers were dissatisfied with bureaucratic hierarchies but were unwilling to embrace markets. The "entrepreneurial government" celebrated by Osborne and Gaebler provided one vision of a third path.

By the late 1980s, there was a growing consensus that the EPA should place a far greater emphasis on pollution prevention. Prevention was deemed vital because once created, pollution cannot be eliminated, only transformed into a more benign form. Congress promoted this shift toward pollution prevention with the passage of the Pollution Prevention Act of 1990, according to which Congress found that:

- There are significant opportunities for industry to reduce or prevent pollution at the source through cost-effective changes in production, operation, and raw materials use. Such changes offer industry substantial savings [and] help protect the environment and reduce risks to worker health and safety.
- The opportunities for source reduction are often not realized because existing regulations, and the industrial resources they require for compliance, focus upon treatment and disposal, rather than source reduction; existing regulations do not emphasize multi-media management of pollution; and businesses need information and technical assistance to overcome institutional barriers to the adoption of source reduction practices. . . .
- Source reduction is fundamentally different and more desirable than waste management and pollution control. (42 USC §§ 1310, 13102, et seq.)

Congress decried "the historical lack of attention to source reduction" and directed the EPA to "establish a source reduction program which collects and disseminates information, provides financial assistance to States," and "facilitate[s] the adoption of source reduction techniques by businesses." The agency was directed to "establish an annual award program to recognize a company or companies which operate outstanding or innovative source reduction programs." Moreover, it was required to "identify opportunities to use Federal procurement to encourage source reduction" (42 USC § 13103).

A 1992 EPA memorandum on the definition of "pollution prevention" noted that it "requires a cultural change—one which encourages more anticipation and internalizing of real environmental costs by those who may generate pollution, and which requires EPA to build a new relationship with all of our constituents to find the most cost-effective means to achieve those goals" (Habicht 1992). Regulators would need to delegate far greater authority to regulated parties and provide them with the flexibility to generate innovations in product and process designs and introduce new internal management systems. Although the new orientation did not find much of an expression in the George H. W. Bush presidency, it would become a central component of REGO under Clinton.

Reinvention became a core element of the Clinton regulatory agenda. Vice President Gore, working with a staff of 260, was responsible for the National Performance Review, a comprehensive effort to promote REGO and generate reform proposals. Gore made the case for REGO in a series of highly publicized media events. In time, virtually all regulatory agencies would consider how the core principles of REGO might be applied in their agencies. Some agencies, like the EPA, created offices of reinvention to centralize and coordinate the reform efforts. The central goals were to simplify regulations, streamline processes, eliminate bureaucratic redundancy, increase flexibility, and enhance responsiveness to external stakeholders.

Although the attraction of REGO can be partly attributed to President Clinton's Democratic Leadership Council centrism, the broader political climate left few other options open. Initially, concerns with the deficit and debt inherited from the Reagan and Bush administrations precluded a substantial expansion of regulatory budgets or commitments. More important, the 1994 midterm elections placed Congress under the unified control of the Republican Party for the first time in four decades. Armed with the Contract with America, the new majority was intent on scaling back the regulatory state, eliminating unfunded mandates and government takings, and forcing heightened attention to compliance costs and cost-benefit analysis more generally. Under these conditions, REGO was one of the few options that would prove to be consistent with the larger shift in the ideological and partisan composition of Congress.

■ Reinventing the Environmental Protection Agency

The EPA was a perfect candidate for reinvention. It was first among regulatory agencies in terms of both its budget and the costs imposed on the economy. Moreover, there was something of a consensus regarding some of the core problems. First, critics noted that the EPA had too great a reliance on command-and-control instruments, prescriptive rules, and design and technology standards. Performance standards, it was argued, could allow regulated parties the flexibility to achieve regulatory goals more cost-effectively. Second, the commitment to media-specific regulation had the perverse effects of focusing attention on media-shifting rather than pollution prevention, while forcing regulated parties to comply with multiple permit processes simultaneously. Integrated regulation and an emphasis on preventive strategies could prove far more effective. Finally, the strong reliance on command-and-control instruments and the imposition of heavy fines contributed to regulatory adversarialism. Litigation sapped scarce resources and resulted in unnecessary delays.

In 1993, EPA administrator Carol M. Browner issued a policy statement titled "New Directions for Environmental Protection," which reiterated the core principles of the Pollution Prevention Act and emphasized the importance of making pollution prevention central to the EPA's mission. Browner noted that a key component of pollution prevention had to be new partnerships with industry: "Collaborative efforts with industry or public agencies in many cases can help us achieve results through pollution prevention more quickly than could be obtained through regulation alone," because "regulations often do not reach the more complicated corporate decisions needed . . . to reduce pollution and energy consumption. We must encourage these efforts by entering into partnerships with public and private organizations where such cooperation can produce tangible environmental results" (Browner 1993). In 1995 the Clinton administration released a report titled "Reinventing Environmental Regulation," which noted:

> We have learned that pollution is often a sign of economic inefficiency and business can improve profits by preventing it. We have learned that better decisions result from a collaborative process with people working together, rather than from an adversarial one that pits them against each other. And we have learned that regulations that provide flexibility—but require accountability—can provide greater protection at a lower cost. (Clinton and Gore 1995: 2)

Rather than continuing the media-specific regulations of the past, "attention must shift to integrated strategies for whole facilities, whole economic sectors, and whole communities." Rather than continuing to apply a "one size fits all" approach to regulation, the EPA must "efficiently tailor solutions to problems." Rather than using standard indicators of agency activity, success "will be measured by achieving real results in the real world, not simply by adhering to procedures." REGO would "encourage innovation by providing flexibility with an industry-by-industry, place-by-place approach to achieving standards." Regulated parties would be encouraged to "accept their responsibility for environmental stewardship" and "make environmental protection a strategic consideration" (Clinton and Gore 1995: 4–5).

The EPA's strategic plan, issued in 1997, emphasized the same set of themes. It clearly identified the limitations of the existing regulatory system and stated a case that could have been drawn from any number of external critiques:

> Insufficient flexibility in regulatory requirements that produce increasingly smaller levels of return can impose additional costs on industries and communities. Prescriptive controls can discourage technological innovation that could help lower costs and achieve environmental benefits beyond those achieved under current mandates. More importantly, a system focused largely on "end-of-pipe" pollution simply is not effective at addressing a number of emerging risks, such as polluted runoff or ozone depletion. (EPA 1997: 8)

Given resource constraints, it was argued, the EPA should form partnerships to leverage the financial, technical, and intellectual resources of corporations, public interest groups, and government at other levels. As the strategic plan explains, "many companies now have mature environmental management programs, knowledgeable and experienced staff, and access to technological advancements" that make them "capable of not just meeting, but exceeding, today's national standards." This trend in corporate environmental management and "the interest in exceeding requirements" led the EPA to note: "in time, our national environmental standards may come to represent a performance floor to maintain, rather than a ceiling to reach" (EPA 1997: 13)

The REGO efforts went beyond promising reports. In 1995 alone, twenty-five projects were introduced at the EPA, with new programs emerging every year thereafter. Some projects—such as Project XL—had broad, economywide significance, whereas others are more narrowly focused on a specific issue or industry. In 1997 the EPA also created its Office of Reinvention, under the direction of a new associate administrator, to manage the REGO initiatives. In addition, the EPA created a new Reinvention Action Council, to coordinate efforts across the agency's offices. Given that many of the initiatives would require the cooperation of multiple offices that were used to functioning independently, such a body could potentially prevent bureaucratic politics from undermining reinvention (see Rosenbaum 2000).

Partners for the Environment

Partners for the Environment, a collection of national and regional projects, promoted collaboration between the EPA and more than 11,000 organizations, including businesses, citizen groups, state and local governments, universities, and trade associations (see EPA 1998c). By the end of the Clinton presidency, the partnership included a plethora of programs (see Table 6.1) covering most environmentally sensitive industries. In each case, the EPA (often in cooperation with other agencies) worked with industry actors to facilitate innovations in technologies, products, and processes that would obviate the need for traditional enforcement and remediation by preventing pollution at the source. The EPA estimated that in 2000 alone, the partners realized emission reductions of 37 million metric tons (carbon equivalent) for greenhouse gases, 158,173 metric tons for nitrogen oxides, and 288,627 metric tons for sulfur dioxide. In addition, the partners saved 603 million gallons of water and 769 trillion British thermal units of energy, as well as money: $5.9 billion in 2000 compared to $4.1 billion in 1999 (http://www.epa.gov/partners/about/index.htm).

The EPA created a number of programs to address specific components of corporate environmental policy. For example, the agency established its

Table 6.1   Partners for the Environment Programs

Agstar	Indoor Environments Program
Climate Wise Recognition Program	Landfill Methane Outreach Program
Coalbed Methane Outreach Program	Natural Gas Star Program
Common Sense Initiative	Pesticide Environmental Stewardship Program
Design for Environment Program	Project XL
Energy Star Buildings Program	Ruminant Livestock Efficiency Program
Energy Star Office Equipment Program	State and Local Outreach Program
Energy Star Residential Program	33/50 Program
Energy Star Transformer Program	Transportation Partners
Environmental Accounting Program	US Initiative on Joint Implementation
Environmental Leadership Program	Voluntary Aluminum Industrial Program
Green Chemistry Challenge	Water Alliances for Voluntary Efficiency
Green Chemistry Program	Waste Minimization National Plan
Green Lights Partnership	WasteWise Program

Source: http://www.epa.gov/partners.

Design for Environment Program in 1992, under the authority granted in the Pollution Prevention Act of 1990. The program is an attempt to reduce or prevent environmental impacts across the life cycle through product and process redesign. This program, explicitly based on concepts "pioneered by industry," was initiated by, and housed in, the Office of Pollution Prevention and Toxics. Through the program, the EPA created "voluntary partnerships with industry, universities, research institutions, public interest groups, and other government agencies." The prevention office used the program partnerships as a means of providing technical support and analysis and collecting and disseminating information that "promotes the incorporation of environmental considerations into the traditional business decision-making process" (EPA 2001a: 1)

The Design for Environment Program focused on introducing and disseminating cleaner technologies in a number of industries. The process involved developing a substitutes assessment for cleaner technologies that provided information on the environmental impact and economic performance of competing technologies and production methods (EPA 1996). The Printed Wiring Board Project, for example, developed alternative technologies and processes to reduce the use of water and energy and the generation of toxic wastes. The project was promoted through close collaboration with the Institute for Interconnecting and Packaging Electronic Circuits and a grant to the University of Tennessee's Center for Clean Products and Clean Technologies. Similar projects were initiated for adhesives, automotive refinishing, computer displays, flexography, garment and textile care, gravure printing, industrial and institutional laundry, lithography, metal finishing, and screen printing. In each case, the Design for Environment team forged alliances with industry actors and trade associations.

The EPA's Green Chemistry Program was created as part of the larger Design for Environment Program to stimulate pollution prevention research in the design and synthesis of chemicals, and established a clear and ambitious set of goals:

> EPA's Green Chemistry Program promotes the research, development, and implementation of innovative chemical technologies that accomplish pollution prevention in a scientifically sound and cost-effective manner. To accomplish these goals, the Green Chemistry Program recognizes and supports chemical technologies that reduce or eliminate the use or generation of hazardous substances during the design, manufacture, and use of chemical products and processes. More specifically, the Green Chemistry Program supports fundamental research in the area of environmentally benign chemistry as well as a variety of educational activities, international activities, conferences and meetings, and tool development, all through voluntary partnerships with academia, industry, other government agencies, and non-government organizations. (http://www.epa.gov/greenchemistry/whats_gc.html)

The Green Chemistry Program employed a set of partnerships with industry, trade associations, academic research centers, government agencies, national laboratories, international organizations, and advocacy groups. It relied on EPA cooperation with the American Chemistry Council, the American Petroleum Institute, and the Society of the Plastics Industry (all of which had self-regulatory programs of their own), as well as with top firms in the chemical industry, including BF Goodrich, Dow Chemical, Dow Corning, E. I. DuPont de Nemours, Eastman Kodak, Polaroid, Rochester Midland, and Solutia.

■ From Promotion to Regulation

Many of the above-mentioned programs focused on the promotion and dissemination of new innovations. As the EPA attempted to integrate these programs with existing regulations, however, the difficulties became palpable. As a generalization, reinvention occurred at the margins or was appended onto existing structures without altering the underlying regulatory design. As Daniel J. Fiorino observes:

> Much has been made of the "reinvention" of environmental regulation in the 1990s. However, nearly all recent efforts to reinvent environmental regulation in the United States have come to little more than a tinkering with specific elements of a highly complex system. These efforts aim, for example, to graft flexibility onto parts of an inflexible whole by inviting

company proposals for exemptions from rules. They propose reductions in administrative burdens by expediting permitting, consolidating reporting, or replacing paper with electronic transactions. However laudable these improvements may be, they rarely, except rhetorically, deliver the systemic change that the term "reinvention" implies. (1999: 442)

As the EPA sought to create greater opportunities and incentives for corporate environmental innovations, its success was constrained by the same factors cited in making the case for REGO. It is difficult to promote reforms to increase flexibility within a system that is premised on the use of command-and-control policy instruments, prescriptive rules, and media-specific regulation. Two examples of how these tensions have manifested themselves are notable: the EPA's position on audit immunity, and its experiences with Project XL.

Measuring Environmental Performance: The Costs of Self-Policing

Corporations with a commitment to environmental improvements usually employ an environmental management system (EMS). In essence, an EMS is an environmental application of total quality management. Corporations assess current environmental performance, identify problems, assign responsibility for their management, and evaluate progress, before starting the process anew. If the EPA wants companies to be proactive and go beyond regulation, it should promote the dissemination of quality environmental management systems. During the 1990s, the EPA's Emerging Strategies Division (renamed the Performance Incentives Division in 2000) worked to promote EMS adoption and to develop environmental performance indicators and procedures for evaluating performance. More important, the EPA participated in the development of the ISO 14000 series of international standards promulgated by the International Organization for Standardization (ISO) in Geneva. ISO 14001 establishes the key features of a quality EMS and provides a mechanism for third-party auditing and certification (see Chapter 9).

A company that employs an EMS needs to collect information on performance to determine whether it is having the intended impact on targeted objectives. It may conduct these audits with an internal team; it may rely on independent third-party auditors to evaluate performance (a necessity for firms seeking certification under ISO 14001). One would assume that the EPA would be highly supportive of environmental audits, given the positive role they can play in providing managers with the information they need for self-regulating environmental impacts and taking corrective action when problems are discovered. Yet the EPA's position on audits created difficulties for companies intent on enhancing their capacity for environmental management.

Businesses face a rather difficult situation with respect to audits, which may generate evidence of regulatory violations that could increase vulnerability to prosecution and civil litigation. To the extent that regulators force disclosure and penalize firms, they create disincentives for audits. If companies refuse to conduct thorough audits, they may be unaware of problems and incapable of taking corrective action. If they try to veil audits with lawyer-client privilege, the costs may prove prohibitive. Ironically, the quality of corporate environmental management may depend on preserving the secrecy of some corporate documentation. Critics retort that profit-seeking corporations will manage impacts only if they fear regulatory sanctions. The higher the probability of detection and prosecution, the greater the incentive for preventative action (see Johnson 1997).

Many of the very corporations that speak the language of heightened corporate environmental responsibility, and tout the merits of corporate environmental management as an alternative to regulation, were active in lobbying for an environmental audit privilege in the 1990s. According to Christopher Bedford, advocates of audit secrecy asked "elected state and federal representatives to shield critical environmental corporate documents in exchange for a simple assertion by management that, 'you can trust us to clean up our own affairs'" (1996: 3). Legislation providing for privilege and immunity was introduced in every state, and several states provided audit privileges, penalty immunities, or both. Although state laws could impact state regulatory practices, they did little with respect to the EPA, which consistently rejected corporate privilege. As the agency's audit policy noted:

> Although EPA encourages environmental auditing, it must do so without compromising the integrity and enforceability of environmental laws. . . . The Agency remains firmly opposed to statutory and regulatory audit privileges and immunity. Privilege laws shield evidence of wrongdoing and prevent States from investigating even the most serious environmental violations. Immunity laws prevent States from obtaining penalties that are appropriate to the seriousness of the violation, as they are required to do under Federal law. Audit privilege and immunity laws are unnecessary, undermine law enforcement, impair protection of human health and the environment, and interfere with the public's right to know of potential and existing environmental hazards. Statutory audit privilege and immunity run counter to encouraging the kind of openness that builds trust between regulators, the regulated community and the public. . . . Privileged information is unavailable to law enforcers and to members of the public who have suffered harm as a result of environmental violations. The Agency opposes statutory immunity because it diminishes law enforcement's ability to discourage wrongful behavior and interferes with a regulator's ability to punish individuals who disregard the law and place others in danger. (EPA 2000: 29–30)

The EPA reserved "its right to bring independent action against regulated entities for violations of Federal law that threaten human health or the environment, reflect criminal conduct or repeated noncompliance, or allow one company to profit at the expense of its law-abiding competitors" (2000: 32). State privilege and immunity laws, in short, would have no impact on the agency's decision to prosecute.

The EPA attempted to reduce disincentives through its self-disclosure policy. Where voluntary audits revealed violations and companies promptly disclosed this fact and corrected the problem, the agency would "not seek gravity-based (i.e., non-economic benefit) penalties" and would "generally not recommend criminal prosecution." The EPA would reduce gravity-based penalties by 75 percent, more generally, when violations were reported, even if they were not discovered through audits (Rodgers 1996; EPA 1995). Was the self-disclosure policy sufficient? Miri Berlin notes that the policy was "discretionary," failed to "create evidentiary privilege," and, as a result, did not "provide companies with effective incentives to audit" (1998: 624). There is some evidence that many corporations continued to conduct audits. Data released by the EPA's Office of Regulatory Enforcement suggest that self-disclosure occurs with some frequency and that the EPA routinely responds to self-disclosure with a reduction in penalties (EPA 2000). For example, when GTE voluntarily reported 600 violations of the Emergency Planning and Community Right to Know Act and the Clean Water Act, involving 314 GTE facilities in twenty-one states, the EPA imposed a penalty of $52,264, an amount "equal to the amount of money saved by the company during its period of noncompliance." Given GTE's "outstanding cooperation in voluntarily disclosing and promptly correcting" the violations, the EPA waived $2.38 million in potential penalties (EPA 1998b: 1).

Despite the anecdotal evidence, the issue of information remains a nettlesome one. Corporations cannot be held accountable for their environmental impacts, unless there is a high degree of transparency and the results of audits are opened to the public. Yet such disclosure may create greater vulnerability to litigation, thereby reducing the incentives for auditing. As a generalization, the EPA will not release self-disclosed documents under the Freedom of Information Act until after a case has been settled. Even then, the documents will not be released if they contain confidential business information. In the end, the challenge for the EPA is to discover some means of preserving the incentives for self-regulation while simultaneously fostering the transparency and accountability necessary to convey legitimacy.

Project XL: Flexibility Within an Iron Cage

The EPA touted Project XL (for "eXcellence and Leadership") as the crown jewel of reinvention. It was created to give "regulated entities an opportunity to develop models for a new, performance-based environmental management system for the next century—one that emphasizes better bottom-line results." By design, Project XL was envisioned as a means of overcoming many of the dysfunctional features of the regulatory system in hopes of promoting innovations and superior performance:

> Participants are given the flexibility to develop common sense, cost-effective strategies that will replace or modify specific regulatory requirements, on the condition that they produce greater environmental benefits. Based on the premise that these participants know better than the federal government how to reduce their pollution, Project XL reduces the regulatory burden and promotes economic growth while achieving better environmental and public health protection. (EPA 1998c: 41)

The EPA anticipated hundreds of proposals with the goal of rapidly approving some fifty pilot programs. These expectations proved optimistic. The reasons are highly suggestive of the difficulties inherent in reconciling reinvention and existing institutions.

As of December 2003, Project XL had received over ninety-five proposals. Based on my analysis of EPA data (http://www.epa.gov/projectxl), there is sufficient information to arrive at some tentative conclusions. First, proposal approval was a lengthy process, particularly in the early years of Project XL. Of the proposals that were submitted in 1995, the average length of time between submission and signing of the final project agreement was 26.7 months, some 2.2 years. Proposals submitted in 1996 languished for an average of 33.5 months, or 2.8 years. Only one proposal submitted in 1997 survived the process, with 40.0 months between submission and final project agreement. In 1998 the EPA responded to this situation by reengineering the process, which resulted in the time requirements falling to 17.9 months in 1998, 11.0 months in 1999, and 6.8 months in 2000.

The successful proposals submitted between 1995 and 2000 represent a mix of large corporations and public agencies, ranging from the Department of Defense's Elmendorf Air Force Base (1996) to the Narragansett Bay Commission (1999). During the period as a whole, 56.25 percent of successful proposals (twenty-seven out of forty-eight) came from corporations, whereas 43.75 percent (twenty-one) came from public agencies. It is interesting to note, however, that 76.19 percent of the successful proposals submitted by government agencies were submitted in the period following the process reengineering. It is impossible, as a result, to determine how much of the reduction in the approval time was attributable to changes in process, and how much was a product of changes in the nature of the applicants or the complexity of the proposed projects.

The costs of proposing, amending, and reviewing projects were significant. According to an analysis of private facilities that submitted proposals in the first six months of Project XL, the average transaction costs were $350,000 for the facilities and $110,000 for the EPA regional office. By dividing the sample into low-cost and high-cost firms (based on whether they were above or below the $540,000 median), it became clear that costs were related to the complexity of proposals: "Every one of the facilities in the high-cost category requested either an agreement covering more than one facility or a waiver of the requirement to get new air permits every time the production process changes (in exchange for an aggregate cap on air emissions). By contrast, none of the facilities in the low-cost category requested such a waiver, and only one submitted a proposal involving more than one facility." Approximately half of the costs of participating in Project XL were incurred through interactions with the EPA's regional offices and in seeking final EPA approval. High-cost firms claimed that some 62 percent of proposal development costs arose through regulatory interactions with the EPA, whereas a mere 5 percent were incurred through the development of the preliminary proposal and an additional 16.2 percent through stakeholder negotiations (Blackman et al. 2001: 6, 9, 7).

Unquestionably, the delays and costs associated with successful proposals constitute an important part of the story. Equally important, however, is the high failure rate. In the first three years of Project XL, fully 72.5 percent of the proposals were rejected, formally withdrawn, or became inactive. The EPA rejected the proposals of firms currently involved in enforcement proceedings. In a few cases, proposals were rejected because the same flexibility could be achieved through other programs. The EPA rejected proposals most commonly, however, because applicants could not guarantee superior environmental performance (SEP). As the EPA noted in rejecting one proposal: "your proposal would not deliver the superior environmental results which the XL program was designed to foster. Overall, your proposal presents both environmental positives and negatives, but in my judgment, not the sort of superior environmental performance envisioned in the XL criteria" (Gardiner 1995).

The quid pro quo—greater flexibility in exchange for superior environmental performance—was a key source of weakness. As Alfred A. Marcus, Donald A. Geffen, and Ken Sexton explain:

> The problem with this framework is how to define SEP and how to work out trades between different levels of SEP and different levels of flexibility. . . . Granting regulatory relief and thereby operating flexibility provides a company with tangible economic benefits. These benefits must be balanced by environmental gains that would not be otherwise achieved. Because the flexibility has to be "paid for" with superior performance, a company must show that the environmental benefits it offers otherwise would not have been gained. This criterion can be difficult to satisfy. Because definitions of SEP and flexibility are vague, companies considering participation in XL are presented with a level of risk that is hard for them to accept. (2002: 163)

Ambitious experiments involve a great deal of uncertainty. As the EPA demanded guaranteed results, negotiations became protracted and filled with opportunities for challenges and obstruction. "By making it easier for dissenters to raise objections that the SEP offered is not good enough, it stands in the way of deals being consummated" (Marcus, Geffen, and Sexton 2002: 163).

In a number of cases, applicants decided to withdraw their proposals. These withdrawals provide a clear picture of some of the tensions inherent in REGO. For a policy to promote meaningful innovation, the flexibility to experiment must be combined with a regulatory realization that all innovations involve risks of failure. Firms will be unlikely to accept these risks if they fear prosecution. Indeed, some applicants were concerned that the EPA retained excessive prosecutorial discretion to punish unsuccessful experiments. Take the case of 3M, a company widely recognized as an innovator in environmental management that had consistently exceeded regulatory requirements. The process was characterized by lengthy dealings with EPA and ongoing questions as to whether Project XL approval was necessary, given that 3M was already producing superior environmental performance without the requested flexibility. More important, the EPA was willing to allow for greater flexibility only if the company would work under the provisions of a consent decree. As 3M explained when withdrawing its application: "3M and other potential Project XL permit applicants are troubled by an implementation approach that relies on consent decrees or any other form of the government's 'enforcement discretion.' Neither the Project XL program nor individual Project XL permits should be considered as operating in 'violation' of environmental law. On the contrary, we strongly believe that the performance of facilities in this program will be 'beyond compliance' of emission limits and will provide numerous additional environmental benefits" (Zosel 1995).

Other proposals faltered as escalating resource demands vanquished any economic incentives to continue. After a three-year effort to develop a secondary emissions offsetting project under XL, for example, Union Carbide withdrew its proposal, noting "the resources needed to develop data sufficient to support the . . . project exceed the value to us of going forward" (Boroughs 1998). Other applicants withdrew their proposals because they had become frustrated with costly delays. For example, the city of Anaheim, California, withdrew its proposal well into the process, citing "considerable delays" in the EPA's "internal review/approval process" that resulted in considerable frustration and disappointment on the part of Anaheim department staff (Aghjayan 1997). In this case, a proposal to retrofit an infrequently used plant became mute. Growing electricity demand during the two-year approval period led the city of Anaheim to place the plant under heavier usage without the improvements proposed under Project XL.

In part, delays must be viewed as a byproduct of a process that demands high levels of stakeholder involvement. Successful proposals have usually evolved through extensive meetings with stakeholders. Consider an XL project at Intel's Maricopa County facility. A proposal to implement a facilitywide cap on air emissions to replace individual permit limits for different air emission sources was introduced on June 30, 1995. From January through October 1996, Intel held some 100 stakeholder and working group meetings, each lasting four to six hours (Rosenbaum 2000: 179). The meetings included representatives from Intel, the EPA, the Arizona Department of Environmental Quality, Maricopa County, the city of Chandler, Don't Waste Arizona, the Santa Clara Committee on Occupational Safety and Health, the Silicon Valley Toxics Coalition, and the Community Advisory Panel, representing local interests. Following the approval of the final project agreement, Intel held quarterly, semiannual, and annual stakeholder meetings, and placed exhaustive material online to maintain high levels of transparency (EPA 1999: 4).

Exhaustive stakeholder consultation that led to consensus only occasionally proved insufficient to convince the EPA to relinquish control. In one interesting case, the Bureau of Water Works for the city of Portland successfully negotiated a final project agreement before holding a series of stakeholder meetings. Despite the apparent success, it ultimately withdrew from the agreement, citing the endless demands imposed ex post by the EPA. The letter notifying the EPA of the decision explained:

> During the several formal stakeholder meetings as well as during ongoing community interactions associated with program implementation, we have been struck by the differences between the community's concerns and needs and EPA's. In particular, stakeholders strongly supported (and continue to support) our efforts. . . . EPA's concerns during this same time were typically more focused on program clarifications and enhancements. We became concerned that EPA's comments were raising potentially significant financial, policy, or implementation issues, and we were unable to see how we could resolve these issues without considerable additional investment of limited resources. . . . The consistency of this input as well as the lack of interest of these stakeholders in EPA's issues made us question the relevance of EPA's concerns, especially in the light of what we saw as the growing workload and associated time commitment necessary to resolve the issues raised. In the end, we concluded that continuing to work on the XL agreement detracted from our ability to implement the program. Our decision to withdraw is directly related to our belief that our community benefits significantly more from actual implementation of the program than from continuing to invest our limited resources in achieving recognition. (Rosenberger 1999)

In response, the EPA engaged a number of points raised in the above-quoted letter. Most interesting was its contention that as a stakeholder, it was first among equals. As the agency noted: "EPA's position in the group of direct participant stakeholders is unique. EPA's positions on policy and technical issues represent an assortment of Agency interests ranging from programmatic and technical expertise . . . to obligations under Federal statutes. No other stakeholder would hold or be responsible for this same range of perspectives." In fact, "community stakeholders often rely on EPA to provide technical expertise not available locally and consequently to safeguard their interests in that way" (Findley and Lund 1999).

Although one might be rightly skeptical of the ultimate impact of Project XL, there were some striking successes. Intel Corporation, considered a showcase for Project XL, achieved results far superior to those required both by regulations *and* the FPA. It attained greater than expected reductions in volatile organic compounds, nitrogen oxides, carbon monoxide, sulfur dioxide, particulates, aggregate combined organic and inorganic hazardous air pollutants, phosphine, sulfuric acid, and arsine. At the same time, it exceeded its goals for recycling water and solid and hazardous wastes. It met these goals while employing an ambitious system of stakeholder consultation (see EPA 1999). While this case is suggestive of what is possible, one cannot tell how many other firms did not pursue comparable achievements because they found the regulatory demands, delays, and costs to be greater than any potential benefits. Intel had to find a means to promote innovative experiments, increase flexibility, reduce regulatory transaction costs, and allow those who would experiment to do so with the understanding that failures will not be met with regulatory actions. This required that the EPA negotiate the constraints imposed by its own structure and the demands for certainty of results inherited from the original regulatory design. The key challenge for the EPA proved to be insurmountable.

■ Conclusion

Few would deny that government should be more effective, efficient, flexible, and results-oriented. Yet REGO was, at best, a partial success. The original regulatory design prioritized certainty of results over competing values. The delays, redundancies, adversarial relationships, and high regulatory transaction costs were not a product of chance. Theoretically, one could remedy many of these problems through greater regulatory delegation. Yet delegation provides greater flexibility (and a host of related benefits) at the cost of greater uncertainty. In the end, regulators were unwilling to make this trade-off. By all indicators, EPA bureaucrats permitted REGO to occur at the margins of the agency, but guarded the EPA's core functions. As Marcus, Geffen, and Sexton conclude: "many of the agency's top management were reluctant to use successful pilots to foster additional change in the regulatory system. . . . In EPA's view, reinvention initiatives might provide new tools that could augment and improve the existing system, not replace it with something new or different that might compromise the environmental protection the agency was obliged to preserve" (2002: 42).

7

Of Partnerships and Paralysis: Voluntarism and the End of Reform

M any of the central principles associated with the reinvention of government could enhance the quality of regulation. In theory, new approaches to pollution management could be disseminated throughout the regulatory and corporate community, with potentially important implications for the design of future regulations. Unfortunately, theory collided with reality in the 1990s. The core features of regulatory design placed significant constraints on what might be accomplished by Clinton-era reinvention. If there were a single lesson that one could glean from the reinvention of the 1990s, it would be this: regulatory design matters. Of course, one might seek to change the underlying regulatory design through new legislation. The EPA's regulatory mandates were established by statute; they could be changed by statute as well. However, there were no sustained efforts to pass such legislation in the 1990s. Republican control of Congress after the fateful 1994 midterm elections essentially foreclosed this option. Yet without statutory change, REGO would stand in tension with existing regulatory design, often degenerating into voluntary initiatives that would support policy without fundamentally changing the logic of environmental protection. Even less satisfactory, however, one might employ voluntary initiatives as a surrogate for policy. This is the course that appears to have been taken during the presidency of George W. Bush.

The 2000 election was met with great trepidation by environmental advocates, who feared a return to what they viewed as the bleak days of the Reagan presidency. Many of the subsequent evaluations of the Bush environmental record portrayed a full-blown crisis wherein the new administration was systematically dismantling the nation's environmental policies and stripping powers and resources from the EPA. Yet many of the claims were rather hyperbolic, designed, one may suspect, to elicit a political response. A more dispassionate examination of the Bush record suggest that while there was little ground for celebration, there was also little ground for the black despondency that seemed to envelop the environmental community. As a generalization, the administration eliminated or revised proposals or practices that were symbolic (e.g., the Kyoto Protocol), unworkable (e.g., the New Source Review process), or enfeebled by constraints imposed by Congress and litigation (e.g., EPA supervision of states in setting total maximum daily loads in water pollution). At the same time, there were lost opportunities. Once problematic proposals or practices were discarded, they were often replaced by proposals that were underdeveloped or failed to be fully implemented.

But what of reinvention? Would EPA reinvention continue under the new administration? Certainly, a Republican administration led by an MBA should be more supportive of voluntary initiatives, regulatory flexibility, and market-based instruments. Rather, reinvention seemed to take the form of voluntary initiatives. There were no concerted efforts to integrate these initiatives into the larger regulatory structure. More troubling, where pressing problems emerged, there were no efforts to introduce new legislation. Rather, voluntary initiatives were offered as a substitute for policy. Given the dearth of new environmental legislation (the last statutory expansion of regulation occurred in 1990), and the reduced pace of regulatory rule making, the reliance on regulatory voluntarism raises particular concerns. Voluntary initiatives may reinforce mandatory regulations. Whether they can serve as substitutes for public policy is questionable. This chapter begins with an assessment of the key features of the Bush environmental record, and then explores the issue of reinvention, or more correctly, the end of reinvention.

■ Continuity and the Bush Environmental Record

The 2000 elections pitted Vice President Al Gore, a dedicated environmentalist, against a Texas governor with a questionable environmental record and strong alliances with the oil industry. In the words of the Sierra Club's Carl Pope and Paul Rauber, if elected, "Bush could be expected to manage the nation's environment much as he has managed that of Texas, which leads the nation in industrial toxic air pollution and in the number of facilities that violate clean-water standards" (2000: 35–36). Following the controversial Bush victory, the negative appraisals continued to mount. One critic noted in a powerful critique of the Bush presidency: "this administration has compiled the worst environmental record of any administration in history." The Bush administration immediately "set about the task of systematically and unilaterally dismantling over thirty years of environmental and natural resources law" and engaged in "a full-fledged ideological crusade to deregulate polluters, privatize public resources, limit public participation, manipulate science, and abdicate federal responsibility for tackling national and global environmental problems" (Parenteau 2004: 363). Before exploring areas of change, areas of continuity should be considered.

Some critics of the administration expected the election to mark a return to the battles of the Reagan years. Ken Conca, for example, predicted: "we can expect a replay of the political dramas of the Reagan-Watt era" (2001: 29). The Reagan administration's efforts to change the direction of environmental policy had several components. First, all agencies were required to meet onerous new regulatory review requirements under Executive Order 12291. Second, President Reagan appointed an EPA administrator who was highly skeptical of the agency's mission. Third, the EPA was forced to endure a loss of one-third of its operating budget—cuts that found their clearest expression in the loss of one-fifth of its staff (see Chapter 5). Finally, there were significant reductions in enforcement, as a product of both the opposition of EPA appointments and the sharp cuts in agency resources.

In the years following the Republican resurgence of 1994, the Clinton administration had little hope of getting new environmental legislation through Congress. Given the contentious political climate, it back-loaded the agenda and adopted a common strategy of issuing a large number of "midnight regulations" in the weeks before the Bush inauguration (Judis 2001). On January 20, 2001, the new Bush administration issued a blanket freeze on these regulations, including a number of environmental regulations that, among other things, would have extended federal protection to some 58 million acres of national forest lands and toughened arsenic standards for drinking water (Kriz 2001a). This freeze resembled that which occurred in the Reagan presidency, and led to fears that the freeze would be combined with a new system of regulatory review.

The topic of regulatory review is fully explored in Chapter 5. As noted there, in 1993 the newly inaugurated President Clinton signed Executive Order 12866, formally revoking the Reagan-era orders. The new system of regulatory review was explicitly framed as a repudiation of, and departure from, the Reagan-Bush presidencies. In 2001 the newly inaugurated President Bush chose, in contrast, to retain the system put into place by his predecessor. There is anecdotal evidence that the Office of Management and Budget's Office of Information and Regulatory Affairs has been far more vigorous in its enforcement of the Clinton executive order, forcing agencies to meet a higher standard with respect to the application of cost-benefit analysis. Figure 7.1 provides a graphical representation of the percentage of EPA submissions that have been approved by the OMB-OIRA without revision (i.e., not found consistent with changes, returned for significant revisions, or withdrawn altogether by the agency). Two things are made abundantly clear in the figure. First, the OMB-OIRA has become far more

Figure 7.1 EPA Rules Approved by OMB-OIRA Without Revision, 1981–2005

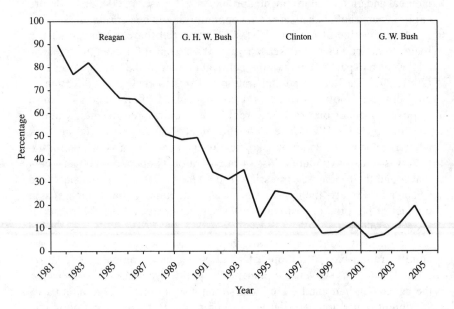

Data source: General Services Administration and Office of Management and Budget, http://
reginfo.org.

activist in its review of rules since 1981, regardless of the partisan control
of the presidency. It would appear that it has gained a degree of independence since its creation. Second, when comparing the role of OMB-OIRA in
the Clinton and Bush presidencies, there is little evidence of a sharp departure. Rather the story appears to be one of continuity.

Agency appointments did not follow the Reagan pattern. Upon the election of George W. Bush, the alarm of environmental advocates was partially
assuaged by the selection of Christine Todd Whitman to head the EPA.
Whitman was a high-profile appointee and a moderate voice in the
Republican Party. As New Jersey governor, she had imposed vigorous controls on air pollution and promoted land preservation. There was nothing in
Whitman's actions as EPA administrator to suggest that she was an opponent of environmental regulation. For example, on February 28, 2001, she
reinstated rules that had been subject to the regulatory freeze requiring
large, diesel-powered vehicles to reduce their emissions by 95 percent and
requiring oil companies to cut by 97 percent the sulfur of diesel fuel
(Nierenberg 2001). She also declared her support for a 2001 Supreme Court
decision that rejected a challenge to the EPA's authority to set air pollution
standards regardless of industry compliance costs (Kriz 2001a). Similarly,

in March 2002, when the US Court of Appeals for the D.C. Circuit upheld the 1997 EPA guidelines for ozone levels and particle emissions, finding them neither arbitrary nor unreasonable, Whitman responded: "This was one that we vigorously defended. . . . We had sound science behind this rule. This was a vindication of our efforts to protect Americans from health problems from the air" (Tucker and Grunwald 2002: A1).

Despite Whitman's best efforts, skepticism regarding the administration's environmental commitment continued to build. The administration made several politically maladroit announcements that created some concern. In addition to the sixty-day freeze on Clinton's midnight regulations, on March 13, 2001, the administration reneged on a Bush campaign pledge to regulate carbon dioxide, citing the incomplete scientific knowledge on the role of carbon dioxide in global warming and economic impacts. One week later, the administration stressed the same theme of scientific uncertainty when it announced its decision to delay an EPA rule setting new arsenic standards for drinking water (Nierenberg 2001). On March 28, 2001, the administration announced its rejection of the Kyoto Protocol, which addresses global climate change. These actions, when taken as a whole, raised persistent concerns that environmental policy would be dictated by the White House, thereby reducing the impact that Whitman would have on policy.

The controversy over carbon dioxide regulation and Kyoto provided clear evidence of Whitman's marginalization and White House control over environmental policy. In early March 2001, Administrator Whitman assured participants at a European environmental summit in Trieste, Italy, of the new president's campaign commitment to the regulation of carbon dioxide emissions and his intentions of including mandatory caps in a new initiative, Clear Skies. As news of the summit filled the media, Republicans in Congress and representatives of the energy industry lobbied the White House, demanding that the president reverse his position on carbon dioxide caps and strengthen his opposition to Kyoto. On returning from the summit, Whitman was summoned to the Oval Office, where she was informed of the president's decision to abandon carbon dioxide regulations. Whitman's interpretation of this event was unambiguous: "The president's decision was meant to mollify the antiregulation elements of the far-right base, and it was made with too little regard for what is in fact a serious problem, or for how it would be received by both moderates in the United States and our allies overseas" (Whitman 2005: 178). In May 2003, Whitman announced her resignation from the EPA. Environmental groups portrayed her exit as symbolic of a larger struggle between the EPA and the White House. Industry groups, never enthusiastic about her appointment and disappointed in her support for regulations, welcomed her resignation (Pianin and Gugliotta 2003).

Many critics were not surprised by this chain of events, and believed that the administration had decided to emphasize a proindustry energy policy, and that environmental protection would have to be subjugated to that larger initiative. On the campaign trail and thereafter, Bush called for greater incentives for the coal and oil industry, for expanded offshore drilling, and for opening up Alaska's Arctic National Wildlife Refuge (ANWR) for exploitation. Even if new drilling technology could reduce the environmental impacts on the ANWR—a serious point of contention among critics—drilling would have, at best, a modest impact on US energy supplies (Kriz 2001b). Concerns over the environmental ramifications of energy policy stimulated a heavy mobilization of key interest groups, the largest coordinated environmental campaign in a decade (Fonder 2002). The controversies were exacerbated by the decision to assign policy development to the newly created National Energy Policy Development Group, chaired by former Halliburton CEO, Vice President Cheney. The activities of the energy group were veiled in secrecy, opening the door to conflicts with Congress when the General Accounting Office's attempts to gain access to materials related to the energy deliberations were rebuffed under claims of executive privilege (Milbank 2001). Moreover, as Whitman would note in her post-EPA memoirs, she found her participation on the task force to be "an eye-opening encounter with just how obsessed so many of those in the energy industry, and in the Republican Party [had] become with doing away with environmental regulation." The members of the task force "placed the blame for America's energy woes squarely on the nation's environmental laws and regulations" (Whitman 2005: 182).

Despite ongoing concerns about White House control of the environmental policy, subsequent appointees shared Whitman's support for the agency's mission. Whitman's successor, Utah governor Michael Leavitt, was the nation's longest-serving governor, with a reputation for forging compromises between environmentalists and business. Leavitt's appointment was viewed as emblematic of the administration's commitment to increased devolution to the states and greater reliance on collaborative regulation (Allen and Milbank 2003). Following the Bush reelection, Leavitt was nominated as the new secretary of health and human services, and was replaced by Stephen Johnson, a career EPA bureaucrat and the first professional scientist to hold the position. Given these appointments, there was little evidence that President Bush was appointing administrators who were uniformly opposed to the EPA's mandate.

What of the EPA's budget? Although the Reagan presidency was marked by the deepest budget cuts in the EPA's history, the Bush record has been largely one of continuity with that of the Clinton administration. In April 2001 the administration proposed a $7.3 billion budget for fiscal year 2002. Although this sum may appear gargantuan, it nonetheless represented a $500 million reduction from the 2001 fiscal year budget, including a $10 million cut in enforcement resources that threatened to shrink the enforcement staff by some 9 percent. Simultaneously, the administration proposed to fund an additional $25 million in grants for state-level enforcement and an additional $25 million for environmental assessments within the states. For critics, the devolution of authority raised serious concerns, given the mixed enforcement records at the state level (Pianin and Grunwald 2001). Other agencies with environmental duties faced budget cuts as well, including the US Geological Survey, the National Oceanic and Atmospheric Administration, the Army Corps of Engineers, the National Park Service, the Fish and Wildlife Service, and the National Science Foundation (Nierenberg 2001).

The controversies of the early days, when combined with the anticipated budget cuts, reinforced fears that the Bush presidency would mark the beginning of diminishing budgets and dwindling staff resources. Yet the empirical record suggests something far different. Budgets remained relatively stable in nominal terms: at the end of Bush's first term, the EPA budget stood at $7.6 billion, approximately the same as it had been in 2000 with comparable stability in staffing. It would increase to $7.8 billion in 2005, the first year of Bush's second term in office, largely on par with the highest level of inflation-adjusted spending during the previous administration. Although some could make a reasoned case that this level of funding is insufficient given the enormous growth in the EPA's mandate and the size of the economy since the 1970s, it was more difficult to substantiate the charge that the EPA had suffered draconian budget cuts under Bush. There was little in the budgetary record to suggest anything other than continuity.

Although the Bush environmental policy engendered its share of controversies, the most important issue may be the least visible: regulatory enforcement. Levels of enforcement rarely attract the same attention as bold policy pronouncements or highly publicized controversies. Nonetheless, their impact can be quite profound. During the Bush presidency, there have been periodic leadership vacuums in enforcement. The assistant administrator of the Office of Enforcement and Compliance Assurance, the top enforcement position in the EPA, remained highly unstable. Bush's first choice for the position, Donald Schregardus, withdrew his name from consideration, anticipating difficulties in Senate confirmation. The president's next nominee was John Peter Suarez. Although Suarez had little experience in environmental regulation (his previous position had been a federal prosecutor and director of the New Jersey Division of Gaming Enforcement), he was ultimately confirmed on August 1, 2002, more than eighteen months into the new administration. Suarez's tenure was short. He resigned his position on January 30, 2004, to assume a position with Wal-Mart, leaving this critical position open once more. Eric Schaeffer, a former director of the Office of Regulatory Enforcement who left the EPA during the New Source Review controversy (see below), argues that the decision "to leave the enforcement program rudderless" was part of a larger strategy that included dramatic reductions in the agency's enforcement budget, the use of jurisdictional barriers between agencies to thwart enforcement, a greater delegation to the states, conservative judicial appointments, excessive intervention by lobbyists via Congress, and a fetish for innovation over enforcement (Schaeffer 2002).

Much of Schaeffer's critique requires a qualitative judgment. However, data on criminal and civil enforcement are good enough (see EPA 2003d, 2004e) to draw some conclusions about the Bush presidency and make some useful comparisons with the Clinton enforcement record. First, criminal enforcement. The EPA does not prosecute its own criminal cases but makes referrals to the Justice Department, which prosecutes the cases, seeking indictments that may result, ultimately, in trials before a federal district court. Changes in the vigor of enforcement should find an expression in the number of criminal cases initiated, the number of referrals, and the magnitude of punishments. An examination of the data suggests that during its first term, the Bush administration initiated an annual average of 465.5 criminal investigations, 11 percent fewer than did the Clinton administration (mean of 522.5). While the number of investigations was lower during the period, the Bush EPA referred, on average, 244.7 cases per year to the Justice Department (2001–2004), approximately 6 percent above the Clinton annual mean of 231.1 cases. Referrals are important to the extent that they result in successful prosecutions. The comparative evidence is ambiguous. The cases successfully prosecuted during the Bush presidency resulted in a larger number of years of imprisonment (an annual mean of 162.5 years, compared with a Clinton mean of 132.9 years), but a lower level of fines (an annual mean of $68.75 million for Bush, compared with $76.6 million for Clinton).

When comparing criminal enforcement under Clinton and Bush, several caveats are in order. First, fines and imprisonment are the end products of a complex set of events involving the EPA, the Justice Department, and the courts. It is difficult to attribute their magnitude to presidential appointees. Second, cases are developed over the course of multiple years. Undoubtedly, some of the cases prosecuted to a successful conclusion during the Bush presidency were initiated during the prior administration. Thus, one would expect that lower levels of criminal inspections under Bush would find their ultimate expression in a subsequent drop in referrals. Finally, these numbers do not directly speak to the environmental significance of individual cases.

What of civil enforcement? In 2000 the Clinton EPA conducted 20,337 inspections, a slight reduction over the levels achieved in previous years.

The number of inspections conducted under the Bush EPA fell to 17,560 in 2001, before increasing steadily to 21,000 by 2004. Civil investigations fell even more precipitously, from 660 in 2000 to 366 in 2001, before recovering somewhat to 455 by 2004. Given that inspections and investigations are an important part of the regulatory process, one would expect these declines to undermine civil enforcement. When the EPA discovers a regulatory violation, it issues an administrative compliance order directing an entity to take corrective action or refrain from a given activity. In 2000, the last year of the Clinton presidency, the EPA issued 3,388 administrative compliance orders. In the next four years, the number of orders fell from this peak to 1,250 in 2002, before increasing to a Bush first-term high of 1,807 in 2004. The EPA can issue administrative penalty complaints in response to civil violations. It can also refer civil cases to the Justice Department. The Bush administration issued administrative penalty complaints more frequently than did the Clinton presidency (an annual mean of 1,800.8 per year for Bush's first term, compared with 1,489.4 for Clinton). Civil referrals declined sharply under Bush (a mean of 318.3 referrals per year for Bush, versus a mean of 360.4 per year for Clinton). Administrative penalties were 35 percent higher, on average, during the Clinton presidency (an annual mean of $34.4 million per year, compared with a mean of $25.5 million per year under Bush). On the other hand, judicial penalties were 28 percent larger during Bush's first term (an annual mean of $89.75 million, compared with an annual mean of $69.9 million under Clinton).

What conclusions can one draw based on these data? While enforcement lagged under Bush, the departures were not significant. However, the one area where there seems to be the greatest departure involves inspections and investigations. Given that cases may take several years to develop, these reductions can have long-term implications. There is a related trend worth noting: a heightened reliance on compliance assistance. During the REGO activities of the 1990s, the EPA expanded technical assistance to firms in the hope of preventing violations. By 2000, EPA compliance assistance reached some 351,000 entities. This number increased dramatically in each subsequent year, reaching 731,000 in 2004. These two trends, when combined, may suggest a profound shift in the nature of enforcement—a point that will be developed in greater detail below.

■ Changing the Direction of Environmental Policy

In large part, the Bush environmental record has been one of continuity. Yet there have been some significant changes during the Bush presidency as well, most of which generated a high level of negative publicity. As a generalization, the policies (or in the case of Kyoto, the proposed policy) were not having the intended impact on the problem in question, largely as a result of design decisions made in previous administrations or constraints imposed by Congress, the courts, or the vigor of state implementation. As a generalization, the administration sought to replace policies with initiatives that were underdeveloped or insufficient to address the problems in question, as is clearly apparent in four examples: global climate change, the New Source Review process, the Clear Skies Initiative, and EPA oversight of total daily maximum loads.

Global Climate Change and the Kyoto Protocol

As noted above, President Bush withdrew support for the Kyoto Protocol in March 2001, citing the uncertainty of the scientific case and the costs of compliance. The withdrawal from Kyoto was greeted with great scorn by administration critics. Bush was portrayed as a unilateralist who was beholden to the fossil fuel industry and big business (a critique that would reappear with the Iraq War). One critic predicted: "Global warming could do to George W. Bush what the Vietnam War did to Lyndon Johnson 33 years ago—leave him with a prematurely crippled, one-term presidency" (Gelbspan 2001: 12). Despite the vitriolic responses, US participation in Kyoto may have been a dead letter regardless of Bush's announcement. Under the Constitution (Article II, Section 2), treaties do not go into force unless they receive the concurrence of two-thirds of the Senate. During the Clinton administration, the Senate had shown little enthusiasm for Kyoto. In July 1997 it unanimously (95–0) passed the Byrd-Hagel Resolution (S. Res. 98, 105th Congress, 1st session), stating that the United States should not be a signatory to any agreement (specifically Kyoto) that would result in "serious harm to the economy" or mandate commitments for developed countries without simultaneously imposing specific scheduled commitments on developing countries. President Clinton apparently understood the Senate's message; he never submitted the treaty for ratification. There was little reason to believe that the treaty, as it existed in 2001, would receive the constitutionally required two-thirds concurrence.

What would take the place of Kyoto? In a speech on February 17, 2002, President Bush reaffirmed the nation's commitment to the United Nations Framework Convention on Climate Change and outlined a new strategy for climate change that would reconcile the need for economic growth with the reduction of greenhouse gas emissions. Bush stated: "Our nation must have economic growth—growth to create opportunity; growth to create a higher quality of life for our citizens. Growth is also what pays for investments in clean technologies, increased conservation, and energy efficiency." Bush announced a commitment "to reduce our greenhouse gas intensity by 18 percent by the year 2012," thereby preventing "over 500 million metric tons of greenhouse gases from going into the atmosphere over the course of the decade" (Bush 2002).

The focus on greenhouse gas intensity was a departure from the Kyoto Protocol, which required reductions in aggregate emissions. Greenhouse gas intensity captures the amount of gases emitted relative to gross domestic product (GDP), thereby focusing on efficiency gains in fossil fuel use. Given that greenhouse gas intensity fell by 16 percent during the 1990s due to efficiency gains, the goal of achieving an 18 percent reduction by 2012 was viewed as painfully modest. More troubling, the proposed reductions in greenhouse gas intensity would be accompanied by a growth in aggregate emissions. In 1991 the United States released 1.3 billion tons of carbon emissions, an amount that increased to 1.5 billion tons by 2003. Given anticipated rates of economic growth, an 18 percent reduction in greenhouse gas intensity would result in an increase in emissions to 1.8 billion tons (Friedman and Bierbaum 2003).

President Bush announced several means of achieving the reductions in greenhouse gas intensity, all of which involved voluntary efforts or financial support for new technologies (e.g., voluntary agreements with industry; the promotion of clean coal, renewable energy, and nuclear power; and an almost $1 billion investment in energy conservation technology and renewable energy sources). Bush also announced his intention of budgeting $4.6 billion over the next five years in clean energy tax incentives to promote the purchases of hybrid and fuel cell vehicles, residential solar energy, and investments in wind, solar, and biomass energy production. "If, however, by 2012, our progress is not sufficient and sound science justifies further action," the president noted, then "the United States will respond with additional measures that may include broad-based market programs as well as additional incentives and voluntary measures designed to accelerate technology development and deployment" (Bush 2002). These initiatives may have been welcomed, but they were not substitutes for mandatory caps on greenhouse gas emissions.

New Sources and Clear Skies

Outside the area of global climate change, the administration's air pollution efforts focused on the New Source Review (NSR) process. The Clean Air Act amendments of 1977 grandfathered existing power plants from complying with the technological standards mandated under the Clean Air Act of 1970, on the assumption that they would be retired and replaced with new facilities. However, none of the grandfathered plants were retired, and none installed state-of-the art pollution technologies, even though many embarked on multimillion-dollar upgrades. In essence, they used the loophole created in the 1977 amendments as a source of economic advantage

(Wenzler 2002). The NSR process was created to require that these plants, when they undergo significant modifications, obtain a permit mandating the use of best available pollution control technology. In 1993 the newly created Office of Enforcement and Compliance Assistance discovered that a large number of facilities had expanded production without submitting to the NSR process. In 1999 the EPA referred some fifty-one cases to the Justice Department for prosecution, citing a failure to comply with the NSR provisions. Some fourteen of those cases involved the electric utility industry (John and Paddock 2004). By the end of the Clinton administration, the EPA was positioned to vigorously enforce regulations that had languished for decades (Barcott 2004; Urstadt 2004). These efforts were bearing fruit: twenty-one defendants (including seven electric utilities) settled out-of-court, agreeing to pay penalties of $79 million and invest some $4.6 billion to upgrade their facilities, with an additional $93 million for other environmental improvements (John and Paddock 2004). Several parties refused to settle, arguing that they had engaged in routine maintenance designed to extend the life of existing facilities.

The Bush administration moved quickly to clarify the issue of what constituted a "major modification." According to the EPA, the improvements to the NSR program would remove "needless regulatory barriers to pollution control and prevention projects," encourage plant modernization, provide "operating flexibility by establishing stringent pollution caps," and create "incentives for facilities to install state-of-the-art pollution controls by providing operational flexibility for facilities that install 'clean units'"(EPA 2002b). Whitman advised utilities that had been charged with violating the NSR that they might suspend settlement talks until the conclusion of rule making—advice that precipitated the resignation of Eric Schaeffer, the head of the Office of Regulatory Enforcement (Parenteau 2004: 374; Schaeffer 2002).

In December 2002 the administration issued a final rule to provide regulated parties with greater flexibility in meeting regulatory requirements (67 Fed. Reg. 80186, December 31, 2002). Units that installed state-of-the-art pollution controls would be deemed "clean units," and changes to these units could occur without going through the NSR process. Owners could obtain plantwide applicability limits for their facilities, whereby the EPA would treat an entire facility as a single unit with a single emissions cap. If major changes within the facility did not exceed the applicability limits, the owners would be exempted from having to obtain an NSR permit. Finally, in 2003 the EPA announced its final rule on what would constitute significant modifications. It exempted equipment replacement from NSR review if total costs did not exceed 20 percent of the replacement value of the entire process unit; if it involved replacing existing components of a process unit with identical (or functionally equivalent) components; if it did not alter the basic design; or if it did not cause the unit to exceed the highest level of emissions experienced over the previous ten years (68 Fed. Reg. 61247, October 27, 2003).

The new rule, scheduled to go into effect on December 24, 2003, raised serious concerns for critics who anticipated that old coal-fired utilities would simply rebuild an entire facility in phases while avoiding regulatory requirements, thereby vitiating the intent of the NSR process. There was also opposition to the baseline for determining whether the NSR was applicable. In response, fourteen states and several public interest groups challenged the rule and filed suits in the US Court of Appeals for the D.C. Circuit. Although the court stayed the effective date of the NSR rule changes pending resolution of the suits, on June 24, 2005, it affirmed the Bush administration's approach to calculating the polluting emissions baseline. Although the NSR process was reinstated, the decision was sufficiently complex that all sides claimed victory (Eilperin 2005), and conflicting decisions by other courts suggest that the controversy was far from resolved.

As the Bush EPA worked to revise the NSR process, it moved forward with a much more ambitious effort: the Clear Skies Initiative, which constituted its only major legislative proposal and, if passed, would have constituted the first substantial set of amendments to the Clean Air Act since 1990. The proposed legislation was submitted to Congress in July 2002 and reintroduced as the Clear Skies Act of 2003. The act proposed federally enforceable emissions caps for nitrogen oxides and sulfur dioxide for all fossil fuel–fired electric generators greater than twenty-five megawatts. Caps would also be established for mercury emitted by coal-fired electric utilities. Clear Skies called for a 73 percent reduction in sulfur dioxide by 2018. Starting from a 2000 baseline of 11.2 million tons, the legislation set a target of 4.5 million tons for 2010, with further reductions to 3.0 million tons by 2018. Clear Skies also called for a 67 percent reduction in nitrogen oxides by 2018. Starting from a 2000 baseline of 5.1 million tons, the legislation created an interim target of 2.1 million tons (2008) and an ultimate target of 1.7 million tons (2018). With respect to mercury, the legislation called for a 69 percent reduction from the 2000 baseline of 48.0 tons, with an interim target of 26.0 tons (2010) and an ultimate goal of 15.0 tons (2018). As with Title IV of the Clean Air Act amendments of 1990, the key policy instrument would be a cap-and-trade system. Units would be subjected to continuous emissions monitoring and reporting. They could bank or sell excess allowances under a system of trading. Owners and operators of units that exceeded allowances would be subject to penalties equal to the excess emissions times the average sales price, combined with an offsetting of allowance reductions in the subsequent year.

Clear Skies received heavy criticism from environmentalists and industry (Crane 2003). Environmentalists were chiefly concerned that the initiative did not regulate carbon dioxide, a major greenhouse gas. Given that industry is responsible for some 37 percent of the carbon dioxide releases in the United States, this omission is of some consequence, particularly when combined with the retreat from Kyoto (John and Paddock 2004). Moreover, while the goals seemed ambitious, their achievement was contingent on compliance costs. The legislation proposed so-called safety valve provisions for the regulated pollutants. If the marginal costs of removing the pollutants exceeded various cost thresholds ($4,000 per ton for sulfur dioxide and nitrogen oxides, $35,000 per pound for mercury), the EPA could "borrow" allowances from a following year's auctions to increase the supply and thus reduce the price of the allowances. It is unclear how long such borrowing would be sustained. The EPA admitted that, given current technologies, the second-phase reductions in mercury would exceed the safety valve threshold by 2010, although technological advances in the interim could allow power plants to achieve these reductions at a lower cost (EPA 2003c).

Critics were also dissatisfied with the proposed reductions. The EPA has estimated that if all power plants were required to meet the standards applied to new facilities, the result would be a 70 percent reduction of sulfur dioxide and nitrogen oxides—gains that could prevent some 14,000 premature deaths resulting from various respiratory diseases and cancer (John and Paddock 2004). Yet critics argued that existing provisions of the Clean Air Act, if vigorously enforced, could achieve greater reductions in emissions than envisioned under the Bush proposal. Indeed, the Clean Air Task Force, the National Environmental Trust, and the US Public Interest Research Group Education Fund estimated that, over the first ten years, the proposal would result in increases of 850,000 tons of nitrous oxides, 2.5 million tons of sulfur dioxide, and 21 tons of mercury (Hunter 2002). There were also concerns regarding the mercury provisions. Clear Skies treated mercury like other pollutants, allowing for the use of a cap-and-trade approach and extending the compliance timetable. Given the toxicity of mercury and the fact that much of the emissions are deposited within 100 miles of the source, many challenged the use of trading (Levine 2004; Urstadt 2004). Some analysts (see Burtraw and Krupnick 2003) remained unconvinced that the issue was one of regulatory instruments, however, noting that critics mistakenly conflate emissions trading and the relatively modest reductions mandated under Clear Skies.

In response to these concerns, competing pieces of legislation were introduced for Senate consideration. Two bills, sponsored by Senator Jim Jeffords (I-VT) and Senator Thomas R. Carper (D-DE), were directly responsive to the president's proposal. The Jeffords Bill (S. 366, 108th Congress) was far more ambitious than the administration's proposal; the Carper Bill (S. 843) was introduced as a compromise between Clear Skies and Jeffords. Both of the alternative bills set lower sulfur dioxide, nitrogen oxide, and mercury allowance caps than did Clear Skies. The Carper Bill disallowed trading in mercury altogether. Most significant, both alternatives proposed emission caps for carbon dioxide, thereby extending regulations to the major greenhouse gas associated with global climate change (for a detailed comparison, see Resources for the Future 2004). Both alternatives strengthened enforcement by disallowing safety valves and increasing the penalties for noncompliance with the Bush proposal, which would have charged the owner the cost of the emission allowances and reduced the subsequent allowances by the amount of the violation.

The political battles surrounding Clear Skies were intense. Environmentalists portrayed the administration's proposal as a significant rollback of the nation's regulatory commitments; industry advocates viewed all of the competing proposals as either unattainable under existing technologies or far too costly. The debates were complicated by EPA actions, including its failure to acknowledge its internal analyses, which concluded that the reductions in sulfur dioxide, nitrogen oxide, and mercury envisioned by the Carper Bill could be achieved at an additional cost of some two-tenths of a cent per kilowatt hour (Gugliotta and Pianin 2003). Moreover, in 2003, Senators John McCain (R-AZ) and Joseph Lieberman (D-CT) shifted the debate to engage the broader issue of climate change with their proposed Climate Stewardship Act of 2003 (S. 139). The bill proposed a comprehensive, economywide cap-and-trade program for greenhouse gases that would cap 2010 emissions at 2000 levels. Although it failed Senate passage (43–55), the composition of the vote suggested greater bipartisan support than one might have expected for revisions to the Clean Air Act that regulate greenhouse gases. Given the multiple concerns and intense opposition, Clear Skies remained stalled in the legislative process.

Rather than battling through a sharply divided Congress, the Bush EPA made the decision to adopt an administrative strategy. On March 10, 2005, the EPA issued its Clean Air Interstate Rule, thereby using the rule-making process to implement the Clear Skies cap-and-trade program for sulfur dioxide and nitrogen oxides. The Clean Air Interstate Rule is not as comprehensive as Clear Skies insofar as its coverage is limited to twenty-eight eastern states and the District of Columbia. But it does impose a comparable set of targets. Five days later, the EPA issued its Clean Air Mercury Rule for coal-fired power plants. Despite ongoing disagreements about whether to regulate mercury as a toxic chemical, the rule treated it as a normal pollutant and adopted a cap-and-trade system. The new rules may render the New Source Review irrelevant for utilities in affected states. Rather than working under an NSR permit, utilities will have greater flexibility in meeting caps (e.g., by purchasing pollution allowances on the market). Given the high salience of the New Source Review process and ongoing concerns about the toxicity of mercury, one should not be surprised that both rules were quickly the subject of lawsuits and petitions for reconsideration filed by state governments, environmental groups, electric utilities, and business associations, and resolution of all of the issues should prove to be a protracted process (see Eisner, Worsham, and Ringquist 2006: 188–189). Although critics may view the administrative strategy as evidence that the new policy could not stand public scrutiny, a Resources for the Future analysis of the new rules suggests that the benefits greatly exceed the costs, even if greater reductions could be achieved through more stringent controls of mercury and nitrogen oxide (see Palmer, Burtraw, and Shih 2005).

Water Pollution and Total Daily Maximum Loads

Under the Clean Water Act, states were required to set quality standards for bodies of water based on their designated use. These standards would find expression in the "total maximum daily load," the maximum sum of the allowable amounts of a single pollutant from all contributing point and non-point sources. Success in water pollution control was contingent on state action, and states were slow to define and implement maximum-load regulations. A failure of states to meet their obligations stimulated lawsuits in thirty-eight states and court orders requiring that maximum loads be enforced by the states or the EPA itself. The Clinton administration responded by issuing a rule in July 2000 under which the EPA would directly oversee state implementation of maximum-load rules. However, Congress added a rider to the appropriations bill prohibiting the EPA from spending money to implement the rule (Cavanagh, Hahn, and Stavins 2001: 16–17). In December 2002 the Bush administration formally withdrew the Clinton-era rule strengthening oversight of maximum loads. According to the EPA press release announcing the decision, the 2000 rule was deemed to be "unworkable based on reasons described by thousands of comments and was challenged in court by some two dozen parties" (EPA 2002a). In any event, the congressional appropriations riders had rendered the issue moot. The key question became: What would the EPA do, in lieu of the rule, to strengthen state compliance with the maximum-load regulations?

In January 2003 the EPA announced plans for a national water quality trading policy that would extend market-based instruments to the regulation of water pollution. The new program was based on the experiences gained from pilot programs initiated under the EPA's 1996 draft framework for watershed-based trading (see EPA 2003e). The new policy would permit companies and treatment plants to buy credits from other facilities in a watershed that had exceeded water quality standards (Pianin 2003). According to the EPA, trading had clear advantages: "flexible approaches to improving water quality could save $900 million annually compared to the least flexible approach. . . . Market-based approaches can also create economic incentives for innovation, emerging technology, voluntary pollution reductions and greater efficiency in improving the quality of the nation's waters" (EPA 2003e: 2).

The EPA required that trading be consistent with the Clean Water Act. All water quality trading would have to occur within a watershed (or an area with an approved total maximum daily load), thus ensuring that standards would be maintained by any trades. Trading would be limited, initially, to nutrients (e.g., total phosphorus and total nitrogen) and sediment loads. The agency recognized that trades in other pollutants might be beneficial, although, given the higher potential risks, it stated that trading programs "should receive a higher level of scrutiny to ensure that they are consistent with water quality standards" and would be approved "on a case-by-case basis where prior approval is provided through an NPDES permit, a [total maximum daily load] or in the context of a watershed plan or pilot trading project that is supported by a state, tribe or EPA." While the agency clearly stated that it did not support the trading of persistent bioaccumulative toxics, it stated that it would "consider a limited number of pilot projects . . . to obtain more information regarding trading of" these toxins (EPA 2003e: 4).

Environmental Defense, the Natural Resources Defense Council, the National Wildlife Federation, and the Sierra Club objected to the newly announced policy on multiple grounds. There were concerns that trading would occur without caps. As Environmental Defense objected: "For trading to be effective, the total amount of pollution should be capped from all key sources. . . . Without a cap, trades may not reduce pollution, but merely reallocate it among sources" (Environmental Defense 2003). Although the trading system was not formally a cap-and-trade system, trades would occur within the limits set by total maximum daily loads and de facto caps on pollution levels, and would not be approved where they might exceed these limits. One might argue that limits set by maximum loads were insufficient, but this is an analytically separable issue. One might also note that the potential cost savings associated with trading could pressure more states to comply with the maximum-load requirements. There were concerns, moreover, that any policy would have to prohibit trades in toxic pollutants rather than leaving the door open to toxic trading via its support for future pilot programs. As Rena Steinzor (2003) of the Center for Progressive Regulation noted: "one person's 'pilot project,' if replicated often enough, is another person's entire program."

In December 2004 the EPA announced trading in five watersheds: Lake Tahoe (California and Nevada), Bear River (Idaho, Utah, and Wyoming), Kalamazoo River (Michigan), Cape Fear (North Carolina), and Passaic River (New Jersey). Although it is impossible to predict the performance of water quality trading, there is cause for skepticism given the role of the states. Recall that it was the very failure of the states to execute their duties that set the stage for these changes in policy. Whether trading will become a core component of water pollution regulation will depend, ultimately, on the behavior of states that have proven reticent to meet their obligations to date.

* * *

What can one conclude from these examples? First, on the face of things, the decisions to depart from the Kyoto Protocol, revise the New Source Review process, and revoke the Clinton executive order strengthening enforcement of total maximum daily loads were not unreasonable. Kyoto was nothing more that a symbol absent Senate ratification. The NSR process was so imprecise that utilities had avoided it with abandon. Congress had constrained the execution of the Clinton executive order through appropriations riders. Second, given the charged political atmosphere surrounding these (and other) environmental issues, environmental advocates were able to portray these decisions as part of a concerted attack on environmental policy without giving the slightest indication of the underlying weaknesses. Third and most important, in each case the proposed solutions appeared to be far less than what was possible. Reductions of greenhouse gas intensity, for example, are undoubtedly warranted. But they would not substitute for mandatory regulations reducing aggregate greenhouse gas emissions. Water trading might provide a means of achieving greater efficiencies, but without adequate enforcement of maximum-load regulations, it would be of little import. In essence, enfeebled policies were replaced by underdeveloped policies.

■ Reinvention as Substitution

Although references to the reinvention of government disappeared in the George W. Bush administration, the basic commitment to relying on voluntary public-private partnerships continued to flourish. Rather than reinforcing policy, however, these partnerships more often served as a substitute. As partnerships flourished, inspections and investigations declined. Moreover, there was clear empirical evidence that the generation of significant rules fell to a level comparable to what existed during the Reagan presidency. As noted in Chapter 5, under a series of executive orders the EPA has been required to submit economically significant rules for OMB review. The number of economically significant rules reviewed per year is a good indicator of the level of regulatory development. As the data in Figure 7.2 reveal, the flow of significant EPA rules increased steadily beginning with the imposition of mandatory review in 1981 and continuing to 1995, at

Figure 7.2 Economically Significant EPA Rules, 1981–2005

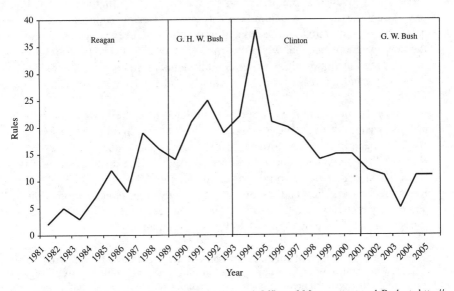

Data source: General Services Administration and Office of Management and Budget, http:// reginfo.org.

which point it began to decline. This decline accelerated in the Bush presidency. Thus, during the first term of the Clinton presidency, the EPA submitted an average of 25.5 significant rules per year to the OMB for review, a number that fell to 15.5 during the second term. During the first Bush term, new rules fell to an annual average of 9.75.

As the generation of new rules fell to a twenty-year low, new public-private partnerships flourished. With one exception (to be explored in greater detail in Chapter 10), nothing was done to integrate these partnerships into policy. Consider the example of climate change. Pursuant to the president's new position of climate change, in February 2002 the Bush administration launched its Climate Leaders Program, a voluntary partnership with businesses that were committed to reducing greenhouse gas intensity. Participants committed to conducting an inventory of the emissions of the six major greenhouse gases from their facilities, related to the electricity they purchased. They agreed to work with the EPA to set reduction targets that exceeded business-as-usual within their industries. The initial eleven participants grew to fifty-four within the next two years, a list that included a number of top corporations in the US economy (e.g., 3M, Alcoa, General Motors, IBM, United Technologies, and US Steel) responsible for some 6 percent of GDP (http://www.epa.gov/climateleaders). While participants pledged significant greenhouse gas reductions, several observations are in order. First, given that the participants are drawn from a list of firms that have already exhibited a commitment to environmental management, one can question how much of the reductions would have been achieved absent the new program. Second, while the goals may be ambitious, they are voluntary. One must question whether commitments to greenhouse gas reductions will stand the test of time, particularly if the costs compromise profitability.

An even more ambitious effort was initiated to address toxic and hazardous wastes, through the Resource Conservation Challenge, a REGO-style partnership designed to prevent the generation of wastes. In *Beyond RCRA,* a "vision paper" charting a future course, the EPA noted the difficulties of past regulatory efforts—for example, the "chilling effect" of the Resource Conservation and Recovery Act on recycling, reuse, reclamation, and energy recovery, and the excessive focus on "end of the pipe" solutions. It envisioned a future that few would find objectionable:

> The year is 2020, and America's wasteful ways are a thing of the past. New technologies and a changed economic climate, combined with enlightened government policies and a pronounced shift in societal and corporate attitudes have resulted in dramatic decreases in the volumes and toxicity of industrial wastes generated by the country's industries. Materials that were once considered wastes suitable only for landfilling are now continually reused and recycled, and "industrial ecology" has become the mantra of corporate executives across the nation. Landfills are becoming obsolete—the small volumes of wastes that actually need disposal are carefully managed under an efficient and environmentally protective system that features a mix of economic incentives, voluntary measures, and regulatory controls. Cleanup of most contaminated sites has been largely completed, and thousands of areas once known as brownfields have been put back into productive use. (EPA 2003b: 1)

The achievement of this future would require "developing new approaches for conserving resources, reducing the amount of toxic materials in society and the toxicity of materials that remain, and managing wastes properly" (EPA 2003b: 1).

The Resource Conservation Challenge, a joint effort of the Office of Solid Waste and the Office of Pollution Prevention and Toxic Substances, has established important objectives: "When it is economically feasible . . . to reduce what comes into the waste management cycle, using pollution prevention, waste minimization, source reduction, and manufacturing process and/or product design changes" (EPA 2004f: 2–3). In its five-year strategic plan (EPA 2004f), the Environmental Protection Agency notes that it would be guided by five basic principles: product stewardship (i.e., promoting environmentally friendly design), the beneficial use of materials (i.e., increasing recycling and the use of industrial byproducts), energy conservation, priority and toxic chemical reduction in waste, and the "greening" of government (i.e., government recycling and environmentally preferable purchasing).

As with other REGO-style initiatives, voluntary partnerships provide the primary means of achieving these goals. While some of these partnerships were inherited from the Clinton administration (e.g., WasteWise), others found their genesis in the George W. Bush presidency. The Coal Combustion Partnership, for example, was created in 2004 through the joint efforts of the EPA, the American Coal Ash Association, the Utility Solid Waste Activities Group, the Department of Energy, and the Federal Highway Administration, and had 110 charter members drawn largely from industry. The partnership was created to promote the "beneficial use" of coal combustion products (e.g., in highway construction, Portland cement), thereby reducing the use of virgin resources and the flow of wastes into landfills. Members receive technical support, networking opportunities, and public recognition through annual awards and the use of the partnership logo.

While such voluntary initiatives are unobjectionable when taken by themselves, they are best viewed in context. As the Resource Conservation Challenge took shape, a failure to fund cleanups took a toll. The Bush administration, unlike its predecessor, failed to promote the reauthorization of the Superfund, which had expired in 1995. Funding depended wholly on general revenues, and congressional appropriations fell dramatically, to an annual average of $1.3 billion during the Bush presidency (see Dealey 2004). These resource reductions had a predictable impact on the pace of cleanups. In response to congressional inquiries about the slowing progress on Superfund cleanups, the EPA's inspector general cited a $174.9 million shortfall for 2003 and noted: "limited funding prevented EPA from beginning construction at all sites or providing additional funds needed to address sites in a manner believed necessary by regional officials, and caused projects to be segmented into phases and/or scaled back to accommodate available funding" (EPA 2004b: 3).

Although the Bush administration failed to push for a reauthorization of the Superfund tax or additional appropriations, it promoted the Small Business Liability Relief and Brownfields Revitalization Act of 2002 (Public Law 107-118) to liberalize liability under CERCLA and create greater incentives for investment (EPA 2004h). The act eliminated the liability of prospective purchasers, even if they investigated the site and were aware of contamination. It also exempted owners or continuous landowners if they did not contribute to contamination, and clarified the so-called innocent landowner defense. Furthermore, exemptions were provided for small businesses responsible for small volumes of contamination, and residential households and small businesses that disposed of municipal solid waste (Collins 2003: 316–319). Because the broad definition of liability under CERCLA undermined the incentives for development, there was a strong justification for legislative action. However, as Flannary P. Collins notes, this relief comes at a price: "the amendments may force the government, and especially the EPA, to assume too much of the liability and its cost. The EPA's assumption of liability and cost is especially problematic given the 1995 termination of the tax provisions funding cleanups. . . . The result may be a decrease in the extent of environmental cleanup" (2003: 328).

■ Conclusion

Voluntary partnerships may generate positive results, although the penchant for self-reporting of accomplishments without third-party verification makes any assessment of performance difficult. Nonetheless, if backed with mandatory regulations and vigorous enforcement, they may make a useful contribution to the regulatory system, compensating for some of the limitations of the original regulatory design. Alternatively, partnerships can serve as convenient substitutes for more vigorous regulatory action. The partnerships undertaken by the George W. Bush administration seemed to follow this latter course. Reductions in investigations and enforcement, great increases in compliance assistance, and dramatic reductions in the generation of significant rules provided the context within which these experiments were situated. Even if programs like Climate Leaders were unobjectionable, few would suggest that they were an adequate substitute for the regulation of carbon dioxide emissions. Similarly, one must view the Resource Conservation Challenge in a broader context wherein the designation of new sites is lagging, cleanups have been starved for resources, and there are no efforts to reinstitute the funding mechanism or seek sufficient budgetary authority.

There is great potential for extending regulatory capacities through voluntary programs, but only if they are explicitly integrated with regulations. This, in turn, requires a significant alteration in basic regulatory design. There was some movement in this direction during the Bush administration with the National Environmental Performance Track, discussion of which is reserved for Chapter 10. With this singular exception, voluntary programs have either supplemented regulation or served as a pale substitute for regulation. We shall return to this theme in subsequent chapters as part of a larger consideration of the opportunities for transforming the existing system of environmental protection into a system of environmental governance that would make full use of markets, associations, and standards without sacrificing the benefits of public regulation.

Part 3

The Emerging System of Green Governance

8

From Greed to Green: Corporate Environmentalism and Management

Pollution is often presented as the textbook case of market failure. Corporations generate pollutants and, by design or indolence, force the costs onto society. In the absence of regulations, it is argued, corporations will pollute with abandon in the quest to maximize profits. Yet there is a growing trend of corporate environmentalism. Companies are voluntarily managing their pollution as a means of gaining market advantage, often going well beyond the requirements imposed by regulators. This trend contradicts the predictions of generations of regulatory analysts. Some observers have gone as far as to suggest that a growing subset of firms should be freed from regulations altogether, given their progressive practices and performance records that are well beyond compliance. Others respond that the innovations in environmental management have been a response to regulatory pressures without which firms would happily return to the predicted pattern of behavior, and that, therefore, it is necessary to retain a strong regulatory posture while providing firms with maximum flexibility to meet—and hopefully exceed—regulatory requirements. This chapter examines the phenomenon of corporate environmentalism, exploring its driving factors, strengths, and limitations.

■ Why Would Businesses Turn Green?

There is incontrovertible evidence that a growing number of businesses are voluntarily managing pollution and generating results that exceed regulatory requirements. At first glance, this seems counterintuitive. Top management has a fiduciary responsibility to maximize shareholder value. As a standard financial management text states: "management's primary goal is *stockholder wealth maximization,* which . . . translates into *maximizing the price of the firm's common stock*" (Brigham and Gapenski 1997: 14). In an age when corporate cost-cutting is ubiquitous, how can one explain the decision to invest resources in environmental management and green production? Although one might argue that managers have embraced a new ethic of corporate social responsibility, it is far more practical to view environmental measures in instrumental terms and ask: How can green production contribute to the bottom line?

What drives corporate innovation? This fundamental question is critical for anyone attempting to make sense of corporate environmentalism. As a generalization, corporations innovate in an attempt to gain competitive advantage. Following Michael E. Porter, corporations can seek sustainable competitive advantage in two ways: through lower costs or through differentiation. In the first case, they can pursue a generic strategy of cost leadership, whereby they seek to become the low-cost producer in their industry. If a company can approximate the levels of differentiation in the market, it should be able to "translate its cost advantage directly into higher profits than competitors." Alternatively, a firm may adopt a differentiation strategy, whereby it "seeks to be unique in its industry along some dimensions that are widely valued by buyers" (1985: 13–14). Both of these generic strategies are relevant to innovations in environmental management. First, consider the connection between corporate environmentalism and cost-based advantages. A firm might seek to eliminate waste streams and minimize the use of hazardous materials in order to reduce disposal costs and exposure to litigation. These cost reductions, in turn, might allow a company to assume a position of cost leadership. Alternatively, a business might identify customers who are willing to pay a premium for goods and services produced in environmentally friendly ways. In either case, market forces might be powerful enough to lead firms to employ technologies and strategies that enhance the environment and the bottom line, either through cost or differentiation.

Green Consumers

The most common argument one encounters in the popular press is that green consumers will be a key driver in corporate environmentalism. A brand image of environmental responsibility may be vitally important, given evidence from opinion polls that citizens strongly value environmental quality. Moreover, there is much anecdotal evidence that green consumerism is on the rise. For example, Church & Dwight Co. Inc., maker of Arm & Hammer products, estimates that its green image is the source of 5–15 percent more revenues per year. Well-known brands like Ben and Jerry's, the Body Shop, and Tom's of Maine attribute their past success to socially conscious consumers (Ottman 1998). Although these case studies are well-known, one should not be too quick to draw lessons from anecdotal evidence. Indeed, market research suggests that even if environmentalism is popular, it does not translate into purchase decisions for most of the population, especially if these decisions require consumers to pay price premiums.

The *Green Gauge Report,* a study of Americans' environmental knowledge and behavior conducted annually by Roper Starch Worldwide, routinely reveals that environmental consumers have relatively weak commitments. They are willing to pay relatively modest premiums for ecologically friendly products. Although a majority of the population claim to be environmentally minded, most consumers place environmental impact well behind other decision criteria, such as past experience, price, brand recognition, personal recommendations, and convenience when making consumption decisions (see Setlow 2001; Speer 1997). As Joel Makower, editor of the *Green Business Letter* explains:

> A funny thing happened on the road to the environmental marketplace: the greener products didn't sell. Surveys cast blame on substandard products, higher prices for "green" items, unfamiliar brands, and products requiring changes in consumer behavior. Those market research surveys told only part of the story. Consumers would gladly make the greener choice—if the product didn't cost more or require a change of habits, if it could be purchased where one already shopped, if it came from a trusted brand, and if it was at least as good as its competition. (http://www.rand.org/scitech/stpi/ourfuture)

Andrew J. Hoffman may be correct when he notes, "the best that marketers can expect is that in cases of price parity, environmental attributes can break the tie" (1999: 250).

Green Contracting and Procurement

A second and more important market force emanates from the business community itself. Companies do not exist in isolation, but are enmeshed in a complex network of commercial relationships. Companies that have made a commitment to green production may impose environmental performance requirements throughout the supply chain. That is, they may demand that suppliers and distributors meet high environmental standards and provide verifiable evidence of their performance. One means by which companies can demonstrate their commitment to potential customers is through certification under standards promulgated by trade associations and national or international standard-setting organizations. Although a detailed discussion of standards is reserved for Chapter 9, it is useful to note here that certification under ISO 14001, the international standard for environmental management systems, is an important means of providing evidence of environmental performance. As Konrad von Moltke and Onno Kuik explain:

Standards are unlikely to play a major role in sales to individual consumers but intermediate points on the product chain are likely to require proof of appropriate certification so as to be able to support claims relating to the environmental impact of products or services. In other words, large corporations involved in complex product chains are likely to require the respect of the appropriate standards by all of their suppliers. In addition there exists a possibility that government procurement will move towards requiring one of these standards for the acquisition of major products or from large enterprises wishing to participate in the procurement process. (1997: 5)

To understand how these pressures might come to bear, consider the example of Ford Motor. Between 1996 and 1998, Ford achieved ISO 14001 certification for all of its more than 140 plants located in twenty-six countries. All facilities were held to the same standards, regardless of variations in national regulatory requirements. In December 1999, Ford required that all of its 150 suppliers certify that at least one manufacturing site was ISO 14001–compliant by the end of 2001, with all manufacturing sites certified by July 1, 2003. With assets of more than \$295 billion (2002), the decision to require ISO certification placed pressure on firms hoping to retain or build relationships with Ford. While Ford is a most striking example, the pattern is not unusual: the extended sense of responsibility that accompanies corporate environmental policy has led a number of large firms to make similar demands. Regardless of the power of green consumer markets, the business-to-business market should continue to force a greening of industry.

The trend in the business-to-business market is reinforced by changes in government procurement practices. The vast majority of Organization for Economic Cooperation and Development (OECD) countries have green procurements policies in place, thereby making environmental performance (and in some cases ISO 14001 certification) a factor for companies seeking to win government contracts (OECD 1999: 35–40). Green procurement was introduced in the United Stated during the presidency of Bill Clinton, who in 1998 issued Executive Order 13101 (63 Fed. Reg. 49643, September 16, 1998), which required agencies to engage in "environmentally preferable purchasing." Under the provisions of the order, "environmentally preferable" means "products or services that have a lesser or reduced effect on human health and the environment when compared with competing products or services that serve the same purpose. This comparison may consider raw materials acquisition, production, manufacturing, packaging, distribution, reuse, operation, maintenance, or disposal of the product or service." The order applies to all acquisition types, from basic supplies to entire buildings. The US federal government is the world's largest single consumer. It can use its market power to force corporations to change their

practices if it makes environmental impacts central to procurement decisionmaking. If EO 13101 increases the percentage of contracting decisions
based on environmental impacts—and participation in one of many voluntary standards programs is recognized as an indicator of environmental
quality—government procurement should create irresistible pressures for
corporate environmentalism.

Green Capital

Consumer markets, business-to-business markets, and government contracting are becoming increasingly green. These pressures are reinforced by the
growing role of environmental and social performance in capital markets.
Credit banks, institutional investors, and insurers are increasingly integrating environmental performance into their decisionmaking processes and are
"starting to shun companies which do not manage their environmental and
social risks properly, and to favor those that are eco-efficient" (Blumberg,
Korsvold, and Blum 1996: 22). This makes good business sense insofar as
high levels of environmental risk may compromise future revenue streams.

Similarly, socially responsible investors, once painfully small in number, are growing rapidly. Between 1995 and 2003, assets in social investment funds grew 40 percent faster than all professionally managed assets.
These assets constituted some $2.14 trillion in the United States, and some
11.3 percent of the total assets under professional management in 2003. To
be certain, social portfolios are screened for a number of different kinds of
investments, including tobacco, gambling, and weapons. However, most
social investment funds use multiple screens, including screens for environmental performance. They actively screen out securities of companies with
records of poor environmental performance and seek out companies with
good environmental performance and green products (see Social Investment
Forum 2003).

Screened investment funds have outperformed unscreened funds for
some time, reflecting the growing empirical evidence that firms with higher
environmental standards have better financial performance than their counterparts with less stringent standards (see Dowell, Hart, and Yeung 2000;
Russo and Fouts 1997). Some critics have attributed this performance
record to the fact that social funds invest more heavily in high-tech industries—the very industries that were greatly overvalued by the stock market
bubble of the late 1990s. Yet performance remained strong even during the
bear market of 2001–2002. In fact, during 2002, poor market performance
and waves of corporate accounting scandals created a $10.5 billion outflow
from the total assets of diversified equity funds in the United States. During
this same period, the assets in socially responsible funds experienced an
inflow of $1.5 billion (Social Investment Forum 2003).

In sum, environmental performance is becoming increasingly important as an indicator of economic performance and as a means of attracting capital and green investors (see Reed 1998; Schmidheiny and Zorraquin 1996). Once investments have occurred, the threat of divestiture or hostile shareholder resolutions may force companies to maintain fidelity to past commitments. Capital markets can be viewed—along with green consumers and the business-to-business and government procurement markets—as forces strengthening the incentives for environmental management.

■ Developing the Capacity for Green Production

Corporate environmentalism is a relatively recent phenomenon. In part, the market forces described above were not sufficiently developed until recent decades. More important, the operational demands of integrating environmental policy and business strategy may well have been impossible for more than a handful of firms prior to the late 1980s. During the 1970s, large businesses created the capacity for environmental management, largely in response to the new regulatory statutes. The responsibility for regulatory compliance was commonly assigned to environment, health, and safety departments. As a generalization, a "green wall" separated these activities from core business functions that top management viewed as being essential to the bottom line. As staffing expanded and the regulatory demands and potential liabilities escalated, the importance attributed to environmental management grew within US corporations. Increasingly, responsibilities were assigned to officers at the vice presidential level and new structures were created to coordinate environmental responsibilities throughout the organization, creating a context more supportive of change (Schot and Fischer 1993).

There is a second trend that deserves attention. During the past two decades, a growing number of companies have adopted advanced manufacturing systems, often in response to the competitive threat posed by Japanese firms. These firms incorporated total quality management to engineer product defects out of their systems. They developed flatter, more participatory organizational structures to incorporate workers at all levels of the firm into a process of continuous improvement. They looked holistically at the supply chain and used "just in time" processes to reduce inventory costs and coordinate activities within the production process, often with the support of advanced management information systems. Many of these firms adopted very high performance thresholds and made quality and flexibility core elements of their corporate cultures (see Flynn, Sakakibara, and Schroeder 1995; Lei, Hitt, and Goldhar 1996). There is a growing body of research that concludes that these advanced manufacturing systems provided a platform for subsequent efforts in pollution prevention. As Richard

Florida notes: "firms that are innovative in terms of their manufacturing processes are likely to be more imaginative in addressing environmental costs and risks. . . . At bottom, adoption of advanced manufacturing systems creates substantial opportunity for adoption of green design and production strategies since both draw upon the same underlying principles—a dedication to productivity improvement, quality, cost reduction, continuous improvement, and technological innovation" (1996: 80).

Does It Pay to Be Green?

There are many anecdotes that illustrate the ways in which firms have derived profits from their environmental programs. Take the example of 3M, an early innovator in this area, which introduced its Pollution Prevention Pays program in 1975. Pollution was portrayed as an indicator of inefficient processes and waste, and thus its prevention was directly linked to corporate financial performance. Between 1975 and 1992, 3M introduced over 3,000 projects designed to prevent pollution. These projects, when aggregated, saved 3M more than $500 million. Other companies, including Dow Chemicals and Chevron, emulated 3M and achieved significant cost savings as a result (Ehrenfeld 1999). While anecdotal evidence is illustrative, the proposition that pollution prevention pays has also been subjected to systematic analysis. Michael Russo and Paul Fouts's study (1997) of the relationship between environmental performance and profitability in 243 firms revealed that environmentally proactive firms had a higher return on assets, particularly in high-growth industries where investments in new technologies and process redesign carried fewer risks than in slow-growth or mature industries. Similarly, a statistical analysis of eighty-three firms by Robert D. Klassen and D. Clay Whybark revealed that, as corporate investments were "increasingly allocated to pollution prevention technologies, manufacturing performance improved in the areas of cost, speed, and flexibility" (1999: 606) This relationship undoubtedly reflects the fact that firms most likely to adopt a pollution prevention program or high-quality environmental management system are usually companies that have made previous investments in advanced manufacturing techniques that have a positive impact on quality control, inventory costs, and on-time delivery (see Hart and Ahuja 1996).

One can make a compelling case that market forces reward environmentally proactive firms. Yet one must treat with caution claims that it *always* pays to be green. This is true for several reasons. First, environmental investments are not created equal. Simply seeking a correlation between environmental expenditure and profitability does not suffice. As Stuart L. Hart explains, if a company's environmental spending is "dominated by 'yesterday's waste' and 'today's emissions' the company is paying dearly for environmental management but receiving few of the operating or strategic benefits. The objective is to minimize the expenditures" in these areas, in favor of "investments in 'today's processes and products' and 'tomorrow's technologies and markets" (1999: 84–85). Hart argues that the return on investment on reactive programs is negative, yet that these investments often constitute 90 percent of the total corporate effort in environmental management. Conversely, proactive initiatives (e.g., investments in pollution prevention) may provide a return on investment in excess of 60 percent, but make up less than 10 percent of the portfolio (see also Schaltegger and Figge 1998).

If statistical associations between expenditures and profitability tell us little without getting to a more detailed examination of how these expenditures are allocated, there are even more profound concerns when we consider issues of causality. There is clear empirical evidence that companies that have made prior investments and innovations in advanced manufacturing systems are more likely to make the transition to green production. This raises an important question: Are we looking primarily at the relationship between advanced manufacturing systems and profitability? Have we reversed the chain of causality altogether, such that companies that are more profitable are more likely to make proactive environmental investments? The causality problem is not exclusive to corporate environmentalism, but has emerged in analyses of corporate social responsibility more broadly. As Jean B. McGiore, Alison Sundgren, and Thomas Schneeweis conclude: "Prior performance is generally a better predictor of corporate social responsibility than subsequent performance. Thus, associations found between concurrent social responsibility and performance may partially be artifacts of previous high financial performance. Firms with high performance and low risk may be better able to afford to act in a socially responsible manner" (1988: 869).

None of this is to say that corporate environmental policy cannot have positive implications for the bottom line. In fact, there is a wealth of data on companies that have translated their environmental concern into cost and differentiation advantages. They have adopted a common set of environmental policy tools. However, one must be cautious in making the more general claim that green production is always profitable and that, thus, one can rely solely on market incentives to deliver environmental quality. It is necessary to examine how companies translate environmental commitment into a pattern of action.

■ From Policy to Practice

Corporate environmentalism begins with the definition of a corporate environmental policy. Yet corporate environmental policies are not created equal. One can place environmental policies into three broad categories. First, there are relatively vacuous statements of values that are designed primarily for public relations purposes (undoubtedly printed with soy inks on recycled paper). Second, and in contrast, others describe the company's commitment to regulatory compliance, explaining in variable detail how the organization will guarantee regulatory compliance. Third, and most interesting for present purposes, are policies that establish a commitment to proactive environmental stewardship. These policies often proclaim a commitment to go "beyond compliance" to achieve levels of environmental quality that are far greater than those required by law. They often present, in some detail, the means by which this will be accomplished. Moreover, they accept an expansive sense of corporate accountability for the impacts of their products and services across the life cycle. They integrate this responsibility into product and process design, making a commitment to finding substitutes for toxic substances, conserving energy and resources, and maximizing their use of recycled inputs. Finally, they hold suppliers and distributors to the same standards, spreading their commitment across the value chain (Brophy 1996a, 1996b).

The propensity of a firm to adopt any of the core environmental tools will depend on what it hopes to accomplish. At a bare minimum, a firm may simply hope to bring its operations into regulatory compliance. At a somewhat more ambitious level, it might seek to introduce process changes to achieve greater productive efficiencies and reduce the risk of future regulatory liabilities. Firms that are even more proactive may seek to redesign products to reduce their environmental impacts and differentiate their products from those of less environmentally sensitive competitors. Product innovations, even more than process innovations, may positively impact on a firm's reputation and increase customer loyalty. Finally, some firms may seek to redefine markets or create altogether new markets, while simultaneously exiting traditional markets (Reed 1998: 3). The further a firm moves along this continuum, from compliance to market creation, the more central environmental policy tools will be to corporate operations. The "green wall" that frequently separates the environmental officers from corporate management becomes less impenetrable, as environmental impacts become central to product and process design.

Ecoefficiency

Businesses have long understood the impact that efficiency has on the bottom line. By reducing the inputs per unit of output, they can gain cost advantages that can translate into competitive advantages in the marketplace. The understanding of efficiency evolved in recent decades to incorporate quality and the prevention of waste in all its manifestations. In corporate environmental policy, the quest for efficiency has been harnessed to reduce environmental impacts. Ecoefficiency entails "the delivery of competitively-priced goods and services that satisfy human needs and bring quality of life, while progressively reducing environmental impacts and resource intensity throughout the life cycle, to a level at least in line with the earth's estimated carrying capacity" (DeSimone and Popoff 1997: 47). According to the International Chamber of Commerce and World Business Council for Sustainable Development (1998), ecoefficiency places seven distinct demands on business: "(1) Reduce the material intensity of goods and services, (2) Reduce the energy intensity of goods and services, (3) Reduce toxic dispersion, (4) Enhance material recyclability, (5) Maximize sustainable use of renewable resources, (6) Extend product durability, and (7) Increase the service intensity of goods and services." To achieve these ends, businesses must closely examine the products they use, the resources and waste associated with the products, and the extent to which changes in design and production can economize on resources and reduce pollution without sacrificing the services demanded by customers. This, in turn, requires the adoption of a more holistic view of what is produced and how it is produced.

Life-Cycle Approaches

Life-cycle analysis is often presented as being critical to achieving higher levels of ecoefficiency. It entails moving beyond a simple concern with productive efficiencies and market outcomes—the traditional focus of corporate decisionmakers—to a far more inclusive vision that extends from cradle to grave (or reincarnation, if we consider recycling). The concern extends upstream to the extraction of raw materials, and downstream through distribution, consumer use, and recycling, revalorization, or disposal. Life-cycle analysis rests on two normative assumptions. First, the company is responsible for the environmental impacts connected with its products and services, even it they fall outside the boundaries of the productive unit, as traditionally understood. Second, this expanded responsibility translates into accountability: businesses must seek to reduce the impacts across the life cycle. These assumptions may prove controversial. They require corporations to voluntarily internalize costs that are rarely reflected in market prices. Moreover, they may require actions that could compromise short-term profitability (e.g., increasing product durability to reduce waste streams). These decisions could well place a firm at a disadvantage in mature industries characterized by severe price competition. Moreover, the holistic orientation that life-cycle analysis demands may run afoul of organizational culture, insofar as it demands that managers integrate corporate functions and staffs that may be formally separate within the firm (see Fussler and James 1996: chap. 14).

Process Redesign and Design for Environment

Corporate environmentalism demands a change of perspective. The traditional perspective viewed pollution as an "end of pipe" problem to be addressed (if at all) through investments in pollution control technologies. Under the new perspective, businesses that discover sources of pollution through life-cycle analysis can adopt a preventive strategy and engineer some pollution out of the system through basic design decisions. The adoption of a more holistic perspective and a commitment to eliminating pollution via design are essential, given that "80–90 per cent of the total life cycle costs associated with a product are committed by the final design of the product before production or construction actually begins," and that "waste resulting from the product creation, use, and disposal are largely determined by original design" (Welford 1996: 142).

Product and process redesign can address at least six different factors. First, it can examine energy used in production. Are there more energy-efficient processes available? Second, it can address the composition and minimization of industrial process residues. Can less toxic or environmentally harmful chemicals be substituted for those currently in use? Third, it can address the selection of materials. How can the amount of materials used (especially toxic materials) be minimized? How can the proportion of recycled materials be maximized? Are the best materials being used when one considers the impact of materials extraction and global resource limitations? Fourth, it can examine the packaging, transportation, and installation of the product. Is the product designed to reduce the emissions and waste generated in getting the product to the customer? Fifth, it can explore the environmental interactions that occur while a product is being used. What residues are generated? How much energy is consumed as the product is used? If the product is dissipated into the environment through use (e.g., surface coatings), what is the impact? Sixth, it can consider the demands of recycling. Can modular designs be used to recycle entire components? Can products be designed for easy disassembly and use standard materials to facilitate recycling? These kinds of questions, when explicitly addressed during the design of a product, can have significant importance for the environmental impact of a given product (see Graedel and Allenby 1996).

One can make a useful distinction between process redesign and product redesign. Process redesign entails the effort to discover more ecologically acceptable means of producing existing goods, without necessarily making changes to the actual product. Take the example of firms in the pulp and paper industry. Boise Cascade responded to controversies over logging forests for paper by engaging in "fiber farming," planting hybrid cottonwood trees as row crops near its facilities to reduce logging and transportation costs. In 1998, 25 percent of the pulp used for white paper was made from this fiber (Boise Cascade 1999). Consider the bleaching of paper. To reduce or eliminate the resulting dioxin and the associated cleanup costs, firms developed oxygen, ozone, and peroxide as bleaching agents. Finally, the printing industry has innovated with water-based and soy inks to eliminate the volatile organic compounds in petroleum-based inks (Porter and van der Linde 1995: 123). In each case, processes were altered to reduce environmental impacts without fundamental changes in product design.

Often, life-cycle analysis will reveal significant environmental gains that can be achieved through product redesign or a design for environment program. According to a primer on the program: "Design for Environment . . . seeks to eliminate the potential negative environmental impacts that result from a particular product or process through its entire life cycle by systematically assessing, evaluating, and addressing these potential problems during product development. By considering environmental issues during design, problems are addressed at the outset. . . . [T]he greatest impact at the lowest cost is usually realized only when improvements are incorporated into initial designs" (Digital Equipment Corporation and Massachusetts Institute of Technology Program on Technology n.d.: 2). In addition to reducing environmental impacts, a design for environment program may provide a firm with a means of managing costs and differentiating products in an increasingly green marketplace.

Rank Xerox, the Xerox Corporation's European affiliate, provides an excellent example of how life-cycle analysis and a design for environment program can be applied. Every new product undergoes life-cycle analysis to identify and reduce environmental impacts. Efforts are made to use as small a number of materials as possible, to facilitate recycling. In addition, Xerox adopts designs based on commonality, with the goal of using components that can be shared with other products. Parts and materials are also designed for durability, to maximize the opportunities for reuse. Products are designed for disassembly, through the use of modular components and snap fastenings to minimize damage. Design also focuses on recyclability. Materials are marked using the international plastic marking system, to facilitate identification and sorting for recycling. Design also emphasizes environmental, health, and safety standards, so that all products will meet or exceed the most demanding standards in any market. Finally, the design process explicitly addresses customer environmental requirements, minimizing energy and materials use. The design for environment work at Xerox has reduced the number of parts and made it possible to recondition and reuse a large number of components on everything from toner cartridges to copying machines (Fussler and James 1996: 242–243).

Another example can be found at General Motors, whose Design and Manufacture for the Environment Committee—which includes representatives from the company's car and truck platforms, Delphi, and participants from Isuzu, Opel, Saab, and Vauxhall—directs engineers to incorporate design for environment concerns directly into product design. Engineers address material and energy utilization, use of recycled materials, energy consumption, and waste; select materials to facilitate recycling; and design the product to facilitate dismantling. GM's "Green Initiative" was applied as a pilot project in the 1999 Chevrolet Silverado and GMC Sierra. As a result of this design for environment work at GM, mercury was eliminated from underhood lamp switches, preventing the potential release of more than one ton of mercury per model year. Gains in fuel efficiency saved 157,505,000 gallons of gas over the life of the model year. A new solder-less design in power and signal distribution areas eliminated eighteen tons of lead per model year. Redesign of brakes to double their life expectancy prevented the generation of more than 6,000 tons of scrap brakes per model year. The use of hydroforming frame technologies reduced steel scrap by 19,800 tons per model year. The redesign of radiator side air baffles to use recycled tires eliminated 140,000 tires per model year. The example of GM reveals that a series of small design alterations can, when combined, make a significant contribution to pollution prevention (General Motors 1998: 19).

How far can design for environment go? In most cases, changes in product design will be incremental, as in the case of GM. However, in some cases design for environment may find its ultimate expression in industrial ecology. The holistic perspective associated with industrial ecology is perhaps its most distinctive feature:

> In an industrial ecology, unit processes and industries are interacting systems rather than isolated components. This view provides the basis for thinking about ways to connect different waste-producing processes, plants, or industries into an operating web that minimizes the total amount of industrial material that goes to disposal sinks or is lost in intermediate processes. The focus changes from merely minimizing waste from a particular process or facility, commonly known as "pollution prevention," to minimizing waste produced by the larger system as a whole. (Richards, Allenby, and Frosch 1994: 3)

Here the goal is to develop processes and systems holistically, with an eye to producing byproducts that can be used as inputs in other production processes rather than discarded as waste. Alternatively, a firm might develop entirely new product lines simply because they can consume existing waste streams. Where industrial ecology is applied in its broadest sense, efforts may be made to cluster businesses that consume each other's waste as inputs into their own products (DeSimone and Popoff 1997: 52–53). This has been the goal behind the co-location strategy adopted by BASF, a German chemical company. In helping to design chemical industries in

China, India, Indonesia, and Malaysia, BASF created industrial ecosystems such that the waste from one facility was consumed as raw material in a neighboring facility (Hart 1997: 71).

Environmental Management Systems

An environmental management system is designed to orient an organization toward the progressive reduction of environmental impacts, rather than focusing on changes in product and process design. As an application and extension of total quality management, it is designed to promote a Deming Cycle of continual improvement (W. Edwards Deming originated the "plan, do, check, set" cycle for total quality management). Indeed, many companies describe their systems as being oriented toward "total *environmental* quality management." Some companies have designed organization-specific systems. Others, in contrast, have created systems to meet the requirements of standards established by international bodies (e.g., the International Organization for Standardization's ISO 14000 series, the European Union's ecomanagement and audit scheme), national standards bodies (e.g., the British Standards Institute's BSI 7750), or trade associations (e.g., the American Chemistry Council's Responsible Care Program). The precise features of an EMS vary by standards (see Starkey 1996).

As a generalization, the EMS standards require that an organization execute several related tasks. First, it must create an environmental policy that states, in broad terms, its goals. Second, it must identify the environmental aspects of the functions executed in its facilities. Third, it must use the information on environmental aspects and regulatory requirements to establish environmental goals and objectives, and design the programs necessary for their realization. Regulatory compliance is viewed as a minimum expectation. Fourth, it must implement the policy by assigning responsibility, providing the necessary training, documenting procedures, and disseminating information on these procedures throughout the organization. Fifth, it must subject the process to periodic review through audits conducted internally or by third parties. Finally, the organization must review progress in meeting its objectives and make adjustments to achieve continuous improvement (Nash and Ehrenfeld 1999).

Critics often discount the significance of environmental management systems on several grounds. First, the mere existence of an EMS tells us little; its impact will depend on management commitment and resource flows. Second and related, because the various EMS standards specify a process in broad terms without mandating specific performance thresholds, it is difficult to evaluate performance. In sum, critics might conclude that an EMS may create a formal process yet fail to have a substantial impact on environmental quality. Improvements—where they occur—may assume a glacial pace. Yet the mere existence of an EMS may create a public impression of proactive stewardship.

Despite the validity of these criticisms, there is a rapidly growing body of evidence that a quality EMS has been important to companies that have gone beyond regulatory requirements in their environmental performance (see Coglianese and Nash 2001). A survey of more than 580 manufacturing plants reveals some important information. First, as one might expect given what was stated earlier, firms with an EMS had larger dedicated environmental staffs and employed advanced manufacturing systems (including total quality management and "just in time" inventory control). Second, a much larger percentage of EMS plants employed environmental performance indictors to monitor regulatory compliance, waste and emission reduction, and energy use. Third, when compared with their non-EMS counterparts, a far larger percentage of EMS plants reported that they derived in-plant environmental benefits from recycling, air emission reductions, solid waste reductions, and electricity use. Fully 79 percent of the EMS plants cited their EMS as the source of their in-plant improvements. The quality and quantity of data on EMS performance continue to grow as analysts explore the sources of successful environmental management (Coglianese and Nash 2001; Florida and Davidson 2001).

Environmental Auditing and Reporting

Companies routinely conduct compliance audits to determine whether they are violating regulations, with an eye to remedial action. However, an environmental audit has a loftier goal. Firms with an environmental management system may use this data to improve internal management systems and report the results to investors, contractors, and other key stakeholders through the periodic release of environmental, health, and safety reports. Critics of corporate environmentalism may discount the significance of internal audits. Information is released voluntarily and may be presented in a highly selective and stylized fashion to create the impression of success. In response, critics have stressed the importance of third-party verification and compliance with standard reporting protocols.

While audits could be conducted by internal or external auditing teams, the latter may carry far greater benefits. As compliance with EMS standards or association codes becomes important for succeeding in government procurement, capital, and business-to-business markets, external audits and third-party registration may become necessary. Moreover, external audits and third-party registration may carry greater weight with regulators. External auditing, however, is a two-edged sword. Audits may reveal environmental problems before they are discovered by regulators, thus allowing businesses to remedy the situation. Yet, in the United States, firms are required to report any regulatory violations to the EPA, thereby increasing vulnerability to regulatory penalties and private civil suits. Business associations have lobbied for audit privilege and immunity provisions in state and federal law, albeit with limited success. The EPA rejects immunity outright and rejects protections established in state law.

While concerns about the provision of audit information abound, a growing number of businesses issue annual corporate environmental reports. By the end of the 1990s, several hundred companies around the globe—including over 35 percent of the world's 250 largest corporations— were publishing such reports (see Kolk 2000; Rondinelli and Berry 2000; Sutherland 2000; White 1999). The proliferation of reporting is easily understood. As Pamela Buxton notes: "Corporate social responsibility matters more than ever. Sound social, ethical and environmental practices have graduated from optional extras to key parts of business strategy. . . . In a climate where transparency is key, companies are aware it is not just their financial bottom line that matters, but a new 'triple bottom line' of financial, environmental, and social performance. With such high stakes, it's no wonder the need for a well designed social/environmental report has moved up the corporate agenda" (2000: 33).

The propagation of corporate environmental reports has created a distinct problem. As Allen L. White notes: "the very growth of such disclosure . . . has led to an enormous volume of inconsistent and unverified information. If the information of interest to stakeholders is not presented in a coherent, uniform framework, the resulting confusion and frustration may well stall the momentum toward greater disclosure" (1999: 32). In this context, it may prove difficult for businesses to communicate their performance records. Indeed, as John C. Stauber and Sheldon Rampton observe: "U.S. businesses spend an estimated $1 billion a year on the services of anti-environmental PR professionals and on 'greenwashing' their corporate image" (1996: 16). When companies invest heavily in environmental public relations, it can be difficult for genuine performers to convey their records with sufficient clarity.

To remedy this situation, a number of organizations have initiated efforts to standardize reporting. The most important effort to date has come from the Coalition for Environmentally Responsible Economies (CERES). It introduced its Global Reporting Initiative in late 1997 to design globally applicable guidelines for preparing enterprise-level sustainability reports. The initiative's guidelines require that reports include: a CEO statement; key indicators of environmental performance; a profile of the reporting entity; sections describing policies, organization, and management systems, stakeholder relationships, management performance, operational performance, and product performance; and a sustainability overview (see http:// www.globalreporting.org/guidelines). The initiative's guidelines require that complying firms provide highly specific information for each of the above categories. For example, under key indicators of environmental performance, businesses are to report key environmental, social, and economic issues and impacts associated with operations, products, and services; the number, volume, and nature of accidental or nonroutine releases to land, air, and water, including chemical spills, oil spills, and emissions resulting from upset combustion conditions; indicators of occupational health and safety; total energy use; total materials use other than fuel; total water use; quantity of nonproduct output returned to process or market by recycling or reuse by material type and by on- and off-site management type; quantity of nonproduct output to land by material type and by on- and off-site management type; emissions to air, by type; discharges to water, by type; indicators of social and economic aspects of operational performance; and major environmental, social, and economic impacts associated with the life cycle of products and services, with quantitative estimates of such impacts. A similar level of detailed reporting is required under other categories.

The Global Reporting Initiative's guidelines require the voluntary disclosure of far more information than could be demanded under existing regulations. Moreover, the guidelines require that such information be released using a common set of metrics, thus allowing for comparisons across companies and over time. Businesses might be concerned that the initiative would force them to disclose evidence of environmental failures and that such disclosures could make them appear to be far less committed to environmental management than businesses that provided highly stylized reports that contain little in the way of performance data. Despite this risk, as of January 2006, 768 organizations from around the world report performance using the Global Reporting Initiative format. Participants from the United States include a number of industrial giants, such as 3M, Abbot Laboratories, Alcoa, Anheuser-Busch, AT&T, Bristol-Myers-Squibb, ChevronTexaco, Citigroup, DuPont, Ford Motor Company, General Motors, Hewlett Packard, IBM, International Paper, Johnson & Johnson, Marathon Oil, McDonald's Corporation, Motorola, Nike, Polaroid, Proctor & Gamble, Sunoco, the Dow Chemical Company, United Parcel Service, and Weyerhaeuser.

■ Evaluating Corporate Environmentalism

Students of environmental policy should celebrate the growing trend in corporate environmentalism. Corporations combine actors with the best knowledge about markets, products, inputs, production processes, capital, supply chain pressures, and the suitability of available control technologies. If they have the incentives to achieve higher levels of environmental performance, one must assume that this knowledge will allow them to achieve gains that could never be dictated by public regulations, and to do so efficiently. Moreover, because many of these corporations have placed a heavy reliance on environmental management systems, one should assume that they will have the organizational capabilities to respond to new environmental challenges as they occur. Finally, one may suspect that market forces will force a rapid dissemination of corporate innovations throughout the economy.

While there is room for celebration, there is also room for healthy skepticism. There are hard limits to what can be accomplished in a voluntary system. Corporate managers have the primary fiduciary responsibility to maximize shareholder wealth. Voluntary environmental investments will continue as long as they reinforce this larger end. After the most egregious waste streams have been managed and the risk of future liabilities has been brought into acceptable ranges, managers may search for profitability gains elsewhere. Moreover, effectiveness may be limited by consumer demands. Companies may view a successful policy as one that allows them to produce the goods the market demands in more environmentally friendly ways, even if the products themselves contribute to environmental degradation. It is instructive that the automotive industry has simultaneously embraced environmental management and the demand for ever-expanding fleets of sport utility vehicles. In the end, one might ask whether the net impact of producing fuel-efficient cars without an environmental policy would be more positive than the current mix of policies and practices.

Finally, we must be concerned with issues of accountability. Corporate environmentalism carries serious problems of information asymmetry. Consumers, communities, and citizens have only as much information about environmental practices as companies wish to release. There is no Freedom of Information Act that can be used to mandate the disclosure of corporate information. The information asymmetries have important implications for citizens who rightfully demand accountability over environmental practices. They also have important implications for firms with a genuine commitment to green production, which are forced to compete with waves of corporate greenwash and to make their claims stand out above the sea of public relations. Some of these firms have made themselves highly accountable through third-party auditing and the release of information (both good and bad) in a standardized format, but this remains the exception. Differentiation-based competitive advantages can be fully exploited if and only if there is sufficient quality information. If information is of questionable value, consumers may find it impossible to discriminate on the basis of environmental performance, thereby obviating the incentives for corporate environmentalism.

What are the implications for regulatory design? First, it would be a mistake to design regulations that neglect differences in corporate performance and capabilities. Firms with a documented record of exemplary performance could be granted far greater flexibility, whereas firms that lack environmental commitment or the requisite organizational capabilities may demand vigorous oversight. Second, regulatory design should focus on the problem of information. Regulations could mandate the universal release of audited performance information. Of course, regulations do not provide the only means to these ends. Trade associations and standard-setting organizations can also play a major role. They can have a powerful impact on corporate incentives as well as on corporate behavior.

Green by Association:
Code- and Standard-Based
Self-Regulation

We often judge the performance of environmental regulation in light of changes in the concentrations of principal pollutants, assigning regulators the credit (or blame) for the results. Unfortunately, policy analysts often forget that "policy outcomes" are more correctly viewed as the product of a complicated set of relationships and decisions, many of which are only indirectly shaped by public policy. Changes in pollution levels are also the product of factors that are difficult for regulators to control, including the self-regulatory activities of trade associations, market and supply chain pressures, and changes in the design of processes and products at the level of the firm. Regulations constitute one factor in a complex configuration of institutions and forces. This chapter considers the role of trade associations and standard-based self-regulation. It begins with a consideration of information scarcity and the problems it creates for environmental protection. The core argument is that association codes and standards can attenuate many of the information-related problems that have bedeviled regulatory reform while reinforcing green market forces.

■ Information Scarcity and Environmental Protection

As argued in earlier chapters, the regulatory system created in the 1970s has contributed to significant gains in environmental quality in virtually every media. Yet there is reason to fear that the original regulatory system has reached the limits of what it can accomplish. The major sources of pollution are now in compliance. For firms that are in compliance, a new challenge presents itself: to promote even higher levels of performance. Further advances will require changes in product and process design at the level of the firm that are difficult to impose from above using traditional regulatory instruments. Rather it may be necessary to delegate greater authority to corporations that possess the greatest knowledge about their technologies, products, and markets, and create incentives for innovations in pollution control and prevention.

As noted in Chapter 6, the Clinton administration pursued a regulatory reinvention program designed, in large part, to promote ongoing corporate innovations. Despite the ongoing efforts at experimentation, there were myriad problems, including the lack of a coherent model, ongoing regulatory adversarialism, and the decision to graft REGO initiatives onto a system premised on the need for command-and-control regulation (Fiorino 1999). The core problems, however, were the demand for certainty of results and, more important, information scarcity. Regulators found it difficult to monitor corporate performance, particularly if each firm pursued novel paths to pollution reduction. The centerpiece of REGO, Project XL, often demanded greater certainty of results than applicants could provide, thereby imposing regulatory transaction costs that undermined the incentives for participation and depressed participation rates (Blackman et al. 2001; Marcus, Geffen, and Sexton 2002).

Information problems also play a role in limiting the power of green market forces. As noted in Chapter 8, many corporations have made important strides in controlling their environmental impacts. These firms have come to view environmental performance as being intimately connected to their primary goal of maximizing shareholder wealth. Companies have employed a number of tools in pursuit of green production. For firms hoping to achieve cost-based advantages, the translation of environmental performance into profitability is relatively unproblematic. If they can reduce production costs and future liabilities by managing or eliminating waste streams, their success should find an expression in prices and profit margins. In contrast, firms that hope to realize differentiation-based advantages face significant challenges. These advantages can be achieved when consumers value qualitative differences and are willing to pay a price premium (or, at the very least, give preferential treatment to products that have the valued characteristics when they are offered at competitive prices). For firms to achieve differentiation-based advantages through green production, two things must be in place. First, there must be a desire to discriminate on the basis of environmental performance in consumer, business-to-business, government procurement, and financial markets. Second, these actors must have access to economical sources of quality information on corporate performance. If the costs of assessing environmental performance are too great, green market forces will fail to reward firms with a positive environmental record. To the extent that firms find it difficult to convey accurate information in a sea of corporate greenwash, they may rationally conclude that green production does not provide a meaningful means of achieving differentiation-based advantages.

In each case, information—or, more correctly, information scarcity—is a source of concern. Regulators might be willing to delegate greater authority to corporations. Delegation, however, opens the door to a host of agency problems and increases the demand for exhaustive information on performance. Corporations might be willing to invest more in environmental management if they felt that these investments would generate a stream of benefits in the marketplace. These benefits might be difficult to capture if consumers, businesses, investors, and government procurement agents distrust publicly available information on corporate environmental performance.

Principals, Agents, and Governance

Principal-agent relationships exist wherever one party delegates authority to another party. Whether we are speaking of a patient consulting a physician, a corporation contracting with a supplier of specialized components, or Congress assigning new regulatory duties to a regulatory agency, a common set of problems emerge. Delegation is necessary because of an asymmetry of information and capabilities: a patient does not have expertise in diagnosing and treating illnesses; Congress lacks the capacity to regulate the environmental practices of corporations. Although the principal delegates authority on presumption that the agent will exercise it faithfully, there is always some uncertainty. The same information asymmetries that necessitate delegation subsequently limit the capacity of principals to monitor and assess the behavior of their agents. The principals, as a result, are at all times vulnerable to miscommunication, shirking, and opportunistic behavior. The problems of control are real and exist in most interorganizational relationships. An entire body of theory has emerged in economics to explore the problems of agency (see Barzel 1989; Eggertsson 1990). Agency theory has also been appropriated with varying success by many scholars interested in studying political-administrative relationships in the area of regulation (see Eisner, Worsham, and Ringquist 1996; Waterman and Meier 1998).

According to agency theorists, a variety of strategies may be used to limit the potential for opportunism within a principal-agent relationship: principals may specify tasks with great precision, they may require agents to abide by detailed and exhaustive written rules, they may create internal oversight mechanisms and accounting techniques to control resource flows. Three factors, however, limit the efficacy of such mechanisms. First, information asymmetry may limit the specificity of any rule system. Second, there is a trade-off between accountability and efficiency. Resources devoted to monitoring agent behavior and compliance are unavailable for other purposes. Third, the adoption of mechanisms to enhance control may foster procedural rigidity, undermining robustness, adaptability, and efficiency.

The key point is straightforward: attempts to control for potential opportunism may claim significant resources and prove prohibitively costly in terms of agent performance (see Williamson 1985).

The difficulties of managing information scarcity and principal-agent relationships are a major force in the evolution of economic governance regimes (see Campbell, Hollingsworth, and Lindberg 1991). Following Oliver E. Williamson (1985), efforts to manage agency problems impose transaction costs, and one would expect actors to develop modes of governance that allow them to economize on these costs. Principals can try to reduce the impact of informational asymmetries in a variety of ways. They can craft contracts that cover every possible contingency as a means of reducing agent discretion. When delegation entails highly specific and complicated responses on the part of agents, principals may combine detailed contracts with third-party monitoring (what Williamson refers to as "trilateral governance"). At the extreme, principals may introduce long-term exclusive contracts ("bilateral governance"), acquire the agent via merger, or develop an in-house production capacity ("unified governance"). In each case, they must be cognizant of the transaction cost implications of alternative governance mechanisms.

Research on transaction cost economics and governance, while concerned primarily with commercial relations, may prove useful for understanding alternative means of dealing with some of the information problems identified above. Take the case of the EPA. One can view the exhaustive environmental legislation of the 1970s as an attempt by principals in Congress to manage the uncertainty of delegating authority to the newly created EPA. As the costs of this strategy became apparent, the EPA embraced REGO in the 1990s. Most reinvention and reform efforts have entailed providing greater flexibility to regulated parties, opening the door to a new set of agency problems. Performance was difficult to monitor and regulators feared that corporations would shirk their duties. Thus the provision of greater flexibility was contingent on the provision of exhaustive information on agent performance and guarantees of superior environmental performance in some hypothetical future. The analytical demands of processing this information limited the scope of reform; large regulatory transaction costs dissuaded many companies from participating. The costs obviated any anticipated benefits.

A comparable set of problems emerged in green markets. Corporations may hope to exploit differentiation-based advantages through green production. Consumers, business contractors, investors, and government procurement agents may hope to discriminate on the basis of environmental performance. However, the costs of monitoring corporate behavior—the collection and processing of information in a sea of corporate greenwash—imposes significant transaction costs. These costs, in turn, may induce green market failure, thereby limiting the extent to which markets and supply chain pressures can be used to promote higher levels of environmental quality.

In these cases, the need for delegation in an environment of information scarcity creates pressures for changes in governance structures. The costs of directly monitoring agent activities may prove prohibitive. In the context of regulation, bilateral and unified governance (e.g., nationalization) are not plausible options. In contrast, trilateral governance may prove quite effective. In essence, government could delegate authority, then rely on qualified third parties—standard-setting organizations demanding external audits and certification—to monitor agent behavior. This model has performed fairly well in the regulation of corporate securities, for example. In the context of corporations seeking to exploit differentiation advantages, the same solution could provide a means of reducing the information costs that consumers, contractors, investors, and procurement agents would otherwise be forced to shoulder, thereby increasing the likelihood that they will discriminate on the basis of environmental performance.

Historically, trade associations and standard-setting organizations have played a vital role in alleviating problems of information scarcity. By developing codes of conduct and standards for products and processes, they can reduce the uncertainties described above. While one might not have much information on specific firms, if products meet the industry standards for design and performance, this lack of information may not be definitive. To the extent that trade association codes and international standards govern corporate environmental performance and firms can certify that they have met the standards in question, they may have a role to play in affecting environmental outcomes and reducing some of the informational problems described above.

■ Trade Associations and Corporate Self-Regulation

Trade associations are ubiquitous in capitalist economies. At a minimum, they serve a promotional function (e.g., marketing industry products). However, they can also coordinate the behavior of their members along many other dimensions. As J. Rogers Hollingsworth, Phillippe C. Schmitter, and Wolfgang Streeck note:

> In all modern economies, companies have associated with each other to collect information about production levels and prices, to conduct joint research and development, to promote standardization, to engage in technology transfer and vocational training, to channel communication and influence to state agencies, to formulate codes of conduct, to negotiate with labor, and even to decide on prices, production goals, and investment strategies. (1994: 7)

At the extreme, trade associations may serve a self-regulatory function, designing industry standards, coordinating production and pricing decisions, monitoring performance, and punishing members for noncompliance. The actual functions executed by associations will depend on many factors, including levels of competition within an industry, an industry's location in the product cycle, whether specific functions are permitted under national laws, whether the associations have the human and financial resources, and whether businesses perceive a need for collective representation.

Historically, trade associations were relatively weak in the United States. In the first decades of the twentieth century, antitrust enforcement focused heavily on horizontal restraints of trade as per se violations of the Sherman Act. This prosecutorial focus led many companies to pursue consolidation rather than associations as means of coordinating activities (McCraw 1986). The importance of associations grew dramatically in the next several decades, however, as a result of World War I mobilization, the associationalism of the 1920s, and the efforts to integrate associations into various New Deal recovery agencies (see Eisner 2000a). Nonetheless, associations remained quite weak in comparative perspective. Understaffed and weakly developed as organizations, they were discounted by businesses and the government. As Graham K. Wilson notes, in the United States "this organisational weakness represented, ironically, political strength. Businesses organised little to protect their collective interests . . . because [their] collective interests were little challenged" (1990: 48). Yet things changed in response to the wave of new social regulations and growing foreign competition. Trade associations that had languished for decades underwent an organizational renaissance, one that brought greater resource flows and responsibilities (see Vogel 1989).

By the 1990s, associations were deeply engaged in shaping public policy, developing codes of conduct for members, and serving self-regulatory functions. Many began to coordinate their members' environmental performance with environmental codes (see Gunningham and Rees 1997; Teubner, Farmer, and Murphy 1994) and the provision of various kinds of services (e.g., peer review of corporate procedures, training). In the United States, the Institute of Nuclear Power Operations, the American Chemistry Council, the American Petroleum Institute, and the American Forest and Paper Association, among others, have ambitious self-regulatory programs. Although self-regulation has often been a response to salient events, it has been far more than an exercise in public relations. The best self-regulatory programs provide detailed design specifications for environmental management systems and require external auditing, with large sanctions for noncompliance (e.g., loss of association membership). Unfortunately, self-regulation is often voluntary, and noncompliance carries few credible sanctions (see Gunningham 1995; Howard, Nash, and Ehrenfeld 2000; King and

Lenox 2000; Rees 1994, 1997). An examination of the self-regulatory activities of the American Forest and Paper Association and the American Chemistry Council can help provide a better understanding of how trade associations manage the behavior of their members.

The American Forest and Paper Association and Sustainable Forestry

The past two decades have witnessed several environmental controversies involving the forest and paper industry. The most salient controversy involved the northern spotted owl. Because it breeds primarily in old-growth forests, the survival of the specie came in conflict with the forest industry, particularly after 1990, when the US Fish and Wildlife Service listed the northern spotted owl as endangered under the Endangered Species Act. Although limitations on the harvesting of wood from old-growth forests was of minimal importance to the industry, the controversy nonetheless portrayed the industry as an enemy of the environment and could open the door to expanded regulation of industry practices and limit access to logging on public lands.

The American Forest and Paper Association (AFPA) responded to this state of affairs by developing its Sustainable Forestry Initiative (SFI) in 1994. The initiative is based on a commitment to meeting market demand while "using environmentally responsible practices that promote the protection of wildlife, plants, soil, air and water quality to ensure the future of our nation's forests." According to the AFPA, the initiative promotes the following:

- Broadening the implementation of sustainable forestry by employing an array of economically, environmentally and socially sound practices in the conservation of forests—including appropriate protection, growth, harvest and use of those forests—using the best scientific information available.
- Ensuring long-term forest productivity and conservation of forest resources through prompt reforestation, soil conservation, afforestation and other measures.
- Protecting the water quality in streams, lakes and other waterbodies.
- Managing the quality and distribution of wildlife habitats and contribut[ing] to the conservation of biological diversity by developing and implementing stand and landscape-level measures that promote habitat diversity and the conservation of forest plants and animals including aquatic fauna.
- Managing the visual impact of harvesting and other forest operations.
- Managing Program Participant lands of ecologic, geologic, cultural or historic significance in a manner that recognizes their special qualities.
- Promoting the efficient use of forest resources.
- Broadening the practice of sustainable forestry by cooperating with forest landowners, wood producers, consulting foresters and Program

Participants' employees who have responsibility in wood procurement and landowner assistance programs.

- Publicly reporting Program Participants' progress in fulfilling their commitment to sustainable forestry.
- Providing opportunities for the public and the forestry community to participate in the commitment to sustainable forestry.
- Promoting continual improvement in the practice of sustainable forestry and monitor[ing], measur[ing] and report[ing] performance in achieving the commitment to sustainable forestry. (http://www.aboutsfi.org/about_principles.asp)

These objectives are translated into a detailed set of performance measures and indicators (Sustainable Forestry Board 2002). A decade after introduction of the Sustainable Forestry Initiative, more than 130 million acres of forestland had been certified and the program had received the endorsement of nineteen state legislatures and a number of environmental groups (see Abusow 2005).

The Sustainable Forestry Initiative is impressive on several counts. First, as noted above, the broad principles are combined with very detailed performance measures and indicators that are available to the public. They are not merely symbolic statements of the industry's respect for the environment. Second, unlike many other trade associations, the AFPA does not make its environmental program optional for members. Rather, SFI membership is a condition of AFPA membership. In addition to being in compliance with all laws and regulations, participants are required to collect significant amounts of information on their resources, establish detailed plans for meeting the SFI objectives, assign responsibilities, and develop information on key indicators. Compliance with the SFI must be verified by third-party auditors (the AFPA provides very detailed information on verification and certification principles and procedures, and on the qualification criteria for verifiers). According to the AFPA, it has asked seventeen members to leave the association for noncompliance. As a result, membership conveys important information about environmental performance. Companies that attain certification through third-party auditing are allowed to place the "SFI Participant" label on their products. Manufacturers, publishers, and retailers that purchase from SFI participants can use the label.

Third, and most impressive, the AFPA has increased accountability by bringing external stakeholders into key positions in the Sustainable Forestry Initiative. The SFI is overseen by a board that has the responsibility of reviewing and developing the SFI standard and verification procedures. The board comprises fifteen members, two-thirds of whom are drawn from outside the industry. In 2005 the board included the president and CEO of the Nature Conservancy, the president of Resources for the Future, the sustainable forestry representative of the National Association of State Foresters, the CEO of International Conservation, the president of the Conservation Fund, and a dean emeritus from the College of Forest Resources at the University of Washington. The AFPA has also created an external review panel comprising representatives of environmental, academic, and government organizations, ranging from the chairman of the Conservation Fund to a representative from the US Department of Interior. The panel conducts independent reviews of the SFI and the accuracy of its annual report.

The American Chemistry Council and Responsible Care

In 1985, Canada's Chemical Producer Association responded to the Union Carbide chemical leak in Bhopal, India, and introduced Responsible Care, an EMS-based self-regulatory initiative. In 1988 the Chemical Manufacturers Association (subsequently renamed the American Chemistry Council) followed suit, making Responsible Care available for association members and partners (http://www.americanchemistry.com). The program spread rapidly across the globe and in 2005 was employed by trade associations in some fifty-two nations. Responsible Care focuses on promoting continual improvement in environmental, health, and safety performance. To this end, American Chemistry Council members must ascribe to a set of guiding principles that emphasize the need to prioritize environmental and health concerns and the importance of stakeholder engagement. The council has also designed a series of codes addressing environmental and health concerns. The codes most relevant to environmental management include community awareness and response, pollution prevention, process safety, distribution, employee health and safety, and product stewardship.

In 1999 the American Chemistry Council's board of directors asked companies to establish at least one goal, make performance improvements toward realization of that goal, and communicate that goal and performance to the public and the council. The hope was to use this information to better understand progress within the industry, identify areas of need, and exhibit continuous performance improvement to the public. The American Chemistry Council required members and partners to engage in annual self-evaluation and reporting with respect to their performance in meeting each of the codes. In so doing, they had to report on distinct performance measures promulgated by the association. The council also relied on a "mutual assistance network" that allowed members to pool experiences and information on best practices. Yet unlike the SFI, Responsible Care did not require third-party auditing. Rather it employed a management verification process. Verification teams consisted of peers (i.e., member-company representatives), a contractor, and community representatives.

Critics were quite skeptical of Responsible Care, noting that during the 1990s the American Chemistry Council spent $1–2 million annually to implement the program in member facilities, while devoting in excess of $10 million annually in advertising its commitment (Fischer et al. 2005: 22). But did Responsible Care make a difference in performance? According to a study of code compliance by Jennifer Howard, Jennifer Nash, and John Ehrenfeld, it elicited "the greatest and most uniform response from companies in areas visible to outsiders. In other areas, companies' actions may differ widely, even though they all report that they conform equally with code requirements." As one might expect, "companies that saw environmental practices as marginal to the organization tended to treat Responsible Care as an important tool in external image manipulation, and a relatively unhelpful vehicle for internal change. Those firms that saw Responsible Care as an important tool . . . had taken EHS [environment, health, and safety] matters seriously before Responsible Care but recognized that aspects of the program went beyond their traditional concerns" (2000: 77, 76). The key conclusion that one might have reached a decade after the introduction of Responsible Care was that its value depended on a firm's preexisting internal commitment to environmental stewardship. However, there were great opportunities for opportunistic behavior as long as self-regulation was not backed with requirements for mandatory audits and explicit sanctions for noncompliance (King and Lenox 2000).

Subsequently, things changed as the American Chemistry Council strengthened Responsible Care (International Council of Chemical Associations 2002: 62). In 2004 it replaced the management verification process with mandatory certification by independent, accredited auditing firms. All members were required to have their headquarters certified by December 31, 2005, and initial certification for remaining facilities by December 31, 2007. Although it is too early to evaluate the impact of these changes, if third-party certification requirements are enforced and backed with serious sanctions, one can predict that participation in Responsible Care will make a significant and verifiable difference in corporate performance.

The key lesson is that associations, as self-regulating entities, can offer many benefits. If compliance is mandatory and codes are sufficiently rigorous—as is the case with the AFPA—association membership can be viewed as an indicator of environmental performance. This helps firms that are hoping to capture differentiation-based advantages by reducing the information costs. At present, however, there is great variation in association codes and enforcement activities. For example, many associations do not make their codes mandatory. Others, like the American Chemistry Council, are in a state of transition. Association membership, when taken alone, may not provide quality information for consumers, contractors, financiers, and government procurement agents hoping to discriminate on the basis of environmental performance.

■ International Environmental Standards

Historically, product standards have been critical in facilitating market exchange and mass standardized production. They reduce information, transaction, and production costs, and allow for competition in commodity markets (Sykes 1995). Trade associations, government agencies (e.g., the Commerce Department), and national standards associations (e.g., the American National Standards Institute) have been key actors in the development of domestic standards. In the past several decades, the importance of international standards and metastandards (i.e., standards for processes) has grown with the rise of international composite production and global telecommunications, computer, and financial systems (Uzumeri 1997). Potentially, international standards can be of great importance in shaping corporate environmental performance. If they are sufficiently rigorous and performance is verified, certification can convey important information to consumers, businesses, investors, and governments hoping to discriminate on the basis of environmental performance. Differentiation-based advantages are dependent on economical sources of accurate information. In global markets, where information scarcity can be particularly onerous, standards can play a vital role in reducing the costs of making sense of corporate claims and disparate national regulatory requirements.

The international environmental management system standards have been developed by the International Organization for Standardization, a Geneva-based international nongovernmental organization that serves as a federation of standards bodies from some 130 nations. The ISO is perhaps best known for the ISO 9000 series of quality control standards. Certified compliance with ISO 9000 has become necessary for firms hoping to gain access to corporate and governmental bid lists. The ISO 14000 series of environmental management standards is rapidly assuming the same status with respect to environmental performance.

The Path to International Environmental Standards

In anticipation of the 1992 Earth Summit, the UN Conference on Environment and Development contacted the ISO and the International Electrotechnical Commission in the hope of stimulating greater business participation. The World Business Council for Sustainable Development, in turn, encouraged standard-setting organizations to become more involved in environmental self-regulation. The ISO and the International Electrotechnical Commission had been contemplating the need for global environmental standards since 1991, when they formed the Strategic Advisory Group on the Environment, consisting of representatives of twenty countries, eleven international organizations, and over a hundred environmental experts. The driving concern was the potential impact of incompatible national environmental standards on trade, and the potential for standard-based environmental protectionism. The advisory group recommended that the ISO create a new technical committee to develop voluntary standards. The ISO complied and created Technical Committee 207 in 1993 (see Drobny 1997). By way of background, the ISO does not directly develop standards. Rather it creates a structure in which national representatives work cooperatively to develop standards through a series of committees and subcommittees. Each nation, in turn, creates technical advisory groups and subgroups to represent its interests in the ISO committees and subcommittees. The technical advisory groups and subgroups combine a diverse set of experts from standard-setting bodies, industry, government agencies, and advocacy groups (Tibor and Feldman 1997). The EMS standards were assigned to the ISO's largest technical committee, the newly created Technical Committee 207, which comprised sixty-seven participating members, eighteen observing members, and representatives of forty-two liaison organizations.

The US technical advisory group is accredited by the American National Standards Institute to represent the United States in the development of standards. It included 510 individuals representing 405 companies, organizations, associations, and government agencies. Thus, Fortune 500 companies work with trade associations, environmental groups (including the Environmental Defense Fund, the National Wildlife Federation, the Global Forest Policy Project, and the Environmental Law Institute) and government agencies (including the Environmental Protection Agency, the Department of Energy, and the National Institute of Standards and Technology) in the development of standards.

Because participation is self-funded, the technical advisory groups (and the ISO more broadly) are not as diverse as they would appear to be based on their formal rosters. There is, quite predictably, a strong corporate bias. As Konrad von Moltke and Onno Kuik note: "while environmental management systems have been designed to reflect objective criteria of good practice they will almost inevitably also reflect the resources and the attitudes of those involved in their elaboration. . . . The practical work of ISO is undertaken in an elaborate committee structure that is dominated by representatives of larger corporations. Government agencies play a limited role" (1997: 5). The same may be said of labor, consumer, and environmental advocacy groups, and less developed countries. The barriers to participation by less developed countries are many, including costs of participation, reliance on the English language, and perceived dominance of OECD nations. This is a serious problem, given past resistance to "ecoimperialism" and the impact that development in less developed countries may have on the larger dynamic of global environmental degradation. As Naomi Roht-Arriaza observes, "while participants in the ISO process seem aware of the dangers posed by a lack of developing country participation, concern has not translated into action by the ISO Secretariat" (1995: 5).

The financial wherewithal of the largest corporate participants is combined with powerful commercial incentives for participation. As noted earlier, many corporations have emphasized environmental performance as part of a larger business strategy, and the realization of differentiation-based advantages is contingent on their capacity to exhibit their commitment to market actors. Moreover, many firms have made heavy investments in advanced manufacturing systems and ISO 9000 quality control systems. They have a powerful stake in securing environmental standards that are compatible with these earlier investments. Indeed, one should not be surprised that the ISO 14000 standards were explicitly designed to "piggyback" on earlier ISO 9000 systems. Many of the key features of the two series, the basic steps in the process, and the required control systems are comparable. As a result, firms that are ISO 9000–compliant are at a substantial advantage in pursuing 14000 certification (see Hersey 1998).

The ISO Environmental Management System Standards

ISO 14001 and 14004, both published in 1996, provide the standards for the design and implementation of an environmental management system (Ritchie and Hayes 1998; Schiffman, Delaney, and Fleming 1997). ISO 14001 defines an EMS as "that part of the overall management system that includes organizational structure, planning activities, responsibilities, practices, procedures, processes, and resources for developing, implementing, achieving, reviewing and maintaining the environmental policy." An organization's environmental policy, in turn, is defined as a "statement by the organization of its intentions and principles in relation to its overall environmental performance which provides a framework for action and for the setting of its environmental objectives and targets." Because the ISO 14000 series is designed to meet the needs of organizations regardless of size or industrial focus, it does not dictate the content of the environmental policy. Rather it requires that the policy be "appropriate to the nature, scale, and environmental impact of its activities, products, or services." The policy must articulate "a commitment to comply with relevant environmental legislation and regulations, and with other requirements to which the organization subscribes." This must be combined with a commitment to continuous improvement and pollution prevention. In addition, the policy must provide "the framework for setting and reviewing environmental objectives and targets." It must be "documented, implemented, maintained, and communicated to all employees" and made "available to the public."

The emphasis placed on continuous improvement might be of some concern when viewed in isolation. After all, improvements could occur at a glacial pace. However, these concerns are mitigated, in part, by the fact that the goal of continuous improvement is placed upon the foundations of an additional requirement that firms be in compliance with all relevant laws and regulations. As John Braithwaite and Peter Drahos explain: "What is distinctive about using the principle of continuous improvement to guide international standard-setting is that once that principle is enshrined as a standard, it structurally induces upward rather than downward movement in the global norm." ISO 14001 "create[s] a platform below which standards cannot fall, by mandating compliance with local law and on top of that requiring continuous improvement in environmental management" (2000: 282). Rather than serving as a ceiling, then, domestic regulations become a floor, and standards compel ongoing gains in environmental performance that might not exist when regulations are taken by themselves.

Under the ISO standards, an organization must comprehensively identify the environmental aspects of its activities. It then must generate objectives and targets that reflect the environmental impacts (their scale, severity, likelihood, and duration), regulatory or legal exposure, the relative costs and benefits associated with the corrective actions, and the demands of key stakeholders (Ritchie and Hayes 1998: 46). These objectives and targets must be quantified where practicable, and placed on a timetable. Responsibility for realizing the goals must be assigned throughout the organization and matched with necessary human, technological, and financial resources. ISO 14001 requires that organizations adopt "documented procedures to monitor and measure on a regular basis the key characteristics of its operations and activities" (§ 4.5). This requires, at minimum, that targets be represented by valid indicators, monitoring equipment be installed, calibrated, and maintained, and data on performance be collected on a periodic basis. Where performance data reveal that the organization is failing to achieve sufficient progress toward its targets or is not complying with environmental regulations, ISO 14001 requires the organization to investigate the causes, adopt corrective actions, and document, communicate, and evaluate the changes (§ 4.5.2). While ongoing monitoring is vital, ISO 14001 requires that comprehensive audits be conducted on a periodic basis (§ 4.5.4) (the key features of EMS audits are presented in ISO 14010).

The ISO 14000 series establishes a set of standards for guiding environmental management within the confines of an organization. It is critical that these activities be communicated to external audiences. In this context, third-party verification and registration are correctly viewed as vital components of a credible EMS (ISO 1998; Guerra 1997). Compliance must be certified by third-party auditors who have met the accreditation standards imposed by their national accreditation bodies. Accredited audit teams must provide a comprehensive analysis of EMS design, implementation, performance, and documentation. As a result of the evaluation, the audit team may determine that the organization has met all the requirements of ISO 14001. If there are deficiencies, an organization may be required to conduct corrective actions, which are to be verified by the audit team. Alternatively, an organization may fail to meet the specifications of ISO 14001 or the audit team may discover serious regulatory violations, either of which will result in disapproval. Following certification, firms must submit to periodic surveillance audits to verify compliance. As Kevin Hersey notes: "since this is a process of establishing goals, it has no true end. Maintaining ISO certification requires both internal and external audits on an ongoing basis" (1998: 29).

In sum, ISO 14001 certification conveys, at minimum, that an organization is in compliance with all relevant laws and regulations, that it has a well-designed environmental management system oriented toward continuous improvement and pollution prevention, that key personnel have been trained to execute their duties, that each aspect of the EMS has been exhaustively documented, and that the performance of the system has been inspected by accredited auditors. Given that ISO 14001 is an international standard, certification should convey the same information regardless of the national origin of the organization in question. It thus carries obvious advantages over trade association codes, which may vary widely with respect to their rigor and enforcement.

The Global Dissemination of ISO 14001

The International Organization for Standardization published its most recent survey of ISO 14001 certification in 2004, including information through the end of calendar year 2003 (ISO 2004). An analysis of these data reveals several things of interest. First, growth in certification has been rapid (see Figure 9.1). By the end of 1996—the year that ISO 14001 was released—1,491 organizations in 45 countries were certified as compliant. By the end of 1998, there were 7,887 certified organizations in 72 countries. By the end of 2004, there were 90,569 certified organizations in 127 countries. Second, and equally striking, the figures provide resounding evidence that firms in the United States have been far less likely to receive certification than their counterparts in Europe or Asia. The United States had 34 certified organization in 1996, 1,052 by the end of 2000, and 4,759 by the end of 2004. While this growth rate appears striking at first glance, the number of certifications is far less impressive when seen in perspective. At the end of 2004, US firms held 5.3 percent of the world's ISO 14001 certificates, a surprisingly low figure given that the United States is responsible for about one-quarter of world gross national product (GNP). European nations, in contrast, held 44.0 percent of the certificates, followed by East Asian countries, which held some 39.7 percent. When seen in comparative perspective, the United States had

Figure 9.1 World and US ISO 14001 Certificates, 1995–2004

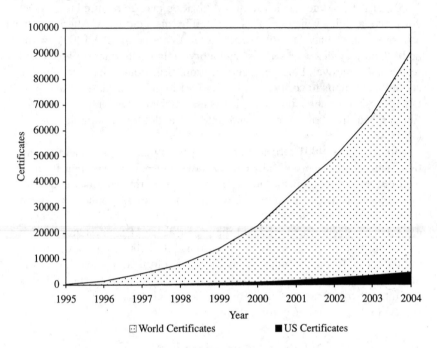

Data source: International Organization for Standardization 2004.

fewer certified organizations than Japan (19,584), China (8,862), Spain (6,473), and the United Kingdom (6,253), and a number comparable to Italy (4,785) and Germany (4,320). Indeed, when adjusted for GDP, the differences are even more striking, as illustrated in Figure 9.2, which reports levels of certification among OECD countries when adjusted for GDP.

Although the United States is responsible for generating one-quarter of the world's GNP, it can claim 5.3 percent of ISO certificates. When adjusted for GDP, the United States has a lower level of certification than any other OECD country (3.2 firms per $10 billion), including Mexico (4.3 firms per $10 billion). Its performance simply pales in comparison with Sweden (142.8 firms per $10 billion) and Finland (79.3 per $10 billion). Yet for a host of reasons, one would expect US firms to be at the forefront of participation in ISO 14000. As noted earlier, there were high levels of corporate representation in the framing of the standards themselves. The US technical advisory group represented literally hundreds of US firms (including DuPont, Merck, IBM, Unisys, Arco Chemical, Exxon, Mobil Oil, Allied-Signal, AMP, 3M, Texas Instruments, Motorola, Georgia-Pacific, International Paper, Caterpillar, AT&T, DEC, Kodak, Proctor & Gamble, B.

Figure 9.2 ISO 14001 Certificates Adjusted for GDP, 2004

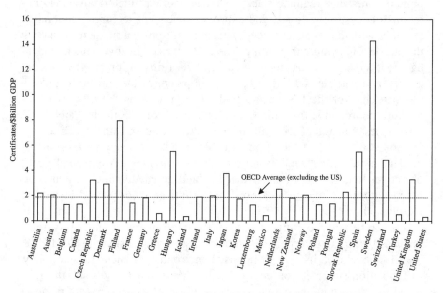

Data source: Organization for Economic Cooperation and Development (GDP) and International Organization for Standardization 2004 (certificates).

F. Goodrich, James River Corp., Weyerhauser, Raytheon, and ALCOA). Moreover, several trade associations participated in the deliberations (including the American Petroleum Institute, the American Forest and Paper Association, the American Society for Quality Control, the American Society of Mechanical Engineers, NSF International, the Chemical Manufacturers Association, the American Industrial Hygiene Association, the American Textile Manufacturers Institute, and Underwriters Laboratories).

As well, there appeared to be a supportive regulatory environment. As shown in Chapters 5 and 6, the regulatory debates have been replete with claims regarding the excessive costs and rigidities associated with command-and-control regulation. Critics of regulation have commonly argued that regulations should leverage private sector innovations. These critiques have not been reserved for conservative think tanks and the business press. As Clinton EPA head Carol M. Browner noted: "regulations often do not reach the more complicated corporate decisions needed to evaluate design, manufacturing, packaging, distribution and marketing practices to reduce pollution and energy consumption. We must encourage these efforts by entering into partnerships with public and private organizations where such cooperation can produce tangible environmental results" (1993).

As the above quote suggests, the ISO 14000 series was developed at a point in time when regulators acknowledged (perhaps rhetorically) the limitations of existing policies, and expressed an intent to forge cooperative relations with the regulated under the banner of reinvention, thereby making the puzzle all the more interesting. The EPA invested in environmental management system development as part of its reinvention of government efforts, and participated fully in the development of the standards. Indeed, the vice chair of the US technical advisory group was the EPA standards network coordinator from the Office of Prevention, Pesticides, and Toxic Substances. Outside of the walls of the EPA, President Clinton's Executive Order 13148 (April 21, 2000) required each federal agency to develop and implement an EMS "which shall include measurable environmental goals, objectives, and targets that are reviewed and updated annually" and combined with performance measures that "shall be incorporated in agency facility audit protocols" (§ 401b).

If anything, the support for environmental management systems increased with the George W. Bush administration. Pursuant to EO 13148, the EPA developed its own EMS-based environmental management policy. In a position statement on environmental management systems, the EPA noted that it would "encourage widespread use of EMSs across a range of organizations and settings" and would "encourage the use of recognized environmental management frameworks, such as the ISO 14001 standards, as a basis for designing and implementing EMSs that aim to achieve outcomes aligned with the Nation's environmental policy goals" (EPA 2002d: 2). Moreover, President Bush appointed Jim Connaughton to lead the Council on Environmental Quality. Connaughton, who served on the US technical advisory group to Technical Committee 207, kept the ISO apprised of the administration's efforts to implement ISO 14001 in various government agencies (Husseini 2003).

Regulatory Reluctance Breeds Self-Regulatory Reluctance

The EPA was involved in the drafting of ISO 14001 and has been quite supportive of the use of environmental management systems. It has invested in a series of EMS pilot programs over the course of the past two presidential administrations and, in 2000, it created a new regulatory green track, the National Environmental Performance Track, which provides a number of benefits to firms with a record of superior performance and a quality EMS (see Chapter 10). Yet the *general* support for environmental management systems remains ambiguous on two points, and oddly rigid on a third. The resulting climate of uncertainty may discourage firms from making investments in ISO 14001 systems with third-party certification.

First, there is great ambivalence over the relationship between an EMS and regulation. As the EPA noted in a report suggestively titled *EPA's Strategy for Determining the Role of Environmental Management Systems in Regulatory Programs:*

> EPA will continue to promote the widespread adoption of EMS, while exploring the potential value of linking EMSs to regulatory structures— either in terms of improving the regulatory structure, encouraging EMSs, or both. EPA is interested in exploring the use of EMSs as an alternative within the regulatory structure through careful experimentation. The experimentation will be grounded in a defined set of policy ideas and questions to test, and will assure a high standard of health and environmental protection. Previous experiences and current understanding of EMSs reveal certain fundamental tensions that suggest the need for such experimentation before EPA can consider program changes. Participation in informed experimentation will provide EPA and its regulatory partners with greater understanding and more complete information on the potential benefits and drawbacks of incorporating EMSs into the regulatory structure. (EPA 2004c: 3)

As this suggests, the EPA remains uncertain as to how best to integrate environmental management systems and regulations after more than a decade of experimentation and debate.

A second source of uncertainty is evident when one seeks to discern whether the EPA regards an ISO 14001–compliant EMS as being preferable to its alternatives. An EMS based on the "plan, do, check, act" cycle can be developed in accordance with a global standard (like ISO 14001) requiring third-party certification, or in accordance with a trade association code requiring *or* recommending second-party certification. It can be customized to meet the needs of a firm without regard to any specific code or standard wherein the public must simply rely on a company's assurances that its system is providing the promised results (see Gereffi, Garcia-Johnson, and Sasser 2001). The EPA's support for environmental management systems does not constitute a commitment to ISO 14001 as *the* EMS standard of choice. Indeed, the EPA notes that, "for the past several years, pursuant to the EMS Position Statement, EPA has been involved in a wide range of activities designed to facilitate EMS adoption, including those based on ISO 14001 and other models" (EPA 2004c: 1). At first glance, this may appear to be a trivial issue. Yet an ISO 14001 EMS requires third-party certification, which depends, in turn, on the EMS meeting the standard's rigorous requirements and on evidence that the organization is in compliance with all relevant laws and regulations. As a result, certification conveys information important to market actors and, potentially, regulators. The recognition of multiple competing standards may lead firms to question whether the additional costs of certification and ongoing surveillance audits will be greater than any additional regulatory benefits.

There are useful distinctions that one can make between the events in the United States and the European Union. In the EU, a decision was made in 1993 on a standard for environmental management systems; its relationship to ISO 14001 was clearly defined, thereby reducing uncertainty and regulatory transaction costs. The European Union's ecomanagement and audit scheme (see Gouldson and Murphy 1998: chap. 4; Starkey 1996) is, by design, comparable to ISO 14001, insofar as it focuses on the design of a comparable EMS. However, it is more rigorous than ISO 14001 in that it requires that firms make publicly available an environmental statement including a profile of environmental impacts and audited information on performance on a site-specific basis. The European Commission explicitly presents ISO 14001 as a steppingstone to the ecomanagement and audit scheme, and it has designed processes to allow firms to avoid duplication in making the transition and maintaining dual certification. As a result, co-certification is quite common. There are questions as to the future status of the scheme relative to EU environmental policies (see van Gestel 2005). However, an early decision regarding a single EMS standard avoided much of the uncertainty that prevailed in the United States (Delmas 2002: 7–11).

Returning to the US case, the third failure of the EPA has been its remarkable rigidity on the status of information gained via environmental audits. Under ISO 14001, firms must audit their performance to evaluate their environmental management systems, measure progress, and revise goals. Moreover, before a company can be certified, it must submit to third-party audits and subsequent compliance audits thereafter. One would assume that the EPA would be highly supportive of environmental audits, given the positive role they can play in providing important information for managers seeking to track corporate environmental performance. However, as shown in Chapter 6, the EPA's policy on audit immunity has created potential disincentives to employ an EMS requiring third-party audits.

A survey of over 30 percent of ISO 14001–certified US firms as of November 1998 revealed that the very factors noted above have been constraints to the adoption of ISO 14001 (Delmas 2002). Some 69 percent cited lack of regulatory flexibility, 62 percent cited uncertainty with regulatory agencies' utilization of EMS audit information, and 60 percent cited potential legal penalties from voluntary disclosure as important constraints. Given that the survey excluded firms that did not implement ISO 14001, the results understate the magnitude of the problem. As Magali Delmas notes, "in a competitive market in which a contract loss due to non-compliance could irreparably damage the prestige and finances of a company, ISO 14001 offers [an] organized approach to managing environmental issues. . . . However, the process of acquiring ISO 14001 certification might be costly if there is uncertainty about regulatory agency commitment to the standard" (2002: 14). The conclusion could not be clearer:

self-regulatory reluctance has regulatory origins (see also Khanna and Anton 2002).

Self-regulatory reluctance may carry consequences beyond US borders. There is much to suggest that firms in developing countries seek ISO 14001 certification when they hope to contract with ISO 14001–compliant firms in wealthy nations (see, e.g., Christmann and Taylor 2001). The failure of US firms to embrace ISO 14001 may limit the incentives for the dissemination of standards in nations lacking credible regulatory structures. Moreover, the failure to embrace ISO 14001 may increase the costs of participating in future ISO standards. In 2002 the ISO began work on a new set of standards (ISO 14064) for greenhouse gas accounting and verification that could be implemented with ISO 14001 environmental management systems (see Boehmer and Chert 2003). These standards, yet to be completed, could harness market and supply chain forces to reinforce climate change policies whether or not the firms are headquartered in nations participating in the Kyoto Protocol. The US withdrawal form Kyoto has created a gap that cannot be filled with voluntary programs, like Climate Leaders, that rest on self-reporting. It is questionable whether credible alternatives can be introduced without more fundamental shifts in the prevailing culture of regulation in the United States.

■ Conclusion

The number of firms certified under the global EMS standard has grown rapidly since 1996. Trade association codes and ISO 14001 are beginning to merge in some interesting ways (e.g., in 2002 the American Chemistry Council introduced a new Responsible Care ISO 14001 certification option whereby members could simultaneously meet the requirements of Responsible Care and the ISO standard). Pressures for certification are spreading through supply chain pressures, and there is no evidence that the growth in certification is abating. Yet one should not view the ISO 14000 series as a panacea. Critics argue that the importance of ISO 14001 can be easily overstated. The standards are far more concerned with the integrity of the process than with the magnitude of the results (Fiorino 2004: 415). Yet certification requires compliance with laws and regulations and, on that platform, a commitment to continuous improvement. Given that certification depends on periodic surveillance audits to verify compliance, one can assume that certification conveys important information regarding environmental performance and corporate capacities. Nonetheless, one may not be satisfied with the mere existence of a certificate relative to the more exhaustive disclosure of information required under the European Union's ecomanagement and audit scheme.

Moreover, as with any voluntary system of corporate self-regulation, profitability may place hard limits on what will be accomplished. ISO 14000 demands creation of the organizational capacity for more ambitious environmental management goals. The key uncertainty is how management will use these capabilities. One can have a quality EMS in place and set relatively modest goals. A firm may have met all of the requirements for certification and remain committed to producing goods that have deleterious ramifications for the environment. The auto industry has embraced ISO 14001, but continues to produce sport utility vehicles. In the end, *what* is being produced may be as critical as *how* it is being produced, and standards are concerned with the latter issue. Nonetheless, one should not make the perfect the enemy of the good. Standard-based self-regulation forces changes that could not be dictated by regulation, while providing an economical source of information to reinforce green market pressures.

There is little question that ISO 14001 certification can meet some, but not all, of the difficulties discussed earlier in the chapter. Although a full discussion of the potential role of standards in regulatory reform will be reserved for later chapters, one can briefly note some of the positive roles that ISO 14001 could play if the EPA were to come to closure on the role of the standard. As exhibited in Chapter 5, the EPA was hesitant to provide firms with greater flexibility without guarantees of superior environmental performance and costly flows of information. These demands severely compromised the performance of Project XL. It might prove far more effective to formally recognize ISO 14001 certification as evidence that firms are meeting their obligations and have developed the capacity for greater self-regulation. Future experiments might be extended to a larger universe of actors if regulators were to recognize certification.

To use the language adopted earlier, standards with external auditing and certification could be adopted as a core component of a broader system of environmental governance. Governance regimes will evolve with or without the active direction of regulators. Historically, the state has shaped governance through policies affecting property rights, corporate organization, and permissible forms of intercorporate relations, although the results have usually been a byproduct of policy decisions made for other reasons (Lindberg and Campbell 1991). Critics correctly note that ISO 14001 would be more effective if it focused on the environmental impact of products rather than simply defining the key feature of environmental management systems. They are also correct in arguing that standard-based self-regulation would achieve a higher level of legitimacy if standards were to mandate the release of more voluminous performance data (e.g., audit reports). A regulatory commitment to integrating standards into a regulatory system can facilitate efforts to strengthen standard-based self-regulation and address concerns of critics. It can also leverage private sector accomplishments as a means of furthering regulatory change while strengthening green market forces. Before this can occur, regulators and policy analysts must have a greater appreciation for the initial observation of this chapter: environmental quality is driven by a host of factors beyond regulation, including the self-regulatory activities of trade associations, market and supply chain pressures, and changes in the design of processes and products at the level of the firm. Ideally, regulations would be part of a larger integrated system of environmental governance.

10

Public-Private Hybrids and Environmental Governance

Environmental quality is the outcome of the behavior of a host of public and private actors embedded in a dense network of relationships. As the previous several chapters suggest, changes in industrial practices are the result of many factors, including public regulation, the self-regulatory activities of trade associations, market and supply chain pressures, and the introduction of new process and product designs at the level of the firm. It would be difficult to attribute the reduction in pollution since 1970 solely to the enforcement efforts of the Environmental Protection Agency. At the same time, it would be implausible to argue that corporations would have pursued the same innovations in environmental management without ongoing regulatory pressures. Unfortunately, the relationships between the regulated and the regulators are permeated by distrust. Regulators often impose constraints and transaction costs that undermine the incentives for corporate self-regulation and innovation and thus have a negative impact on the evolution of environmental governance regimes.

Some examples drawn from previous chapters provide useful illustrations of how these tensions are exhibited. As noted in Chapter 6, even when the EPA has charted a course of reinvention, success has been hampered by excessive regulatory transaction costs. In the case of Project XL, for example, participants cited interaction with regulators as being the greatest source of costs. Ongoing demands for information and guarantees of superior environmental results were often sufficient to undermine the incentives for participation. In Chapter 9, we explored the ISO 14000 series of standards. Certification under ISO 14001 requires periodic compliance audits. If a firm engages in self-auditing and discovers regulatory violations, it is required by law to report that fact to the EPA. The EPA has rejected pleas for audit immunity and routinely imposes fines on firms that have self-reported violations. At first glance, one might ask: Why should violations of environmental regulations go unpunished? Yet the lack of audit immunity means that firms that are making voluntary investments in environmental management systems in hope of creating the capacity to achieve levels of environmental performance superior to what might be demanded by policy, do so at the risk of increasing their exposure to penalties and civil suits. Under these circumstances, they may simply decide that the potential costs of exposure are simply too great. Regulatory adversarialism may undermine precisely the patterns of behavior that regulators should hope to promote.

Regulatory adversarialism and the resulting failure to coordinate regulatory and corporate activities can impose large opportunity costs. When the EPA oversees the behavior of firms that have verified records of environmental performance, it squanders scarce resources that might be better deployed for alternative purposes. As noted in Chapter 8, the firms that have been most likely to implement successful corporate environmental policies have developed an impressive set of organizational capabilities, often through the adoption of advanced manufacturing techniques and the creation of management information systems. There is an entire universe of firms that have not made comparable investments, because of their small size or because they operate in price-sensitive commodity markets with narrow profit margins. As a generalization, these firms may have checkered compliance histories and lack the expertise to redesign products and processes to achieve genuine gains in performance. Such firms demand closer regulatory oversight; they could benefit from ongoing consultation with regulators and compliance assistance. One might argue that any resources devoted to regulating companies with excellent performance records would be better redeployed to focus on the firms that demand closer regulatory oversight.

This chapter explores public-private hybrids designed to effectively integrate public regulation and corporate or associational self-regulation. The chapter begins with an examination of the Dutch covenants, an innovative instrument adopted in the Netherlands to employ associations as implementation agents. Next the chapter examines two recent regulatory experiments in the United States: the HPV Challenge Program and the National Environmental Performance Track. Although both programs hold great promise, they have been hampered by basic problems of regulatory design. The chapter concludes with some reflections on how these programs might be changed to increase their effectiveness. The changes presented here will be developed in greater detail in Chapter 14, which explores the larger issue of making the transition from traditional environmental protection regulation to a broader system of green governance.

■ Public-Private Hybrids

Environmental policymaking is fraught with an uncertainty that stems from several sources. First, environmental policy is characterized by extreme complexity. Policymakers are forced to work at the intersection of multiple scientific and social scientific disciplines. They must make decisions in a dynamic environment characterized by changing technologies, new pollutants, and evolving scientific knowledge. Second, the uncertainty stems from severe problems of information asymmetry. Regulators do not have access to detailed information on specific product designs, production processes, technologies, and environmental performance. This knowledge exists at the level of the firm (and is often decentralized within corporate organizations). Third, uncertainty is a product of politics. As noted in Chapter 3, the EPA is enmeshed in a complex institutional network in which policymaking and policy implementation are highly decentralized and subject to pressures of partisanship and interest group politics.

How can one manage high levels of uncertainty? The most common approach has been the adoption of command-and-control regulatory instruments. They provide a greater certainty of results. One can more or less guarantee, for example, that the universal application of a particular pollution control technology will have specific results on emissions levels. These results may come at a high cost, insofar as many firms may be overregulated in a regulatory regime based on command-and-control instruments, whereas others could achieve far greater results at a lower marginal cost. A second approach to managing uncertainty could be to delegate authority to the corporations that possess the greatest information. The underlying presumption is that market incentives will be sufficient to promote higher levels of environmental performance. As detailed in Chapter 8, however, one can question whether these incentives will create sufficient pressure for environmental innovation, particularly in the absence of supportive policies. Moreover, the sacrifices in public accountability are particularly great. Delegation increases uncertainty regarding performance, thereby creating the kinds of agency problems explored in Chapter 9. In a regulatory system that prioritizes certainty of results, the uncertainty inherent in regulatory delegation may prove unacceptable.

While both of these strategies might be adopted for managing uncertainty, there is a third option that has gained far greater support in recent years: the creation of public-private hybrids. Uncertainty is managed through ongoing negotiation and collaboration. Regulated parties are given greater latitude in developing pollution control strategies, thereby harnessing their detailed knowledge and using it to promote innovative solutions to pollution. At the same time, corporate innovations are placed within a broader regulatory framework, thereby creating greater accountability than might exist in a purely market-based approach. The single best example of public-private hybrids can be found in the Dutch covenant system.

Dutch Covenants

> When it comes to addressing the major environmental problems, the government is the obvious institution to oversee all parties, activities and processes having an impact. . . . It is the job of governments to bring parties together and to stimulate the necessary private sector initiatives. Governments must promote the development of knowledge and help in the implementation of new technology. They create the circumstances for businesses, citizens, and lower administrative levels to do their own jobs. In addition, governments will also have to play a steering role. It is the government that creates the frameworks and preconditions and modifies them where necessary. (Netherlands Ministry of Housing, Spatial Planning, and the Environment 2003: 28)

This quote, drawn from a summary of the Netherlands' fourth national environmental policy plan, is indicative of the way Dutch regulators envision their role in environmental protection. The strict, hierarchical relationships inherent in US-style regulation are rare in the Netherlands. Rather than viewing environmental quality as being primarily the product of government action, Dutch regulators understand that it is the result of successful governance wherein the state coordinates or steers the activities of a multitude of actors in a cooperative setting. Before examining Dutch environmental regulation in more detail, it is necessary to explore some of the contextual factors that facilitate this approach to environmental protection.

The Netherlands is a small country of some 41,526 square kilometers, less than twice the size of New Jersey. With more than 16 million people, it is also characterized by a high population density. Population pressures, combined with heavy exploitation of agriculture resources and heavy industry, have reinforced the salience of environmental protection. Although environmental regulation in the Netherlands dates back to the water boards of the Middle Ages, its modern environmental era began in the early 1970s, almost precisely when comparable changes were occurring in the United States. In 1971 the nation created its Directorate-General for Environmental Protection. Drawing on an earlier body of environmental law, the directorate began to regulate business on a media-specific basis, setting ambitious environmental goals and adopting command-and-control instruments (in particular, permits). Regulatory performance consistently fell below expectations. Although many of the critiques of command-and-control regulation that were common in the United States were equally applicable to the Dutch case, the response to poor regulatory performance could not have been more dissimilar (Hofman 1998).

The Netherlands has long been characterized by its corporatist structures and its "consensus democracy." To understand the context of the response, it is necessary to explore three features of Dutch society: ideological "pillarization" and its implications for the private sector, corporatist systems of interest intermediation, and the importance of consensus democracy (Kickert 1996). The term *pillarization* refers to the fact that Dutch society has been divided vertically by ideology and religion, rather than horizontally by social classes as a response to sixteenth-century Protestant-Catholic divisions. By the twentieth century, there were clear divisions between Protestants, Catholics, Socialists, and Liberals. Moreover, each of the pillars had developed its own set of social and economic institutions (e.g., labor associations, trade associations, political parties, schools). The state often worked through these associations, thereby leading to a merging of the public and private.

As a means of managing the struggles between labor and capital, the Netherlands developed a number of corporatist institutions in the late nineteenth and twentieth centuries. Corporatism describes "a coordination of national negotiations in which state agencies endow major private economic associations with quasi-public authority. This can be used to arrive at binding commitments with the force of legislation and to discipline members" (Maier 1984: 40). For example, as a means of preventing inflation, a government agency could vest authority in business and labor peak associations and engage in tripartite negotiations covering wages and prices. In addition, the Netherlands was characterized by consensus democracy. A strong cultural orientation toward compromise and consensus rather than adversarial conflict has led to stable coalition governments and a political culture that places a premium on democratic deliberation (Kickert 1996). Corporatism and the emphasis placed on consensus have been particularly important in shaping the regulatory process. Combined, they provide a system "adopted to handle societal conflict" and "cope with policy uncertainties. The consensual setting allows for open, decentralized, and flexible policy processes that may facilitate learning-oriented policymaking" (Arentsen, Bressers, and O'Toole 2000: 602).

The Dutch system of environmental protection is widely recognized for its innovative nature (Lotspeich 1998). The system has two key components: national environmental policy plans and covenants. Although the Dutch system evolved along more-or-less traditional lines during the 1970s and 1980s, things began to change rapidly in 1989, following the publication of the National Institute for Public Health and the Environment report *Concern for Tomorrow*. The report provided a broad overview of environmental conditions and concluded that the current end-of-the-pipe technologies were insufficient to prevent environmental degradation and create a foundation for sustainable development. Indeed, it found that integrated regulation combined with pollution reductions of 70–90 percent would be necessary for the nation to achieve a position of sustainability. That same year, the government released its first environmental policy plan, titled "To Choose or to Lose." The plan set the goal of achieving significant reductions in several pollutants. For example, it set binding goals of 70–90 percent reductions in sulfur dioxide, ammonia, volatile organic chemicals, and nitrogen oxide emissions by 2010, using 1985 as a baseline. Since 1989, three additional national environmental policy plans have been issued, evaluating performance and establishing new and often more ambitious goals. To achieve these goals, the housing and environment ministry called for new approaches to managing environmental protection (Beardsley, Davies, and Hersh 1997).

This new approach involved the government entering into a consultative and cooperative relationship with industry through the negotiation of covenants. Covenants are best defined as "legally non-binding agreements between organisations and their stakeholders, often trade organisations and the government, in which goals for environmental performance are collectively agreed and monitored" (Spence, Jeurissen, and Rutherfoord 2000: 961). The process of negotiating and implementing covenants has been widely recognized as a highly innovative way of making policy under conditions of uncertainty and complexity (Janicke and Jargens 2000). Economic sectors are represented by "target groups." At present, there are target groups for agriculture, industry, refineries, energy companies, retailers, transportation, the building industry, waste disposal companies, and the water sector. Participants arrive at agreements over what constitutes best practice for a given industry, and identify valid and realistic performance measures (Spence, Jeurissen, and Rutherfoord 2000: 951). They then negotiate the terms of covenants that translate the goals of national environmental policy into specific objectives, identifying the necessary pollution control activities, pollution targets, and timetables. Rather than focusing exclusively on pollution by medium, moreover, the covenants engage nine broad crosscutting themes: climate change, acidification, eutrophication, toxic and hazardous pollutants, soil contamination, waste disposal, nuisance, groundwater depletion, and resource dissipation. Ultimately, the covenants are signed by the government and the trade associations. Within the terms of the covenants, firms in the relevant industry develop detailed four-year plans, which are subsequently reviewed by permitting authorities at the local levels. Since provinces and municipalities create their own environmental policy plans to reflect the goals established in the national policy plans, this provides a means of integrating regulation along multiple geographical levels. Companies are required to publicize their plans and publish annual progress reports on meeting the goals of the covenants. Thus, cooperative negotiations at the national level are translated into firm-level plans approved by local officials and involving voluminous self-reporting of environmental performance.

The benefits of the covenants are obvious. Participating firms are given the flexibility to innovate within a relatively stable context, while avoiding the costs and rigidities associated with command-and-control regulation. Because most covenants have "escape clauses" allowing firms to defect from agreements if costs become too great, the risks of participation are manageable. Regulators realize benefits as well. Corporations and trade associations have far greater information on productive technologies, processes, and performance, creating ongoing problems of information asymmetry. Regulators can gain access to this information via the self-reporting requirements and thereby promote innovations that may allow for greater gains in environmental protection. Moreover, they can better target scarce enforcement resources on firms that have chosen not to participate in the covenant system. As one might expect, there have been concerns on the part of environmental groups that the covenants do not provide sufficient accountability. The government and trade associations are the sole participants; environmental groups do not have an established role in the process and there are no formal channels for challenging the agreements (Beardsley, Davies, and Hersh 1997).

How has Dutch environmental policy performed? The record is positive but mixed based on the figures released in the 2000 *Environmental Data Compendium*. On the positive side, the Dutch have realized success in reducing air pollution. The average annual concentration of particulate matter fell from an average of forty micrograms per cubic meter in early 1992 to less than thirty-five in 2000. The concentration of nitrogen dioxide was twenty-one micrograms per cubic meter in 2000, compared with the European air quality standard of forty, although this standard was exceeded in the largest Dutch cities. Chronic levels of benzene, sulfur dioxide, and ozone have also significantly declined, to levels below the European air quality standards (Netherlands National Institute for Public Health and the Environment 2002: E1.5, E1.7, E1.10).

The Dutch have also realized gains in water pollution, although they have been mixed given the difficulties inherent in heavy reliance on commercial agriculture. Dutch regulators set two threshold levels for water pollution: the maximum allowable concentration (MAC) and the desired quality standard (DQS). The MAC is the concentration at which no negative health consequences can be expected (or, in the case of carcinogens, the mortality risk can be brought to a level of 10^{-6}). The DQS is a more stringent standard at which concentrations would have a negligible impact on the environment. The goal is to achieve this level of water quality by 2010. The country's *Environmental Data Compendium* reports data for various bodies of water and nationally and regionally managed water more generally. Let us restrict our focus to nationally managed waters. In the area of heavy metals in fresh surface water, the progress between 1985 and 2000 was substantial, in many cases exceeding the DQS. Cadmium concentrations fell from 0.47 micrograms per liter to 0.17 (MAC: 2.0, DQS: 0.4). Chromium concentrations fell from 9.6 to 2.2 micrograms per liter (MAC: 84.0, DQS: 2.4). Copper concentrations fell from 9.1 to 5.4 micrograms per liter (MAC: 3.8, DQS: 1.1), a great reduction but not sufficient to meet either standard. Mercury concentrations fell from 0.09 to 0.04 micrograms per liter (MAC: 1.20, DQS: 0.07). Nickel concentrations fell from 8.7 to 6.7 micrograms per liter (MAC: 6.3, DQS: 4.1). Lead concentrations fell from 7.3 to 5.1 micrograms per liter (MAC: 220.0, DQS: 5.3). Zinc concentrations fell from 70 to 25 micrograms per liter (MAC: 40, DQS: 12). The Dutch have had less success in controlling nitrogen and phosphorous concentrations in fresh surface waters and nitrates in groundwater, failing to meet the guideline values for MAC and European Union standards. Similarly, the record has been mixed for groundwater quality, depending on substance and soil type. With respect to pesticides in soil, the record is mixed as well, with a number of prohibited pesticides above the DQS (Netherlands National Institute for Public Health and the Environment 2002: E2.2, E2.4, E4.3, E3.3).

Can the Dutch covenant serve as a model? One cannot simply transplant covenants without the larger corporatist framework within which they are embedded. Corporatist systems provide a high level of stability and a long-term orientation that is "more prone to producing cooperative results." In contrast, a pluralist system seems heavily prone to "self-maximization and atomistic behavior." Where there are agreements, participants have incentives to defect and free-ride on the behavior of those who do not (Matthews 2001: 496). As a generalization, the preconditions for a corporatist system of interest intermediation do not exist in the United States (see Wilson 1982). The most important limitations come in the area of association membership. Trade associations play an important role in facilitating dialogue and negotiation in the Dutch system; they can provide member firms with the technical resources necessary to meet larger regulatory goals. While membership levels are low in many nations, including the United States, peak association membership is compulsory in the Netherlands, and trade association membership is almost universal (Spence, Jeurissen, and Rutherfoord 2000: 950–951).

■ The United States: Toward Regulatory Hybrids?

Although the United States does not have anything remotely comparable to the Dutch covenants, a number of regulatory experiments hold the potential for evolving into public-private hybrids. Some of these experiments have been discussed in Chapter 6. Although many of the Clinton administration's

REGO efforts expired with little appreciable impact on regulation, two programs that survived and expanded during the presidency of George W. Bush hold promise for extending regulatory capacity: the HPV Challenge Program and the National Environmental Performance Track. In both cases there are significant problems of regulatory design that compromise performance.

The HPV Challenge Program

The basic information necessary to inform regulatory priorities is often lacking. While the gaps in water quality data are stunning, as noted in Chapter 4, they pale in comparison to the gaps in data on high production volume (HPV) chemicals (i.e., chemicals with annual production levels of 1 million pounds or more). In the past two decades, reports on the chemical industry focused attention on a disturbing fact: regulators had little data on the toxicity and environmental impacts of the vast majority of industrial chemicals used in the United States. According to an Environmental Defense report titled *Toxic Ignorance,* "even the most basic toxicity testing results cannot be found in the public record for nearly 75% of the top volume chemicals in commercial use. In other words, the public cannot tell whether a large majority of the highest-use chemicals in the United States pose health hazards or not—much less how serious the risks might be, or whether those chemicals are actually under control. In 1998, the EPA reported that 43% of high production volume chemicals had no publicly available data on basic toxicity and only 7% had a full set of basic data" (1997: 7). The Chemical Manufacturers Association (subsequently renamed the American Chemistry Council) arrived at similar conclusions, thereby creating a consensus among regulators, advocates, and industry.

The result of this consensus was the HPV Challenge Program, implemented by the EPA's Office of Pollution Prevention and Toxics. The program, developed jointly by the EPA, Environmental Defense, and the American Chemistry Council, was designed to enlist the voluntary efforts of industry to develop and make publicly available information that could support the assessment of risks from the 2,782 HPV chemicals reported in 1990 under the "inventory update rule" of the Toxic Substances Control Act. During the sign-up period (March 1999 through December 2000), companies, trade associations, or industrial consortia could voluntarily sponsor chemicals. Sponsorship entails a commitment to provide an initial assessment of existing data, conduct new testing where necessary, and make the data publicly available. For each HPV chemical, the end result would be a screening-information dataset (SIDS)—a set of screening data developed by the OECD and consisting of basic physical-chemical data, environmental fate and pathway data, ecotoxicity data, and toxicological data (see 65 Fed.

Reg. 81686). Chemicals that failed to receive sponsorship would be added to the "priority testing limit" of the Toxic Substances Control Act (§ 4[e]). All testing was to be completed by the end of 2004, at which time the EPA would analyze the submissions to determine which of the HPV chemicals posed sufficient risks, in order to justify further analysis and, potentially, regulation (EPA 2004g).

HPV Challenge represents a new level of cooperation among actors that often have been embroiled in adversarial relations. On at least two counts, the program appears to be a success. First, sponsorship levels (and by implication, the willingness of companies to devote resources to regulatory goals) have been rather impressive, given the voluntary nature of the program. As of January 2000, 2,123 chemicals had received sponsorship, a number that would increase to 2,238 by January 2004 (the EPA permitted participation after the close of the sign-up period). Second and related, the program went far in allowing the EPA to manage high levels of information scarcity and conserve on regulatory resources. The EPA calculates that 59 percent of the data reported under the program—some 6,800 studies—had already been collected by companies but were previously unavailable to the public (EPA 2004g: 7).

Despite these positive accomplishments, the basic incentive structure, combined with informational asymmetries, opens the door to a host of problems. Corporations have monopolistic control over information that, if released, could increase vulnerability to civil liability, mandatory testing, and regulatory control. At the same time, the EPA lacks the administrative capacity to verify the screening-information dataset. Under the current design of HPV Challenge, the EPA has no alternative other than to assume that the data provided by corporate sponsors provide an accurate portrayal of the chemicals in question. One should not be surprised that the program has had its share of difficulties. First, the process has been bedeviled by slow submission rates. When companies sponsor a chemical, they formally state their "start year"—the year they will submit their test plan, which provides a robust summary of existing data—and state their strategy for filling gaps in the data. Though the EPA designed the program to spread submissions evenly across the years, submissions have consistently fallen behind schedule. As noted in a 2003 evaluation conducted by Environmental Defense: "Hundreds of sponsors have decided to delay initiation of data development for their chemicals, thereby 'back-loading' the program's schedule and jeopardizing timely completion of the program" (Denison and Florini 2003: viii). The EPA is hesitant to accept responsibility for the slow compliance rate, noting: "Voluntary programs, such as the HPV Challenge Program, operate exclusively on the basis of industry commitments for participation. If industry fails to respond to such initiatives, the Agency will be less able to achieve effective new chemical screening efficiently" (EPA 2003a: 105).

Second, there is the issue of orphan chemicals. As of 2004, some 571 chemicals lacked sponsors. The EPA determined that many of these chemicals no longer met the criteria for HPV chemicals, thereby reducing the list of orphans to 330 (EPA 2004g: 58). The core problem was not an inability to identify the companies producing orphan HPV chemicals. Companies that report producing the highest number of orphans include Kopper Industries (thirteen orphans), US Steel (ten orphans), BASF (eight orphans), Dow Chemical (eight orphans), and Exxon Mobil Chemical Company (six orphans). Rather, responsible parties offer a number of rationales for their decision to eschew sponsorship. A survey of 202 companies conducted for Environmental Defense (Denison 2004) noted a host of rationales, including claims that the company no longer produced or imported the chemical, that the company believed that it was safe, and that the company was but one of several producers. In the end, an analysis of the responses led to the conclusion that the decision not to sponsor a chemical was justified in 29 percent of the cases.

Third, the US sponsors have increasingly abandoned the US process for its less rigorous international counterpart. The HPV Challenge Program competes with the HPV Initiative of the International Council of Chemical Associations (ICCA), which in turn is tied to the HPV SIDS Program of the OECD. Companies, associations, and consortia can sponsor chemicals under the ICCA initiative, which subsequently submits data to the OECD for screening-level hazard assessment in a SIDS initial assessment meeting. In order to avoid duplication of efforts, the EPA recognizes commitments under the ICCA initiative, although companies seeking recognition are not required to submit their data to the EPA. The EPA exempts parties from meeting preexisting obligations should they decide to migrate from the HPV Challenge to its ICCA counterpart. Increasingly, firms have availed themselves of this option. In 2000, 100 percent of the 2,123 chemicals were sponsored solely under the HPV Challenge Program. By July 30, 2004, only 56.2 percent (or 1,248 chemicals) were solely within HPV Challenge; 38.3 percent were sponsored under the ICCA (851 chemicals), with an addition 5.5 percent (123 chemicals) under dual sponsorship (EPA 2004g: 49).

The decision to embrace the ICCA process is a logical response to potential regulatory and civil liability. It is managed by a trade association, thereby reducing concerns that might arise from sharing data directly with regulators. More important, the ICCA process does not require submission of test plans for public comment, nor does it result in the immediate public release of information, unlike the EPA process, which maintains a 120-day public comment period and disseminates information via the Internet with little delay. As the EPA notes: "The number of chemicals that have moved from the HPV Challenge Program to ICCA HPV Initiative raises a concern because the data submitted under ICCA are not as readily publicly accessible" (2004g: 49). Finally, the ICCA/OECD process moves at a relatively slow pace. While the EPA anticipated that 974 chemicals should have made it through the SIDS initial assessment meeting by July 2004, only 229 chemicals—24 percent of the expected number—actually did (EPA 2004g: 50).

The fourth and final problem with the HPV Challenge Program is particularly profound. Despite the generation of data, one must note that the program has been restricted to a grossly outdated list of HPV chemicals drawn from the 1990 "inventory update rule" of the Toxic Substances Control Act. Since the list was finalized, several hundred new HPV chemicals have entered the stream of commerce. As an Environmental Defense report noted: "the Challenge program does not extend to these 'new HPVs' except insofar as companies independently elect to sponsor them. To date, 112 of the 735 'new HPVs' have been sponsored, leaving 623 unsponsored—one-quarter as many as were available for sponsorship within the scope of the original HPV Challenge Program" (Denison 2004: iv). Given the rapid introduction of new HPV chemicals unaffected by the EPA's program, it is unclear whether any effort to analyze risks and set future regulatory priorities will in fact focus regulatory attention on the chemicals of greatest concern. In sum, though the HPV Challenge Program has yielded some positive results, performance has been compromised by a host of problems that could have been easily anticipated.

The National Environmental Performance Track

Regulatory green tracks are voluntary programs designed for firms that have a strong record of environmental performance. As a generalization, entry into green tracks is restricted to firms that exhibit a record of regulatory compliance (or performance "beyond compliance"), commit to continuous improvement, and implement an environmental management system (see Chapter 8). The basic assumption underlying green tracks is that high-performing firms have the capacity for greater self-regulation, subject to regulatory oversight. They should be rewarded with public recognition, greater flexibility in meeting regulatory requirements, and lower inspection priorities. If these firms are given greater flexibility, it is assumed that they will be more innovative in developing pollution control and prevention strategies and that these innovations, in turn, will contribute to greater gains in environmental quality and will be disseminated through the economy. If collaboration and cooperation are promoted, participants should also learn from each other's experiences. Regulators should benefit as well. The granting of a lower inspection priority to high-performing firms should free enforcement resources to focus on companies that are more likely to evade their regulatory obligations. Moreover, green tracks create a context for policy-related learning as regulators gain a better understanding of the merits of alternative policy instruments.

During the 1990s, states began to experiment with regulatory green tracks. The Multi-State Working Group on Environmental Management Systems—a consortium of state agencies, the EPA, nongovernmental organizations, industry representatives, and academics—provided an important network for conducting research on the regulatory implications of corporate environmentalism and sharing results (Speir 2001). These experiments found an expression at the national level in 1996, when EPA Region 1 created its Star Track Program, whose primary goal was to promote the expanded use of environmental management systems and compliance audits, with a particular focus on management systems that met the features specified by ISO 14001. Participation was restricted to a select set of firms with an established compliance auditing program, a record of compliance, and a commitment to continuous improvement in environmental performance and pollution prevention. Participants were required to submit to comprehensive audits on an annual basis to verify that they were in compliance with all federal, state, and local regulations. If noncompliance was discovered, the participant was required to implement a corrective and preventive action plan. In addition, the noncomplying participant was required to conduct an EMS audit using an EPA audit protocol, identify areas for improvement, and create an implementation plan for making the required changes. The results were to be certified by a third party and publicly disseminated.

Star Track participants were given several rewards. First, they were given limited penalty amnesty for violations detected through self-audits, if corrected within a given period of time—an important, if selectively applied, correction to the problems cited in Chapter 6. Second, they were assigned a lower inspection priority, reflecting EPA recognition that Star Track participants were less likely to run afoul of regulations. Third, they received so-called express-lane service for permits and other regulatory actions, reducing the red tape and delays that constitute some of the greatest costs of regulation. Finally, firms with the best performance records were recognized through special "environmental merit" awards. The fourteen participants included large corporations from a variety of sectors, ranging from pharmaceuticals to sporting goods to information technology.

In response to the experiences with Star Track, the EPA introduced the National Environmental Performance Track (NEPT) in 2000 (EPA 2001c). Organizations interested in participating in the NEPT need to employ a high-quality EMS that includes an environmental policy statement committing the organization to compliance, pollution prevention, continuous improvement, and the sharing of environmental performance data with the public. Prior to applying to the NEPT, applicants must have their environmental management systems assessed through a third-party audit using the

Performance Track's independent assessment protocol. Participants must also demonstrate past environmental compliance and a commitment to continuous improvement. Applicants can be rejected if they have a record of criminal convictions or repeated and significant civil violations, or if they are actively involved in investigations or prosecutions. They must document their commitment to improvement for the current and prior year in at least two aspects of their activities in at least one of the following stages: the upstream stage (e.g., material procurement), the input stage (e.g., material and resource use), the nonproduct outputs stage (e.g., pollution emissions), and the downstream stage (e.g., environmental impacts of products). In each case, the EPA is interested in actions that have taken the organization beyond compliance. Applicants must also commit to specific improvements in at least four aspects of their activities in at least two stages of the process. Finally, they must have a commitment to public outreach (http://www.epa.gov/performancetrack/program/standard.htm).

The EPA offers a host of benefits for participants. First, the agency provides public recognition of NEPT firms. The EPA informs elected officials of firms in their states that have joined the NEPT, establishes links to the firms' program descriptions on its website, and profiles the firms in articles in the trade press. As well, participants that actively publicize the NEPT program and encourage other firms to join are qualified to receive a Performance Track Outreach Award and use the Performance Track logo. A second benefit is enhanced networking. The EPA sponsors regular conferences, regional roundtables, and teleseminars to promote information sharing. Its 2004 member conference, for example, included presentations on topics ranging from marketing the NEPT program, to innovations in environmental management systems, to interacting with state regulators. The NEPT also has a mentoring program that matches new or potential participants with top-performing facilities that can provide technical assistance and information on best practices within the industry. A third benefit is a low inspection-priority status. Finally, the EPA provides a host of regulatory and administrative incentives, including flexible permits, faster response time for requests for alternative compliance requirements, extended accumulation time for hazardous wastes under the Resource Conservation and Recovery Act, and streamlined reporting and reduced paperwork requirements.

As of 2005 the National Environmental Performance Track had 337 members (culled from a list of over 500 applicants), including a collection of industrial giants (e.g., 3M, Anderson Corporation, Bridgestone/Firestone, E. I. Dupont de Nemours and Co., IBM, International Paper, Johnson & Johnson, Lockheed Martin, Monsanto Company, Motorola, Nestlé USA, Pfizer, Raytheon, Ricoh Electronics, US Steel). It has also forged relationships with a host of associations through its Performance Track Network, which includes a number of trade associations (e.g., the American Chemistry Council, the American Furniture Manufacturers Association, the American Textile Manufacturers Institute, the National Association of Chemical Distributors, the National Paint and Coatings Association, the North American Die Casting Association, the Steel Manufacturers Association, the Synthetic Organic Chemical Manufacturers Association) (EPA 2004a: 22–24).

The number of NEPT members is somewhat difficult to assess on three counts. First, the EPA counts each facility as a separate member. Fully 65.6 percent of NEPT members are facilities that belong to multifacility organizations. Johnson & Johnson, for example, accounts for forty facilities, 11.8 percent of total NEPT membership. If each organization were counted once regardless of the number of facilities, NEPT membership would fall from 337 to 162. Second, although the NEPT was designed to engage corporations, over 6 percent of the members are drawn from the public sector, including the 173rd Fighter Wing of the Air National Guard, the NASA Ames Research Center, and Dinosaur National Monument. Third, the organizations vary dramatically in their potential environmental impact. It is difficult to compare Fortune 500 manufacturing firms (like 3M, Monsanto, and International Paper) and some of the seemingly less significant members (like the Mammoth Cave Hotel or the Badlands Lodge, complete with twenty-two cabins, a full-service dining room, and a gift shop).

My analysis of the applications and progress reports of NEPT participants reveals that the mix of organizations has only become more biased toward small organizations over time (http://yosemite.epa.gov/opei/ptrack.nsf//famembers?readform). In their applications, NEPT participants characterize their organizations by number of employees (under 50, 50–99, 100–499, 500–1000, and 1000+). Of the 135 organizations that joined the NEPT in 2001, 57.0 percent had 500 or more employees, compared with the 14.1 percent that had 99 or fewer employees. As shown in Figure 10.1, large organizations have become increasingly rare compared to their smaller—and less significant—counterparts. Indeed, of the fifty-three new participants in 2005, 47.2 percent had 99 or fewer employees, compared with the 26.4 percent that had more than 500 employees.

How has the Performance Track performed? In its third annual report, the EPA cited some seemingly impressive statistics. Since the program's inception, members have reduced energy use by 8.47 trillion British thermal units, water use by 1.34 billion gallons, hazardous materials use by 16,420 tons, solid waste by 582,213 tons, hazardous waste by 8,321 tons, emissions of greenhouse gases by carbon monoxide by 1.6 tons, emissions of nitrogen oxides by 3,898 tons, and emissions of sulfur dioxide by 16,257 tons. Participants have increased their use of reused and recycled materials by 76,695 tons, and conserved 7,871 acres of land and habitat. At the same

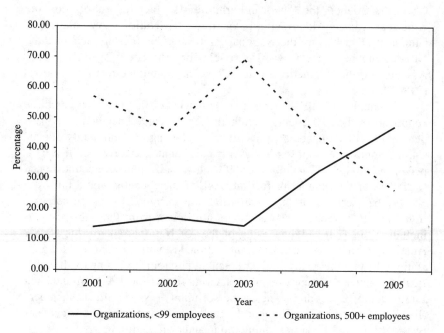

Figure 10.1 Size of NEPT Participants, 2001–2005

Organizations, <99 employees   - - - Organizations, 500+ employees

Data source: Environmental Protection Agency, National Environmental Performance Track.

time, water discharges have increased by 19,421 tons due to declining performance at two large facilities (EPA 2005a: 12). At first glance, such statistics do seem impressive. However, in a clear departure from Project XL,
which demanded guarantees of superior results and massive flows of information, under the Performance Track the EPA is content with self-reporting
without verification by regulators or third parties. Under these conditions, it
is impossible to determine what proportion of these results is genuine and
what proportion is mere puffery. Moreover, given that many of the larger
participants in the NEPT are firms with widely recognized reputations for
proactive environmental practices, one must imagine that some of the
reported results would have occurred in the absence of the program.

There is nothing objectionable about the NEPT. But one may be dubi-
ous that it constitutes the beginning of a more significant shift in regulatory
design. In the past, the EPA has been hesitant to relinquish control and permit complex experiments to go forward. While some of this hesitancy may
be assigned to the strength of the bureaucratic culture, one cannot fail to see
difficulties in managing the kinds of agency problems discussed earlier. In
Project XL, the EPA was willing to grant the flexibility to innovate only in
exchange for guarantees of superior environmental performance and volu-

minous flows of information. The resulting regulatory transaction costs were sufficient to depress participation rates. Although there have been no systematic studies of costs incurred under the NEPT, a 2005 assessment conducted by the Environmental Council of the States noted:

> There is a need to reduce transaction costs, both for agencies in developing and implementing these programs, and for facilities that choose to participate in them. EPA and states also need to provide better incentives faster to attract and retain program participants. In addition, greater flexibility is needed to allow states to utilize performance-based programs to achieve state-specific environmental goals and address environmental problems. (2005: 4)

For the NEPT to become the foundation of a genuine multi-tiered system of hybrid regulation, it must expand beyond the relatively small universe of firms that are currently participating. At the same time, some means must be discovered to generate verifiable performance data. Securing greater certainty of results without creating prohibitively large regulatory transaction costs is an enormous challenge that has yet to be met.

■ Regulatory Design and Regulatory Hybrids

The HPV Challenge Program and the National Environmental Performance Track are examples of programs that hold great promise. Unfortunately, they are plagued by broader regulatory design problems that exacerbate rather than manage information scarcity. There are ways to manage information scarcity that facilitate delegation (e.g., mandatory information disclosure, code-based associational self-regulation, and standard-based self-regulation backed with third-party certification). As a policy instrument, mandatory information disclosure can be remarkably effective in compensating for informational asymmetries—a major source of market failure. Moreover, mandatory information disclosure has been relatively unobjectionable when compared with more invasive regulatory instruments. Similarly, standard-based self-regulation with third-party certification has become a norm in many industries, as exhibited by the heavy reliance on ISO 9000 quality control standards and, increasingly, ISO 14001 environmental management system standards. Mandatory information disclosure would render the HPV Challenge Program unnecessary. When combined with changes in governance, it could expand participation and strengthen the performance of the National Environmental Performance Track.

The HPV Challenge Program focuses on a list of chemicals that is fifteen years out of date, with no mechanism for addressing emerging HPV chemicals, which have been entering the stream of commerce at a rapid pace. As the EPA's analyses reveal, the vast majority of the new data provided under HPV Challenge already existed. Corporations simply had little incentive to make the data public. One should anticipate that any incentives created by HPV Challenge will disappear if sponsorship results in new regulations or significant civil lawsuits or both. There is a simple remedy for this situation: new requirements that corporations develop and publicly disclose a screening-information dataset for any chemical manufactured or imported in quantities beyond a given threshold (e.g., the current threshold of 1 million pounds per year). If information disclosure were combined with third-party verification, the screening system could provide a more accurate portrayal of environmental and health impacts. A more rigorous requirement, such as that imposed for pesticides under the Federal Insecticide, Fungicide, and Rodenticide Act (see Bosso 1987), might be deemed optimal, insofar as it would force manufacturers to prove with reasonable certainty that their product, when used properly, would cause no harm to human health and no unreasonable risks to the environment. Yet even in the absence of a more rigorous standard, mandatory disclosure of a screening dataset would provide the EPA with the information necessary to make rudimentary risk assessments, without having to rely on corporate voluntarism. Moreover, if the experience with the Toxic Release Inventory is any guide, mandatory disclosure may create internal pressures for greater self-regulation, and decisions to eschew use of chemicals that may raise public or regulatory concerns.

Although the EPA celebrates the accomplishments of NEPT participants, the program is beset by two information-related problems. At the front end, the relatively low participation rate may be a product, in part, of the difficulties of gaining entry to the program. In Project XL, the approval process became a significant bottleneck, limiting the number of potential participants. The second problem is more profound. Unlike Project XL, in the NEPT the EPA is now content with self-reporting of accomplishments without third-party verification. It is impossible to determine whether this reflects a shift in regulatory postures or an overreaction to Project XL's problems. One can anticipate that the NEPT, as currently construed, will have minimal impacts on regulatory design.

A simple solution to the first problem would be to permit all corporations with ISO 14001 certification automatic entry into the NEPT. Growth in ISO 14001 certification has been rapid, as shown in Chapter 9, although regulatory reluctance has limited certification in the United States. Given that the vast majority of NEPT participants are already ISO 14001–certified (72.59 percent of the 135 organizations that joined in 2001 and 73.58 percent for organizations that joined in 2005), one can surmise that firms interested in the NEPT may already have experience with ISO 14001. Moreover, the EPA has experience with ISO 14001. The agency participated in its development and has been investigating the potential role of the standard for nearly a decade (EPA 2004c). Granting automatic entry to certified firms would carry several benefits and no obvious costs. First, certification conveys precisely the kind of information that would be necessary to identify firms that should receive greater flexibility in meeting regulatory requirements (i.e., information on whether a firm has a high-quality EMS, has a commitment to continuous improvement, and is in compliance with all environmental laws and regulations). Because companies must submit to periodic surveillance audits to verify ongoing compliance, this information should be relatively current. Finally, since corporations assume the costs of inspection and certification, the reliance on standards can conserve scarce regulatory budgets.

As noted by the Environmental Council of the States, participation is not simply a function of transaction costs. There is a need for "better incentives faster to attract and retain program participants. . . . Incentives must deliver significant business value to potential program participants." Such incentives include streamlined permitting, reduced frequency of inspections, and "direct financial incentives such as access to government environmental research grant money," "reduced or waived permitting fees," and "preferences for program participants in federal and state contracting and procurement" (2005: 4, 10, 12). The EPA is currently developing a host of new incentives (e.g., flexible air permits, expedited permit renewal under the National Pollutant Discharge Elimination System, and streamlined permits under the Resource Conservation and Recovery Act). Since the Clinton presidency, the United States has had an environmentally preferable purchasing program to reward green firms through procurement. As noted in Chapter 7, the Resource Conservation Challenge is explicitly exploring green procurement as one means of creating incentives for greater self-regulation. However, the extension of new incentives may be difficult to justify absent some means of verifying performance, and the resource demands associated with verification could be sufficient to vanquish the benefits of participation.

Fortunately, the second problem—verifying performance—is easily managed through a similar mechanism. As noted above, the EPA has formed partnerships with several trade associations through its Performance Track Network. The EPA could work with these associations to develop reporting protocols and identify key performance indicators and standard reporting metrics on an industry-specific basis. Some associations, like the American Chemistry Council, have already developed a set of environmental codes that are tailored to the specific features of the industry and compatible with ISO 14001. Under ISO 14001, all firms undergo periodic surveillance audits. By requiring that audits include the indicators developed cooperatively with trade associations, the EPA would have access to verified performance data, which are currently lacking. An additional benefit is clear: the competition between associations and regulators—so evident in the HPV Challenge Program—would be reduced.

■ Conclusion

Regulation in complex issue areas is an information-intensive business. The constraints imposed by information scarcity force regulators to select among two alternative paths, both of which carry significant costs. The first path, many would argue, has been fully exploited. Mandatory technological standards have been imposed; most firms are in regulatory compliance. For the past decade, regulators have been seeking means of extending regulatory capacity under severe resource constraints while creating the incentives for corporations to go beyond compliance through various forms of partnerships and voluntary initiatives. Yet as noted in this and previous chapters, the second path of regulatory delegation does not fully eliminate the knowledge problem. Rather it recasts it as an agency problem. There are means of managing informational asymmetries and monitoring agent performance. Mandatory information disclosure and standard-based self-regulation with third-party verification constitute two promising instruments that could go far in resolving the difficulties inherent in regulatory delegation. The EPA has extensive experience in the area of information disclosure and ISO 14001. By integrating these instruments into the existing arsenal of regulatory policy tools, the EPA could compensate for some of the core problems of regulatory design, essentially creating the foundations for public-private regulatory hybrids that could leverage private sector resources and manage information scarcity without sacrificing public accountability. We shall return to this topic in far greater detail in Chapter 14.

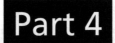

Part 4

Regulating the Global Commons from the Bottom Up

11

Beyond the Tragedy
of the Global Commons

G lobalization has become one of the dominant features of the contemporary era. Rather than constituting some end-state, it is more
useful to understand globalization as a process involving the growing international movement of goods, services, ideas, and people (see
Micklethwait and Wooldridge 2003). Moreover, rather than being a linear
process leading inexorably to a borderless world, globalization has often
been quite chaotic and unbalanced. The growth that has accompanied globalization has resulted in massive increases in incomes both in wealthy and
less developed countries (LDCs) as exhibited by life expectancies.
According to the World Bank, "Between 1980 and 1998, the world's average life expectancy at birth rose from 61 to 67 years, with the most dramatic
increases occurring in the low- and middle-income countries." Moreover,
since 1970, "life expectancy worldwide has risen on average by 4 months
each year" (http://www.worldbank.org/depweb/english/modules/social/life).
At the same time, improved incomes and life expectancies have fueled population growth. With a global population of over 6 billion—and an
increased population of some 200,000 people per day—the environmental
ramifications of extended life expectancies could be calamitous if the consumption patterns of developing countries mirror those of their wealthier
neighbors. As one analyst observes: "it is difficult to imagine the consequences, for example, of providing private automobiles to each of China's
300 million city dwellers or enough factory-raised animals to feed
Kentucky Fried Chicken to the non-vegetarian portion of India's population.
Two hundred years of industrial development in the North occurred largely
at the expense of the lands, resources, and people of the South. Where will
the middle classes of the developing world's cities find the equivalent
resources to appropriate in the name of development?" (Tokar 1997:
171–172).

Despite all of the benefits associated with globalization, critics are quick to observe that liberalization has imposed a high environmental cost. Rainforests and unique ecosystems are disappearing at an unprecedented rate, exacerbating global climate change and undermining biodiversity. Pressured by poverty and the need to attract foreign investment, LDCs have neglected environmental protection. Wealthy nations fuel this process by demanding an endless flow of cheap goods that can only be provided if governments in LDCs permit labor and environmental practices that would be illegal in the United States and Europe. Reflective of, and contributing to, the uneven nature of the globalization process, the world has yet to develop an institutional infrastructure capable of offering regulatory solutions to global environmental problems. This is not to say that global institutions do not exist. Where they are the most developed, however, they are designed explicitly to accelerate trade liberalization as an engine of economic growth.

In the United States, the criticisms found the clearest expression in the "Battle in Seattle," the 1999 protests against the World Trade Organization (WTO). Tens of thousands of protesters demanded that the WTO temper its support for free trade with a commitment to environmental protection and the rights of indigenous people, while opening trade talks to democratic participation. There was a simple message behind the media images of tear-gassed protesters, shattered windows, and police lines shielding the WTO dignitaries: growth carries incalculable environmental costs that many are unwilling to accept. Yet some analysts found the objections of the protesters to be self-defeating. There is much to suggest that environmental quality becomes more salient once a population reaches a given level of income. Wealthier nations invest in environmental protection; LDCs are forced to address more pressing problems such as pervasive poverty, a dearth of social services, and high infant mortality rates. Absent some system of international wealth redistribution, trade provides the best single engine of growth and the only practical means of raising the incomes of poorer nations to a point where they will begin investing in environmental protection. The key problem, however, is that many rapidly growing nations engage in a pattern of growth that may deliver irreversible environmental damages and high cleanup costs (Vinod and Belt 1997).

One hypothesized relationship between per capita income and levels of environmental quality can be represented by a bell-shaped or inverted U-shaped curve often referred to as the environmental Kuznets curve (EKC) (the original Kuznets curve described the relationship between national income levels and levels of inequality). A simplified version of the environmental Kuznets curve is presented in Figure 11.1. The implications of the EKC hypothesis are relatively clear. During the early stages of industrialization, one should expect to witness growing levels of environmental degradation. However, at a certain level of per capita income, growth provides

Figure 11.1 The Environmental Kuznets Curve

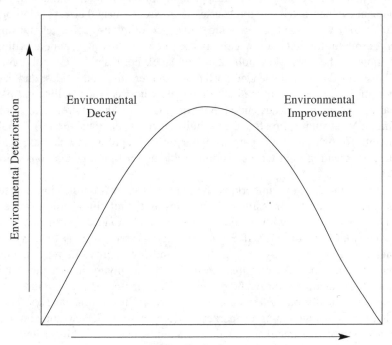

Environmental Decay

Environmental Improvement

Environmental Deterioration

Per Capita Income

Source: Yandle, Bhattarai, and Vijayaraghavan 2004.

the resources necessary to reverse past damages. As a generalization, "if economic growth is good for the environment, policies that stimulate growth (trade liberalization, economic restructuring, and price reform) should be good for the environment" (Yandle, Bhattarai, and Vijayaraghavan 2004: 29). Econometric studies that apply cross-sectional observations across countries or regions find that development drives increases in air and water pollution until per capita income reaches a level of $5,000 to $8,000, at which point pollution levels begin to decline. Indeed, there is evidence to suggest that the EKC may be flatter than originally believed, reflecting technological change, changes in the composition of output, and improvements in regulation (Dasgupta et al. 2002: 147, 148, 152).

Some researchers have questioned the empirical support for the EKC, even if the hypothesis makes theoretical sense (see Deacon and Norman 2004). The critiques often focus on the underlying assumptions, "among others, that all nations in the sample are following the same development path; that they are developing independently of one another; and that development can be treated like the 'cause' of an environmental effect" (Margolis 2002: 6). Even if one can conclude that the pollution-income relationship conforms to the EKC, a few caveats are in order. First, it may be useful to distinguish between flow pollutants and stock pollutants. Flow pollutants, like sulfur dioxide, suspended particulate matter, nitrogen oxides, and carbon monoxide, cause immediate damages, whereas stock pollutants, like various municipal wastes and carbon dioxide, harm the environment in the future. Most studies find that the pollution-income relationship for flow pollutants follows the EKC pattern, whereas stock pollutants increase with income, creating long-term pollution problems for future generations (Lieb 2004).

Second, and more important, the impact of growth on the environment is contingent on the investment in policies and institutions: "Improvement of the environment with income growth is not automatic but depends on policies and institutions. GDP growth creates the conditions for environmental improvement by raising the demand for improved environmental quality and makes the resources available for supplying it. Whether environmental quality improvements materialize or not, and when and how, depend critically on government policies, social institutions and the completeness and functioning of markets" (Panayotou 1997: 468). In sum, one cannot simply assume that growth will automatically yield higher levels of environmental quality in the long run and that all of the environmental damage done during the development process will be reversible. Yet there is relatively strong empirical and theoretical support for the proposition that growth and environmental improvements are causally connected. To the extent that institutions and public policies provide a critical intervening variable, the policy prescriptions are equally clear. Trade liberalization should be combined with investments in the regulatory capabilities of LDCs. International assistance in this endeavor could flatten the EKC, thereby reducing the environmental costs of growth.

The protests against the WTO may have provided a vivid illustration of the discontent with free trade and its potential impacts. Yet the global economic system is premised on a shared commitment to free trade, which has been in place since the end of World War II. Any discussion of global regulation must begin with a discussion of trade and its connection to growth.

■ A Primer on Trade Liberalization

A political commitment to free trade is a relatively recent event. Traditionally, tariffs provided an important source of government revenues and allowed domestic producers to charge higher prices than would be possible under competitive conditions. Moreover, by providing nations with differential treatment, trade policy could be used to maintain international alliances. In the United States, protectionism reached a high point in 1930, with the passage of the Smoot-Hawley Act. As one might expect, high tariffs stimulated retaliation and created great barriers to international commerce, thereby exacerbating the global depression of the 1930s. Following the dark days of the Great Depression and World War II, the United States spearheaded the expansion of trade through the promotion of liberalization. Advocates believed that free trade would contribute to peace by prohibiting the kinds of policies that sparked economic nationalism. As a generalization, nations with high levels of economic interdependence rarely go to war. At the same time, advocates believed that free trade would provide an engine of economic growth. A new international regime was created under the General Agreement on Tariffs and Trade (GATT); successive rounds of trade negotiations led to massive tariff reductions, creating the foundations for an international economy.

The economic argument in support of free trade was based in the theory of comparative advantage normally attributed to David Ricardo (see Ruffin 2002). The theory—a mainstay of most introductory economics texts—is simple yet profound. Every nation can produce some goods more efficiently than other goods. While a nation might pursue a path of self-sufficiency or autarky, such a policy carries a high cost by preventing specialization and the realization of economies of scale. It is in the best interest of a given nation to specialize in the production of the goods for which it has a comparative advantage and trade with other nations that have a comparative advantage in producing other goods. In the end, all nations can benefit from the exploitation of comparative advantage. Note that the argument is not that all nations will benefit equally; while every nation has a comparative advantage in certain goods (e.g., it can produce product X more efficiently than product Y), some nations may not have an absolute advantage in producing anything. Even under these conditions, they will gain from free trade.

GATT was premised on a faith in comparative advantage and a commitment to nondiscrimination. Members were given the status of "most-favored nation," and agreed to apply the same tariff rate to any member that was made available to all other GATT members. Under the principle of national treatment, members were obliged to treat the goods imported from a member nation no differently than they treated goods produced by local industries. They cannot, for example, impose specialized taxes or regulations designed to create disadvantages for imports once they enter the domestic market. Between 1947 and 1967, a series of six negotiating rounds resulted in significant reductions in tariffs. However, negotiations became far more complicated subsequently, as attention shifted to various nontariff barriers (e.g., government procurement policies, product standards, and subsidies). The reduction of nontariff barriers proved contentious, because they often meet the demands of local constituencies or are designed to achieve domestic goals (see Carbaugh 1998: chap. 7).

The World Trade Organization, Free Trade, and Sustainable Development

Despite its half-century history, GATT was created as a temporary measure. It was replaced by the World Trade Organization, which was created in 1995 as a permanent organization. Located in Geneva, Switzerland, the WTO has 147 members responsible for 97 percent of international trade. It is responsible for overseeing the implementation of some 30,000 pages of trade agreements (both inherited from GATT and revised in the past decade), resolving trade disputes, and creating a forum within which members can initiate new negotiations. The preamble to the Marrakech Agreement, which created the WTO, clearly recognized the importance of promoting free trade *and* sustainable development. It noted that members recognize that "their relations in the field of trade and economic endeavor should be conducted with a view to raising standards of living . . . while allowing for the optimal use of the world's resources in accordance with the objective of sustainable development, seeking both to protect and preserve the environment and to enhance the means for doing so in a manner consistent with their respective needs and concerns at different levels of economic development" (WTO 2004: 4–5).

Although the WTO has been the focus of many groups claiming to represent the interests of the developing world, it is important to note that less developed countries constitute three-quarters of the WTO's members. The WTO seeks to make decisions by consensus. If a vote is called, however, the principle of "one country, one vote" leaves no question as to the ability of LDCs to shape the outcome. Reflecting the role of LDCs, the fourth ministerial conference, in Doha, Qatar, which began in November 2001, focused very heavily on issues of concern to LDCs and the need to promote sustainable development. The ministerial declaration of November 14, 2001, noted: "we shall continue to make positive efforts designed to ensure that developing countries, and especially the least-developed among them, secure a share in the growth of world trade commensurate with the needs of their economic development. In this context, enhanced market access, balanced rules, and well targeted, sustainably financed technical assistance and capacity-building programmes have important roles to play" (WTO 2001: para. 2). Moreover, it reaffirmed the commitment to sustainable development and directly addressed the tension between development and the environment:

> We are convinced that the aims of upholding and safeguarding an open and non-discriminatory multilateral trading system, and acting for the protection of the environment and the promotion of sustainable development can and must be mutually supportive. We take note of the efforts by members to conduct national environmental assessments of trade policies on a voluntary basis. We recognize that under WTO rules no country should be prevented from taking measures for the protection of human, animal or plant life or health, or of the environment at the levels it considers appropriate, subject to the requirement that they are not applied in a manner which would constitute a means of arbitrary or unjustifiable discrimination between countries where the same conditions prevail, or a disguised restriction on international trade, and are otherwise in accordance with the provisions of the WTO Agreements. (2001: para. 6)

Given the apparent recognition of issues of concern to LDCs and the commitment to norms of sustainable development and environmental protection, one must question why the WTO and the international trade regime have continued to be the target of discontent. Perhaps critics are simply unaware of the WTO's position on sustainable development and the positive implications of growth for the environment? One does not mobilize dissent with nuanced discussions of WTO protocols and the EKC. There is an alternative explanation that may be more compelling: the WTO may herald the importance of sustainable development while doing little to translate its concerns into policy because, first, it assumes that free trade will reinforce the goal, and, second, it assumes its actions should focus on a single goal—ongoing liberalization.

The WTO has clearly proclaimed its support for environmental protection and sustainable development. The core question is how the WTO views this commitment in reference to its larger set of trade-related commitments. In 1994 the WTO created its Committee on Trade and the Environment to explore the relationships between trade and sustainable development and to make recommendations regarding necessary modifications to WTO rules. Although the committee has met several times a year, there is no evidence to suggest an appreciable transformation of the WTO's mission. Indeed, the organization is clear about its core mission: "WTO Members recognize . . . that the WTO is not an environmental protection agency and that it does not aspire to become one. Its competence in the field of trade and environment is limited to trade policies and to the trade-related aspects of environmental policies which have a significant effect on trade" (WTO 2004: 6). The WTO argues that members should be free to develop nationally specific environmental protection policies "provided that they do not discriminate between imported and domestically produced like products (national treatment principle), or between like products imported from different trading partners (most-favoured-nation clause)" (WTO 2004: 7). Moreover, GATT allows WTO members to adopt policies that are inconsistent with GATT principles if they are "necessary" to protect human, animal, or plant life or health, or to conserve exhaustible natural resources (Article XX[b, g]). However, when such policies are challenged, the WTO has focused on whether the same end can be achieved through other means and whether they "result in arbitrary or unjustifiable discrimination" and "constitute a disguised restriction on international trade" (WTO 2004: 51). In the end, the support for free trade trumps environmental protection. Although world leaders have repeatedly noted their concern over the WTO's position, "it remains far from clear that governments are now ready to amend existing WTO rules to buffer environmental laws from trade challenges" (French 2000: 123). The benefits of trade liberalization have been far too attractive.

The core position adopted by the WTO is a simple one: "to a great extent, trade liberalization is not the primary cause of environmental degradation, nor are trade instruments the first-best policy for addressing environmental problems" (WTO 2004: 22). According to the WTO, liberalization can have several positive effects on the environment. First, it can allow for greater efficiency through competition, thereby conserving on resources. Second, it can reduce poverty via trade expansion, thereby allowing for the "encouragement of a sustainable rate of natural resource exploitation." Third, it can increase "the availability of environment-related goods and services." Finally, it can improve the conditions "for international cooperation through a continuing process of multilateral negotiation." Given that past commitments to financial and technology transfers from wealthy nations to LDCs have not been fulfilled, the WTO argues, these benefits become "fundamental to help them achieve sustainable development" (2004: 23).

Thus, while the WTO clearly recognizes the importance of the environment, this recognition has not materially altered its commitment to trade liberalization. Domestic regulatory policies and multilateral environmental agreements are deemed acceptable to the extent that they do not impose any unnecessary restrictions on free trade or undermine the most-favored nation and national treatment clauses. The WTO would clearly welcome an ambitious multilateral environmental program that provided financial support and technology transfers from wealthy nations to LDCs. However, in the absence of new international environmental institutions, free trade, it is argued, remains the best possible policy for promoting global environmental quality.

■ **Free Trade: A Regulatory Race to the Bottom?**

Free trade could be a source of grave concern if it leads, inexorably, to a regulatory race to the bottom. The basic argument makes implicit sense.

Wealthy democracies that impose stringent regulatory requirements force companies to assume costs that undermine their competitiveness in global markets. Corporations may respond by moving production facilities to LDCs that seek to attract investment by offering weak environmental standards and ineffective enforcement. Over time, these "pollution havens" will serve as a magnet for dirty industries. Wealthy nations, in turn, will seek to stem the exit of core industries by sacrificing their own regulatory standards. The result is a regulatory race to the bottom driven by the quest for profitability and facilitated by free trade. This argument, a mainstay of many critiques of globalization, provides the basis for potential remedies ranging from trade sanctions to universal environmental standards.

Although there is clear evidence that compliance costs are substantially higher in wealthy democracies (Jaffee et al. 1995), the larger argument receives little empirical support. A wealth of studies have failed to find evidence that foreign investment in LDCs is driven by regulatory costs in wealthy nations or that the outflow of dirty industries to LDCs is greater than the inflow of new investments to nations with high regulatory standards (Albrecht 1998; Eskeland and Harrison 1997; Tobey 1990; van Beers and van den Bergh 1997). At first blush, this seems counterintuitive. After all, corporations seek to maximize profits and regulatory costs are the highest in wealthy nations. Yet one can only make unambiguous predictions if nations were alike with respect to infrastructure, labor force, governmental stability, protection for property rights, resource endowments, and proximity to markets. As one study concludes: "the costs of pollution control should not be overestimated: even with respect to heavily polluting industries, pollution control costs hardly more than 3% of total output, and most of these costs are a necessary condition for any proper operation. In the light of the differences—in the cost of labour, capital and transactions, and in political and economical risk—between developing and highly developed economies, the role of lower environmental standards, if there is one, can be only minor" (Janicke, Binder, and Mönch 1997: 472).

Additional empirical validation can be found in a statistical analysis of a sample of US-based multinational enterprises (MNEs) involved in manufacturing or mining in countries with a per capita GDP below $8,000 (in 1985 dollars), drawn from the Standard and Poor's list of 500 corporations, for the period 1994–1997 (Dowell, Hart, and Yeung 2000). The MNEs differed in their environmental standards. The first interesting fact is that of the eighty-nine firms in the sample, a majority adopted stringent global standards that exceeded US standards, whereas approximately half the number adopted the weaker local environmental standards instead. Over the period under analysis, twelve firms upgraded their standards, whereas only six downgraded their standards. The analysis yielded an important finding: MNEs with investments in poor countries *and* global environmental standards that exceed US standards had higher market values than those that adopted the standards of the host nations (for those that adopted US standards, the relationship between environmental standards and market value was positive but statistically insignificant). Indeed, MNEs that adopted the more stringent global standards had market values that were $8.6–$10.4 billion greater, on average, than those that adopted lower standards, and market values appreciated quickly once firms adopted higher environmental standards (Dowell, Hart, and Yeung 2000: 1069–1071).

This raises an important issue: all firms are not created equal. The analysis clearly suggests that "'quality' firms adopt high environmental standards independent of local requirements, and generate less pollution, while lower-quality firms engage in a 'race to the bottom,' as a means of gaining short term financial advantage" (Dowell, Hart, and Yeung 2000: 1071). The decision to adopt higher global standards and apply them uniformly to all facilities makes sense on a number of grounds beyond those introduced in Chapter 8. By applying a single standard, firms can reduce the costs of monitoring and evaluating performance, while disseminating improvements to all of their facilities. Moreover, firms that adopt higher standards may prevent future investments required to adapt to changing local standards. Finally, they can use their self-regulatory capacities strategically by pushing for more stringent regulations in host countries, thereby forcing additional costs on local competitors.

The impact of globalization on national regulatory standards is an important issue, given the arguments regarding the ways in which policies are shaped to attract investments. The regulatory race to the bottom is often referred to as the "Delaware effect" (a reference to the process by which states liberalized their incorporation requirements to compete for corporate charters; Delaware won this contest by providing the most liberal requirements in the nation). In *Trading Up,* David Vogel notes that there are clearly cases of the Delaware effect in the conflict between economic integration and regulation. Yet, he concludes, the relationship between trade and environmental regulation is much more consistent with the "California effect" (a reference to the capacity of California, with its large consumer market and strong environmental movement, to force a regulatory race to the top). Vogel notes: "True, the steady growth of regulation has interfered with trade, while trade agreements are increasingly interfering with regulation. But what is more significant is that, on balance, both global and regional economic integration have *increased* while consumer and environmental standards have become *stronger.*" Reinforcing the findings reviewed above, he notes that corporations producing in multiple markets have an interest in common product and environmental standards. Moreover, because companies in wealthy nations have a greater capacity to meet high standards, stringent regulations can be a source of competitive advantage. "Political jurisdictions which have developed stricter product standards force foreign producers in nations with weaker domestic standards either to design products that meet those standards or sacrifice export markets." These firms, in turn, have an incentive to make the domestic regulations in their host nations more stringent, since they have already met these standards to gain access to foreign markets (Vogel 1995: 249, 261).

One might agree with the proposition that, in the long run, trade's effects on the environment will be positive. After all, there is little question that trade has been an important engine of growth for less developed countries. Nations that have embraced market liberalization have been far more successful than those that have attempted to use some combination of trade restrictions and industrial policies to promote the development of strategic industries, as exhibited by the rapid and sustained growth of a number of Asian economies relative to their Latin American counterparts. Moreover, there is much research supporting the position that environmental quality is income-dependent. Once nations reach a certain level of wealth, they devote greater resources to environmental protection (as suggested by the EKC). Finally, as Vogel argues, economic integration can unleash a "regulatory race to the top" in national environmental standards.

With all of the potentially positive impacts of trade and development on the environment, one might still reject the Panglossian conclusions of many analysts. One might argue that we do not have the luxury of waiting for long-term improvements. The positive changes envisioned by the advocates of the EKC may come to fruition only if development is combined with investments in institution building. More important, some problems, such as global climate change, may be far more difficult to reverse at some future point in time. Others problems (e.g., the global loss of biodiversity and unique ecosystems) are irreversible. Even if we assume the most roseate conditions, there remains a strong justification for the creation of new international regulatory institutions.

■ The Challenges of Global Regulation

Let us assume that trade liberalization has positive environmental ramifications. To the extent that it forces greater efficiency, it should create incentives for producers to reduce the resource demands of production. To the extent that it improves the national income of less developed countries, it should increase both the demands and the resources available for investments in environmental protection. To the extent that firms headquartered in LDCs are required to meet higher standards to compete in international markets, they should reinforce this trend by demanding more stringent regulations in their home markets. Yet, as critics will quickly note, there are a host of environmental problems that cannot be managed domestically and cannot be easily reversed—if at all—in some hypothetical future. Even if the World Trade Organization and the advocates of liberalization are correct, one might conclude that there remains a strong theoretical case for international regulation.

Even if the case could be made for international regulation, the task of creating functional international regulatory institutions offers a set of seemingly intractable challenges. International relations scholars have yet to arrive at a consensus over behavioral assumptions (see Vig 1999: 3–5). In the immediate post–World War II period, realists conceived of states as having an innate desire to dominate one another; war was largely an inevitable byproduct of this desire. Neorealists have brought a greater sophistication to the analysis of international relations, arguing that states are self-interested actors that conceive of the international arena as an anarchic environment. They seek to maximize their strength relative to other nations and participate in international organizations and agreements only to the extent that such activities contribute to the broader goal. One might view this perspective as being an antiquated inheritance of the Cold War. Yet as Stephen M. Walt observes, since the Cold War, the United States "has called repeatedly for greater reliance on multilateralism and a larger role for international institutions, but has treated agencies such as the United Nations and the World Trade Organization with disdain whenever their actions did not conform to U.S. interests. It refused to join the rest of the world in outlawing the production of landmines and was politely uncooperative at the Kyoto environmental summit. Although U.S. leaders are adept at cloaking their actions in the lofty rhetoric of 'world order,' naked self-interest lies behind most of them . . . realism is likely to remain the single most useful instrument in our intellectual toolbox" (1998: 43).

The advocates of other analytical perspectives (e.g., liberals, neoliberals, institutionalists) are skeptical of the behavioral assumptions underlying (neo)realism. Moreover, they question the utility of viewing the state as a unitary actor when it is, in fact, a complex constellation of institutions often pursuing different goals and representing potentially irreconcilable constituencies. Under these alternative assumptions, the potential for cooperation may be far greater than one might otherwise imagine. State behavior is often conditioned by norms, institutions, and long-standing relations of cooperation and dependency that circumscribe the naked pursuit of national interest and focus attention on the benefits of collective action. In many policy areas, regimes have emerged to structure the cooperation and interaction of nations. According to Stephen D. Krasner, regimes are "implicit or explicit principles, norms, rules, and decision-making procedures around which actors' expectations converge in a given area of international relations" (1983: 2). Such regimes have evolved in several policy areas, ranging from telecommunications standards to the control of chlorofluorocarbons.

Perhaps the gulf between realists and their critics are not that great. Some, like Robert Jervis, argue that the gap separating realism and neoliberalism has been exaggerated. Both "start from the assumption that the absence of a sovereign authority that can make and enforce binding agreements creates opportunities for states to advance their interests unilaterally and make it important and difficult for states to cooperate with one another." Indeed, Jervis continues, neoliberals do not necessarily see more cooperation that realists; "rather, neoliberalism believes that there is much more unrealized or potential cooperation than does realism, and the schools of thought disagree about how much conflict . . . is unnecessary or unavoidable in the sense of actors failing to agree even though their preferences overlap" (1999: 43, 47). In fact some scholars have derived institutional positions from realist assumptions (see, for example, Keohane 1984). One can assume that states make rational calculations to gain power in an anarchic environment, and that these calculations and an understanding of the preferences of other nations create opportunities for cooperation. Under conditions approximating the one-stage Prisoners' Dilemma game, states understand that mutual defection from cooperation is the most common outcome, but that it is a suboptimal outcome that limits their capacity to realize joint gains. Hence they develop institutions or regimes to manage the interaction and reduce the probability of mutual defection. Although preferences do not change as a result of institutions, institutions can reduce uncertainty about the behavior of other actors (Hasenclever, Mayer, and Rittberger 1996: 184–185). Yet all of this might be of little more than scholarly value if, as John J. Mearsheimer notes, "what is . . . impressive about institutions, in fact, is how little independent effect they seem to have had on state behavior" (1994: 47).

If realists are correct in their portrayal of the international arena, the prospects for global environmental regulation would appear to be bleak. Most environmental regulations strive to produce public goods. Given the key feature of a public good—nonexcludability—a rational, self-interested actor would have strong incentives to engage in free-riding, particularly if participation by competing states depresses its economic competitiveness and compromises its capacity to project influence in the international arena. If, in contrast, the critics of realism are more on the mark, there would appear to be greater hope. Yet even optimists would seem to agree that there are limits to the sacrifices nations are willing to make in the name of overarching principles and policy objectives. Certainly, nations may be willing to sacrifice some measure of success in a highly competitive international political economy in the name of environmental protection. However, as the politics surrounding the Kyoto Protocol suggest (see Chapter 12), the domestic economic impacts of international agreements may be sufficient to prevent ratification even if the costs of inaction are potentially catastrophic. At the end of the day, international treaties must be ratified by legislative bodies, and legislators are subject, at all times, to electoral pressures.

Beyond the uncertainty over the behavior of nation-states, one must consider the technical tasks of constructing international institutions. At the very least, institutions must be capable of aggregating preferences, defining goals, monitoring performance, backing policy with credible threats, and imposing costs on the most powerful (see Weaver and Rockman 1993a). Preference aggregation and goal definition are extraordinarily difficult, given the diversity of actors and the above-noted uncertainty regarding behavioral assumptions. Most global environmental agreements will impose costs on actors at different levels of development and may have serious consequences for national economic development strategies. In some cases, these costs can be offset by financial transfers. Under the Montreal Protocol, for example, wealthy nations created a multinational fund to cover some of the costs of reducing the production and consumption of ozone-depleting chemicals. In the case of the Kyoto Protocol, the failure to impose restrictions on the practices of developing countries would have significant consequences for support in the US Senate.

Assuming that one could define goals with some care, the implementation problems are enormous. Policy is most effective when it punishes marginal departures from prescribed norms of behavior (see Barrett 1999). By focusing on marginal violations, actors can be forced to change patterns of behavior before too much damage is done. Moreover, assuming that punishments should be proportional to the magnitude of the violations in question, actors in the international arena may not have the political will to punish massive violations with commensurate penalties. In a highly integrated world economy, such sanctions—trade blockades, for example—could have widespread economic ramifications, punishing the guilty *and* the innocent alike. One suspects that such sanctions, particularly if contemplated against a powerful nation, would never be imposed. As regulated parties came to understand this fact, the regulations would be violated as soon as the costs became too great. In the end, the policies would soon become largely symbolic.

Although enforcement at the margin is preferable to enforcement targeting large violations, an enforcement regime that focuses on marginal violations increases administrative costs. First, it is, by definition, information-intensive. To detect marginal violations, one must have access to fine-grained information on performance. Problems of information scarcity have bedeviled regulation in the United States, as shown in previous chapters. The difficulties on a global scale would make the domestic problems seem trivial by comparison. There are technological remedies—continuously monitoring technologies have been a key component of acid rain regulations in the United States, for example. But the monitoring of daily performance can be quite difficult, particularly on a global scale, where one will encounter vast differences both in the financial resources available for monitoring and in the capacity of domestic regulatory agencies to collect information. Granted, parties may agree to engage in self-monitoring and self-reporting, but the veracity of reporting will come into question, particularly if nations are hesitant to sacrifice national interest in the name of environmental goals. In short, one would predict that the climate of information scarcity, when combined with the existing incentive structure, would produce massive agency problems that would be difficult to manage.

Second, there must be a capacity for evaluating the information that is collected and identifying violations. The analytical demands would require nothing short of a gargantuan bureaucracy, the costs of which could be difficult to imagine. In practice, these duties could be assumed by national regulatory authorities. However, this raises, once again, significant concerns with a domestic analog. As noted in Chapter 4, the lack of regulatory capacity at the state level has compromised regulatory performance in the United States. As with the problem of information scarcity, the difficulties of relying on a decentralized administrative structure would be far greater on a global scale than within the confines of a single nation-state. Domestic constituencies would have to support the policies in question and create and fund the regulatory capacity necessary to detect violations and impose penalties.

Building International Regulatory Regimes: A Bottom-Up Approach

There is a set of conditions that would appear ideal in setting the foundations for global regulatory regimes. First, there should be a strong domestic commitment to the regulations in question. Most environmental regulations require that significant long-term costs be imposed on regulated parties in the hope of achieving a future stream of benefits. It is difficult to argue that such regulations can be successfully maintained absent domestic support. Ideally, nations with compatible domestic commitments would create international institutions as a means of coordinating their efforts and pooling information. This could open the door for various forms of cooperation (e.g., emissions trading, joint research and development) that would benefit all parties.

Second and related, it is beneficial if a nation can use its domestic regulatory structures to administer the policies in question. If there is any strong message from the chapters that constitute Part 2 of this book, it is this: institutions matter. The decisions one makes with respect to agency design, the selection of policy instruments, and the requirements for monitoring performance will have an important impact on the performance of policy. As the discussion of regulatory reinvention noted (see Chapter 6), efforts to create new regulatory capacities, regardless of their justification and intellectual merits, can easily flounder if they prove incompatible with existing bureaucratic routines. Rather than creating new international regimes and *then* seeking to create the domestic creating regulatory capacities necessary for implementation, one should reverse this chain of events and view domestic capacities as setting a hard limit on what can be accomplished internationally. Unfortunately, even the most sophisticated proposals for global regulatory systems often pay scant attention to issues of enforcement and administration, viewing them as matters to be addressed in some hypothetical future (see Aldy, Barrett, and Stavins 2003).

Third, the new regime would be compatible with the most developed international regime currently in place—the trade regime administered by the WTO. As noted earlier, there is a strong argument to be made for the proposition that trade can have positive impacts on environmental quality in less developed countries. Trade can have a positive impact through the dissemination of higher environmental standards—the so-called California effect. Moreover, insofar as trade has been an important engine of economic growth, it can push incomes up the environmental Kuznets curve, increasing both the demand for, and the resources for, investments in environmental regulation. Regardless of the environmental merits of free trade, one would not expect nations to willingly sacrifice the economic benefits of trade for gains in environmental quality.

We have, in essence, a contrast between "bottom-up" and "top-down" approaches to the construction of international commitments. Global regulation provides us with an interesting irony: global regulatory institutions should be most successful precisely where they are least needed. That is, if there is strong domestic support, if there are supportive domestic regulatory institutions, and if these are compatible with existing international commitments to free trade, one would expect a far greater likelihood of success. Similarly, global regulatory institutions should be difficult or impossible to create if they compel actors to engage in patterns of action that are difficult to reconcile with domestic political commitments and regulatory institutions. This irony will be illustrated in detail in Chapter 12 through an examination of two international regulatory experiments: the Montreal Protocol and the Kyoto Protocol. In the case of the Montreal Protocol, the efforts to regulate the use of chlorofluorocarbons and reverse stratospheric ozone depletion were successful, in part, because they had strong domestic support and could use domestic regulatory institutions to implement policy. The Kyoto Protocol, in contrast, lacked these key features (and much more).

■ Conclusion

In light of the difficulties of developing functional international regulatory institutions, one must question what kinds of alternatives exist. Some have argued that in the face of these difficulties we should put an end to globalization in the name of environmental quality. Herman E. Daly argues: "Cosmopolitan globalism weakens national boundaries and the power of national and subnational communities while strengthening the relative power of transnational corporations. Since there is no world government capable of regulating global capital in the global interest, and since the desirability and possibility of a world government are both highly doubtful, it will be necessary to make capital less global and more national." For Daly, globalization is a "standards-lowering competition to reduce wages, externalize environmental and social costs, and export natural capital at low prices while calling it income" (1994: 187). Such calls, echoed by the antiglobalization protests of recent years, seem difficult to justify given the empirical research reviewed in this chapter. Others have concluded that international (and even domestic) regulatory institutions are unfeasible or undesirable relative to markets, which provide the best means of addressing environmental problems. If expanded trade drives gains in income and environmental quality via the environmental Kuznets curve, market forces can promote green production in firms, and private initiatives like the ISO 14000 series of standards can reinforce environmental values in trade and across the supply chain, perhaps there is little need for governmental intervention.

There is a middle road, one that preserves the benefits of free trade and markets while developing institutions to coordinate the actions of nations with common commitments. There are examples of international environmental regulatory regimes that have accomplished things beyond what might have been accomplished via market forces and corporate or associational self-regulation when taken alone. The Montreal Protocol, which addresses substances that deplete the ozone layer, is the clearest case in point. In a relatively brief period of time, the primary sources of stratospheric ozone depletion were removed from the stream of commerce, resulting in significant gains in environmental quality. An examination of the Montreal Protocol may provide useful lessons for thinking about the strengths and limitations of the most recent foray into international institution building, the Kyoto Protocol.

12

From Montreal to Kyoto

W hen environmental policy advocates confront critics of international regulation, they often point to the Montreal Protocol as evidence that such policies can be effective. There is a strong consensus that the protocol was a key element in successful international efforts to regulate chemicals, chlorofluorocarbons (CFCs) in particular, that deplete ozone. It follows that if the international community can ban CFCs and reverse damage to the ozone layer, it should be able to manage other problems such as global climate change. Or does it? This chapter challenges the assertion that the success of the Montreal Protocol should be a source of inspiration for the advocates of the Kyoto Protocol, which addresses global climate change. Most of the factors that made the Montreal Protocol a success are absent from the latter. As will become clear, the "bottom-up" path to regulation exhibited in the case of Montreal is quite different than the "top-down" approach inherent in the Kyoto Protocol (see Morrisette 1989 for a compelling analysis of the bottom-up process leading to Montreal).

■ Regulating Ozone Depletion: The Montreal Protocol

Virtually all models of the policy process begin with agenda setting. Before elected officials turn their attention to an issue, they must have reason to believe that it is sufficiently salient to generate political returns. Although definitional imprecision can be of great value in building coalitions, ambiguity may prove terminal when attempting to design credible solutions. Ozone depletion constitutes one of those rare cases when a problem can be defined and quantified with great precision. Ozone depletion was clearly documented as a result of scientific research. Ground-based ozone measurements were initiated in 1956 and supplemented by satellite measurements in the 1970s. Although thinning of ozone was occurring in many areas, the ozone hole over Antarctica became emblematic of the larger problem. Not only was the problem easily defined and quantified, but it also had potentially catastrophic implications for human health. Stratospheric ozone absorbs ultraviolet-B radiation from the Sun, preventing it from reaching Earth's surface. The ozone layer helps stabilize global temperature and protects plant life and aquatic systems from damage. Exposure to ultraviolet-B radiation causes a host of problems for humans, including an increased incidence of skin cancer and cataracts and a weakening of immune systems, with additional impacts on ecosystems (Cutchis 1974). Given these features, one should not be surprised that ozone depletion became highly salient and moved onto the policy agenda in the United States and other industrialized democracies.

The science of ozone depletion is well developed, eliminating another source of ambiguity in making the transition from problem definition to policy design. Ozone depletion is the product of halogen source gas emissions, particularly gases containing chlorine or bromine. CFCs constitute the most important category of halogen source gases. Chlorofluorocarbons, hydrochlorofluorocarbons (HCFCs), and other halons are inexpensive to produce and have a wide range of consumer and industrial applications (e.g., refrigeration, air conditioning, propellants, cleaning, fire extinguishers). Most halogen gases do not react with other substances in the troposphere, the layer of the atmosphere closest to the Earth's surface. However, as air motion pushes them into the stratosphere and they are subjected to ultraviolet radiation, they are converted into chlorine monoxide and bromine monoxide—reactive halogen gases that destroy stratospheric ozone. Although the natural air movements will return reactive halogens to the troposphere, where precipitation will deposit them back on Earth's surface, this will occur only after they have spent years in the stratosphere and the damage to the ozone layer has been done. Although some halons are largely destroyed in the troposphere, others have a very long atmospheric lifetime (i.e., the amount of time required for 60 percent of the substance to be converted or destroyed). Thus, whereas CFC-12 has an atmospheric lifetime of 100 years, methyl bromide (an agricultural fumigant) has a lifetime of well under a year. Given the underlying science, the solution was relatively straightforward: policy should prevent the emission of halogen source gases. With existing CFC concentrations and long atmospheric lifetimes, any regulatory response would not provide benefits for decades to come (Fahey 2003: Q8–12).

The Domestic Response

The movement toward the regulation of ozone-depleting chemicals began in earnest in 1976. Although the exuberance of the first Earth Day in 1970 had diminished, there was nonetheless a supportive climate of public opinion. In one poll conducted in 1976 by the Roper Center, 32 percent of respondents believed that the impact of aerosols on the destruction of the ozone layer constituted a serious problem. By 1980, 62 percent of respondents would characterize ozone depletion as a somewhat serious (25 percent) or very serious (37 percent) problem. Moreover, in 1976 there was clear willingness to translate these concerns into changes in consumer behavior. In a Roper poll, 63 percent reported that they could do without aerosol spray cans with no difficulty, with another 33 percent noting that they could do so with some added inconvenience.

In this favorable climate, the EPA began working to address CFCs within existing regulatory programs. In October 1976 it used its regulatory authority for pesticides to notify producers, formulators, and registrants that CFCs should be discontinued unless essential, warning that a failure to discontinue use of these propellants could lead to the cancellation of product registration (a de facto ban). Moreover, after April 15, 1977, all pesticide products containing CFCs had to be labeled with a consumer warning. The EPA had also created a work group on chlorofluorocarbons (including representatives of the Food and Drug Administration and the Consumer Product Safety Commission) to coordinate the development of new regulations. In December 1976, EPA administrator Russell Train announced: "Our increasing awareness of the environmental effects of chlorofluorocarbons upon the stratosphere has made it clear that we must initiate the regulatory process without further delay." To that end, he announced the EPA's goal, by April 1977, of developing regulations for nonessential aerosol uses of CFCs, as well as the agency's intention to investigate alternatives. The ultimate goal was to issue final regulations, within two years, to reduce halon gas emissions. Moreover, the United States began working on an international response. In October 1976, member nations of the North Atlantic Treaty Organization were asked to work with the United States to develop national regulations and consider an international convention (Train 1976).

In March 1977 the EPA ordered the phaseout of "nonessential" fluorocarbon aerosols in consumer products such as deodorants, hair sprays, and household cleaners. The regulatory response was strengthened in the next several years. A ban on the manufacture of bulk fluorocarbons for aerosols went into effect on October 15, 1978. A ban on the production of spray products using CFC propellants went into effect on December 15, 1978. Finally, the ban on interstate shipment of stocks of these products went into effect on April 15, 1979, although products already in stock could be sold until supplies were depleted (EPA 1978).

The early regulatory response was in some ways surprising. The United States had a heavy commercial stake in ozone-depleting chemicals. DuPont and General Motors developed CFCs in 1928 for refrigeration, and new applications were discovered on a regular basis, driving an ever-expanding market. Indeed, world production doubled every five years up to 1970 (Parson 1991: 2). Within this growth market, the United States was the world's largest single producer of CFCs. In 1975, when the issue first came onto the policy agenda, the United States produced 737 million pounds of CFCs. The EPA estimated that a restriction on nonessential uses of CFCs would reduce production to 47 percent of the 1975 total (Train 1976). Given the growing antiregulatory sentiment of the period, the decision to move aggressively in introducing domestic restrictions was striking, driven by issue salience.

The domestic regulatory response and publicity surrounding the nonessential use of ozone-depleting substances had a powerful impact on the market for CFCs. As Richard Elliot Benedick, US negotiator for the Montreal Protocol, explains: "In 1976–78, US media interest, promoted and nurtured by some scientists, legislators, and environmental organizations, stimulated decisions by millions of individual consumers that led to the collapse of the domestic market for CFC aerosol sprays even before there was any government regulation" (1999). Domestic production fell by some 50 percent, with a 25 percent reduction in global production. As consumers demanded non-CFC aerosols and producers worried about future restrictions, corporations began to fund research on chemical substitutes. DuPont invested some $3–4 million per year into the search for a marketable substitute, a figure that would continue to escalate over the next decade. In 1980, research into substitutes was combined with concerted industry lobbying to stall further regulations. A new 400-member industry group, the Alliance for Responsible CFC Policy, questioned the scientific foundations for CFC regulations and the wisdom of imposing unilateral domestic regulations—claims that found a more responsive audience in the Reagan administration (Parson 1991: 7).

In sum, strong domestic support and regulatory action preceded international action. Although the United States was at the forefront of CFC regulation, it was not alone. Canada, Denmark, Norway, and Sweden joined the effort to ban CFCs as aerosol propellants. The Netherlands mandated warnings on aerosol cans, while West German industry imposed a one-third reduction in CFC aerosols. The European Economic Community required members to freeze production and reduce the use of CFCs as aerosols by 30 percent by 1981. In short, something of an international consensus existed prior to the development of an international agreement on CFCs (Miller and McFarland 1996; Morrisette 1989). Under these conditions, one might correctly view the resulting international convention as a means of coordinating the actions of parties with a domestic commitment and creating mechanisms to pressure nations that had yet to regulate CFCs.

The Path to Montreal

International concern over stratospheric ozone depletion began in 1977, as the United States was beginning to implement its domestic phaseout of nonessential CFCs. A March 1977 meeting in Washington, D.C., sponsored by the United Nations Environment Programme (UNEP) brought together representatives from thirty-three nations. The meeting resulted in the World Plan of Action for the Ozone Layer, an agreement to cooperate in conducting research on the chemistry of ozone depletion and its environmental and health ramifications. It also created the Coordinating Committee on the Ozone Layer to compile research and develop recommendations connected to the world action plan.

In 1981, UNEP created a legal and technical working group to draft a global ozone-protection framework convention. In March 1985, forty-three nations agreed to the Vienna Convention for the Protection of the Ozone Layer. The convention created a framework within which parties could agree to take "appropriate" measures to protect the ozone layer without making firm commitments to specific actions. Most significant, it created both a context for cooperating in research and a process by which the Conference of the Parties could develop and adopt subsequent protocols to create mutually binding obligations, such as those assumed under the Montreal Protocol and its subsequent amendments (DeSombre 1999). Two months after the Vienna Convention was signed, British researchers reported the discovery of holes in the ozone layer over Antarctica. While there remained some uncertainty as to whether the holes were the product of natural processes or ozone-depleting substances, they became a salient symbol of the need to take swift action and propelled rapid action on a protocol.

Industry opposition to further CFC regulation had grown in intensity during the early 1980s. As noted in Chapter 5, the Reagan administration's economic recovery program was premised on the need to eliminate costly regulations. Anne Gorsuch's tenure as EPA administration, when combined with unprecedented budget reductions and OMB-mandated regulatory review, created a powerful roadblock to new regulations. However, following the resignation of Gorsuch and ongoing pressure from Congress and the environmental community, President Reagan worked to reduce the negative publicity surrounding his environmental record by appointing supportive leadership to the EPA, including William Ruckelshaus and Lee Thomas. The change in leadership was combined with a shift in the US position on international controls on CFC production. DuPont played a key role in redirecting the administration's position. It announced in 1986 that marketable substitutes could be available in five years. Seven months after DuPont's 1986 announcement, EPA administrator Lee Thomas declared US support for an immediate freeze in CFC consumption, with phased reductions to a global ban (Parson 1991: 10–11, 15).

As the negotiations over the Montreal Protocol approached, the Reagan administration began to express its skepticism. Richard Elliot Benedick reports that in spring 1987, "a backlash flared up from anti-regulatory ideologues within the Reagan administration, who seemed to have realized belatedly that the negotiations for a strong treaty might actually be on their way to success" (2004: 12). The US position, which had evolved to call for an initial 50 percent reduction, was challenged by Interior Secretary Don Hodel and a special interagency group. Secretary of State George Schultz insisted that the ultimate decision should be made by President Reagan. Opposition to a protocol mounted within the administration, and Secretary Hodel made highly publicized comments that "hats and sunglasses" were a sufficient solution to skin cancer.

In June 1987 the Senate passed a resolution (S. Res. 266), on a vote of 80–2, expressing the sense of the Senate that: "(1) the President should endorse the original position of the United States in ongoing international negotiations to protect the Earth's ozone layer; and (2) the United States should continue to seek an international agreement which will provide for an immediate freeze in the production of the major ozone depleting chemicals at 1986 levels, an automatic reduction of not less than 50 percent in the production of such chemicals, and the virtual elimination of such chemicals." President Reagan responded to the resolution and sent an "eyes-only" personal cable to Benedick, who was attending a fortieth-anniversary celebration of the Marshall Plan in Berlin. In Benedick's words: "Ignoring the advice of some of his closest political friends, the President completely endorsed, point-by-point, the strong position of the State Department and EPA. Is it possibly a coincidence that President Reagan, who later characterized the Montreal Protocol as 'a monumental achievement,' had been operated on in recent months to remove skin cancers from his face? Only his dermatologist may know for certain" (2004: 13).

The Montreal Protocol mandated a staged reduction in the production and consumption of fully halogenated chlorofluorocarbons (CFC-11, CFC-12, CFC-113, CFC-114, and CFC-115), classified as Group I substances. Production was to be frozen at the 1986 level as of 1990, followed by a 20 percent reduction by 1994 and a 50 percent reduction by 1999. The Group II substances included three key halons that were to be frozen at the 1986 levels by 1993. The protocol had important implications for trade, essentially eliminating the incentives for nations to profit from the reduction in production within signatory nations. The bulk importation of controlled substances from nonparty states was prohibited one year after the protocol went into force. Importation of products containing CFCs from nonparty states was banned three years later. The protocol provided developing countries with some special provisions, including a ten-year grace period on the phaseout and a vague guarantee of aid and technology transfers to promote the transition to CFC alternatives.

Entry into force required ratification of eleven signatory nations responsible for at least two-thirds of the global consumption of ozone-depleting substances (using the 1986 baseline). The United States ratified the Montreal Protocol on April 21, 1988; the ratification requirements were met by December 1988 and the protocol entered into force on January 1, 1989. Although developing countries were slow to ratify (for reasons explored in some detail below), after subsequent amendments the number of nations that ratified the protocol increased to 188. The Montreal Protocol has been amended on several occasions, accelerating the phaseout, expanding the protocol to additional substances, and strengthening the incentives for developing countries. These events were driven by new research suggesting that ozone depletion was occurring faster than originally believed.

One should not minimize the role of industry in shaping the US position on the Montreal Protocol and subsequent expansions. As noted earlier, in 1986 DuPont announced that marketable substitutes could be available in five years. Dupont had steadily increased its research into substitutes—research that reached a level of $30 million by 1988—and this research had been sufficiently fruitful as to allow the company to announce its support for a global phaseout and its plans to stop producing CFCs and halons by 1999. By 1988, DuPont announced the development of competitively priced CFC substitutes that could be used in a host of applications (Miller 1989: 547). The successful development of CFC substitutes "changed the market conditions and forced other CFC manufacturers to follow suit" (Haas 1992: 221). From the perspective of DuPont, an expansion of Montreal could be viewed as an opportunity to open new markets for CFC substitutes, thereby replacing a low profit-margin commodity with high-margin patent-protected chemicals.

The London Amendment of 1990. The Montreal Protocol was designed so that the phaseout schedules could be revised in response to periodic scientific and technological assessments. Although much was known about the science of ozone depletion, the underlying research continued to evolve, with important implications for policy. The first set of revisions came in the form of the London Amendment, negotiated at the second Conference of the Parties in June 1990. The protocol was amended to extend regulation to additional fully halogenated chlorofluorocarbons (CFC-13, CFC-111, CFC-112, and CFC-211 through CFC-217). Under the amendment, consumption would have to be reduced to 80 percent of the 1989 baseline by 1993, with a further reduction to 15 percent by 1997 and a phaseout by 2000. In addition, carbon tetrachloride (a substance used as a refrigerant, propellant, and solvent) was placed on a schedule for a complete phaseout by 2000, with an intermediate target of 15 percent of the 1989 baseline by 1995. Methyl chloroform (a solvent and fumigant) was regulated as well, with a complete phaseout scheduled for 2005 and intermediate targets of 70 percent and 30 percent of the 1989 baseline by 1995 and 2000 respectively. Moreover, the trade restrictions were tightened to include a complete ban on imports of controlled substances from, and exports to, states that were not parties to the protocol (UNEP 2000: 326–328).

The amendments also created a new financial mechanism to assist developing countries. By June 1990 it became clear that the participation by developing countries would pose a problem (less than a third had signed the protocol, including three of the thirteen nations that would soon become the greatest consumers of CFCs). China and India threatened to reject the protocol unless they were compensated monetarily. Wealthy nations, in turn, realized that the long-term success was contingent on the participation of developing countries (Connolly and Keohane 1996). With the London Amendment, industrialized nations decided to create a financial mechanism, a large multilateral fund to assist developing countries in meeting their compliance costs. The assistance would come in addition to other financial transfers currently in place rather than as a substitute. Recipients would receive aid only if they assumed phaseout obligations with performance monitoring. The new fund, with an initial budget of some $113 million, increased incentives for participation. Over the course of the next three years, fifty additional developing countries—including the largest prospective CFC consumers—ratified the protocol (see Mitchell and Keilbach 2001). By the end of 2003, contributions to the fund had totaled some $1.7 billion (http://www.unmfs.org/general.htm).

The Copenhagen Amendment of 1992 and beyond. Under the Clean Air Act amendments of 1990 (§ 604), the EPA was authorized to impose limits on the production and consumption of ozone-depleting substances through the use of allowance caps and tradable permits. The timetables for reductions and phaseout were in keeping with those specified under the Montreal Protocol. However, in February 1992 the United States announced that, in response to new scientific research, it would unilaterally accelerate the timetable for CFCs, halons, carbon tetrachloride, and methyl chloroform, with a complete phaseout on December 31, 1995. In addition, it would review new evidence on the need to control use of methyl bromide. The United States was not alone in moving beyond the protocol. Both Germany and Switzerland had announced bans on CFCs and other ozone-depleting substances by the end of 1995.

In November 1992, at the fourth Conference of the Parties in

Copenhagen, EPA administrator William K. Reilly endorsed new amendments to the Montreal Protocol, noting: "we must accelerate the phaseout of CFCs, halons, carbon tetrachloride, and methyl chloroform. The difference between phaseout at current treaty requirements and an acceleration as announced for the United States by President Bush earlier this year is a potential reduction of one million cancers and 10,000 deaths through the year 2075 in the United States." He went on to note that "the United States has championed the need for decisive action to control methyl bromide," arguing that "the environmental threat from this chemical cannot be denied. . . . We must act now to reduce its use and to phase out its production and consumption by the year 2000" (Reilly 1992). The parties agreed to an accelerated timetable for the phaseout of chlorofluorocarbons, carbon tetrachloride, and methyl chloroform, from 2000 to the end of 1995. The timetable for the phaseout of halons was accelerated to the end of 1993. The amendment introduced control measures for HCFCs, which had been used as substitutes for CFCs as refrigerants and aerosols. Although HCFCs have a shorter atmospheric lifetime and are thus less of a concern than CFCs, they are still a source of regulatory concern. Under the Copenhagen Amendment, consumption of HCFCs was frozen at the 1989 baseline (plus 3.1 percent of the 1989 consumption) in 1996, with reductions to 65 percent by 2004, 35 percent by 2010, 10 percent by 2015, and 0.5 percent by 2020, with a complete phaseout by 2030. The amendment further introduced control measures for both production and consumption for two new groups of substances, hydrobromofluorocarbons, scheduled for a complete phaseout by 1996, and methyl bromide, which was to be frozen at 1991 levels by 1995 (UNEP 2000: 334–342).

The Montreal Amendment, negotiated at the ninth Conference of the Parties in September 1997, was the only amendment that did not extend the protocol to new substances or accelerate timetables. Rather it mandated that parties create systems for licensing the import and export of "new, used, recycled and reclaimed controlled substances." In contrast, the Beijing Amendment, negotiated at the eleventh Conference of the Parties, in 1999, extended the Montreal Protocol to cover bromochloromethane, a feedstock in the manufacture of biocides. Under the Beijing Amendment, consumption and production of bromochloromethane was banned as of January 1, 2002. In addition, the timetable for HCFCs and baseline calculations were modified. Most important, the imports of HCFCs from, and exports to, states that are not parties to the protocol were banned as of January 1, 2004 (UNEP 2000: 343–348).

The Performance and Lessons of the Montreal Protocol
The Montreal Protocol has been celebrated as the single clearest example of a successful global environmental policy. As UN Secretary-General Kofi

Annan noted in a 2004 address, the Montreal Protocol was a "remarkable success." He explained: "When the Montreal Protocol on Substances that Deplete the Ozone Layer was signed in Montreal 17 years ago, it was not at all clear that it would be possible to phase out ozone-depleting substances within the short period envisaged by the agreement. Today, more than 90 per cent of the global production and consumption of those substances has indeed been phased out. Moreover, consistent progress is being made towards reducing and eliminating any remaining production and consumption." Annan went on to note that the success of the protocol should be an inspiration to "the parties to other multilateral environmental agreements" (Annan 2004). Perhaps. Before we consider the lessons of the Montreal Protocol, let us consider its performance.

As noted previously, ozone-depleting substances have a long atmospheric life. Some CFCs (e.g., CFC-12) will contribute to a reduction of ozone for up to a century. As a result, the recovery of the ozone layer will lag behind policy interventions. Nonetheless, progress to date has been impressive. As the Scientific Assessment Panel of the Montreal Protocol noted in its 2002 assessment of ozone depletion:

> Global observations show that the total combined effective abundances of anthropogenic chlorine-containing and bromine-containing ozone-depleting gases in the lower atmosphere (troposphere) peaked in the 1992–1994 time period and are continuing to decline. Furthermore, observations indicate that the stratospheric abundances of ozone-depleting gases are now at or near a peak. Thereafter, stratospheric ozone should increase, all other influences assumed constant, but ozone variability will make detection of the onset of the long-term recovery difficult. For example, based on assumed compliance with the amended and adjusted Protocol by all nations, the Antarctic ozone "hole," which was first discerned in the early 1980s, is predicted to disappear by the middle of this century—again with all other influences assumed constant. (UNEP and WMO 2002: 18)

Despite this positive evaluation, greater results will not be forthcoming for some time: "The ozone layer will remain particularly vulnerable during the next decade or so, even with full compliance. With the atmospheric abundances of ozone-depleting substances being near their highest, the human-influenced perturbations will be at or near their largest" (UNEP and WMO 2002: 18). Indeed, the best-case scenario—that is, if there is continued compliance with the Montreal Protocol—is a return to pre-1980 ozone conditions by 2050 (see Levinson and Waple 2004; DeSombre 2004). How does one explain the success of the Montreal Protocol? What are the lessons for future international environmental agreements?

Peter M. Haas argues that the strong regulatory regime created under the Montreal Protocol is difficult to understand through the lens of neorealism. It "ran contrary to U.S. domestic particularistic interests, which opposed regulation, and also differed from a contemporary assessment of the aggregate national interest." Rather than focusing narrowly on national interest, one must turn attention to the ecological "epistemic community," "a knowledge-based network of specialists who shared belief in cause-and-effect relations, validity tests, and underlying principled values and pursued common goals." This community united atmospheric scientists and officials from government agencies in multiple nations and in UNEP. Members of the community shared information and developed an intellectual consensus regarding the nature of the ozone depletion and the most efficacious responses. Moreover, Haas argues, "the first countries to actively encourage global controls were those in which the epistemic community and the tradition of proenvironment sentiment were the strongest: the United States, Canada, Finland, Norway, and Sweden" (Haas 1992: 188, 187, 215).

Epistemic communities are particularly well developed in the area of environmental protection and may be effective in framing prevailing understandings of causality and feasible policy responses and promoting policy diffusion; they may shape actors' understanding of their own self-interest (see Hasenclever, Mayer, and Rittberger 1996: 206–210; Jervis 1999). Yet it is unclear that winning the argument is sufficient. The existence of epistemic communities may be important only when nations perceive that they are vulnerable to environmental problems and their capacity to manage the problems could be positively affected by international cooperation (Sprinz and Vaahtoranta 1994: 80). If this is true, then ideas may be best conceived as intervening variables (i.e., allowing actors to understand how best to pursue their self-interest given the problem at hand and the capabilities of existing and potential international structures).

Detlef Sprinz and Tapani Vaahtoranta, for example, seek to understand the position adopted by nations with respect to the Montreal Protocol. They argue that one can predict a nation's behavior by considering two dimensions: ecological vulnerability and abatement costs. If a nation has a high level of vulnerability to environmental problems, it is far more likely to favor strict regulations. There are two reasons why a vulnerable nation might advocate international regulations: "unilateral abatement activities may be insufficient to substantively improve the state of its environment," and "it would like to avoid putting its polluting industries at a comparative disadvantage in international markets" (1994: 79). Both reasons were clearly operative in the case of the Montreal Protocol. Yet the greater the abatement costs, the more hesitant countries should be to promote international regulations. This argument would lead one to predict that while the United States had high levels of ecological vulnerability (as reflected by high levels of skin cancer), it would not aggressively promote international regulation due to its heavy commercial stakes in CFCs. While this prediction would hold true up into the mid-1980s, the United States rapidly changed its position in 1986–1987, when it began to promote a comprehensive ban. The explanation for the shift in the US position is likely attributed to the development of commercial substitutes. Because the costs of abatement changed, the United States changed its calculation of the extent to which its interests could be furthered by a strong international regime.

The case of the Montreal Protocol reveals several important lessons. First, the clarity of the problem and the popular salience almost guaranteed that ozone depletion would move onto the policy agenda. The popular concern over the potential health risks—in particular, the heightened risk of skin cancer—created a demand for a policy response. The EPA responded by initiating regulatory controls of ozone-depleting substances—a decision that was reinforced by new statutory authorization from Congress. The regulation of ozone-depleting substances did not require the creation of new regulatory instruments or capacities. Second, one cannot deny the importance of economic incentives in the story. Popular concerns found a clear expression in patterns of consumer behavior. The growing demand for non-CFC aerosol sprays created powerful market forces for a corporate response. Moreover, the seeming inevitability of regulations on CFCs and other ozone-depleting substances led DuPont and other producers to invest heavily in the development of substitutes. Once substitutes were discovered, international action could create new markets for patented chemicals. Thus, while the US chemical industry was initially resistant to new regulations and organized to challenge the foundations of policy, new market opportunities eroded this resistance and opened the door to more vigorous regulator efforts—a rarity in the Reagan-Bush era.

The role of incentives is evident in the very design of the protocol and its use of trade restrictions as a policy tool. By converting the parties to the Montreal Protocol into a de facto trade cartel, the new regime eliminated the incentives for noncompliance. States that refused to ratify the protocol would not be able to trade controlled substances with member nations. International markets were used quite effectively as a means of reinforcing the goals of policy. The economic incentives for regulation remained strong under the Montreal Protocol. As Bruce Yandle notes: "In 1988, when the EPA announced the CFC restriction, the agency indicated that the phasedown would generate windfall profits of $1.8 billion to $7.2 billion by the end of the century for American producers of CFCs" under the assumption that legitimate producers would dominate the market for CFCs and, ultimately, their substitutes. Although the protocol created a black market for CFCs, "the promise of phase-down profits must have comforted major CFC producers and provided powerful incentives for the world's major CFC substitute producers to monitor government enforcement of the CFC phaseout" (1999: 38).

Thus, before attention turned to the negotiation of specific protocols, the United States and other key nations had already made a domestic commitment employing its domestic regulatory structures. The commitment was bolstered by public opinion and the potential for new economic opportunities in the market for CFC substitutes. Given the nature of the problem, however, these commitments would not have a significant impact on the underlying problem unless there were an international component. The continued production and consumption of ozone-depleting substances outside nations that had made a domestic commitment would undercut these investments. Thus there was a strong demand for a protocol and ongoing pressure for expansion and an acceleration. As Nigel Purvis (2003) notes, the connection between domestic commitments and international agreements is vitally important: "Successful international agreements (those that are ratified widely and influence behavior) . . . usually mirror the existing domestic values and interests of the great powers. Efforts to use international agreements to force the great powers to act against their perceived self-interests and priorities rarely succeed. Far more successful are efforts to internationalize approaches already adopted by the most influential nations, such as the Montreal Protocol."

■ Regulating Climate Change: The Kyoto Protocol

Global climate change has been at the center of environmental policy debates for several decades, giving rise to an ambitious international regulatory initiative, the Kyoto Protocol. Many advocates of the Kyoto Protocol were emboldened by the success of the Montreal Protocol. If nations could unite to preserve the ozone layer, certainly they could cooperate to preserve the global climate. After all, climate change constitutes a far more critical threat. Although the case of ozone depletion offers important lessons, they do not support the contention that all global environmental problems are created equal.

Scientific Complexity and Problem Definition

Although observations of climate change date back for a century, the issue gained salience in the 1980s, the warmest decade on record thus far. Droughts and forest fires in 1988 were linked to global warming in cover stories of both *Time* and *Newsweek*. The growing media coverage stimulated calls for action and Senate hearings on controlling carbon emissions (Schneider 1989). In this supportive environment, the World Meteorological Organization (WMO) and UNEP created the Intergovernmental Panel on Climate Change (IPCC) in 1988 "to assess, on a comprehensive, objective, open and transparent basis, the scientific, technical and socio-economic information on climate change that is available around the world in peer-reviewed literature, journals, books and, where appropriately documented, in industry literature and traditional practices" (IPPC 2003: 3). The IPCC is organized into working groups on science, impact and adaptation, and mitigation. In addition, the IPCC has established a task force on national greenhouse gas inventories. The panel publishes a host of technical papers and, periodically, a multivolume assessment report synthesizing research on science, adaptation, and mitigation.

At first glance, the science of climate change would appear to be relatively simple. Atmospheric concentrations of greenhouse gases (carbon dioxide, methane and nitrous oxide, CFC-12, HCFC-22, perfluoromethane, and sulfur hexafluoride) have grown significantly over the course of recent Earth history. Most of these changes can be attributed to human activities, including fossil fuel combustion and changes in land use (e.g., deforestation, commercial agriculture). Although several greenhouse gases have long atmospheric lifetimes and great global-warming potential, carbon dioxide receives the greatest attention in discussions of climate change, due to its heavy concentrations. Although detailed records of carbon dioxide levels have been compiled only since 1957, air bubbles trapped in ice core samples from Greenland and Antarctica have allowed scientists to conclude with some certainty that carbon dioxide concentrations have grown rapidly over the course of the past century. Moreover, these concentrations have altered the balance between radiation coming into the atmosphere and radiation escaping the atmosphere ("radiative forcing"). As a result, global mean surface air temperature has increased since the late nineteenth century (see Vitousek 1994).

While there is a strong consensus that growing greenhouse gas concentrations have contributed to an increase in global mean surface temperature, things become far more uncertain when attempting to predict the future. The emissions of key greenhouse gases in the next century will reflect a number of factors, including population growth, rates of economic growth, patterns of land use and energy consumption, and decisions regarding mitigation. Moreover, there remain important questions about how climate systems will respond to changes in temperature, precipitation, and ocean salinity. Competing assumptions regarding the various key variables can yield very different estimates of future climate change, which in turn affect estimates of economic impacts, the distribution of costs and benefits, and the financial burdens of mitigation and adaptation. Analysts are forced to speak probabilistically of outcomes under multiple competing scenarios.

Consider the predictions issued by the IPCC. Its first assessment report, in 1990, concluded that the next century could bring an increase in global mean temperature of between 1–5 degrees Celsius (1.8–9.0 degrees Fahrenheit), depending on the emissions scenarios (IPCC 1990). By its second assessment report, in 1995, the IPCC had revised its initial projection to an increase of 1–3 degrees Celsius by 2100, with the best estimate being a 2-degree increase in global mean surface air temperature, approximately one-third lower than the best estimate made five years earlier (IPCC 1995: 22). Difficulties stemmed from the variety of scenarios considered by the IPCC, with world population estimates for 2100 ranging from 6.4 billion to 17.6 billion and different estimates of economic growth rates and energy supplies. Moreover, there was a significant amount of scientific uncertainty. The IPCC noted that "many factors currently limit our ability to project and detect future climate change," including "estimation of future emissions and biogeochemical cycling (including sources and sinks) of greenhouse gases" and the "representation of climate processes in models." Furthermore, "future unexpected, large and rapid climate system changes (as have occurred in the past) are, by their nature, difficult to predict. This implies that future climate changes may also involve 'surprises'" (1995: 24).

Given the range of estimates regarding climate change, the predictions of effects were somewhat amorphous. For example, sea levels were expected to rise by 0.15–0.95 meters, although the reliability of the predictions was admittedly low (IPCC 1995: 27). Moreover, the IPCC concluded that climate change would carry a combination of adverse and positive effects that would vary by region and core assumptions. It noted that "policymakers are faced with responding to the risks posed by anthropogenic emissions of greenhouse gases in the face of significant scientific uncertainties." Nonetheless, the uncertainties should be viewed "in the context of information indicating that climate induced environmental changes cannot be reversed quickly, if at all, due to the long time-scales associated with the climate system." Moreover, "decisions taken during the next few years may limit the range of possible policy options in the future because high near-term emissions would require deeper reductions in the future to meet any given target concentration." Delayed action "might reduce the overall costs of mitigation because of potential technological advances but could increase both the rate and the eventual magnitude of climate change, hence the adaptation and damage costs" (1995: 28). By 2001, things had only become more complex. The number of competing scenarios increased to thirty-five, generating a wider range of predicted increases in the global mean temperature (1.4–5.8 degrees Celsius over the period 1990–2100). Sea levels were now projected to rise by 0.09–0.88 meters over the same period, a reduction from the rise of 0.13–0.94 meters predicted in the second assessment (IPCC 2001: 13, 18).

Scientists and social scientists involved in the debates over climate change have been quite frank in their acknowledgment of the uncertainties surrounding the issue. As David G. Victor notes:

> We find it striking that more than two decades of intense research, reflect-
> ing a total investment of perhaps as much as $30 billion worldwide, has
> actually expanded the estimated change in temperature. That investment
> has not narrowed any key estimates of other changes in climate, such as
> the frequency and intensity of storms or the risks of drought. As scientists
> have learned more about the climate system, they have uncovered a vast
> field of unturned stones. (2004: 11)

Given the need to generate long-range forecasts on the basis of dozens of
scenarios with different assumptions regarding key variables, researchers do
not have the luxury of presenting policymakers with simple predictions.
Nonetheless, the kinds of predictions that can be made with a fair amount of
confidence provide a source of genuine concern. One of the consistent mes-
sages is that due to the long atmospheric lifetimes of key greenhouse gases
and the potential for catastrophic events, policymakers do not have the luxury of adopting a "wait and see" attitude.

Political Uncertainty and Public Opinion

While scientists and social scientists may be used to working with uncertainty and probabilistic statements, elected officials crave certainty. Given
the levels of scientific uncertainty, elected officials may rationally avoid
commitments that impose costs on constituents. Critics of policy may magnify uncertainties by arguing that "junk science" is being used to justify
sumptuous research grants and to promote vast forays into state planning.
As two critics note: "A call for doing something about the greenhouse effect
is nothing less then a call for a permanent change in the economic infrastructure of the world. . . . The evidence . . . is ludicrously small given the
attention and money being lavished on the issue. One thing is clear, however: the prevention of any possible greenhouse effect will require a degree of
bureaucratic control over economic affairs previously unknown in the
West" (Bolch and Lyons 1993: 81).

The effects of scientific uncertainty are combined with an additional
problem: global climate change is not a pure "public bad," producing only
socially undesirable results. It will yield a combination of costs and benefits
that will be unequally distributed across the world. While rising sea levels
may be devastating for some nations, others will find adaptation unproblematic and may benefit from extended growing seasons, lower food costs,
and reduced winter heating bills. If nations behave as realists expect—striv-
ing to maximize their power in an anarchic environment—one should not
expect them to incur costs to prevent negative outcomes on distant shores
and for future generations.

There is little question that global climate change has attracted a high
level of media coverage. One indicator of media coverage is a simple count
of newspaper stories with the terms "global warming" or "global climate

change" in the title or lead paragraph. A Lexis-Nexus search of articles in the *New York Times,* the *Washington Post,* and *USA Today* revealed that coverage has fluctuated significantly since the IPCC was created in 1988, peaking in 1992, 1997, and 2001 (see Figure 12.1). The largest number of stories occurred in 2001, the year President George W. Bush announced the US withdrawal from Kyoto. In 2001, 736 stories appeared in these three papers, with 408 stories in the *New York Times* alone. To place these figures in context, in 2001 the *New York Times* ran 15 stories on the Clean Air Act, 30 stories on acid rain, and 21 stories on the changes in the arsenic rule. Indeed, it ran more stories on global climate change than on social security (311), Medicare (380), or Iraq (378).

Given the high levels of media coverage, how was the issue understood by the public? A Gallup poll conducted in March 2001, the peak of media coverage, revealed that only 31 percent of participants believed that global warming would pose a "serious threat" within their lifetimes; 66 percent believed it would not. A poll conducted in April 2001 by the *Los Angeles Times* asked participants to identify the most important problem facing the country. Only 1 percent of the participants listed global warming as their first response. Two polls questioned participants about the US decision to withdraw from the Kyoto Protocol. A Gallup poll conducted in July 2001 revealed that 32 percent approved of the decision, 51 percent disapproved, and 17 percent had no opinion. In a Harris poll conducted a month later,

Figure 12.1 Media Coverage of Global Climate Change, 1988–2004

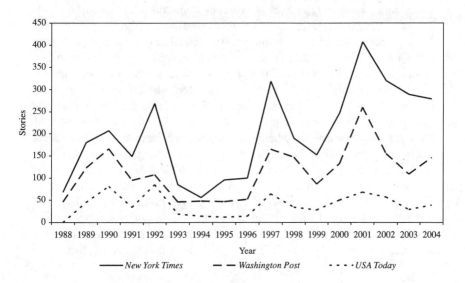

those who said that they had "seen, heard, or read" about the global-warming agreements were asked: "The United States government says that it cannot accept the Kyoto and Bonn agreements to limit emissions of greenhouse gases because they are not based on sound research and would damage the American economy. Do you think the American position is right or wrong?" The poll suggested some shifts in opinion: 42 percent believed the position was right, 46 percent believed it was wrong, and 11 percent were not sure or refused to answer.

According to a Harris poll of September 2002, 74 percent of participants believed "the theory that increased carbon dioxide and other gases released into the atmosphere will, if unchecked, lead to global warming and an increase in average temperatures." Nonetheless, in a Gallup poll conducted in March 2002, participants were perfectly divided over whether news accounts were generally exaggerated (31 percent), generally correct (32 percent), or generally underestimated (32 percent). This ambiguity over the seriousness of the problem may contribute to a general unwillingness to incur costs. In a March 2001 poll conducted by *Time* and CNN, participants were asked about their willingness to support "tough government actions to help reduce global warming" under different scenarios. If the result would be an increase in unemployment, 38 percent would be willing to support the policy, 55 percent would not. If the result would be a mild increase in inflation, 54 percent would support the policy, 39 percent would not. If the policy would force an increase in utility bills, 47 percent would support the policy, 49 percent would not. The poll also asked participants whether they would be willing to pay an extra 25 cents per gallon to reduce pollution and global warming. Respondents were almost equally divided (48 percent would accept an increase in gas prices, 49 percent would not). Of those who would accept a 25-cent increase, only 44 percent would be willing to pay an extra 50 cents per gallon. A comparable question asked two and a half years later in a CBS poll revealed that 18 percent would pay 50 cents extra, 28 percent would pay only 25 cents extra, and 51 percent would reject any increases.

Although opinion polls can be inconsistent and difficult to interpret, one can arrive at four basic conclusions. First, a large majority recognized that global warming was occurring as a result of human activities. Second, there was no consensus on whether the severity of the issue was being accurately portrayed. Third, there was little support for the proposition that global climate change would pose a serious threat to the American way of life in the near term (i.e., within this generation). Fourth, there was little indication of a willingness to incur personal costs (e.g., gas taxes, higher utility bills, unemployment) to reduce global warming. While policy advocates may make the argument that global climate change constitutes a profound problem demanding a significant regulatory investment, the argument has proven unpersuasive for much of the population. This, in turn, has important ramifications for elected officials, a point we shall return to shortly.

The Path to Kyoto

As with the case of ozone depletion, the path to a protocol began with a framework convention. With great fanfare, the United States and a number of other nations signed the United Nations Framework Convention on Climate Change at the 1992 Earth Summit, in Rio de Janeiro, Brazil. Within a year, 166 nations had signed the convention. Nations agreed to collect and share information, develop domestic mitigation programs, and meet via the Conference of the Parties to coordinate efforts and develop protocols. Although the United States signed the convention and participated actively in the Conference of the Parties, it did nothing to develop domestic mitigation programs, excepting some voluntary REGO initiatives. The chief greenhouse gas, carbon dioxide, remained free of mandatory controls.

After several years of intense discussions, the third Conference of the Parties adopted the Kyoto Protocol on December 11, 1997. The Kyoto Protocol required significant reductions in greenhouse gas emissions, with the goal of stabilizing atmospheric concentrations. Industrialized countries (so-called Annex I countries) were assigned primary responsibility for reductions in greenhouse gas emissions. Nations were assigned binding emissions targets (using a 1990 baseline), with the requirement of achieving the reductions by 2008–2012. Emission levels would be averaged over this five-year "budget period." The United States agreed to 7 percent reductions, the European Union to 8 percent reductions, and Japan to 6 percent reductions. Some nations (New Zealand, the Russian Federation, and Ukraine) were required to maintain the 1990 baseline, whereas others (Norway, Australia, and Iceland) were allowed to increase emissions over the baseline from 1–10 percent. Developing nations, in contrast, were under no obligations.

When the protocol was drafted in 1997, most Annex I nations were already producing emissions well above the 1990 baseline. Thus, many nations were agreeing to massive greenhouse gas reductions on a timetable that became increasingly compressed as ratification lagged. Given the high costs of meeting the Kyoto obligations, the protocol established additional mechanisms to permit more cost-effective reductions. Under pressure from the United States, the Kyoto Protocol allowed for emissions permits, trading, and credit for investments in other Annex I countries. Since targets are concerned with net emissions levels, moreover, nations could combine emissions reductions with the creation of new carbon sinks (e.g., through afforestation or reforestation). Finally, Kyoto established a "clean development mechanism" whereby Annex I nations could claim credit for investments in developing countries that had reduced greenhouse gas emissions. Such investments could simultaneously help stabilize aggregate emissions and subsidize the transfer of clean technologies to less developed countries (see Molitor 2000).

Although Kyoto provided the broad outlines of a global system for regulating greenhouse gas emissions, most critical issues regarding implementation and enforcement were left to be determined by the Conference of the Parties. Although the system would rely on self-reporting, there was nothing of substance in the protocol about verification. Although the protocol authorized a system of emissions trading, it was left to the Conference of the Parties to "define the relevant principles, modalities, rules and guidelines, in particular for verification, reporting and accountability for emissions trading" (Article 17). With respect to enforcement, it was once again left to the Conference of the Parties to "approve appropriate and effective procedures and mechanisms to determine and to address cases of non-compliance with the provisions of this Protocol, including through the development of an indicative list of consequences, taking into account the cause, type, degree and frequency of non-compliance" (Article 18). The failure to develop the implementation structure was a profound source of uncertainty for Annex I countries. As Scott Barrett noted: "the negotiators of this agreement were preoccupied with negotiating targets and timetables rather than enforcement or participation mechanisms. This was a mistake. If effective enforcement mechanisms are omitted, and cannot be included subsequently, then the targets and timetables so painstakingly negotiated may not be met" (1999: 137).

Ratification, Withdrawal, Resurrection

To enter into force, the Kyoto Protocol required the ratification of at least fifty-five parties to the convention, including Annex I parties, that accounted for at least 55 percent of the total carbon dioxide emissions for 1990. Although the protocol was met with fanfare, ratification was slow to come. When President Clinton signed the protocol in 1998, he could have no illusions about ratification. In July 1997 the Senate passed (95–0) the Byrd-Hagel Resolution (S. Res. 98), informing the president that

> it is the sense of the Senate that:
> (1) the United States should not be a signatory to any protocol to, or other agreement regarding, the United Nations Framework Convention on Climate Change of 1992, at negotiations in Kyoto in December 1997, or thereafter, which would—
>   (A) mandate new commitments to limit or reduce greenhouse gas emissions for the Annex I Parties, unless the protocol or other agreement also mandates new specific scheduled commitments to limit or reduce greenhouse gas emissions for Developing Country Parties within the same compliance period, or
>   (B) would result in serious harm to the economy of the United States; and

(2) any such protocol or other agreement which would require the advice and consent of the Senate to ratification should be accompanied by a detailed explanation of any legislation or regulatory actions that may be required to implement the protocol or other agreement and should also be accompanied by an analysis of the detailed financial costs and other impacts on the economy of the United States which would be incurred by the implementation of the protocol or other agreement. (Report no. 105-54)

The concerns presented by the Senate deserve some consideration. One of the key areas of dissatisfaction with the protocol was the lack of obligations placed on developing countries. Although current greenhouse gas concentrations are largely a product of wealthy nations, a number of developing countries are experiencing rapid growth, which will bring dramatic increases in their emissions. China, for example, is rapidly moving to the forefront and will surpass the United States as the world's largest greenhouse gas producer by 2015 (Meyerson 1998: 126). Without participation by developing countries, there will be net increases in greenhouse gas concentrations even under Kyoto. Yet developing countries do not prioritize mitigation, given the premium placed on growth as a solution to poverty (see Buchner and Galeotti 2004). The Senate was concerned, moreover, that in its present form, Kyoto would place US businesses at a competitive disadvantage and create new incentives for corporations to move their production offshore to nations that were not bound by the provisions of the protocol (a problem referred to as "emissions leakage").

With lower levels of national income, more pressing concerns (e.g., poverty, infant mortality), and demands for equity, it was difficult to convince developing countries that they should accept greenhouse gas restrictions. Certainly, they might be convinced to participate if given generous emission caps with a surplus of emission credits. But this would be a pyrrhic victory, insofar as the surplus credits would undermine the integrity of Kyoto by alleviating the need for genuine reductions in Annex I nations. Under such conditions, Kyoto might succeed more as a program to secure large bilateral wealth transfers than as a response to global climate change. Indeed, Russian participation was secured, in part, by adopting a 1990 baseline that, in the wake of the collapse of the Soviet Union, provided it with potentially massive windfall profits without the need to make any alterations in emissions levels (Victor 2004: 58–59).

Consider the issue of cost. A 1998 study conducted by the Department of Energy provided a useful comparison of competing estimates of the costs of reducing emissions to the Kyoto target of 7 percent below the 1990 baseline. In the worst-case scenario (carbon costs of $348 per metric ton and without the use of trading, sinks, offsets, and the clean development mechanism), Kyoto would impose an annual cost of $437 billion (1996 dollars) with reduction in GDP of 4.2 percent below projections. Depending on assumptions regarding carbon costs, other models placed 2010 costs at between $102 billion and $105 billion (1996 dollars). If one included the use of trading, sinks, offsets, and the clean development mechanism, the 2010 costs fell dramatically, ranging from $56 billion to $133 billion per year (1996 dollars). Depending on the fiscal policy responses, the Department of Energy concluded that the total annual cost to the economy in 2008–2012 would fall within the range of $77 billion to $283 billion (1992 dollars). The dramatic differences in estimated impacts reflect differences in underlying assumptions and the uncertainty inherent in arriving at such calculations (Department of Energy 1998: 122, 140–141). Whether impacts of this magnitude constitute "serious harm to the economy" is a judgment call for elected officials.

William D. Nordhaus and Joseph G. Boyer presented a disconcerting estimate of costs in an study aptly titled "Requiem for Kyoto." Using an integrated-assessment model of the global economy and global warming, the authors concluded that the net global cost of the Kyoto Protocol is $716 billion in present value. Moreover, the United States would bear almost two-thirds of these costs. Although one might argue that the costs would be justified by the benefits, the authors arrived at a very different conclusion: regardless of the specific components of Kyoto, "the different policies reduce damages by only a modest amount. Indeed, one of the surprises is how little the policies affect the damages from global warming. The reasons are that, because there is so much inertia in the climate system and because the Protocol does not limit the emissions of developing countries, the Kyoto Protocol reduces the global temperature increase by only a fraction of a degree over the next century" (1999: 34). Indeed, given the magnitude of the costs and the limited impact of the Kyoto targets on global mean temperature, the benefit-cost ratio of the protocol was calculated to be one to seven.

Although some imagined that the Senate resolution would provide the Clinton administration with greater leverage in subsequent negotiations, the Senate sent a much clearer message: without significant changes, there would be no possibility of winning the two-thirds majority necessary for treaty ratification (Dewar 1997). In the end, President Clinton clearly understood this reality and never submitted the Kyoto Protocol for ratification. Because the United States was the largest producer of greenhouse gases, its behavior was closely monitored by other industrial countries. As the Clinton presidency drew to a close, only twenty-nine nations had ratified the protocol—a list devoid of Annex I nations.

As noted in Chapter 6, in March 2001 the newly inaugurated President George W. Bush announced his rejection of the Kyoto Protocol, citing scientific uncertainty and reiterating the core concerns of the Byrd-Hagel Resolution. Although the decision stimulated a chorus of denunciations from European officials, as of that date Romania was the only Annex I country to have ratified the protocol. With the ratification by a nation responsible for 1.2 percent of world emissions and the withdrawal of a nation responsible for some 25 percent of global greenhouse gases, many believed that Kyoto was dead. Yet in the years following Bush's announcement, Annex I countries ratified the protocol in increasing numbers. Many wondered whether these ratifications were executed in the expectation that the ratification threshold would not be met. However, in November 2004, Russia ratified Kyoto, thereby pushing the protocol over the threshold necessary for it to enter into force.

The Prospects for Kyoto

The prospects for the Kyoto Protocol remain uncertain. The protocol passed the ratification threshold in 2004 and entered into force less than four years before the beginning of the budget period. Although Russia ratified in the expectation of enjoying a $100 billion credit windfall, the value of these credits may be less than one expected. The United States, long projected to be the primary source of demand in the emissions trading system, is not participating in Kyoto, and members of the European Union have been busy developing an internal emissions trading system that may make it difficult for Russia to extract profits. Regardless, there are significant questions about whether Russia has the institutional capacity to monitor and enforce domestic regulations.

Among Annex I countries, greenhouse gas emissions fell 6.3 percent between 1990 and 2002. However, these changes were driven largely by the massive economic dislocations in economies in transition (former Soviet-bloc nations), which experienced a 39.8 percent reduction in emissions. Excluding the economies in transition, Annex I countries *increased* their emissions by 8.4 percent. Among ratifying nations, Austria, Finland, Italy, and Norway increased greenhouse gas emissions between 5 percent and 10 percent, whereas Canada, Spain, Greece, Ireland, Japan, New Zealand, and Portugal experienced increases of over 10 percent (a distinction shared by the United States and Australia, neither of which ratified the protocol). The United Kingdom and Germany realized significant reductions, of 14.5 percent and 18.5 percent respectively (United Nations Framework Convention on Climate Change 2004: 9, 12). In both cases, reductions were the product of special circumstances, including the restructuring of the UK electricity sector (which resulted in reduced reliance on coal relative to natural gas and nuclear energy) and the collapse of the East German economy following German reunification.

The Kyoto Protocol faces great challenges. There is little probability that most major Annex I countries will be successful in meeting their Kyoto obligations. The enforcement regime has yet to be tested and may not be sufficient to force compliance. More important, if global climate change is to be arrested, the protocol will demand both agreements on more stringent emission targets and the extension of emission controls to developing countries. The broadening of the protocol, in turn, may prove impossible without US participation. With respect to the United States, Kyoto may be important insofar as it focused greater domestic attention on regulating carbon dioxide emissions. While the Bush administration promised a host of voluntary reduction programs and technological innovations to reduce greenhouse gas intensity, several states introduced renewable energy portfolio standards designed to force a reduction in greenhouse gas emissions. Regional credit markets are emerging in the United States; member states of the European Union have gone even further in creating regional markets. It is conceivable that these initiatives, when taken as a whole, may produce a foundation for future cooperation, opening the door to a "bottom-up" pattern of development supporting a post-Kyoto protocol that corrects some of the problems inherent in its predecessor.

■ Conclusion

The central lesson of the Montreal Protocol is a simple one. Domestic regulatory commitments created a firm foundation for international commitments. The scientific case was clear and unambiguous; the consequences of ozone depletion had an immediate impact on citizens' lives and thus became politically salient, creating a demand for domestic regulations. In essence, there was a "bottom-up" process whereby domestic commitments preceded and created a foundation for international action. Rather than making decisions in an international context and then attempting to impose commitments on reluctant participants, negotiators were able to construct the ozone regime on existing national commitments and employ existing administrative capacities. Rather than being *the* solution, the international component was part of a larger system that largely preceded the efforts to design an international regulatory system.

The Kyoto Protocol lacked many of these features. The science of climate change was far more complex, as researchers sought to generate long-term projections from the interaction of competing demographic, economic, and developmental trends. Due to a combination of complexity, uncertainty, and consequences that would occur in the distant future, the issue failed to generate much salience on the part of the public. There were no concerted efforts to extend air pollution regulations to address the chief greenhouse gases. The Kyoto Protocol thus took the form of a "top-down" initiative. Advocates might have hoped that an international protocol could force the necessary changes in public opinion and domestic policy. But in the end, such changes were not forthcoming.

Sustainable Development: Managing the Unmanageable

The Montreal and Kyoto Protocols were ambitious global regulatory efforts. In each case, parties had to commit to significant changes in behavior that would impose immediate adjustment costs. The challenges associated with ozone depletion and climate change are seemingly modest when compared with those associated with sustainable development. Whereas the former focused on controlling the emissions of specific substances and were guided by distinct scientific research programs, sustainable development is concerned with global patterns of production and distribution and engages the broader issues of economics, demographics, equity, and social justice. Definitional imprecision has created significant barriers to creating international agreements comparable to those established for ozone and global climate change. Yet the sustainable development debates have had at least one important impact: they have forced a rethinking of the basic organization of the US system of environmental protection.

■ The Concept of Sustainable Development

For almost two decades, environmentalists and policy analysts have bandied about the term "sustainable development." In 1987 the World Conference on Environment and Development, or Brundtland Commission, released *Our Common Future,* which popularized the concept of sustainable development. The Brundtland Report noted: "Sustainable development seeks to meet the needs and aspirations of the present without compromising the ability to meet those of the future" (United Nations World Commission on Environment and Development 1987: 40). This definition did little to clarify the concept. In the words of one critical review: "Sustainable development is a little like Zen. Everybody talks about it, but few people really know what it is" (Shaw and Murray 1999: 147). Similarly, Herman E. Daly remarks: "Although there is an emerging political consensus on the desirability of something called sustainable development, this term—touted by many and even institutionalized in some places—is still dangerously vague. . . . Sustainable development is a term that everyone likes, but nobody is sure of what it means." With respect to the definition adopted in *Our Common Future,* Daly notes: "While not vacuous by any means, this definition was sufficiently vague to allow for a broad consensus. Probably that was a good political strategy at the time—a consensus on a vague concept was better than disagreement over a sharply defined one" (1996: 1–2).

Definitional opacity is an important issue. As Pierre Crosson and Michael A. Toman observe, "to identify what may be required to achieve sustainability . . . it is necessary to have a clear understanding of what the concept means" (1994: 90). The ambiguity inherent in the term "sustainable development" has allowed for the existence of multiple irreconcilable definitions of the underlying problem and an equally incompatible set of responses (see Goodland and Daly 1996). It is often impossible to determine whether actors debating sustainable development are even engaging the same set of issues. Indeed, while appreciating the underlying sentiments of the concept, Michael McCloskey, chairman of the Sierra Club, fears that the concept is so vague as to offer little guidance for thinking about the future of environmental governance:

> If "the emperor has no clothes on," we must in the end acknowledge it. There was a day when we needed the high hope and the fine inspiration represented by the concept. But today, we need a useable line of thought—an operational reality. We need a line of thought which can be extended rationally into the detail of research, planning and application. And sustainability does not seem to be that thought. What we now fear is that "sustainability" will prove to be no more than a boon to publicists who will paste new labels on old bottles and claim that every project that makes their clients rich is sustainable. In the absence of any operational definition, who is to prove them wrong? (1999: 159)

Is sustainable development a coherent focus for future policy, or simply a vague concept that can be all things to all people?

Let us stipulate that there are profound difficulties with the United Nations' definition. Nevertheless, one might still take seriously the problem of sustainability as recognizing the interrelatedness of various trends in demographics, development, resource depletion, and global climatic change, and calling for a movement away from the narrow policy-specific focus that has characterized environmental protection regulation. As Fritjof Capra and Gunter Pauli note: "the major problems of our time . . . cannot be understood in isolation. They are systemic problems—interconnected and interdependent. Stabilizing world population will only be possible when poverty is reduced worldwide. The extinction of animal and plant species on a massive scale will continue as long as the South is burdened by massive debts" (1995: 2). Given the magnitude of the trends in question and the complexity of their interconnections, one should not be surprised that the proposed responses have demanded efforts to resolve the inherent conflict between existing economic practices and the limitations of the ecosystem.

The Inherent Conflict: Capitalism vs. Sustainability

Since the end of World War II, a liberal trade regime has facilitated rapid growth in the world economy, opening the door to previously unimagined levels of wealth and consumption and an extension of life expectancies, even in the developing world. Although rising incomes provide the foundations for greater investments in environmental protection, growth also generates new patterns of consumption that may have catastrophic implications. One might respond that markets have proven remarkably capable of managing resource constraints in the past. Price changes signal scarcity and create incentives for greater efficiencies and the search for innovations and substitutes. By managing constraints as they arise, one might be able to achieve a form of sustainability. Yet as Michael Common notes: "The attainment of this kind of sustainability could be consistent with massive environmental degradation as normally understood" (1995: 54). It is vital to move beyond the narrow set of concerns of economics:

> Economists emphasise human management in human interests, narrowly conceived, and neglect considerations relating to the functioning of the biosphere and its constituent systems. Ecologists emphasise system function considerations, but cannot relate those to human interests in any direct and simple way. The question which arises is whether there can exist a synthetic approach, which can operationally inform the analysis of human behaviour and debate over how human society should behave. . . . [T]here is such an approach but it necessarily involves imprecision. The sustainability problem can be stated as that of managing human affairs so as to address the problems of poverty and inequality while also minimising threats to ecological sustainability. (1995: 55)

To understand the core problem of sustainability, we must begin with the ecosystem. It sets hard limits on human activity. The biosphere consists of Earth and its atmosphere, the various resources that preserve life, and the processes that impact on the availability of resources. Following Common (1995: chap. 3), when considering resources one can make several useful distinctions. Although there are flow resources that are not impacted by the level or intensity of use (e.g., solar energy), most resources are stock resources. The level and intensity of use affects future availability. Some stock resources—trees or fish populations, for example—are renewable by virtue of their biotic nature. If use is less than or equal to reproduction rates, the stock can be extended indefinitely. Other stock resources, like minerals and fossil fuels, are exhaustible. Resources are consumed and transformed into wastes that are discharged back into the environment. When the flow of waste falls within the environment's assimilative capacity, the transformation process is largely in balance and there is a sustainable system. However, when residual flows exceed the environment's assimilative capacity, this can reduce the ability of the biosphere to absorb wastes and, ultimately, to support life. The lesson seems self-evident: as long as waste flows fall within the assimilative capacity of the biosphere, development would appear to be sustainable.

All of this might be true in a steady-state situation. Unfortunately, the interaction of population growth and changing patterns of resource use threatens to severely compromise Earth's carrying capacity. The carrying capacity of the ecosystem is difficult to determine with respect to levels of population, for several reasons. First, humans, unlike other species, have culturally determined consumption patterns. North Americans and Europeans, for example, consume far more food and energy than their Southern Hemisphere counterparts—consumption patterns that could not be adopted globally (Daly and Cobb 1994: 241). Moreover, humans have a great adaptive capacity. They are far better than other species at altering patterns of resource consumption in response to changing circumstances (e.g., they conserve on scarce resources and develop substitutes). Finally, many nations are engaged in rapid development, which will have profound effects on per capita resource consumption and, ultimately, on the likelihood that the environment's carrying capacity will be stressed at lower rather than higher levels of population. Indeed, the goal of keeping the world's population below some numerical threshold might fail to provide sufficient protection if it is offset by changing consumption patterns. There must be simultaneous efforts to address levels and patterns of resource use (Costanza et al. 1997: 109–110).

Critics may challenge the reliability of population growth trends. There is something of a demographic transition that characterizes nations as they develop. From a state of low life expectancy (a combination of high birth rates and high death rates), they enter a period of rapid population growth (high birth rates are combined with lower death rates). Ultimately, birth rates equilibrate with death rates, resulting in a stabilization and even a reduction of population (Longman 2004; Sinding 2000). However, the demographic transition is a product of industrialization and, as a result, carries with it higher rates of consumption, resource use, and waste generation. Given the large proportion of the world's population that has entered this stage, it is questionable whether the stage of high life expectancy will be reached before the carrying capacity of the ecosystem has been exceeded or the assimilative capacity has been so reduced as to result in irreparable harm (Chiapetta 1998; Daly and Cobb 1994: chap. 12).

■ What Is to Be Done?

The basic structure of the sustainability argument is clear: while capable of assimilation, regeneration, and resilience, the ecosystem has a limited carrying capacity. The impact of human production and consumption can be reduced through the widespread adoption of pollution control technologies and recycling, but not indefinitely. Furthermore, the existing climatic, demographic, and developmental trends may be sufficient to exceed the carrying capacity of the ecosystem, with dire consequences for the quality (and existence) of life. What is to be done? Given the nature of the trends addressed above, one should not be surprised that advocates of sustainable development argue for more than incremental changes. One can identify several possible leverage points, several of which were identified by the United Nation Conference on Environment and Development in its Agenda 21:

> The growth of world population and production combined with unsustainable consumption patterns places increasingly severe stress on the life-supporting capacities of our planet. These interactive processes affect the use of land, water, air, energy and other resources. Rapidly growing cities, unless well-managed, face major environmental problems. The increase in both the number and size of cities calls for greater attention to issues of local government and municipal management. The human dimensions are key elements to consider in this intricate set of relationships and they should be adequately taken into consideration in comprehensive policies for sustainable development. Such policies should address the linkages of demographic trends and factors, resource use, appropriate technology dissemination, and development. Population policy should also recognize the role played by human beings in environmental and development concerns. (1992: § 5.2)

One area that deserves immediate attention is population growth. The world's population is expected to exceed 8 billion people by 2020, with a majority of new growth occurring in less developed countries. Population control can be pursued through a number of means. At the least-invasive end of the continuum, one would find education on family planning combined with access to contraceptives, both of which could be funded through international organizations and foreign aid. At the other extreme, one would find mandatory family caps, such as China's one-child policy. Between these two endpoints, one may find innovative proposals like a cap-and-trade system for procreation permits. Under one proposal, an international organization would set maximum population caps and distribute permits (denominated in units of one-tenth of a child) globally. As potential parents in wealthy nations purchased the rights to reproduce, they would simultaneously subsidize incomes in developing nations and cleaner development (Daly and Cobb 1994: 244–246). Of course, such proposals are more notable for their novelty than their practicality.

While population reduction is necessary, it is not sufficient. The problem is the level of aggregate resource consumption, which is the product of population multiplied by per capita consumption. Slow or negative population growth will not alleviate pressures on overall resource consumption if per capita consumption continues to grow. If we introduce arguments for equity into what is essentially a zero-sum game, any changes would necessarily involve a massive global redistribution of wealth. Policies would have to raise the welfare of the poorest populations while achieving commensurate reductions in the consumption opportunities for the wealthiest. Global wealth redistributions might be achieved in a host of ways. One of the more interesting proposals combines the goal of wealth redistribution with a reduction in global warming. Once one determines the optimal level of greenhouse gas emissions, one could issue pollution permits to nations on the basis of population. These permits could be tradable and freely transferred from nation-to-nation in a market. There is a significant disjunction between national populations and greenhouse gas emissions. The wealthiest nations are currently responsible for a majority of greenhouse gas emissions, reflecting the higher levels of per capita consumption. Under a system of global permitting, developed nations would have to make significant investments in greenhouse gas controls, purchase permits from developing countries, or combine purchases with clean technology transfers (Common 1995: 290–311). The credit system would provide an automatic mechanism for funding green development and reducing global poverty.

There are ways of reducing consumption that would not require an explicit redistribution of wealth. Some proponents of the ecological vision argue that sustainable levels of consumption require a genuine revolution in international economic organization that would counter the trends in trade liberalization and globalization that have promoted maximum production and consumption. As Hartmut Bossel observes, this system carries a number of negative externalities:

> The "free" global market drives regions with very different environmental, resourcial, social, and cultural conditions into competitive struggle. For many it is a struggle for survival, and they have no choice but to sacrifice whatever is available to gain a competitive edge. To stay in the game under increasingly more difficult conditions (spread of poverty, population growth!), others have to follow suit. This produces a downward, reinforc-

ing spiral of ecological degradation, resource overuse, unemployment, income losses, shrinking economy, social destabilization, and sacrifices in health, welfare, and human rights. (1998: 152)

A far more sustainable path, it is argued, would be one in which economic activity is reorganized to occur on a regional rather than a global basis (see Daly 1994). Under regionalization, "each region should be essentially self-sufficient with respect to its basic life support (food, energy, water, building materials, consumer products). This would require regional adaptation to the ecological carrying capacity" and would include "the options of adjusting population and personal demands, as well as enhancing the productivity of the regional ecosystem" (Bossel 1998: 296). Free trade, the centerpiece of the post–World War II system, would be abandoned to promote regionalization and prevent the competitive pressures that have produced the current unsustainable path.

From Theory to Practice (or Vice Versa)
The sustainable development argument is premised on the assumption that existing demographic and developmental trends will combine to undermine Earth's limited carrying capacity. There is no shortage of intellectually stimulating responses, ranging from tradable procreation permits to global transfers of wealth. Yet even the most intellectually inventive and theoretically grounded proposals will falter if they cannot be implemented. Politics is the art of the possible, and the opportunity set available to those seeking a solution to global climate change and unsustainable patterns of development is constrained by existing institutions. In each case, the practical process of translating theory into practice constitutes an insurmountable barrier. As argued in Chapter 11, international regulatory agreements are most likely to be successful when they are backed by strong domestic commitment, can be implemented with domestic regulatory institutions, and are compatible with the trade regime. There are no international institutions capable of imposing such policies and backing them with sanctions, nor is there any indication that nations are willing to sacrifice their sovereignty to make such institutions a reality (see Victor and Skolnikoff 1999).

Any significant commitment to sustainable development will require the passage of new laws and the allocation of resources, both of which will depend on domestic political coalitions. Most grand sustainability schemes have some common elements that would appear to make these kinds of commitments highly improbable. First, each requires an intergenerational and cross-national transfer of wealth. That is, nations must decide to sacrifice consumption today so that there are greater opportunities for future generations in distant lands. Current debates in the United States regarding budget deficits, social security, and Medicare reform reveal little enthusiasm for making such sacrifices, even when the beneficiaries are one's own progeny. Second, the scientific uncertainty, complexity, and imprecision implicit in the sustainable development debates create doubts as to whether such sacrifices will yield the promised benefits in some hypothetical future. As the debates surrounding global climate change suggest, voters have a difficult time processing complex issues and working with uncertainty. Elected officials demand certainty, particularly if they are being asked to impose costs on their constituents.

Moreover, there is a lack of institutional capacity for administering such programs. Certainly, one may counter that international institutions have been created in the past and will doubtless be created in the future. But as shown in previous chapters, the lack of domestic foundations for international policy can prove highly problematic. In the case of the Montreal Protocol, success was contingent, in part, on the preexistence of policies and institutions that could translate commitments to reduce ozone-depleting substances into a pattern of enforcement actions. International agreements served to coordinate the actions of nations that had already made a commitment backed with institutional capacities. Certainly, the Kyoto Protocol contained little detail on the underlying institutional architecture, leaving a host of critical issues to be determined later. But it is still quite unclear how Kyoto will fare as it makes the transition from theory to practice. As a generalization, rather than beginning with theoretical discussions of potential policy remedies, one should begin with a far more practical set of concerns: the kinds of commitments that can be enforced given existing policies and institutions. Unfortunately, the constraints imposed by institutions rarely enter into the debates of international regulation, and when they do, it is as an afterthought.

Finally, efforts to redesign the architecture of the international trade regime in the hope of promoting sustainable development seem equally dim. Trade is widely recognized as the engine of growth in developing and wealthy nations. There is much to suggest that trade has felicitous implications for the environment, both through the prevalence of the "California effect" and through the potential for rising incomes to push nations toward greater environmental investments. The rapid improvements in life expectancy in developing countries would undoubtedly make them unwilling to embrace efforts to limit economic integration, absent compensatory financing. This, in turn, brings us back to the initial question of whether one can sustain domestic coalitions to support these obligations in addition to the costs associated with reduced trade. There seems to be little to suggest that the abandonment of the most successful international regime is a plausible response to concerns over sustainable development.

■ Think Globally, Act Nationally

In 1992 the United Nations Conference on Environment and Development
sponsored the Earth Summit in Rio de Janeiro. At the summit, 179 nations,
including the United States, signed Agenda 21, an action plan focusing on
sustainable development. Rather than embracing grand schemes of sustainability, Agenda 21 envisioned a far more decentralized response. It called
on governments to develop national strategies for sustainable development
and to do so in a broadly participatory fashion. Pursuant to Agenda 21,
President Clinton created a new federal advisory committee, the President's
Council on Sustainable Development (PCSD), via Executive Order 12852
(58 Fed. Reg. 39107, July 21, 1993).

Executive Order 12852 constituted a significant, if subtle, departure
from the sustainability debates as represented in the Brundtland
Commission's report. It defined sustainable development as "economic
growth that will benefit present and future generations without detrimental-
ly affecting the resources or biological systems of the planet." As is clear
from this definition, "economic growth" effectively replaced the goal of
"meeting the needs" of the world's population (the UN's original formula-
tion). Indeed, the White House press release (June 14, 1993) that accompanied the signing of the order noted that the PCSD "represents a ground-
breaking commitment to explore and develop policies that encourage
economic growth, job creation, and effective use of our natural and cultural
resources." Any of the debates regarding constraining consumption or promoting equity in global wealth distributions seemed, at best, tangential to
this charge.

The PCSD members represented a number of federal agencies
(Departments of Agriculture, Commerce, Education, Energy, Housing and
Urban Development, Interior, and Transportation; the Environmental
Protection Agency, the Small Business Administration), state, local, and
tribal organizations (Columbia River Inter-Tribal Fish Commission, Marion
County, Oregon; city of Tulsa, Oklahoma), environmental and advocacy
organizations (Environmental Defense, the Natural Resources Defense
Council, the Center for Neighborhood Technology, the Nature Conservancy,
the Sierra Club, and the Women's Environment and Development
Organization), and a number of corporations (American Electric Power, BP
Amoco, Dow Chemical, Enron Corporation, General Motors Corporation,
and S. C. Johnson & Son). The PCSD was placed under the cochairmanship
of Ray C. Anderson, chairman, president, and CEO of Interface Inc., and
Jonathan Lash, president of the World Resources Institute (see Lash and
Buzzelli 1995).

Following a series of meetings and position papers, the PCSD published an interim report, *Sustainable America: A New Consensus for the Future,* in 1996, and a final report, *Towards a Sustainable America,* in 1999. The underlying assumptions clearly presented sustainability as dependent on growth. As the PCSD noted: "To achieve our vision of sustainable development, some things must grow—jobs, productivity, wages, capital and savings, profits, information, knowledge, and education—and others—pollution, waste, and poverty—must not." Economic growth, environmental protection, and social equity were presented as "mutually reinforcing." Yet there was little question as to which of the three would be assigned primacy: "Economic growth based on technological innovation, improved efficiency, and expanding global markets is essential for progress toward greater prosperity, equality, and environmental quality." Additional environmental progress was possible "because market incentives and the power of consumers can lead to significant improvements in environmental performance at less cost." Further environmental progress would also depend on regulatory reform: "The current regulatory system should be improved to deliver the required results at lower costs." It should "provide enhanced flexibility in return for superior environmental progress." There were additional assumptions regarding the importance of "stabilizing global human population," promoting "steady advances in science and technology . . . to help improve economic efficiency, protect and restore natural systems, and modify consumption patterns," and enhancing education, the flow of information, and participation in decisionmaking. However, the PCSD assigned primary importance to economic growth and supported the kinds of corporate-based efforts discussed in Chapter 8. As the PCSD noted: "Environmental progress will depend on individual, institutional, and corporate responsibility, commitment, and stewardship" (1999: v–vi). While space constraints preclude a detailed analysis of all the PCSD's recommendations, of particular interest here are the recommendations for reconfiguring the nation's system of environmental management.

One of the missions of the PCSD was to "advise the President on the next steps in building the new environmental management system of the 21st century." An environmental management system was presented as "the overall framework of a broader set of institutional and individual influences that affect the environment, including, but not limited to, environmental laws and regulations, corporate stewardship, economic and financial systems, and other features of organized society" (1999: 36). As noted in previous chapters, the EPA has focused primarily on media-specific regulation using command-and-control instruments. The PCSD concluded that the nation needed a new environmental management system that could develop ways of collecting and disseminating useful information on environmental performance, promote the collaboration of various private and public sector actors, and leverage the resources of these actors to promote sustainability.

Several recommendations focused on information. To measure environmental progress, it is essential to "develop and apply agreed-upon sustainable development indicators and collect the necessary data." This, in turn, requires that one "define common metrics for environmental protection . . . to meaningfully inform communities, nongovernmental organizations, regulators, and financial analysts interested in the environmental performance of organizations." It also required investments in information systems and firm-level environmental accounting. Drawing on the European Union's Ecomanagement and Audit Scheme and the ISO 14000 series, the PCSD noted the need for life-cycle analyses that could be used to assign stewardship responsibilities, focus attention of the "delivery of service and value instead of the delivery of material or product," and identify modes of operation that "recognize and reduce environmental impacts" (1999: 44–47).

The PCSD dismissed the "one size fits all" approach inherent in command-and-control instruments, noting: "after decades of evolving environmental regulation, there is growing variation in the way different organizations perform. Some firms have already internalized the need for environmental stewardship into their business; others are simply focused on compliance. Still other firms need a great deal of assistance before they are able to meet environmental requirements at all" (1999: 47). The PCSD suggested that firms that adopt "design for environment, extended product stewardship, eco-efficiency and environmental management systems that include a commitment to continuous improvement" should be "supported and rewarded." Once standards for high performance are defined (i.e., in terms of "compliance history, modern environmental management systems, continual improvement, pollution prevention, reported results, etc."), the council recommended that alternative regulatory strategies be made available:

> Participating companies could propose process-specific operational changes and alternative strategies leading to both high environmental performance and increased profitability. Businesses that outperform existing environmental requirements and continually improve performance over time would benefit from the economic and administrative certainty of such a program. (1999: 48–49)

Such a green track (comparable to the National Environmental Performance Track) could provide far greater incentives to engage in proactive environmental management.

Realizing that an optimal system would be capable of responding to a rapidly changing economic environment, the PCSD emphasized the merits of market-based programs and corporate environmental management systems. However, the mere existence of a corporate environmental policy and EMS was deemed insufficient. "Effective environmental management systems can provide structural support for improving performance if coupled with qualitative and quantitative performance commitments and goals" and combined with third-party certification and auditing. The council presented its determination of what EMS characteristics would be optimal (see Table 13.1). It also recommended the development of "performance goals and program incentives" along with "a critical review of current programs and policies for the accreditation of third-party certifiers and auditors" to facilitate the movement toward this alternative track of regulation (1999: 52–53).

The PCSD recommended that the new system "foster a collaborative regional approach to environmental protection" that would cut across existing jurisdictions while maintaining national standards. It also recommended that policymakers facilitate individual and community involvement through information dissemination and education. Finally, the system must be responsive to concerns derived from the environmental justice debates suggesting that the distribution of pollution and environmental resources has been inequitable, to the disadvantage of low-income and minority communities. An optimal system would "identify risks and protect communities against disproportionate impacts." Indeed, the council noted that such impacts can be prevented if there are mechanisms in place "to ensure that community representatives (not local government officials alone) are collaboratively involved in decisionmaking processes affecting the community" (1999: 55, 58).

After six years of deliberations, the PCSD formally ceased operations on June 30, 1999. During its tenure, several federal agencies created offices or programs that made some reference to sustainable development and

Table 13.1 Recommended Characteristics of Corporate Environmental Management Systems

---

A plant-specific environmental management system, or corporate-level system implemented at the plant level.
Accepted corporate environmental principles, policies, and goals.
Commitment to compliance baselines and continually improved performance.
Identification and prioritization of environmental aspects and impacts.
Environmental performance metrics and indicators.
Sufficient public involvement and public reporting to permit meaningful understanding of facility management, performance, and compliance status.
Pollution prevention, design-for-the-environment, and life-cycle approaches.
Supply-chain and extended product responsibility efforts.
Environmental accounting.
Periodic system evaluation or auditing.
Provisions for corrective and preventive action with regard to identified problems.
Senior-led responsibility and interdepartmental agreement.

Source: President's Council on Sustainable Development 1999: 52.

introduced some sustainability-related initiatives. The EPA's reinvention of government efforts seemed to embody many of the PCSD recommendations. Moreover, in 1996 the EPA created a challenge grant program for sustainable development, ultimately funding some 123 projects searching for innovative solutions to environmental problems. Funding was always quite limited, however, peaking at $5 million per year (see Farrell 1999). The grant program expired in 1999 and many of the sustainable development efforts largely expired with the Clinton administration. There were few traces of the sustainable development agenda at the EPA following the 2000 election. Critics who believed that sustainable development was little more than a trendy catchphrase may have their suspicions confirmed by its rapid movement off the policy agenda. Of course, many agencies, including the EPA, continue to execute policies that were compatible with sustainable development. And the term "sustainable development" was not scrubbed from every government document and website.

The PCSD constituted an important effort to develop a national strategy for sustainable development within a collaborative setting that emphasized participation and consensus building among groups that seldom engage in collective dialogue. Granted, the quest for stakeholder engagement in environmental policy can prioritize consensus over the quality of the resulting recommendations (see Coglianese 1999; Foreman 1998). But as shown in previous chapters, some of the recommendations generated by the PCSD have strong theoretical and empirical justification. In the end, the sustainable development debates in the United States may be significant to the extent that they stimulate further reflection on the limitations of the existing regulatory design and engage actors to cooperate in larger issues of environmental governance. Whether these deliberations have any importance for the evolution of policy remains to be seen, although one cannot be overly sanguine given the strength of existing regulatory design.

■ Conclusion

Although the sustainable development debates have been bedeviled by definitional ambiguity, there is a growing consensus that the combination of unfettered population growth and current patterns of development, consumption, and energy use carry serious implications for the future of the global environment. Although many nations recognize the need for concerted international action, in the end, sustainable development generated "an impossible mandate covering every imaginable environmental issue and goal, little political support, no sense of priorities," and "a Christmas tree approach to agenda setting" (Esty 2001: 75). In September 2002 the United Nations held its World Summit on Sustainable Development in

Johannesburg, South Africa. The ten-year anniversary of the Earth Summit provided a good opportunity to assess how far the international community had come in dealing with the issue of sustainable development. The Johannesburg summit was charged with the task of developing an implementation plan that set targets and timetables for promoting sustainable development. Although the plan would not be legally binding, it was hoped that it would unleash a series of events comparable to those that led to the Montreal Protocol (La Vina, Hoff, and DeRose 2003: 55–56).

In the months leading up to the Johannesburg summit, critics noted that the promise of the Earth Summit had not been translated into action. Although parties developed national strategies and submitted them to the United Nations, they were rarely backed with significant expansions of development assistance for less developed countries or changes in national policies and practices. The summit generated a host of nonbinding agreements. Nations agreed to reduce by half the proportion of the world's population without access to safe drinking water and basic sanitation, by 2015; to reduce by half the proportion of the world's population living on less than $1 per day, by 2015; to reduce by two-thirds infant, under-five, and maternal mortality rates, by 2015; to minimize the adverse health and environmental effects of chemical use and production, by 2020; and to take action to maintain or restore fish stocks to produce a maximum sustainable yields, by 2015 (see Rutsch 2003). However, as James Gustave Speth, chair of Carter's Council on Environmental Quality and former president of the World Resources Institute, notes, there were no "specific, monitorable plans of action" resembling those advocated by many participants. "What emerged instead was either nothing or next to nothing (as, for example, in the cases of renewable energy, desertification, development assistance funding, governance, and globalization) or very general and nonbinding targets with timetables for their accomplishment. The United States and many others typically opposed these targets and timetables, so it was considered a major accomplishment . . . when anything vaguely resembling a target and timetable was agreed upon" (2003: 26).

More troubling, parties seemed to retreat from the positions they had adopted in previous meetings. They refused to agree to targets and timetables for renewable energy sources. Efforts to insert language urging the United States to ratify the Kyoto Protocol were unsuccessful. Moreover, language urging nations to adopt the precautionary principle was softened at the urging of the United States and Japan to advocate a precautionary "approach." While the implementation plan supported ongoing discussions of trade, it did not provide any substantive guidance for reconciling the conflicts between liberalization, development, and environmental quality. In the end, "the failure of governments to adopt and agree on effective means of implementation (including financing issues) and institutional mechanisms, make it likely that the successes of the summit could be rendered meaningless" (La Vina, Hoff, and DeRose 2003: 67).

The Johannesburg summit did not constitute a highpoint for US environmental diplomacy. Although 104 heads of state attended the summit, President George W. Bush was represented by his secretary of state, Colin Powell (whose presentation was interrupted by heckles from environmentalists). "A defining feature at Johannesburg was the unrelenting criticism leveled against the United States by many of those in attendance" (Schmidt 2002: A685). Critics seized on US patterns of energy consumption, the refusal to ratify Kyoto, reliance on agricultural subsidies, and championing of public-private partnerships and private initiatives rather than binding commitments (see Pope 2003). In the end, a decade of debates on the vague concept of sustainable development generated little more than lofty rhetoric and symbolic goals unsupported by enforceable commitments.

While international agreements may not be the most likely path to success in dealing with sustainable development, a more decentralized response is clearly within the range of the possible. Such a response would require a serious effort to rethink the basic structural design of the US system of environmental regulation. Such a consideration began with the reinvention efforts of the 1990s and the deliberations of the President's Council on Sustainable Development. We turn now to a discussion of the future of environmental protection and the potential for constructing a system that simultaneously expands our capacity for managing environmental impacts in the United States and promotes gains in environmental quality in a domestic and global context.

Conclusion

Green Governance
and the Future of
Environmental Protection

M uch of the thinking about political economic relations in the
United States has been shaped by the market-state dichotomy.
Analysts tend to draw distinctions between command-and-control
regulation and market-based instruments, as if this dichotomy could exhaust
the range of possibilities. Since the mid-1980s, social scientists have developed a far more sophisticated understanding of how economic activities are
coordinated in capitalist economies. They have identified the various ways
in which complex public and private organizations coordinate their economic activities and manage their interdependencies. Markets continue to exist
and play an important role, particularly when anonymous and independent
parties engage in decentralized bargaining and transact over relatively simple goods. Contracts, where they exist, are self-liquidating and do not compromise the independence of the parties in question. However, parties often
seek to coordinate their actions through other means as a way of economiz-
ing transaction costs, reducing their vulnerability to opportunism, or managing uncertainty (see Hollingsworth and Boyer 1997; Williamson 1985).

The resulting arrangements are best described as "governance structures." The term *governance* "generally refers to the means for achieving
direction, control, and coordination of wholly or partially autonomous individuals or organizational units on behalf of interests to which they jointly
contribute" (Lynn, Heinrich, and Hill 2002: 6). The debates over governance reflect a broader movement in the organization of political economies
in the contemporary era. As Bob Jessop explains, we are witnessing the "de-
statization of politics," a "shift from the centrality of govern*ment* to more
decentralized forms of govern*ance*." This "involves a shift from the top-
down hierarchical political organization typical of sovereign states to
emphasis on promoting and/or steering the self-organization of interorganizational relations." Rather than focusing on hierarchical relations linking
the state and economy, researchers should investigate the interaction and

coordination among private and public organizations engaged in "reflexive negotiation and mutual learning" and the extent to which this coordination facilitates managing an uncertain and dynamic environment (1999: 389–390).

Where does the state fit into these schemas? J. Rogers Hollingsworth and Robert Boyer argue that the state "is a coordinating mechanism quite unlike any of the others. It is the state that sanctions and regulates the various nonstate coordinating mechanisms, that is the ultimate enforcer of rules of the various mechanisms, that defines and enforces property rights, and that manipulates fiscal and monetary policy. At the same time, the state may also be an economic actor by engaging in production and exchange relations" (1997: 13). Similarly, Leon N. Lindberg and John L. Campbell explain: "States decisively constitute the economy by directly or indirectly influencing the selection of governance regimes. Governance regimes arise from the strategic choices and relative power of economic actors. Hence, we must understand how state actions (or inactions) and state institutional forms may condition or structure the strategic choices and power positions of producers (and other economic actors)" (1991: 361). The state, in short, is an actor and shapes the structure within which governance regimes evolve.

The implications of this shift for environmental regulation and the role of the state are profound. Traditional accounts of regulation envision a hierarchical relationship in which policies are imposed on regulated parties. Whether policy is successful will depend on the technical merits of the policy, resource flows, and the vigor of enforcement. An appreciation of the governance debates leads one to discount the usefulness of this portrayal (see Heinrich and Lynn 2001). As Martijn van Vliet notes, this is part of a larger "shift in focus within the science of public administration from 'monocentric' to 'polycentric' approaches, in which processes of governing and governance are not considered as a relation or a process between a governing actor (the state) on the one had and a to-be-governed object (society) on the other, but as a relation or interaction between two or more 'acting' subjects." The focus shifts to networks of relationships among interdependent organizations engaged in dialogue, knowledge sharing, and collective problem solving (1993: 106, 109–110).

Under the traditional vision of regulation, the state's role was essentially a form of law enforcement. When one views regulation through the lens of governance, the state's role is qualitatively different. Policymakers would be well advised to recognize the rich variety of mechanisms that are used to coordinate economic activities and the ways in which these mechanisms can be used to further regulatory goals. The state must develop cooperative relationships with other organizations (e.g., corporations, trade associations, financial institutions, environmental groups) that create a context for open dialogue, the sharing of knowledge, and the generation and dissemination of innovations (see Fiorino 2001). Traditional modes of regulation may still play a role. However, state coercion will be used as a last resort and as a means of promoting cooperation.

With this in mind, let us consider how markets, corporations, associations, and international standards organizations coordinate economic activities with the end of promoting higher levels of environmental performance. In so doing, let us first consider the state in its nonregulatory capacity. Of course, there is an underlying assumption in this exercise, namely that state regulation should be introduced not as the solution of choice, but as a last resort—a means of compensating for the limitations of private initiatives. One can justify this position through reference to the principle of subsidiarity, which suggests that agents at different levels of association have different tasks. Agents at higher levels of organization should not assume the functions of local agents unless the latter are incapable of executing them (Beabout 1988). One can also justify this position by arguing that the power to make decisions may be best exercised by those who have the best knowledge of products, inputs, productive technologies, cost structures, and organizational capacities, particularly if there are incentives to reduce or prevent pollution. If the incentives are weak or there are significant limitations that cannot be met by agents and associations at other levels, the state has a role to play in addressing *these* specific problems. The benefits of decentralization should include greater cost-effectiveness, higher rates of innovation, greater dynamism, and greater robustness than could ever be achieved through direct regulation. Moreover, to the extent that the incentives cut across national borders, the result can be a system that is not dependent on the efforts of any single regulatory authority—a critical issue in an age of globalization.

The result of such a process will be a system that defies easy characterization, insofar as it represents a unique blending of the public and private. There is a wealth of research to suggest that private parties have a remarkable capacity to develop covenants to manage common pool resources, monitor compliance, and enforce agreed upon norms (see Schlager 2004). In some cases, the state has an important role to play in reinforcing the covenants; in other cases, the covenants are strictly private. However, they are not easily portrayed along a simple state-versus-market dichotomy. As Elinor Ostrom observes: "Institutions are rarely either private or public— 'the market' or 'the state.' Many successful [common pool resource] institutions are rich mixtures of 'private-like' and 'public like' institutions defying classification in a sterile dichotomy" (1990: 14). With this in mind, let us begin our exploration of environmental governance.

■ Constructing Governance
Regimes from the Ground Up

When we consider the foundations of a new system of environmental governance, we do not begin with an institutional abyss. Markets create means of resolving competing uses of scarce resources via the price mechanism. Courts and the legal system allow for the adjudication of disputes and force actors to assume accountability for damages. Following the insights of Ronald H. Coase (1960), regulation may be unnecessary to the extent that property rights are well defined and enforceable and there are no transaction costs. Under these conditions, different rules about liability may affect the distribution of costs among disputants, but the system should provide optimal levels of environmental protection. Coase recognized that transaction costs may prevent parties from defending their rights, thereby creating a justification for regulation, although he remained agnostic as to whether the benefits of such regulations would justify the costs.

In *Free Market Environmentalism,* Terry L. Anderson and Donald R. Leal consider the potential for a property rights–based system. Starting from an economic perspective—that is, environmental issues can be correctly understood as competition over competing uses for scarce resources—they argue that private actors have the knowledge and incentives to manage environmental resources efficiently if property rights are defined, defensible, and divestible:

> At the heart of free market environmentalism is a system of well-specified property rights to natural and environmental resources. Whether these rights are held by individuals, corporations, nonprofit environmental groups, or communal groups, a discipline is imposed on resource users because the wealth of the property owner is at stake if bad decisions are made. Moreover, if private owners can sell their rights to use resources, the owners must not only consider their own values, they must also consider what others are willing to pay. In the market setting, it is the potential for gains from trade that encourage cooperation. . . . When resources are controlled politically, the costs of misuse are more diffused and the potential for cooperation is minimized because the rights are essentially up for grabs. (2001: 4)

Under a property rights–based system, government subsidies that promote the overuse of scarce resources and distort market cues would be eliminated. As a generalization, those who hold the property rights possess the incentives and the information to make rational decisions about competing uses of scarce environmental resources, understanding that they suffer the costs and enjoy the benefits of their decisions.

When property rights are poorly defined, when market mechanisms are subordinated to political decisions, and when voters are rationally ignorant, one can expect much rent-seeking behavior that conveys benefits to mobilized interests and imposes costs on the unorganized public, often with deleterious ramifications for the environment. In contrast, when property rights over a resource like water, minerals, grazing land, or fisheries are defined, defensible, and divestible, one can assume that parties will have the information and incentives to conserve on scarce resources. In some cases such as water, this may require a system of tradable permits that could be assigned to residents at a level that would allow for the preservation of aquifers. Agribusiness in arid climates would have to purchase water rights on markets. If water is sufficiently scarce, the cost of water could undermine profitability, thereby stimulating investments in water-conserving innovations or forcing water-intensive industries to relocate to areas of abundant water (see Anderson and Leal 2001: 90–93). Public policies, in contrast, often subsidize the prices of scarce resources (e.g., subsidized grazing and mining rights, unimpeded access to scarce water), thereby promoting overuse and creating environmental problems that stimulate demands for more invasive forms of state regulation.

A property rights–based system carries several significant difficulties, some of which were anticipated by Coase. First, one can imagine ways of assigning property rights to a scarce resource like water and creating a market for tradable water quotas. It is far more difficult—but not impossible—to assign rights to other resources like clean air. If the past is any guide, resource scarcity creates incentives to define property rights with greater precision; actors develop technologies to defend those rights. Second, it may be exceedingly costly for some parties to determine whether their rights have been infringed upon. Corporations may prove unwilling to voluntarily disclose information on pollution. It may be difficult to allocate responsibility among multiple sources of pollution upstream. For those who are negatively impacted, information asymmetries may limit their ability to understand that their rights have been infringed upon and seek relief. The costs of monitoring behavior are the kinds of transaction costs that Coase understood as providing a justification for regulation. There are remedies for this situation, which will be discussed below. Nonetheless, when actors have information and property rights are well defined, one can expect that they will have greater incentives and information to defend their resources. One can assume, similarly, that corporations will have the incentive to reduce their potential liabilities and respond to resource scarcity through decisions about products, productive technologies, and pollution control investments.

Third, transaction costs may make it prohibitively expensive for some parties to defend their property rights. They may have to engage in political organization, encountering collective action problems and new costs that are greater than the damages in question. Given the costs, it may prove irrational to seek relief and defend one's property rights. Fourth, some environmental issues involve transboundary pollution flows (e.g., acid rain, global climate change). There is an absence of institutions for defending rights on a global scale. Finally, some important environmental assets may be of no instrumental value to individuals. Biodiversity or the preservation of unique ecosystems may be inherently valuable to humankind, but this value may find no expression in a property rights–based system. Thus, such a system may be of limited effectiveness in many environmental arenas.

Corporate Environmentalism

When advocates of property rights–based regimes speak of the market, they clearly understand that corporations are key actors in the market. However, given the analytical focus, corporations are not examined as complex organizations that potentially have the capacity and incentives to manage their environmental impacts. It thus makes sense to consider corporate environmentalism separate from debates over the potential role of property rights. In so doing, one must clearly acknowledge that corporations may adopt a host of strategies to minimize their legal liability and respond to the forces presented above. As shown in Chapter 8, corporations are being driven by market forces to pursue higher levels of environmental quality. Companies have employed a number of tools in pursuit of green production, including life-cycle analysis, design-for-environment, industrial ecology, environmental management systems, and environmental auditing. The adoption of these tools has been most prevalent among firms that made earlier investments in advanced manufacturing systems. An environmental management system, for example, draws on the same kinds of tools applied in total quality management systems. Companies must identify all environmental impacts, design systems for bringing these impacts into acceptable ranges, and, after reviewing the results, begin the process anew. This requires heavy investment in training and management information systems—costs that may be prohibitive for firms that cannot build on earlier investments.

Why would profit-seeking firms voluntarily go beyond regulatory requirements, particularly in a context of global price competition? Although one might wish to assume that corporate boardrooms have become enamored of Deep Ecology, it is more realistic to assume that managers view environmental stewardship as consistent with the maximization of shareholder wealth. They will pursue voluntary pollution reduction efforts to the extent to which such efforts reinforce (or at the very least, do not compromise) profitability. Corporations may see environmental management as having two kinds of positive impacts on competitiveness. First, to the extent that pollution reduction or prevention is a form of waste reduction, environmental management increases resource productivity and thereby reduces costs. It can also lessen or prevent future cleanup costs and allow a firm to proactively manage future liabilities. These cost advantages translate into price advantages that may be rewarded by the market, regardless of whether consumers seek goods produced in environmentally friendly ways.

Second, environmentally sound production or management can allow a company to differentiate its products from those of less green competitors. There are strong market pressures for green production. Beyond consumer markets, there are powerful forces in the business-to-business, government procurement, and financial markets that reward firms that have a positive environmental record. As with cost-based advantages, firms seeking to achieve differentiation-based advances do not need to be staffed with environmentalists who have sublimated the quest for profitability to some higher set of values. Rather, firms can pursue this strategy for purely economic reasons. A verified commitment to environmental management is increasingly a prerequisite of success within many industries, ranging from automobiles to information technology.

The limits of corporate environmentalism. Corporations have the best information regarding their production processes, technologies, and cost structures. They routinely analyze marginal costs and benefits and the cost-effectiveness of competing alternatives. Given the profit incentives and their access to fine-grained information, one can assume that corporate efforts at pollution reduction will be far more efficient than any externally imposed pollution control requirements, particularly if managers are given the flexibility to innovate and respond to the unique features of their enterprises. Given the pace of technological change and investment, one would expect to see far greater dynamism, particularly when compared with rigid state regulations, which are often slow to respond to changing circumstances and frequently lock-in dated technologies. Yet there are some reasons for concern.

If a company is successful in reducing waste streams, the market should effectively transmit information about costs through the price mechanism. Differentiation advantages are more complicated, however. Even if consumers, other businesses, and procurement agents have a desire to discriminate against companies with inferior environmental records, it may mean little unless they have accurate information about corporate accomplishments. Without the mandatory disclosure of information in a standardized format, it may be too costly for market actors to distinguish between corporate greenwash and reliable representations of performance. Thus a first challenge is to increase the flow of credible information to allow markets to function more effectively. Such a flow of information could also reduce the transaction costs associated with efforts to defend one's property rights. Without mandatory disclosure, firms are free to report what they wish. There are no instruments like the Freedom of Information Act to force the disclosure of corporate information. There are ways in which associations, standards, and public policies could remedy these information asymmetries.

There is another concern. Recall that environmental management is viewed as being of instrumental importance: a manager's primary fiduciary responsibility is to maximize shareholder wealth. If a firm designs and implements a quality environmental management system, the level of pollution reduction should reflect larger calculations about what the market will reward. We must assume that profitability creates a hard limit to corporate aspirations. If some firms in an industry refuse to invest in green production and engage in vigorous price competition, they may undermine the incentives for corporate self-regulation. In the end, the levels of pollution control deemed compatible with profitability may be substantially less that what is socially desirable or what might be possible should there be more effective governance on an industrywide level. Once again, standards and public policy could play an important role in reinforcing market cues. Before we consider their role in greater detail, let us turn to a discussion of trade associations.

Associational Self-Regulation

As noted in Chapter 9, a growing body of research has explored the role that associations can play in regulating their members' environmental performance. They can coordinate practices within an industry by promulgating association codes or standards that force members to self-regulate. They can provide resources to assist entities that might lack the means of achieving high levels of environmental performance. In the United States, two important examples in the environmental arena include the nuclear energy and the chemical industries. With the full support of the Nuclear Regulatory Commission, the Institute of Nuclear Power Operations began to serve some self-regulatory functions in the wake of Three Mile Island as a means of preempting additional regulations and increasing safety within the industry (Rees 1994). Similarly, the Chemical Manufacturers Association (subsequently renamed the American Chemistry Council) expanded its self-regulatory functions in the wake of Bhopal, introducing Responsible Care, an EMS-based system designed to reduce environmental hazards in the industry (see Gunningham 1995; Howard, Nash, and Ehrenfeld 2000; King and Lenox 2000). Participants comply with a detailed code of conduct and submit their systems to a management systems verification process involving peer review and auditing.

As self-regulating entities, associations can offer many benefits. Since corporations remain key participants and association codes reflect common products, processes, and technologies within an industry, many of the advantages of corporate environmentalism are retained. At the same time, the problems stemming from information scarcity can be partially managed. If an association requires that members comply with codes and that codes be sufficiently rigorous, consumers can use association membership as an economical indicator of environmental performance. Thus, rather than independently assessing the credibility of corporate environmental reports—a complicated task to say the least—consumers could simply determine whether a company belongs to an association that regulates its members.

Most sophisticated environmental management systems are found in highly profitable firms that have made significant past investments in advanced manufacturing systems. Associations can facilitate participation among less successful firms by subsidizing some of the costs of making the transition to environmental stewardship. By pooling industry experience, sharing pollution control technology, and providing a peer review process for management systems and training programs, they can reduce the costs incurred by firms that failed to develop organizational capacity in the past. Some of this is already occurring. Responsible Care, for example, sends teams of industry actors into chemical facilities to provide a form of peer review. The American Petroleum Institute invests heavily in training, education, and technology dissemination. Building on this model, there is no reason why associations could not underwrite the development of management systems in firms that might find the costs prohibitive.

The limits of associational governance. In theory, an association could compel members to achieve higher levels of pollution control than they might under a decentralized system of corporate environmentalism. Yet such expectations could be imposed on members only if the costs were less than the benefits of association membership (or if membership were necessary for economic survival). For example, the costs of complying with the American Forest and Paper Association's Sustainable Forestry Initiative might be more than justified by the benefits of association membership, since expulsion from the association would effectively foreclose access to the supply chain of members. However, there are distinct limits to what can be achieved under association codes. Members must still realize a profit, and this places constraints on what an association can demand—an important constraint in an era of global competition, where stringent national association codes might only open the door to imports. Corporations have the proximate goal of maintaining profitability; associations have the proximate goal of maintaining or expanding their membership roles and revenues. The extent to which private entities will embrace environmental management will be limited by organizational needs.

Hypothetically, associations could subsidize the costs of participation, thereby partially offsetting these costs. Yet as a greater percentage of firms in an industry abide by environmental codes, the marginal benefits decline. Ironically, the differentiation advantages gained from quality environmental management may dissipate as an industry realizes higher levels of participation. When few firms can be distinguished on the basis of their performance, they are far more likely to appeal to customers who would discriminate on these grounds. However, if a certain level of performance becomes an industry norm and all actors can make a verifiable claim to environmentally sound production, there will be incentives to search for differentiation advantages in other areas.

There is a further difficulty. Trade associations are rarely international organizations. They govern the behavior of industry actors within a given nation (or even within a subnational jurisdiction). If associations adopt stringent performance standards and coordinate the practices of all major members, these same firms may be competing against foreign entities that are not participating in comparable association schemes. As economic activity becomes increasingly global, it is questionable whether associations can play a primary role in self-regulation. There are examples of international cooperation among nationally based associations. Responsible Care, for example, is implemented by chemical associations in forty-six countries and overseen by a Responsible Care leadership group that is part of the International Council of Chemical Associations. Unless this model is broadly disseminated, the pressures of global competition may erode the environmental self-regulatory efforts of national associations and their members.

In sum, although associations can contribute to higher levels of environmental performance, there are once again limitations. One can assume that associations will strive to maintain a balance between meeting the demands of external stakeholders and promoting industry needs—a balance that may limit their willingness to promote high levels of environmental performance. Moreover, the more successful they are in bringing all industry actors into compliance with environmental norms, the greater the incentives for firms to search elsewhere for sources of sustainable competitive advantage. One can imagine ways in which public policies could be crafted to address some of the weaknesses of associational self-regulation. We shall return to this issue below.

International Standards and Self-Regulation

Another means of promoting self-regulation of environmental impacts is through international standards. International standards provide one means of going beyond the limitations of associational governance on a nation-specific scale. As noted in Chapter 9, the prevailing international standards for environmental management are taken from the ISO 14000 series, developed under the auspices of the International Organization for Standardization in Geneva, Switzerland. Companies that wish to be certified as ISO 14001–compliant must design and implement an EMS geared to meet the standards' requirements and initiate a cycle of continuous improvement to reduce environmental impacts. ISO 14001 requires heavy investments in training, personnel, and record-keeping. Certification under the ISO 14001 standard requires external auditing (comparable, in some ways, to external financial auditing), which attests both to an organization's success in meeting the standard's specifications and its compliance with all laws and regulations. Given the infrequency of regulatory inspections, the existence of an ISO 14001 certificate may prove to be a useful indicator of a firm's environmental performance. One should not be surprised, given what was stated above regarding the growing importance of corporate environmental practices, that ISO 14001 certification is necessary for success in many industries. Many firms now require that all first-tier suppliers and distributors be certified as compliant with ISO 14001. Despite popular claims that the globalization of production leads inexorably to a ratcheting down of environmental performance, it is clear that, in many cases, standards have provided a mechanism for improving environmental performance in facilities that are beyond the reach of US environmental regulations.

The limits of standard-based governance. Despite the rapid dissemination of ISO 14001 certification, there are sources for concern. First, ISO 14000 is frequently criticized for its singular focus on process. Firms must meet rather rigorous requirements with respect to EMS design and documentation. Yet the rapidity and magnitude of change in environmental impacts is seen largely as a managerial prerogative. Some firms may set ambitious goals to go well beyond what regulators could ever require; others may be far more modest. In short, the existence of an ISO 14001–certified EMS says little about overall environmental performance other than that it is superior to what might be mandated by laws and regulations. Second and related, while ISO 14001 leads firms to a continuous reduction in environmental impacts, it does not speak to the larger environmental impact of the companies' core products. As noted above, the US automobile industry has embraced ISO 14001 and has forced other firms to follow suit through supply chain pressures. Yet one might question the overall environmental impact when one is simply reducing the waste generated from the production of an ever-expanding fleet of luxury cars, trucks, and sport utility vehicles.

Finally, one must be concerned with participation rates. ISO 14001 rests on the existence of a high-quality EMS, which in turn depends on pre-existing corporate capabilities. Firms that implemented advanced manufacturing systems (e.g., total quality management, "just in time" inventory control, sophisticated management information systems) developed an organizational capacity to manage environmental impacts as well (Florida 1996; Florida and Davidson 2001). The ISO 14000 series was designed explicitly to piggyback on the International Organization for Standardization's ISO 9000 series of quality control standards. Firms that have failed to make these earlier investments may find the transition to ISO 14000 to be prohibitively expensive. Of course, to the extent that there are significant supply chain pressures, compliance and certification costs may be the price of survival. As argued in Chapter 9, regulatory treatment of the standards and information gained during audits has also depressed participation rates, a point that we will return to below.

■ Putting the Pieces Together

The basic components of our stylized world are now in place. In this world, many but not all profit-seeking corporations explicitly manage environmental impacts, thereby reducing or preventing pollution. The goal may be to achieve higher levels of resource productivity and claim cost-based advantages in the market. The goal may be to appeal to green consumers by differentiating their products from the competition. Corporations may want to gain access to the bid lists of corporations that have made environmental performance a key criterion in establishing supplier relationships. They may seek to attract capital from socially responsible investment funds or receive the lower insurance rates that accompany lower levels of environmental risk. They may be concerned about the vulnerability to potential lawsuits in the future, as citizens and communities sue to get compensation for environmental damages. One way of reducing this vulnerability is to manage environmental practices proactively and prevent future events. Regardless of the proximate goal, environmental management is viewed as a means of achieving market advantages that will translate into higher levels of profitability.

Financial institutions and large contractors will not be easily inveigled by symbolic statements of corporate environmental values, even if they are designed with care (and printed with an abundance of soy ink). There is too much corporate greenwash, too many attempts on the part of businesses to create the impression of environmental commitment, even if it bears little connection to corporate practices. Thus, some subset of companies may seek to comply with the environmental codes developed by their trade associations. However, many associations may not have well-established environmental programs, or key potential contractors may find compliance with these codes to be an insufficient indicator of commitment. Thus another subset of firms may seek to implement ISO 14001 and achieve certification.

For some companies, it may be possible to meet the requirements of association codes and ISO 14001 simultaneously or to combine one of these options with participation in the Global Reporting Initiative, a voluntary effort to standardize the release of audited environmental information.

Once companies have made a verifiable commitment to environmental management, they may decide to impose similar requirements on first-tier suppliers and distributors. They may require that companies wishing to bid on contracts acquire ISO 14001 certification. Such a comprehensive vision of environmental impacts is strongly supported by an ISO 14001–compliant EMS. As a result of this decision, supply chain pressures may force additional firms to embark on the road to environmental management, leading to a further expansion in the number of companies that are promoting higher levels of environmental quality regardless of regulatory requirements.

■ Bringing the State Back In

What should be clear by now is this: absent direct regulation, there are a number of forces that have shaped the evolving system of corporate environmental governance. Although this system is uneven and has clear limitations, it is nonetheless significant. Policymakers should integrate some appreciation of these structures into their deliberations over an appropriate state role. They should ask how public policies and institutions can be reconfigured to reinforce the positive contributions and compensate for the more glaring deficits. As the discussion of the President's Council on Sustainable Development in Chapter 13 suggests, this deliberative process has already been initiated, although its impact on policy and practices remains nebulous.

Although it is always attractive to engage in a full-blown redesign of institutions and policies, it is more pragmatic to consider how one might achieve one's results through a practicable rearrangement and modification of current policies and practices. Let us consider three of the most significant limitations here. The first and most obvious limitation comes in the area of information. If firms have credible environmental policies and are seeking differentiation-based advantages, they will be successful only to the extent that they can make their commitments and performance known to relevant stakeholders. If there is too much greenwash, even genuine claims may be discounted by consumers and investors who are rightfully skeptical and unwilling to incur the costs necessary to verify corporate claims. A key question is this: How can policy be used to guarantee that market actors have access to reliable information in a standardized format?

Second, there is the problem of participation. The largest, most profitable firms are also the companies most likely to have the organizational resources necessary to maintain well-developed environmental management systems. Moreover, they are involved in multiple supply chains. As they impose environmental standards on suppliers and distributors, they can force smaller firms to invest in environmental management. However, there is an entire universe of small and medium-sized enterprises that do not have the resources, information, or incentives to invest in a high-quality EMS or reengineer products to prevent pollution. They may be involved in highly price-sensitive markets selling standard components with razor-thin profit margins. The key question concerns how these firms can be convinced to participate in environmental management. Short of some form of direct public regulation, it is difficult to arrive at a solution.

Third, process and performance may be related, but they are not synonymous. A firm may have a quality EMS that meets association standards or achieves ISO 14001 certification or both. Yet it may have very low aspirations with respect to system performance. More likely, companies may discover a clear relationship between environmental management and cost reductions in the initial phases. As they move beyond the most egregious sources of pollution, however, they may discover declining marginal benefits. Under these circumstances, they may rationally pursue profitability gains in areas that have no positive ramifications for environmental quality. Rather than seeking continuing improvements in environmental performance, for example, they may seek to introduce new product features that engender new waste streams. How can firms be convinced, absent direct command-and-control regulation, to adopt sufficiently high performance standards?

Information Disclosure and Green Market Forces

Information scarcity is commonly cited as a source of market failure. Although companies may seek to gain environmentally based differentiation advantages, these advantages exist only if consumers and investors intent on discriminating on the basis of environmental performance have economical sources of quality information on a firm-specific basis. Unfortunately, information on performance can be lost in a sea of corporate greenwash and public relations campaigns designed to create false impressions of environmental stewardship. Although there have been private efforts to standardize reporting, such as the Global Reporting Initiative, they are voluntary. A simple response to this problem is to create legal requirements that all firms disclose environmental performance data using standard indicators, subject to third-party auditing.

Mandatory information disclosure is the cornerstone of capital market regulation in the United States. The Securities and Exchange Commission (SEC) requires all publicly traded firms to report information of material interest to shareholders. It is interesting to note that the SEC also requires the public reporting of environmental impacts. According to the SEC's Regulation S-K:

> Appropriate disclosure also shall be made as to the material effects that compliance with Federal, State and local provisions which have been enacted or adopted regulating the discharge of materials into the environment, or otherwise relating to the protection of the environment, may have upon the capital expenditures, earnings and competitive position of the registrant and its subsidiaries. The registrant shall disclose any material estimated capital expenditures for environmental control facilities for the remainder of its current fiscal year and its succeeding fiscal year and for such further periods as the registrant may deem material. (Reg. § 229.101, Item 101, d[xii])

In practice, companies report only major Superfund liabilities. Regulation S-K could be amended to require more comprehensive disclosure of information on the release of standard pollutants. More will be said about this recommendation below.

Mandatory information disclosure can provide market actors with information that can be valuable in making purchasing, procurement, and investment decisions. It may also directly shape corporate behavior. As noted in Chapter 2, Congress created the Toxic Release Inventory with the Emergency Planning and Community Right-to-Know Act of 1986. Under the inventory, firms were required to disclose information on the use of 654 toxic chemicals. This information, provided in a standard format, was made available through a public database. Evaluations of corporate responses to the Toxic Release Inventory reveal that the program stimulated voluntary reductions of up to 50 percent in reported releases in its first several years (Karkkainen 2001: 287). Comparable responses have been observed in other nations as well (see Afsah, Blackman, and Ratunanda 2000). Mandatory disclosure created new concerns over potential liability, thereby increasing internal pressures for reform. Moreover, the Toxic Release Inventory was introduced at the same time that many companies were implementing environmental management systems to manage impacts. There is every reason to believe that mandatory disclosure of comprehensive environmental performance data, employing standard indicators and third-party verification, could have similar impacts.

Given the diversity of products, processes, and inputs, the use of common performance indicators across the economy might not reveal the most useful information. Ideally, mandatory information disclosure would require the reporting of data on indicators specific to the industry in question. Moreover, it would require that this information be presented in combination with summary statistics such as industry averages and the performance thresholds achieved by top performers (e.g., the top quartile and decile of firms in an industry). Information disclosure is an area ripe for state-association collaboration. Trade associations possess the best information regarding the technologies, inputs, and production processes employed in their industries. As noted above, they have great self-regulatory potential that has yet to be explored by regulators. By working cooperatively with trade associations, the EPA could develop industry-specific reporting protocols and rely on associations to provide industrywide statistics. This information would simultaneously provide market actors the information needed to discriminate on the basis of performance, create targets for firms seeking to improve their performance, and give regulators a means to target more accurately their enforcement resources.

Beyond the National Environmental Performance Track

As noted in Chapter 10, the EPA is currently experimenting with the National Environmental Performance Track. Although it is too early to provide a comprehensive evaluation, the performance of state-level green tracks has been mixed, particularly when they have focused on process rather than performance (Speir 2001). More important, by design, regulatory green tracks engage in cream skimming. They reward the subset of firms that are already exceeding requirements and that have sophisticated management systems in place. As a result, their larger impact on environmental quality may be limited. The key challenge for green tracks is that of making integrated regulation and flexibility available to a larger set of firms in the hope of stimulating innovations without simultaneously relaxing standards. To explore this issue, it is useful to consider the potential role of industry associations.

One can draw a useful distinction between corporate voluntarism and self-regulation (see Gunningham and Rees 1997). Corporate voluntarism involves decisions made on a firm-by-firm basis to employ an EMS and some of the environmental policy tools described in Chapter 8. Self-regulation, in contrast, involves employing industry-level associations to regulate their members. Associations may impose industry codes, set environmental standards, or prescribe EMS design specifications. A number of associations regulate their members through codes, although the quality of codes and enforcement is mixed. Corporate voluntarism and self-regulation have very different regulatory implications. Corporate voluntarism can generate a proliferation of custom-built management systems that are difficult for regulators to evaluate and monitor. Many of the EPA's reinvention initiatives (like Project XL) were designed, nominally, to promote innovations. However, the diversity of systems creates problems of information scarcity for regulators, which respond, quite predictably, by requesting voluminous information and guarantees of superior environmental performance. The resulting regulatory transaction costs thwart participation. As for self-regulation, although industry codes may be easier for regulators to monitor, they will be discounted by corporations to the extent that they stand at tension with regulations. In both cases, the kinds of activities that companies must engage in to have meaningful environmental management systems may increase their vulnerability to regulatory penalties.

The NEPT currently depends on corporate voluntarism; associations have no significant role in the experiment, although many are members of the Performance Track Network. Given the difficulty of overseeing custom-made corporate environmental policies, one would predict that there will be administratively imposed limits to the number of participants or regulatory demands and that delays will prove so onerous as to vitiate any advantages firms might enjoy. The solution to this problem is to delegate far greater authority to associations and integrate them into the performance track, thereby creating a system of government-supervised self-regulation (Priest 1997) or what Ian Ayers and John Braithwaite (1992) refer to as "enforced self-regulation." Ideally, corporate voluntarism would be replaced by a system of associational self-regulation, which in turn would be given some formal recognition and support by regulators, who would be intimately involved in negotiating and overseeing association rules.

The EPA could work with associations in determining the ideal specifications for a corporate environmental management system, tailored to reflect the technologies used in a given industry. Ideally, it would design the systems to be ISO 14001–compliant, so firms could take advantage of international certification and the growing body of knowledge on the performance of ISO 14001 systems. The American Chemistry Council is already implementing an alternative track of Responsible Care that meets the requirements for ISO 14001 certification. Given the limitations inherent in the process orientation of an environmental management system, the EPA could work with associations to develop industry-specific environmental performance indicators to ensure that companies adopt sufficiently demanding pollution prevention goals. Rather than spending scarce resources on monitoring, the EPA could impose third-party auditing requirements (another advantage of ISO 14001–based requirements). In sum, by tailoring regulatory specifications to reflect the products, processes, and technologies predominant in the industry, a green track could be used to create a sector-specific form of regulation that would potentially go beyond the limitations imposed by the existing system.

Employing associations as implementation agents is by no means unprecedented. In the Netherlands, as shown in Chapter 10, environmental standards are set on an industry-specific basis through negotiations with industry associations, which play a central role in supervising member firms and facilitating implementation. Even if the EPA has not used associations in this manner, they have been used in other policy arenas in the United States. Historically, there was heavy reliance on associations as implementation agents during the crises of war mobilization and the Great Depression (see Eisner 2000a). Outside periods of crisis, associations have also served an important role in some regulatory issue areas. For example, the SEC regulates the over-the-counter market through the National Association of Securities Dealers, a decision initiated by the commission when it realized that it could not regulate the highly decentralized industry (Eisner 2000b: 111). The Nuclear Regulatory Commission has delegated some regulatory powers to the Institute of Nuclear Power Operations, an industry association founded in the wake of Three Mile Island with explicit self-regulatory functions (see Rees 1994).

Green Carrots and Sticks

Industry self-regulation—even with government supervision—may raise profound concerns on the part of a public that demands the accountability that has been a hallmark of regulation. Yet it is vital to emphasize that a green track is not a substitute for traditional regulation. Rather it provides higher levels of flexibility for firms that have already exceeded regulatory requirements. Traditional command-and-control regulations must remain in force to create a regulatory floor for all firms other than those that have made a verifiable commitment to meeting the standards of the green track. Of course, it is hoped that the number of green track participants will continue to swell such that traditional regulation would be relevant to an ever-smaller subset of firms. Unfortunately, regulators may discover that most firms might have few—and declining—incentives to participate in a green track. Current benefits, like greater flexibility, integrated permitting, and a low inspection priority, may be outweighed by compliance costs. Moreover, differentiation advantages may disappear as the universe of environmentally responsible businesses expands, leading profit-seeking firms to search for other sources of sustainable advantage that may be less environmentally friendly.

Assuming that new legislation mandating association membership is fanciful at best, the most powerful incentives could be provided through a serious application of the government's procurement powers. Given that government at all levels spends 20 percent of GDP, procurement policies could be used creatively to effect change across the supply chain. Clinton's Executive Order 13101 required agencies to engage in "environmentally preferable purchasing," integrating environmental performance into contracting decisions. Pursuant to the order, each major procuring agency was directed to designate an environmental executive (at the assistant secretary level or its equivalent) to integrate the requirements into agency practices and report procurement decisions to the federal environmental executive (White House Task Force on Recycling 2001: 15–16). Thus far, procurement has focused primarily on recycled goods; the government does not collect data on the dollar value of environmentally preferable purchasing. Yet as shown in Chapter 7, the Resource Conservation Challenge is promoting expanded green procurement to create incentives for greater environmental stewardship.

Building on EO 13101, the federal government could use its procurement power to reinforce green track participation. It could guarantee procurement preferences to participants that offer their products at a price that falls within some reasonable range (e.g., 3–5 percent) of the average bid. These preferences could create incentives to promote ongoing emphasis on green production. Association membership could be promoted by giving priority to firms that both are members of associations that have negotiated agreements with the EPA, and are in compliance with the association codes. Ultimately, one could magnify the impact of procurement across the supply chain by giving the highest preference to firms that contract *exclusively* with other participating firms, where they exist. This would be analogous to Ford Motor Company's decision to require that all its suppliers be ISO 14001–compliant, thereby coercing environmentally responsible management through supply chain pressures.

By now, it should be clear that we are concerned with much more than regulatory reform, as traditionally understood. Rather the focus is placed squarely on how existing governance structures are shaping environmental performance and, within this context, how government policies can reinforce incentives to promote superior environmental outcomes. Far more could be accomplished by incorporating regulatory policies, particularly if they are redesigned to reinforce rather than obviate private sector initiatives. Wherever possible, policies should be reconfigured to minimize the reliance on command-and-control instruments and maximize the reliance on cap-and-trade instruments that have a proven track record of attaining higher levels of environmental quality at lower costs. Certainly, command-and-control instruments may prove to have a vital role for firms that lack the organizational capabilities or resources to employ a quality EMS or engage in pollution trading. Yet even in these cases, one would hope that the establishment of a structure that generates powerful incentives and the flexibility for higher levels of corporate self-regulation, and that creatively employs associations and international standards, would free up substantial budgetary resources that could be redeployed to provide expanded compliance assistance for this subset of underperforming firms.

Ultimately, what is envisioned is a system in which regulated entities could be placed into one of three analytically separable tiers (see Table

14.1). All firms, regardless of their tier, would be subject to mandatory environmental information disclosure. Beyond that, regulatory treatments would vary based on environmental performance and organizational capacity. At the top tier, one would find the subset of firms that have the capacity to engage in self-regulation and meet progressively higher performance thresholds. At an intermediate tier, one would find businesses that are subject to regulations, reporting comprehensive and credible data on performance, and presumably responding to market incentives and incentive-based regulations to achieve higher levels of environmental performance. At the bottom tier, one would find corporations (particularly small and medium-sized enterprises, and firms in highly price-sensitive commodity markets) that experience persistent difficulties in complying with regulations and lack the capacity to move, unassisted, to higher tiers. This bottom tier would receive the bulk of regulatory attention, albeit with special attention to assisting firms in making the transition to the intermediate tier via the provision of compliance assistance and, where appropriate, financial assistance either through direct grants or access to a revolving fund.

In the past, the EPA has been indicted for its rigidity, its imposition of high costs, its focus on technique rather than results, and its persistent "bean counting." Under the system described above, success would be measured not by the number of citations or the magnitude of the penalties, but by the effectiveness of the entire system of environmental governance and the pace with which regulated entities become effectively self-regulating and move to the top tier. Most of the basic components of the system currently exist. The core challenges are to identify the limiting factors and use public policy to fill the gaps and integrate the components. The missing components (e.g., mandatory reporting with industry-specific indicators) would not require a dramatic expansion of regulatory authority or public sector expenditures.

Filling the Gaps

For all its potential merits, the creation of the multi-tiered system of governance described above is not sufficient, when taken by itself, to compensate for all the problems identified in previous chapters. There are two clear examples, both of which require a national response, and neither of which can be addressed adequately through the proposed system of environmental governance. Indeed, in both cases, efforts to strengthen the coercive hand of the state would appear to be necessary if one wanted to realize the full benefits of a less coercive system. These examples work at the local and global levels.

As noted in Chapter 3, the EPA is characterized by a high level of vertical fragmentation. Regulatory duties are delegated to regional offices and to state regulators. Without a credible threat of enforcement, compliance flounders. Voluntarism, self-regulation, and partnerships are of little value if they do not rest on a firm foundation of enforcement. So much of what must

Table 14.1 Multi-Tiered Hybrid System of Regulation

Actors	Instruments	Incentives	Results
Government-Supervised Self-Regulation			
Environmental Protection Agency Trade associations Corporations	Green track Environmental management systems: • ISO 14001 • Industry-specific performance expectations • Third-party auditing	Flexibility Integrated permitting processes Low inspection priority Performance-based procurement preferences Differentiation and cost-based advantages	Performance "beyond regulation" Innovations "Globalization" of performance
Incentive-Based Regulation			
Environmental Protection Agency Corporations	Market-based instruments Environmental management systems: • ISO 14001 • Third-party auditing	Moderate flexibility in regulatory compliance Cost-based advantages	Pollution reductions potentially "beyond regulation" Efficiency gains
Standard Regulation			
Environmental Protection Agency Corporations	Command-and-control instruments Compliance assistance Financing	Avoidance of penalties and negative publicity	Regulatory compliance Promotion of self-regulatory capacity
Regulation by Information			
Securities and Exchange Commission Environmental Protection Agency Corporations	Mandatory information disclosure: • Industry-specific indicators • Third-party auditing	Avoidance of penalties Differentiation-based advantages rewarded by markets	Heightened corporate accountability Information for market and regulators Internal pressure for self-regulation

be done to ensure enforcement is dependent on state-level regulatory capacity. States compile vital information on pollution. They develop implementation plans for air pollution; they are responsible for setting local water quality standards. They play a central role in environmental permitting, inspections, and enforcement. Although it is easy to blame or credit the EPA administrator or the president or both for environmental quality, one must recall that public policy as a pattern of action is far more dependent on what occurs at the implementation stage.

States are wildly uneven in the development of regulatory capacities (see Siy, Koziol, and Rollins 2001), and key sources of poor regulatory performance can often be found within the states. States have been forced to absorb a host of new costs in recent decades, as Congress sought to manage its budgetary problems by shifting burdens to the states. This process was partially abated with the passage of the Unfunded Mandates Reform Act of 1995. The George W. Bush administration has signaled its desire to shift more enforcement duties to the states along with a greater share of the EPA's enforcement budget. While one might support this devolution of authority, it may quickly exceed the capacities of certain states, thereby exacerbating current problems. There is a strong justification for a heavy infusion of federal funds into state environmental agencies where there is clear evidence that a lack of regulatory capacity has prevented effective implementation (Scheberle 2004: 383–385).

One can move from the local to the global to consider an additional example of an area where the kind of system described above may have an insufficient impact: global climate change. As argued in Chapter 12, some of the basic factors that provided a firm foundation for the success of the Montreal Protocol, which addresses ozone-depleting substances, were seemingly lacking in the Kyoto Protocol, which addresses global climate change. Although there were clear differences with respect to the complexity and salience of the two issues, it is more useful to focus on the strong domestic commitment to the regulation of ozone-depleting substances, a commitment that provided a foundation for subsequent international commitments. With the domestic regulations in place, US corporations had incentives to invest in new research and development and promote international agreements as a means of creating new market opportunities and equalizing regulatory costs for foreign competitors.

What are the implications for policy? Rather than viewing international regulation of greenhouse gases as an impossibility, one can instead view the creation of domestic regulations as a critical first step. As discussed in Chapter 7, the Clear Skies Initiative proposed by the George W. Bush administration did nothing to extend regulation to carbon dioxide, despite campaign commitments to the contrary. The competing bills, in contrast, integrated carbon dioxide caps into their multipollutant proposals.

Requiring carbon dioxide caps in new Clean Air Act amendments, combined with mandatory reporting on carbon dioxide emissions (part of the larger mandatory reporting system presented above), could go far in reducing domestic resistance to international measures. Corporations would have greater incentives to reduce their emissions (e.g., market pressures combined with access to government contracts and the NEPT). They would have incentives to invest in alternative fuel technologies that could allow them to claim a commercial advantage. They would be more likely to promote participation in international initiatives if one of the results would be the certainty that all potential competitors were forced to labor under comparable regulatory constraints. Moreover, clear evidence that the United States was assuming responsibility for its greenhouse gas emissions would go far in convincing developing countries to assume commitments to manage greenhouse gases, an important issue given the existing trajectory of development.

The Bush administration sought to harness corporate voluntarism through its Climate Partners Program. While there is some anecdotal evidence that participants have made headway in reducing carbon dioxide emissions, participation was largely limited to firms that already had an established record for exemplary environmental performance. Establishing regulatory caps on carbon dioxide (if sufficiently rigorous), when combined with mandatory reporting of emissions, would create incentives for a much larger universe of firms to seek out innovative solutions. As in the above examples, public regulation is not best understood as an alternative to corporate voluntarism, but as a vital foundation for voluntarism that increases the returns to innovation by preventing nonparticipants from free-riding on the efforts of others.

This recommendation has a strong local component as well. As of 2006, seventeen states, including Texas, Wisconsin, Pennsylvania, and New Jersey, have assumed responsibility for greenhouse gas emissions by introducing renewable portfolio standards for their electrical utilities. In essence, a renewable portfolio standard requires that some proportion of a load-bearing entity's electricity be generated by renewable sources such as solar or wind energy. Although early results are quite positive in Texas, other states have encountered problems that can be attributed to poor policy designs, lack of developed enforcement capacity, and limited information on local variations in production and consumption (Haddad and Jefferiss 1999; Langniss and Wiser 2003).

A renewable portfolio standard may be of limited value in reducing greenhouse gas emissions if it creates incentives for substituting out of more benign energy sources like natural gas. Indeed, analysts debate whether it is more effective to impose carbon caps, a portfolio standard, or some combination of instruments (see Palmer and Burtraw 2004).

Moreover, the impact and dissemination of portfolio standards may well depend on the potential for trading of renewable energy credits between states (and, potentially, nations) (see Victor 2004). Utilities in states with heavy investments in solar energy may, for example, sell some portion of the electricity to utilities in states that do not have the capacity to generate a comparable level of renewable energy at competitive prices. The design and maintenance of a trading system requires heavy investments in analysis and administration, once again suggesting that success in addressing global climate problems at the local level may be contingent on decisions to invest greater federal resources in the development of state-level regulatory capacities and an active EPA role in coordinating trades among states. This, in turn, requires a fundamental change in the EPA's regulatory posture, one that is consistent with the larger argument of this book.

■ Conclusion

This book began with a simple observation: although the US system of environmental protection regulation has generated some impressive gains, there is much to suggest that it has run its course. Future gains in environmental quality may be impossible without a fundamental reconsideration of regulatory design. This reconsideration must take the form of incorporating advances in corporate self-regulation, associational regulation, and standards into the regulatory system and thinking creatively about how public policies can be used to reinforce incentives or compensate for their absence. The decision to reconceptualize regulation—to move from hierarchical relationships, command-and-control instruments, and adversarial politics—will not be easy, given the pressures of partisanship, the complexity of the underlying issues, the vagaries of public opinion, and original decisions regarding regulatory design. Nevertheless, success in extending the environmental gains of the past into the future, and managing a host of emerging environmental problems, may be impossible without a decision to transform the existing system of environmental regulation into a broader system of green governance.

Acronyms

AFPA	American Forest and Paper Association
ANWR	Arctic National Wildlife Refuge
CEQ	Council on Environmental Quality
CERCLA	Comprehensive Environmental Response, Compensation, and Liability Act
CERCLIS	Comprehensive Environmental Response, Compensation, and Liability Information System
CERES	Coalition for Environmentally Responsible Economies
CFC	chlorofluorocarbon
DQS	desired quality standard
EKC	environmental Kuznets curve
EMS	environmental management system
EO	executive order
EPA	Environmental Protection Agency
GAO	General Accounting Office
GATT	General Agreement on Tariffs and Trade
GDP	gross domestic product
GNP	gross national product
HCFC	hydrochlorofluorocarbon
HPV	high production volume
HSWA	Hazardous and Solid Waste Amendments
ICCA	International Council of Chemical Associations
IPCC	Intergovernmental Panel on Climate Change
ISO	International Organization for Standardization
LDC	less developed country
MAC	maximum allowable concentration
MNE	multinational enterprise
NEPT	National Environmental Performance Track
NPDES	National Pollutant Discharge Elimination System

NPV	net present value
NSR	New Source Review
OECD	Organization for Economic Cooperation and Development
OIRA	Office of Information and Regulatory Affairs
OMB	Office of Management and Budget
PCSD	President's Council on Sustainable Development
RCRA	Resource Conservation and Recovery Act
REGO	reinvention of government
RIA	regulatory impact analysis
SARA	Superfund Amendments and Reauthorization Act
SEC	Securities and Exchange Commission
SEP	superior environmental performance
SFI	Sustainable Forest Initiative
SIDS	screening-information dataset
UNEP	United Nations Environment Programme
USDA	US Department of Agriculture
VSL	value of a statistical life
WMO	World Meteorological Organization
WTO	World Trade Organization

Bibliography

Abusow, Kathy. 2005. "Let's Talk About Change: The SFI Program." Paper presented at the 2005 SFI Program annual conference, Portland, ME.

Ackerman, Bruce A., and W. T. Hassler. 1981. *Clean Coal/Dirty Air, or How the Clean-Air Act Became a Multibillion-Dollar Bailout for High Sulfur Coal Producers and What Should Be Done About It.* New Haven: Yale University Press.

Adler, Jonathan H. 2000. "Clear Politics, Dirty Profits: Rent-Seeking Behind the Green Curtain." In *Political Environmentalism: Going Behind the Green Curtain,* edited by T. L. Anderson. Stanford: Hoover Institution.

Afsah, Shakeb, Allen Blackman, and Damayanti Ratunanda. 2000. "How Do Public Disclosure Pollution Control Programs Work? Evidence from Indonesia." Washington, DC: Resources for the Future.

Aghjayan, Edward K. 1997. Correspondence of Edward K. Aghjayan, public utilities general manager, city of Anaheim, California, to Laura Gentile, project manager, EPA. November 8.

Albrecht, Johan. 1998. "Environmental Policy and the Inward Investment Position of US 'Dirty' Industries." *Intereconomics* 33 (4): 186–194.

Aldy, Joseph E., Scott Barrett, and Robert N. Stavins. 2003. *13+1: A Comparison of Global Climate Change Policy Architectures.* Washington, DC: Resources for the Future.

Allen, Mike, and Dana Milbank. 2003. "Utah Gov. Named as Chief of EPA; Nominee Wants Power Moved Out of Washington." *Washington Post* (August 12): A1.

Anderson, Terry L., and Donald R. Leal. 2001. *Free Market Environmentalism.* Rev. ed. New York: Palgrave.

Andreen, William L. 2003. "The Evolution of Water Pollution Control in the United States: State, Local, and Federal Efforts, 1789–1972." *Stanford Environmental Law Journal* 22: 215–294.

Annan, Kofi. 2004. "Secretary-General Says Success of Montreal Protocol Protecting Ozone Layer Should Inspire Parties to Other Environmental Agreements." New York: United Nations.

Arentsen, Maarten J., Hans Th. A. Bressers, and Laurence J. O'Toole. 2000. "Institutional and Policy Responses to Uncertainty in Environmental Policy: A Comparison of Dutch and U.S. Styles." *Policy Studies Journal* 28 (3): 597–611.

Averch, Harvey. 1990. *Private Markets and Public Intervention: A Primer for Policy Designers*. Pittsburgh: University of Pittsburgh Press.

Ayers, Ian, and John Braithwaite. 1992. *Responsive Regulation: Transcending the Deregulation Debate*. Oxford: Oxford University Press.

Barcott, Bruce. 2004. "Changing All the Rules: Bush Administration's Overturning of New Source Review in Pollution Regulation." *New York Times Magazine* (April 4): 38–45, 66, 73, 76–78.

Barrett, Scott. 1999. "International Cooperation and the International Commons." *Duke Environmental Law and Policy Forum* 10: 131–145.

Barzel, Yoram. 1989. *Economic Analysis of Property Rights*. Cambridge: Cambridge University Press.

Baumgartner, Frank R., and Bryan D. Jones. 1993. *Agendas and Instability in American Politics*. Chicago: University of Chicago Press.

Beabout, Gregory R. 1988. "The Principle of Subsidiarity and Freedom in the Family, Church, Market, and Government." *Journal of Markets and Morality* 1 (2): 130–141.

Beardsley, Dan, Terry Davies, and Robert Hersh. 1997. "Improving Environmental Management: What Works, What Doesn't." *Environment* 39: 6–9.

Bedford, Christopher. 1996. "Dirty Secrets: The Corporations' Campaign for an Environmental Audit Privilege." Environmental Action Foundation, Good Neighbor Project for Sustainable Industries, and Communities Concerned About Corporations, Takoma Park, MD.

Benedick, Richard Elliot. 1999. "The Indispensable Element in the Montreal Ozone Protocol." *Columbia Earth Institution: EARTHmatters* 1999 (Fall): 4.

———. 2004. "The Improbable Montreal Protocol: Science, Diplomacy, and Defending the Ozone Layer." Paper presented to the 2004 American Meteorological Society policy symposium, Washington, DC.

Bensel, Richard F. 1984. *Sectionalism and American Political Development*. Madison: University of Wisconsin Press.

Berlin, Miri. 1998. "Environmental Auditing: Entering the Eco-Information Highway." *New York University Environmental Law Journal* 6: 618–655.

Bernstein, Marver H. 1955. *Regulating Business by Independent Commission*. Princeton: Princeton University Press.

Blackman, Allen, James Boyd, Alan Krupnick, and Janice Mazurek. 2001. "The Economics of Tailored Regulation and the Implications for Project XL." Washington, DC: Resources for the Future.

Blumberg, Jerald, Age Korsvold, and Georges Blum. 1996. *Environmental Performance and Shareholder Value*. Geneva: World Business Council on Sustainable Development.

Boehmer, Keven, and Aleg Chert. 2003. "An Emerging Global Standard." *Carbon Finance* (December): 16–17.

Boise Cascade. 1999. *Environmental Perspectives*. Boise, ID: Boise Cascade.

Bolch, Ben, and Harold Lyons. 1993. *Apocalypse Not: Science, Economics, and Environmentalism*. Washington, DC: CATO Institute.

Boroughs, Zulma. 1998. Correspondence of Zulma Boroughs, Union Carbide Corporation, to Gregg A. Cooke, EPA regional administrator. December 18.

Bossel, Hartmut. 1998. *Earth at a Crossroads: Paths to a Sustainable Future*. Cambridge: Cambridge University Press.

Bosso, Christopher J. 1987. *Pesticides and Politics: The Life Cycle of a Public Issue*. Pittsburgh: University of Pittsburgh Press.

———. 2005. *Environment, Inc.: From Grassroots to Beltway*. Lawrence: University of Kansas Press.

Bosso, Christopher J., and Deborah Lynn Guber. 2003. "The Boundaries and Contours of American Environmental Activism." In *Environmental Policy: New Directions for the Twenty-First Century,* edited by N. J. Vig and M. E. Kraft. Washington, DC: Congressional Quarterly.

Braithwaite, John, and Peter Drahos. 2000. *Global Business Regulation.* Cambridge: Cambridge University Press.

Brigham, Eugene F., and Louis C. Gapenski. 1997. *Financial Management: Theory and Practice.* 8th ed. Fort Worth, TX: Dryden.

Brophy, Michael. 1996a. "Environmental Charters and Guidelines." In *Corporate Environmental Management: Systems and Strategies,* edited by R. Welford. London: Earthscan.

———. 1996b. "Environmental Policies." In *Corporate Environmental Management: Systems and Strategies,* edited by R. Welford. London: Earthscan.

Brown, Steven, and Michael J. Kiefer. 2003. "ECOS Budget Survey: Budgets Are Bruised but Still Strong." *ECOStates* (Summer): 10–15.

Browner, Carol M. 1993. "New Directions for Environmental Protection: P2 Policy Statement." Washington, DC: Environmental Protection Agency.

———. 2000. "30 Years of U.S. Environmental Protection." Speech delivered at the Kennedy School of Government, Harvard University, April 17.

Buchanan, James M., Robert D. Tollison, and Gordon Tullock. 1980. *Toward a Theory of the Rent Seeking Society.* College Station: Texas A&M Press.

Buchner, Barbara, and Marzio Galeotti. 2004. "Climate Policy and Economic Growth in Developing Countries: The Impact of Kyoto." *International Journal of Global Environmental Issues* 4 (1): 109–138.

Burford, Anne, and John Greenya. 1986. *Are You Tough Enough?* New York: McGraw-Hill.

Burtraw, Dallas. 2000. "Innovation Under the Tradable Sulfur Dioxide Emission Permits Program in the U.S. Electricity Sector." Discussion Paper no. 00-38. Washington, DC: Resources for the Future.

Burtraw, Dallas, and Alan J. Krupnick. 2003. "A Mercurial Reaction on Mercury?" Washington, DC: Resources for the Future.

Burtraw, Dallas, and Erin Mansur. 1999. "The Effects of Trading and Banking in the SO_2 Allowance Market." Discussion Paper no. 99-25. Washington, DC: Resources for the Future.

Bush, George W. 2002. "President Bush Announces Clean Skies Initiative." Speech delivered at the NOAA Science Center, Silver Spring, MD, February 14.

Buxton, Pamela. 2000. "Companies with a Social Conscience—More Firms Are Publishing Social as Well as Financial Reports." *Marketing* (April 27): 33.

Campbell, John L., J. Rogers Hollingsworth, and Leon N. Lindberg, eds. 1991. *Governance of the American Economy.* New York: Cambridge University Press.

Capra, Fritjof, and Gunter Pauli. 1995. "The Challenge." In *Steering Business Toward Sustainability,* edited by F. Capra and G. Pauli. Tokyo: United Nations University Press.

Carbaugh, Robert J. 1998. *International Economics.* 6th ed. Cincinnati: South-Western College Publishing.

Cavanagh, Sheila M., Robert W. Hahn, and Robert N. Stavins. 2001. "National Environmental Policy During the Clinton Years." Washington, DC: Resources for the Future.

Chiapetta, Sidonie. 1998. "Some Observations on Population, Ecosystems, and Markets." *Journal of Social, Political, and Economic Studies* 23 (3): 241–257.

Christmann, Petra, and Glen Taylor. 2001. "Globalization and the Environment:

Determinants of Firm Self-Regulation in China." *Journal of International Business Studies* 32 (3): 439–458.

Clinton, Bill, and Al Gore. 1995. "Reinventing Environmental Regulation 1995." http://www.epa.gov/reinvent/notebook/19950316.pdf.

Coase, Ronald H. 1960. "The Problem of Social Cost." *Journal of Law and Economics* 3 (October): 1–44.

Coglianese, Cary. 1999. "The Limits of Consensus: The Environmental Protection System in Transition: Toward a More Desirable Future." *Environment* 41 (3): 28–33.

Coglianese, Cary, and Jennifer Nash, eds. 2001. *Regulation from the Inside: Can Environmental Management Systems Achieve Policy Goals?* Washington, DC: Resources for the Future.

Collins, Flannary P. 2003. "The Small Business Liability Relief and Brownfields Revitalization Act: A Critique." *Duke Environmental Law and Policy Forum* 13 (2): 303–328.

Common, Michael. 1995. *Sustainability and Policy: Limits to Economics.* Cambridge: Cambridge University Press.

Conca, Ken. 2001. "Green Politics in the Bush Era: Anti-Environmentalism's Second Wave." *Dissent* 48 (3): 29–33.

Congressional Research Service. 1994. *Risk Analysis and Cost-Benefit Analysis of Environmental Regulations.* Washington, DC.

Connolly, Barbara, and Robert O. Keohane. 1996. "Institutions for Environmental Aid: Politics, Lessons and Opportunities." *Environment* 38 (June): 12–20.

Costanza, Robert, John Cumberland, Herman Daly, Robert Goodland, and Richard Norgaard. 1997. *An Introduction to Ecological Economics.* Boca Raton, FL: St. Lucie.

Crane, Michael. 2003. "Environmental Legislation Watch." *Legal Intelligencer* (October 16): 6.

Cropper, Maureen L., and Wallace E. Oates. 1992. "Environmental Economics: A Survey." *Journal of Economic Literature* 30 (June): 675–740.

Crosson, Pierre, and Michael A. Toman. 1994. "Economics and Sustainable Development." In *The Greening of Industrial Ecosystems,* edited by B. R. Allenby and D. J. Richards. Washington, DC: National Academy Press.

Cutchis, Pythagoras. 1974. "Stratospheric Ozone Depletion and Solar Ultraviolet Radiation on Earth." *Science* 184 (4132): 13–19.

Daly, Herman E. 1994. "Fostering Environmentally Sustainable Development: Four Parting Suggestions for the World Bank." *Ecological Economics* 10: 183–187.

———. 1996. *Beyond Growth: The Economics of Sustainable Development.* Boston: Beacon.

Daly, Herman E., and John B. Cobb. 1994. *For the Common Good: Redirecting the Economy Toward Community, the Environment, and a Sustainable Future.* 2nd ed. Boston: Beacon.

Dasgupta, Susmita, Benoit Laplante, Hua Wang, and David Wheeler. 2002. "Confronting the Environmental Kuznets Curve." *Journal of Economic Perspectives* 16 (1): 147–168.

Davis, Joseph A. 1984a. "Special Report: Hazardous Wastes Superfund Contaminated by Partisan Politics." *Congressional Quarterly Weekly Report* (March 17): 615.

———. 1984b. "Superfund Bill Doomed: RCRA Rewrite Strengthens Hazardous Waste Protections." *Congressional Quarterly Weekly Report* (October 6): 2453.

Deacon, Robert, and Catherine S. Norman. 2004. "Is the Environmental Kuznets

Curve an Empirical Regularity?" Working paper. Santa Barbara: University of California, Department of Economics.

Dealey, Sam. 2004. "Superfund Enters the Presidential Campaign, but Realities Are Unclear." *The Hill* (March 31): 4.

Delmas, Magali A. 2002. "Environmental Management Standards and Globalization." In *Dynamics of Regulatory Change: How Globalization Affects National Regulatory Policies.* International and Area Studies. Berkeley: University of California.

Denison, Richard A. 2004. *Orphan Chemicals in the HPV Challenge: A Status Report.* New York: Environmental Defense.

Denison, Richard A., and Karen Florini. 2003. *Facing the Challenge: A Status Report on the U.S. HPV Challenge Program.* New York: Environmental Defense.

Department of Energy. 1998. *Impacts of the Kyoto Protocol on U.S. Energy Markets and Economic Activity.* Washington, DC.

Derthick, Martha, and Paul J. Quirk. 1985. *The Politics of Deregulation.* Washington, DC: Brookings Institution.

DeSimone, Livio D., and Frank Popoff. 1997. *Eco-Efficiency: The Business Link to Sustainable Development.* Cambridge: MIT Press.

DeSombre, Elizabeth R. 1999. "The Experience of the Montreal Protocol: Particularly Remarkable, and Remarkably Particular." Paper presented at the Third Generation of International Environmental Law Conference, October, Irvine, CA.

———. 2004. "Global Warming: More Common than Tragic." *Ethics & International Affairs* 18 (1): 41–46.

Dewar, Helen. 1997. "Senate Advises Against Emissions Treaty That Lets Developing Nations Pollute." *Washington Post* (July 26): 11.

Digital Equipment Corporation and Business and Environment Massachusetts Institute of Technology Program on Technology. N.d. *Implementing Design for Environment: A Prime*r. Cambridge.

Dowell, Glen, Stuart Hart, and Bernard Yeung. 2000. "Do Corporate Global Environmental Standards Create or Destroy Market Value?" *Management Science* 46: 1059–1074.

Downs, Anthony. 1972. "Up and Down with Ecology: The 'Issue-Attention Cycle.'" *Public Interest* 28 (Summer): 38–50.

Drobny, Neil. 1997. "Environmental Management for the 21st Century." In *Implementing ISO 14000: A Practical, Comprehensive Guide to the ISO 14000 Environmental Management Standards,* edited by T. Tibor and I. Feldman. New York: McGraw-Hill.

Duffy, Robert J. 1997. "Regulatory Oversight in the Clinton Administration." *Presidential Studies Quarterly* 27 (Winter): 71–90.

Eggertsson, Thrainn. 1990. *Economic Behavior and Institutions.* Cambridge: Cambridge University Press.

Ehrenfeld, John R. 1999. "Cultural Structure and the Challenge of Sustainability." In *Better Environmental Decisions: Strategies for Governments, Businesses, and Communities,* edited by K. Sexton, A. A. Marcus, K. W. Easter, and T. D. Burkhardt. Washington, DC: Island.

Eilperin, Juliet. 2005. "EPA Emissions Rule Is Upheld: Judges Back Agency's View on Coal-Fired Plant Upgrades." *Washington Post* (June 25): 8.

Eisner, Marc Allen. 1991. *Antitrust and the Triumph of Economics: Institutions, Expertise, and Policy Change.* Chapel Hill: University of North Carolina Press.

———. 2000a. *From Warfare State to Welfare State: World War I, Compensatory Statebuilding, and the Limits of the Modern Order.* University Park: Pennsylvania State University Press.

———. 2000b. *Regulatory Politics in Transition.* 2nd ed. Baltimore: Johns Hopkins University Press.

Eisner, Marc Allen, Jeff Worsham, and Evan J. Ringquist. 1996. "Crossing the Organizational Void: The Limits of Agency Theory in the Analysis of Political Control." *Governance* 9 (4): 407–428.

———. 2000. *Contemporary Regulatory Policy.* Boulder: Lynne Rienner.

———. 2006. *Contemporary Regulatory Policy.* 2nd ed. Boulder: Lynne Rienner.

Environmental Council of the States. 2001. *State Environmental Agency Contributions to Enforcement and Compliance: A Report to Congress.* Washington, DC.

———. 2005. *Survey of State Support for Performance-Based Environmental Programs and Recommendations for Improved Effectiveness.* Washington, DC.

Environmental Defense. 1997. *Toxic Ignorance: The Continuing Absence of Basic Health Testing for Top-Selling Chemicals in the United States.* New York.

———. 2000. *From Obstacle to Opportunity: How Acid Rain Emissions Trading Is Delivering Cleaner Air.* New York.

———. 2003. "News Release: New Water Pollution Trading Program Lacks Cap to Ensure Effectiveness." New York.

EPA (Environmental Protection Agency). 1978. "Government Ban on Fluorocarbon Gases in Aerosol Products Begins October 15." Washington, DC.

———. 1987. *EPA's Use of Benefit-Cost Analysis, 1981–1986.* Washington, DC.

———. 1995. "Audit Policy: Incentives for Self-Policing." Washington, DC.

———. 1996. *Cleaner Technologies Substitutes Assessment: A Methodology and Resources Guide.* Washington, DC.

———. 1997. *EPA Strategic Plan.* Washington, DC.

———. 1998a. *Chemical Hazard Data Availability Study: What Do We Really Know About the Safety of High Production Volume Chemicals?* Washington, DC.

———. 1998b. "GTE Corrects Violations Through EPA's Self-Disclosure Policy." *Audit Policy Update* 3 (1): 1.

———. 1998c. *Partners for the Environment: A Catalogue of the Agency's Partnership Programs.* Washington, DC.

———. 1999. *Project XL Progress Report: Intel Corporation.* Washington, DC.

———. 2000. "Incentives for Self-Policing: Discovery, Disclosure, Correction and Prevention of Violations." *FRL* 6576–6573 (April 11, 2000).

———. 2001a. *Design for the Environment Program: Partnerships for a Cleaner Future.* Washington, DC.

———. 2001b. *Financing America's Clean Water Since 1987: A Report of Progress and Innovation.* Washington, DC.

———. 2001c. *National Environmental Performance Track: Program Guide.* Washington, DC.

———. 2001d. *The United States Experience with Economic Incentives for Protecting the Environment.* Washington, DC.

———. 2002a. "EPA Proposes to Withdraw Unworkable 2000 TMDL Rule; Continues to Work with Stakeholders to Improve TMDL Implementation on a Watershed Basis." Washington, DC.

———. 2002b. *Myths and Facts About New Source Review Reform.* Washington, DC.

————. 2002c. *U.S. Environmental Protection Agency 2002 Fiscal Year Annual Report*. Washington, DC.

————. 2002d. "United States Environmental Protection Agency Position Statement on Environmental Management Systems." Washington, DC.

————. 2003a. *2003–2008 EPA Strategic Plan: Direction for the Future*. Prepublication copy. Washington, DC.

————. 2003b. *Beyond RCRA: Waste and Materials Management in the Year 2020*. Washington, DC.

————. 2003c. *The Clear Skies Act Technical Support Package*. Washington, DC.

————. 2003d. *FY 2003 Enforcement and Compliance Trends*. Washington, DC.

————. 2003e. *Water Quality Trading Policy*. Washington, DC.

————. 2004a. *Building on the Foundation: Performance Track Second Annual Progress Report*. Washington, DC.

————. 2004b. *Congressional Request on Funding Needs for Non-Federal Superfund Sites*. Washington, DC.

————. 2004c. *EPA's Strategy for Determining the Role of Environmental Management Systems in Regulatory Programs*. Washington, DC.

————. 2004d. *Fiscal Year 2005 Annual Performance Plan*. Washington, DC.

————. 2004e. *FY 2004 End of Year Enforcement & Compliance Assurance Results*. Washington, DC.

————. 2004f. *Resource Conservation Challenge Strategic Plan*. Washington, DC.

————. 2004g. *Status and Future Directions of the High Production Volume Challenge Program*. Washington, DC.

————. 2004h. *Substantial Progress Made, but Further Actions Needed in Implementing Brownfields Program*. Washington, DC.

————. 2005a. *Growth and Renewal: Performance Track Third Annual Progress Report*. Washington, DC.

————. 2005b. *Summary of EPA's 2006 Budget*. Washington, DC.

Eskeland, Gunnar S., and Ann E. Harrison. 1997. "Moving to Greener Pastures? Multinationals and the Pollution Haven Hypothesis." Policy Research Development working paper. Washington, DC: World Bank.

Esposito, John C. 1970. *Vanishing Air: The Ralph Nader Study Group Report on Air Pollution*. New York: Grossman.

Esty, Daniel C. 2001. "A Term's Limits." *Foreign Policy* 126 (September–October): 74–75.

Fahey, D. W. 2003. "Twenty Questions and Answers About the Ozone Layer: Scientific Assessment of Ozone Depletion: 2002." Geneva: World Meteorological Organization.

Farrell, Alex. 1999. "Sustainability and Decision-Making: The EPA's Sustainable Development Challenge Grant Program." *Policy Studies Review* 16 (3–4): 36–74.

Fellmeth, Robert C. 1970. *The Interstate Commerce Omission, the Public Interest, and the ICC: The Ralph Nader Study Group Report on the Interstate Commerce Commission and Transportation*. New York: Grossman.

Fenno, Richard F. 1973. *Congressmen in Committees*. Boston: Little, Brown.

Findley, Chuck, and Lisa Lund. 1999. Correspondence of Chuck Findley, EPA deputy regional administrator, Region X, and Lisa Lund, EPA deputy associate administrator for reinvention, to Michael F. Rosenberger, administrator, city of Portland, Bureau of Water Works. July 1.

Fiorino, Daniel J. 1999. "Rethinking Environmental Regulation: Perspectives on Law and Governance." *Harvard Environmental Law Review* 23: 441–468.

————. 2001. "Environmental Policy as Learning: A New View of an Old Landscape." *Public Administration Review* 61 (3): 322–334.

————. 2004. "Flexibility." In *Environmental Governance Reconsidered: Challenges, Choices, and Opportunities,* edited by R. F. Durant, D. J. Fiorino, and R. O'Leary. Cambridge: MIT Press.

Fischer, Carolyn, Ian Parry, Francisco Aguilar, and Puja Jawahar. 2005. "Corporate Codes of Conduct: Is Common Environmental Content Feasible?" Discussion Paper no. 05-09. Washington, DC: Resources for the Future.

Florida, Richard. 1996. "Lean and Green: The Move to Environmentally Conscious Manufacturing." *California Management Review* 39 (1): 80–105.

Florida, Richard, and Derek Davidson. 2001. "Why Do Firms Adopt Advanced Environmental Practices (and Do They Make a Difference)?" In *Regulation from the Inside: Can Environmental Management Systems Achieve Policy Goals?* edited by C. Coglianese and J. Nash. Washington, DC: Resources for the Future.

Flynn, Barbara B., Sadao Sakakibara, and Roger G. Schroeder. 1995. "Relationship Between JIT and TQM: Practices and Performance." *Academy of Management Journal* 38 (5): 1325–1360.

Fonder, Melanie. 2002. "Enviros Launch Largest Campaign in 10 Years." *The Hill* (February 27): 6.

Foreman, Christopher H., Jr. 1998. *The Promise and Peril of Environmental Justice.* Washington, DC: Brookings Institution.

French, Hilary. 2000. *Vanishing Borders: Protecting the Planet in the Age of Globalization.* New York: Norton.

Friedman, Robert M., and Rosina M. Bierbaum. 2003. "The Bumpy Road to Reduced Carbon Emissions." *Issues in Science and Technology* 19 (4): 55–56, 58.

Friedman, Robert M., Donna Downing, and Elizabeth M. Gunn. 2000. "Environmental Policy Instrument Choice: The Challenge of Competing Goals." *Duke Environmental Law and Policy Forum* 10 (Spring): 327–387.

Furlong, Scott R. 1995. "The 1992 Regulatory Moratorium: Did It Make a Difference?" *Public Administration Review* 55 (3): 254–262.

Fussler, Claude, and Peter James. 1996. *Driving Eco Innovation: A Breakthrough Discipline for Innovation and Sustainability.* London: Pitman.

GAO (General Accounting Office). 1994. *Superfund: Legal Expenses for Cleanup-Related Activities of Major U.S. Corporations.* Washington, DC.

————. 2000. *Water Quality: Identification and Remediation of Polluted Waters Impeded by Data Gaps.* Washington, DC.

Gardiner, David. 1995. Correspondence of David Gardiner, EPA assistant administrator, to Wilbur A. Steger, CONSAD Research Corporation. November 13.

Gelbspan, Ross. 2001. "Bush's Climate Follies." *American Prospect* 12 (13): 11–12.

General Motors. 1998. *1997 General Motors Environmental, Health, and Safety Report.* Detroit.

Gereffi, Gary, Ronnie Garcia-Johnson, and Erika Sasser. 2001. "The NGO-Industrial Complex." *Foreign Policy* 125 (July–August): 56–65.

Glicksman, Robert L. 2004. "The Value of Agency-Forcing Citizen Suits to Enforce Nondiscretionary Duties." *Widener Law Review* 10: 353–394.

Goodland, Robert, and Herman Daly. 1996. "Environmental Sustainability: Universal and Non-Negotiable." *Ecological Applications* 6 (4): 1002–1017.

Goodnow, Frank J. 1900. *Politics and Administration.* New York: Macmillan.

Gouldson, Andrew, and Joseph Murphy. 1998. *Regulatory Realities: The*

Implementation and Impact of Industrial Environmental Regulation. London: Earthscan.

Graedel, T. E., and B. R. Allenby. 1996. *Design for Environment.* Upper Saddle River, NJ: Prentice-Hall.

Gramlich, Edward M. 1998. *A Guide to Benefit-Cost Analysis.* 2nd ed. Prospect Heights, IL: Waveland.

Green, Mark J. 1972. *The Closed Enterprise System: Ralph Nader's Study Group Report on Antitrust Enforcement.* New York: Grossman.

———, ed. 1973. *The Monopoly Makers: Ralph Nader's Study Group Report on Regulation and Competition.* New York: Grossman.

Greer, Jed, and Kerry Bruno. 1996. *Greenwash: The Reality Behind Corporate Environmentalism.* Penang, Malaysia: Third World Network.

Guerra, Antonio. 1997. "The ISO 14001 Registration Process." In *Implementing ISO 14000: A Practical, Comprehensive Guide to the ISO 14000 Environmental Management Standards,* edited by T. Tibor and I. Feldman. New York: McGraw-Hill.

Gugliotta, Guy, and Eric Pianin. 2003. "EPA Withholds Air Pollution Analysis; Senate Plan Found More Effective, Slightly More Costly Than Bush Proposal." *Washington Post* (July 1): A3.

Gunningham, Neil. 1995. "Environment, Self-Regulation, and the Chemical Industry: Assessing Responsible Care." *Law and Policy* 17 (1): 57–109.

Gunningham, Neil, and Joseph Rees. 1997. "Industry Self-Regulation: An Institutional Perspective." *Law and Policy* 19 (4): 363–414.

Haas, Peter M. 1992. "Banning Chlorofluorocarbons: Epistemic Community Efforts to Protect Stratospheric Ozone." *International Organization* 46 (1): 187–224.

Habicht, F. Henry, II. 1992. "EPA Definition of Pollution Prevention." Memorandum from F. Henry Habicht II, EPA deputy administrator. Washington, DC: Environmental Protection Agency.

Haddad, Brent M., and Paul Jefferiss. 1999. "Forging Consensus on National Renewables Policy: The Renewables Portfolio Standard and the National Public Benefits Trust Fund." *Electricity Journal* 12 (2): 68–80.

Hahn, Robert W. 2000. *Reviving Regulatory Reform: A Global Perspective.* Washington, DC: AEI-Brookings Joint Center for Regulatory Studies.

Hahn, Robert W., and Gordon L. Hester. 1989. "Marketable Permits: Lessons for Theory and Practice." *Ecology Law Quarterly* 16: 361–406.

Hamilton, James T. 1995. "Pollution as News: Media and Stock Market Reactions to the Toxics Release Inventory Data." *Journal of Environmental Economics and Management* 28 (1): 98–113.

Harrington, Winston. 2003. "Regulating Industrial Water Pollution in the United States." Discussion Paper no. 03-03. Washington, DC: Resources for the Future.

Harris, Richard A., and Sidney M. Milkis. 1996. *The Politics of Regulatory Change: A Tale of Two Agencies.* 2nd ed. New York: Oxford University Press.

Hart, Stuart L. 1997. "Beyond Greening: Strategies for a Sustainable World." *Harvard Business Review* 75 (1): 66–76.

———. 1999. "Business Decision Making About the Environment: The Challenge of Sustainability." In *Better Environmental Decisions: Strategies for Governments, Businesses, and Communities,* edited by K. Sexton, A. A. Marcus, K. W. Easter, and T. D. Burkhardt. Washington, DC: Island.

Hart, Stuart L., and Gautam Ahuja. 1996. "Does It Pay to Be Green? An Empirical

Examination of the Relationship Between Emission Reduction and Firm Performance." *Business Strategy and the Environment* 5: 30–37.

Hasenclever, Andreas, Peter Mayer, and Volker Rittberger. 1996. "Interests, Power, Knowledge: The Study of International Regimes." *Mershon International Studies Review* 40 (2): 177–228.

Hays, Samuel P. 1978. "Clean Air: From the 1970 Act to the 1977 Amendments." *Duquesne Law Review* 17: 33–66.

Heinrich, Carolyn J., and Laurence E. Lynn, eds. 2001. *Governance and Performance: New Perspectives.* Washington, DC: Georgetown University Press.

Heinzerling, Lisa, and Frank Ackerman. 2002. *Pricing the Priceless: Cost-Benefit Analysis of Environmental Protection.* Washington, DC: Georgetown Environmental Law and Policy Institute.

Hersey, Kevin. 1998. "A Close Look at ISO 14000: The Quest to Improve Environmental Safety." *Professional Safety* 43 (7): 26–29.

Hoffman, Andrew J. 1999. "The Importance of Organizational Change Management for Environmental Decision Making." In *Better Environmental Decisions: Strategies for Governments, Businesses, and Communities,* edited by K. Sexton, A. A. Marcus, K. W. Easter, and T. D. Burkhardt. Washington, DC: Island.

Hofman, Peter. 1998. "Public Participation in Environmental Policy in the Netherlands." *TDRI Quarterly Review* 13 (1): 25–30.

Hollingsworth, J. Rogers, and Robert Boyer. 1997. "Coordination of Economic Actors and Social Systems of Production." In *Contemporary Capitalism: The Embeddedness of Institutions,* edited by J. R. Hollingsworth and R. Boyer. Cambridge: Cambridge University Press.

Hollingsworth, J. Rogers, Philippe C. Schmitter, and Wolfgang Streeck. 1994. "Capitalism, Sectors, Institutions, and Performance." In *Governing Capitalist Economies: Performance and Control of Economic Sectors,* edited by J. R. Hollingsworth, P. C. Schmitter, and W. Streeck. New York: Oxford University Press.

Howard, Jennifer, Jennifer Nash, and John Ehrenfeld. 2000. "Standard or Smokescreen? Implementation of a Voluntary Environmental Code." *California Management Review* 42 (2): 63–82.

Hunter, Natasha. 2002. "Its Clear Skies for Dirty Air: W's Emissions Swapping Plan May Be Dangerous If You Breathe." *American Prospect* 13 (15): 16–18.

Hunter, Susan, and Richard Waterman. 1992. "Determining an Agency's Regulatory Style: How Does the EPA Water Office Enforce the Law?" *Western Political Quarterly* 45: 401–417.

Huntington, Samuel P. 1952. "The Marasmus of the ICC." *Yale Law Journal* 61 (April): 467–509.

Husseini, Ahmad. 2003. "Environmental Achievements of US Administration." *ISO Bulletin* (February 4): 4.

International Chamber of Commerce and World Business Council for Sustainable Development. 1998. "Corporate Management Tools for Sustainable Development." Background document, United Nations Commission on Sustainable Development.

International Council of Chemical Associations. 2002. *Responsible Care Status Report, 2002.* Brussels.

IPCC (Intergovernmental Panel on Climate Change). 1990. *Scientific Assessment of Climate Change: Report of Working Group I.* Cambridge: Cambridge University Press.

———. 1995. *IPCC Second Assessment: Climate Change 1995.* Geneva.

———. 2001. *Summary for Policymakers: A Report of Working Group I of the Intergovernmental Panel on Climate Change.* Geneva.

———. 2003. *Introduction to the Intergovernmental Panel on Climate Change.* Geneva.

ISO (International Organization for Standardization). 1998. *Publicizing Your ISO 9000 or ISO 14000 Certification.* Geneva.

———. 2004. *The ISO Survey of ISO 9000 and ISO 14000 Certificates, Thirteenth Cycle.* Geneva.

Jaffee, Adam B., Steven R. Peterson, Paul R. Portney, and Robert N. Stavins. 1995. "Environmental Regulation and the Competitiveness of U.S. Manufacturing: What Does the Evidence Tell Us?" *Journal of Economic Literature* 33 (1): 132–163.

Janicke, Martin, Manfred Binder, and Harald Mönch. 1997. "'Dirty Industries': Patterns of Change in Industrial Countries." *Environmental and Resource Economics* 9 (4): 467–491.

Janicke, Martin, and Helge Jargens. 2000. "Strategic Environmental Planning and Uncertainty: A Cross-National Comparison of Green Plans in Industrialized Countries." *Policy Studies Journal* 28 (3): 612–632.

Jervis, Robert. 1999. "Realism, Neoliberalism, and Cooperation: Understanding the Debate." *International Security* 24 (1): 42–63.

Jessop, Bob. 1999. "Narrating the Future of the National Economy and the Nation State: Remarks on Remapping Regulation and Reinventing Governance." In *State/Culture: State-Formation After the Cultural Turn,* edited by G. Steinmetz. Ithaca: Cornell University Press.

John, Dewitt, and Lee Paddock. 2004. "Clean Air and the Politics of Coal." *Issues in Science and Technology* 20 (2): 63–70.

Johnson, Catherine W. 1997. "ISO 14000 and Environmental Audits: A Legal Perspective." In *Implementing ISO 14000,* edited by T. Tibor and I. Feldman. New York: McGraw-Hill.

Judis, John B. 2001. "Round Midnight." *American Prospect* 12 (3): 11–12.

Kagan, Robert A., and Lee Axelrad, eds. 2000. *Regulatory Encounters: Multinational Corporations and American Adversarial Legalism.* Berkeley: University of California Press.

Karkkainen, Bradley C. 2001. "Information and Environmental Regulation: TRI and Performance Benchmarking—Precursor to a New Paradigm?" *Georgetown Law Journal* 89 (1): 257–292.

Kelly, E. W. 1987. *Policy and Politics in the United States: The Limits of Localism.* Philadelphia: Temple University Press.

Keohane, Nathaniel O., Richard L. Revesz, and Robert N. Stavins. 1998. "The Choice of Regulatory Instruments in Environmental Policy." *Harvard Environmental Law Review* 22 (1): 313–367.

Keohane, Robert O. 1984. *After Hegemony: Cooperation and Discord in the World Political Economy.* Princeton: Princeton University Press.

Khanna, Madhu, and Rose Q. Anton. 2002. "Corporate Environmental Management: Regulatory and Market Based Incentives." *Land Economics* 78 (4): 539–558.

Kickert, Walter J. M. 1996. "Expansion and Diversification of Public Administration in the Postwar Welfare State: The Case of the Netherlands." *Public Administration Review* 56 (1): 88–94.

King, Andrew A., and Michael J. Lenox. 2000. "Industry Self-Regulation Without

Sanctions: The Chemical Industry's Responsible Care Program." *Academy of Management Journal* 43 (4): 698–712.

Kingdon, John W. 1984. *Agendas, Alternatives, and Public Policies.* Glenview, IL: Scott, Foresman.

Klassen, Robert D., and D. Clay Whybark. 1999. "The Impact of Environmental Technologies on Manufacturing Performance." *Academy of Management Journal* 42 (6): 599–615.

Kolk, Ans. 2000. "Green Reporting." *Harvard Business Review* 78 (1): 15–16.

Kolko, Gabriel. 1963. *The Triumph of Conservatism: A Reinterpretation of American History, 1900–1916.* New York: Free Press.

———. 1965. *Railroads and Regulation, 1877–1916.* Princeton: Princeton University Press.

Konar, Shameek, and Mark A. Cohen. 1997. "Information as Regulation: The Effect of Community Right to Know Laws on Toxic Emissions." *Journal of Environmental Economics and Management* 32 (1): 109–124.

Kopp, Raymond J., Alan J. Krupnick, and Michael Toman. 1997. "Cost-Benefit Analysis and Regulatory Reform: An Assessment of the Science and the Art." Discussion Paper no. 97-19. Washington, DC: Resources for the Future.

Kraft, Michael E. 2002. "Environmental Policy and Politics in the United States." In *Environmental Politics and Policy in Industrialized Countries,* edited by U. Desai. Cambridge: MIT Press.

———. 2003. "Environmental Policy in Congress: From Consensus to Gridlock." In *Environmental Policy: New Directions for the Twenty-First Century,* edited by N. J. Vig and M. E. Kraft. Washington, DC: Congressional Quarterly.

Krasner, Stephen D. 1983. "Regimes and the Limits of Realism: Regimes as Autonomous Variables." In *International Regimes,* edited by S. D. Krasner. Ithaca: Cornell University Press.

Krehbiel, Keith. 1991. *Information and Legislative Organization.* Ann Arbor: University of Michigan Press.

Kriz, Maragaret. 2001a. "Power Struggle." *National Journal* 33 (13): 942–947.

———. 2001b. "Showdown on the North Slope." *National Journal* 33 (9): 634.

La Vina, Antonio G. M., Gretchen Hoff, and Anne Marie DeRose. 2003. "The Outcomes of Johannesburg: Assessing the World Summit on Sustainable Development." *School of Advanced International Affairs (SAIS) Review* 23 (1): 53–70.

Landy, Marc, and Loren Cass. 1997. "U.S. Environmental Regulation in a Competitive World." In *Comparative Disadvantages: Social Regulation and the Global Economy,* edited by P. S. Nivola. Washington, DC: Brookings Institution.

Landy, Marc K., Marc J. Roberts, and Stephen R. Thomas. 1994. *The Environmental Protection Agency: Asking the Wrong Questions, from Nixon to Clinton.* New York: Oxford University Press.

Langniss, Ole, and Ryan Wiser. 2003. "The Renewables Portfolio Standard in Texas: An Early Assessment." *Energy Policy* 31 (6): 527–535.

Lash, Jonathan, and David Buzzelli. 1995. "The President's Council on Sustainable Development." *Environment* 37 (April): 44–45.

Layzer, Judith A. 2002. *The Environmental Case: Translating Values into Policy.* Washington, DC: Congressional Quarterly.

Lei, David, Michael A. Hitt, and Joel Goldhar. 1996. "Advanced Manufacturing Technology: Organizational Design and Strategic Flexibility." *Organization Studies* 17 (3): 501–523.

Levine, Samantha. 2004. "Who'll Stop the Mercury Rain?" *U.S. News & World Report* (April 5): 70–71.

Levinson, D. H., and A. M. Waple. 2004. "State of the Climate in 2003." *Bulletin of the American Meteorological Society* 85 (6): S1–72.

Lewis, Jack. 1985. *The Birth of EPA.* Washington, DC: Environmental Protection Agency.

Lieb, Christoph Martin. 2004. "The Environmental Kuznets Curve and Flow Versus Stock Pollution: The Neglect of Future Damages." *Environmental and Resource Economics* 29 (4): 483–506.

Lindberg, Leon N., and John L. Campbell. 1991. "The State and the Organization of Economic Activity." In *Governance of the American Economy,* edited by J. L. Campbell, J. R. Hollingsworth, and L. N. Lindberg. New York: Cambridge University Press.

Longman, Phillip. 2004. "The Global Baby Bust." *Foreign Affairs* 83 (3): 64–79.

Lotspeich, Richard. 1998. "Comparative Environmental Policy: Market-Type Instruments in Industrialized Capitalist Countries." *Policy Studies Journal* 26 (1): 85–104.

Lynn, Laurence E., Jr., Carolyn J. Heinrich, and Carolyn J. Hill. 2002. *Improving Governance: A New Logic for Empirical Research.* Washington, DC: Georgetown University Press.

Maier, Charles S. 1984. "Preconditions for Corporatism." In *Order and Conflict in Contemporary Capitalism: Studies in the Political Economy of Western European Nations,* edited by J. H. Goldthorpe. Oxford: Clarendon.

March, James G., and Johan P. Olsen. 1989. *Rediscovering Institutions: The Organizational Basis of Politics.* New York: Free Press.

Marcus, Alfred A., Donald A. Geffen, and Ken Sexton. 2002. *Reinventing Environmental Regulation: Lessons from Project XL.* Washington, DC: Resources for the Future.

Margolis, Michael. 2002. "The Impact of Trade on the Environment." Issue Brief no. 02-28. Washington, DC: Resources for the Future.

Matthews, Mary M. 2001. "Cleaning Up Their Acts: Shifts of Environmental and Energy Policies in Pluralist and Corporatist States." *Policy Studies Journal* 29 (3): 478–498.

Mayhew, David R. 1974. *Congress: The Electoral Connection.* New Haven: Yale University Press.

McCloskey, Michael. 1999. "The Emperor Has No Clothes: The Conundrum of Sustainable Development." *Duke Environmental Law and Policy Forum* 9 (2): 153–160.

McConnell, Grant. 1966. *Private Power and American Democracy.* New York: Knopf.

McCraw, Thomas K. 1986. "Mercantilism and the Market: Antecedents of American Industrial Policy." In *The Politics of Industrial Policy,* edited by C. E. Barfield and W. A. Schambra. Washington, DC: American Enterprise Institute.

McGarity, Thomas O. 1991. *Reinventing Rationality: The Role of Regulatory Analysis in the Federal Bureaucracy.* Cambridge: Cambridge University Press.

McGiore, Jean B., Alison Sundgren, and Thomas Schneeweis. 1988. "Corporate Social Responsibility and Firm Financial Performance." *Academy of Management Journal* 31 (4): 854–872.

Mearsheimer, John J. 1994. "The False Promise of International Institutions." *International Security* 19 (3): 5–49.

Melnick, R. Shep. 1983. *Regulation and the Courts: The Case of the Clean Air Act.* Washington, DC: Brookings Institution.

Meyerson, Frederick A. B. 1998. "Population, Carbon Emissions, and Global Warming: The Forgotten Relationship at Kyoto." *Population and Development Review* 24 (1): 115–130.

Micklethwait, John, and Adrian Wooldridge. 2003. *A Future Perfect: The Challenge and Promise of Globalization.* Rev. ed. New York: Random House.

Milbank, Dana. 2001. "Growing Conflict over Presidential Powers; Senate Leaders Ask EPA for Clean Air Documents." *Washington Post* (December 15): A8.

Miller, Alan S. 1989. "Incentives for CFC Substitutes: Lessons for Other Greenhouse Gases." In *Coping with Climate Change: Proceedings of the Second North American Conference on Preparing for Climate Change,* edited by J. C. Topping. Washington DC: Climate Institute.

Miller, Alan, and Mack McFarland. 1996. "The World Responds to Climate Change and Ozone Loss." *Forum for Applied Research and Public Policy* 11 (Summer): 55–63.

Miller, James C., III. 1977. "Lessons of the Economic Impact Statement Program." *Regulation* 1 (4): 16–18.

Mitchell, Ronald B., and Patricia M. Keilbach. 2001. "Situation Structure and Institutional Design: Reciprocity, Coercion, and Exchange." *International Organization* 55 (4): 891–917.

Moe, Terry M. 1989. "The Politics of Bureaucratic Structure." In *Can the Government Govern?* edited by J. E. Chubb and P. E. Peterson. Washington, DC: Brookings Institution.

Molitor, Michael R. 2000. "The United Nations Climate Change Agreements." In *The Global Environment: Institutions, Law, and Policy,* edited by Norman J. Vig and Regina S. Axelrod. Washington, DC: Congressional Quarterly.

Morrisette, Peter M. 1989. "The Evolution of Policy Responses to Stratospheric Ozone Depletion." *Natural Resources Journal* 29: 793–820.

Morriss, Andrew P. 2000. "The Politics of the Clean Air Act." In *Political Environmentalism: Going Behind the Green Curtain,* edited by T. L. Anderson. Stanford: Hoover Institution.

Nash, Jennifer, and John Ehrenfeld. 1999. "Environmental Management Systems and Their Roles in Environmental Policy." Paper presented to the Multi-State Working Group Summit Conference on Environmental Management Systems, November 2–3, Washington, DC.

Nathan, Richard P. 1983. *The Administrative Presidency.* New York: Wiley.

National Advisory Council for Environmental Policy and Technology. 2004. *Final Report of the Superfund Subcommittee of the National Advisory Council for Environmental Policy and Technology.* Washington, DC.

Netherlands Ministry of Housing, Spatial Planning, and the Environment. 2003. *Where There's a Will, There's a World: Working on Sustainability.* The Hague.

Netherlands National Institute for Public Health and the Environment. 2002. *Dutch Environmental Data Compendium.* Bilthoven.

Neustadt, Richard E. 1991. *Presidential Power and the Modern Presidents: The Politics of Leadership from Roosevelt to Reagan.* New York: Free Press.

Nierenberg, Danielle. 2001. "U.S. Environmental Policy: Where Is It Headed?" *World Watch* 14 (4): 12–21.

Nordhaus, William D., and Joseph G. Boyer. 1999. "Requiem for Kyoto: An Economic Analysis of the Kyoto Protocol." Discussion paper. Cowles Foundation, Yale University, New Haven, CT.

OECD (Organization for Economic Cooperation and Development). 1999. *Report by the Environmental Policy Committee on Implementation for the 1996 Recommendation on Improving the Environmental Performance of Governments.* Paris.

Osborne, David, and Ted Gaebler. 1992. *Reinventing Government: How the Entrepreneurial Spirit Is Transforming the Public Sector.* Reading, MA: Addison-Wesley.

Ostrom, Elinor. 1990. *Governing the Commons: The Evolution of Institutions of Collective Action.* Cambridge: Cambridge University Press.

Ottman, Jacquelyn. 1998. "Waste Not: Green Strategies Key to Efficient Products." *Marketing News* (June 22): 12.

Palmer, Karen, and Dallas Burtraw. 2004. "Electricity, Renewables, and Climate Change: Searching for a Cost-Effective Policy." Washington, DC: Resources for the Future.

Palmer, Karen, Dallas Burtraw, and Jhih-Shyang Shih. 2005. *Reducing Emissions from the Electricity Sector: The Costs and Benefits Nationwide and for the Empire State.* Discussion Paper no. 05-23. Washington, DC: Resources for the Future.

Panayotou, T. 1997. "Demystifying the Environmental Kuznets Curve: Turning a Black Box into a Policy Tool." *Environment and Development* 2 (4): 465–484.

Parenteau, Patrick. 2004. "Anything Industry Wants: Environmental Policy Under Bush II." *Duke Environmental Law and Policy Forum* 14 (2): 363–405.

Parson, Edward A. 1991. "Protecting the Ozone Layer: The Evolution and Impact of International Institutions." Cambridge: Harvard University, Kennedy School of Government.

PCSD (President's Council on Sustainable Development). 1996. *Sustainable America: A New Consensus for Prosperity, Opportunity and a Healthy Environment for the Future.* Washington, DC: Government Printing Office.

———. 1999. *Towards a Sustainable America: Advancing Prosperity, Opportunity, and a Healthy Environment for the 21st Century.* Washington, DC: Government Printing Office.

Pianin, Eric. 2003. "EPA to Allow Polluters to Buy Clean Water Credits; Environmental Groups Say Policy Weakens Law." *Washington Post* (January 14): A3.

Pianin, Eric, and Michael Grunwald. 2001. "Bush Plan Shifts Power over Polluters to States; EPA's Enforcement Activities Would Be Scaled Back." *Washington Post* (April 10): A3.

Pianin, Eric, and Guy Gugliotta. 2003. "EPA Chief Whitman to Resign; Former N.J. Governor's Tenure Gets Mixed Reviews." *Washington Post* (May 22): A1.

Pope, Carl. 2003. "Alone in the World." *Sierra* 88 (1): 6–7.

Pope, Carl, and Paul Rauber. 2000. "Why Vote?" *Sierra* 85 (September–October): 32–45.

Porter, Michael E. 1985. *Competitive Advantage: Creating and Sustaining Superior Performance.* New York: Free Press.

Porter, Michael E., and Claus van der Linde. 1995. "Green and Competitive: Ending the Stalemate." *Harvard Business Review* (September–October): 120–134.

Priest, Margot. 1997. "The Privatization of Regulation: Five Models of Self-Regulation." *Ottawa Law Review* 29: 233–288.

Probst, Katherine N., and Diane Sherman. 2004. "Success for Superfund: A New Approach for Keeping Score." Washington, DC: Resources for the Future.

Purvis, Nigel. 2003. "Climate Change Negotiations: A Foreign Policy Perspective." Washington, DC: Brookings Institution.

Rabe, Barry G. 2003. "Power to the States: The Promise and Pitfalls of Decentralization." In *Environmental Policy: New Directions for the Twenty-First Century,* edited by N. J. Vig and M. E. Kraft. Washington, DC: Congressional Quarterly.

Rauch, Jonathan. 1991. "The Regulatory President." *National Journal* 23 (48): 2902–2906.

———. 1999. *Government's End: Why Washington Stopped Working.* New York: PublicAffairs.

Redford, Emmette S. 1954. "The Protection of the Public Interest with Special Reference to Administrative Regulation." *American Political Science Review* 48 (4): 1103–1113.

Reed, Donald J. 1998. "Green Shareholder Value, Hype or Hit?" *Sustainable Enterprise Perspectives.* Washington, DC: World Resources Institute.

Rees, Joseph. 1994. *Hostages of Each Other: The Transformation of Nuclear Safety Since Three Mile Island.* Chicago: University of Chicago Press.

———. 1997. "Development of Communitarian Regulation in the Chemical Industry." *Law and Policy* 19 (4): 477–528.

Reilly, William K. 1992. "Remarks at the Fourth Meeting of the Parties to the Montreal Protocol, Copenhagen." Washington, DC: Environmental Protection Agency.

Reisch, Mark, and David Michael Bearden. 1997. *Superfund Fact Book.* CRS Report for Congress. Washington, DC: Congressional Research Service.

Resources for the Future. 2004. "Legislative Comparison of Multipollutant Proposals S. 366, S. 1844, and S. 843." Washington, DC: Resources for the Future.

Richards, Deanna J., Braden R. Allenby, and Robert A. Frosch. 1994. "The Greening of Industrial Ecosystems: Overview and Perspective." In *The Greening of Industrial Ecosystems,* edited by B. R. Allenby and D. J. Richards. Washington, DC: National Academy Press.

Richards, Kenneth. 2000. "Framing Environmental Policy Instrument Choice." *Duke Environmental Law and Policy Forum* 10 (2): 221–285.

Riker, William H. 1990. "Political Science and Rational Choice." In *Perspectives on Positive Political Economy,* edited by J. E. Alt and K. A. Shepsle. Cambridge: Cambridge University Press.

Ringquist, Evan J. 1993. *Environmental Protection at the State Level: Politics and Progress in Controlling Pollution.* Armonk, NY: Sharpe.

Ritchie, Ingrid, and William Hayes. 1998. *A Guide to the Implementation of the ISO 14000 Series on Environmental Management.* Upper Saddle River, NJ: Prentice Hall.

Rodgers, Kerry E. 1996. "The ISO Environmental Standards Initiative." *New York University Environmental Law Journal* 5: 181–276.

Roht-Arriaza, Naomi. 1995. "Shifting the Point of Regulation: The International Organization for Standardization and Global Lawmaking on Trade and the Environment." *Ecology Law Quarterly* 22: 479–539.

Rondinelli, Dennis A., and Michael A. Berry. 2000. "Environmental Citizenship in Multinational Corporations: Social Responsibility and Sustainable Development." *European Management Journal* 18 (1): 70–84.

Rosenbaum, Walter A. 1998. *Environmental Politics and Policy.* 4th ed. Washington, DC: Congressional Quarterly.

———. 2000. "Escaping the 'Battered Agency Syndrome': EPA's Gamble with Regulatory Reinvention." In *Environmental Policy: New Directions for the Twenty-First Century,* edited by N. J. Vig and M. E. Kraft. Washington, DC: Congressional Quarterly.

Rosenberger, Michael F. 1999. Correspondence of Michael F. Rosenberger, administrator, city of Portland, Bureau of Water Works, to Chuck Findley, EPA deputy regional administrator. April 29.

Ruckelshaus, William D. 1993. "William D. Ruckelshaus: Oral History Interview." Washington, DC: Environmental Protection Agency.

Ruffin, Roy J. 2002. "David Ricardo's Discovery of Comparative Advantage." *History of Political Economy* 34 (4): 727–748.

Russo, Michael, and Paul Fouts. 1997. "A Resource-Based Perspective on Corporate Environmental Performance and Profitability." *Academy of Management Journal* 40 (3): 534–559.

Rutsch, Horst. 2003. "Ensuring Environmental Sustainability: 'Undoing the Damage We Have Caused.'" *UN Chronicle* 39 (4): 50–51.

Sabatier, Paul, and Hank Jenkins-Smith. 1993. *Policy Change and Learning: An Advocacy Coalition Approach.* Boulder: Westview.

Sanders, Elizabeth. 1987. "The Regulatory Surge of the 1970s in Historical Perspective." In *Public Regulation: Perspectives on Institutions and Policies,* edited by E. Bailey. Cambridge: MIT Press.

Schaeffer, Eric. 2002. "Clearing the Air: Why I Quit G. W. Bush's EPA." *Washington Monthly* (July–August): 20–25.

Schaltegger, Stefan, and Frank Figge. 1998. "Environmental Shareholder Value." Study no. 54. Basel: WWZ/Sarasin.

Schattschneider, E. E. 1960. *The Semisovereign People: A Realist's View of Democracy in America.* New York: Holt, Rinehart, and Winston.

Scheberle, Denise. 2004. "Devolution." In *Environmental Governance Reconsidered: Challenges, Choices, and Opportunities,* edited by R. F. Durant, D. J. Fiorino, and R. O'Leary. Cambridge: MIT Press.

Schiffman, Reeva I., B. Tod Delaney, and Scott Fleming. 1997. "ISO 14001 Implementation: Getting Started." In *Implementing ISO 14000: A Practical, Comprehensive Guide to the ISO 14000 Environmental Management Standards,* edited by T. Tibor and I. Feldman. New York: McGraw-Hill.

Schlager, Edella. 2004. "Common-Pool Resource Theory." In *Environmental Governance Reconsidered: Challenges, Choices, and Opportunities,* edited by R. F. Durant, D. J. Fiorino, and R. O'Leary. Cambridge: MIT Press.

Schmidheiny, Stephan, and Federico J. L. Zorraquin. 1996. *Financing Change: The Financial Community, Eco-Efficiency, and Sustainable Development.* Cambridge: MIT Press.

Schmidt, Charles W. 2002. "The Down-to-Earth Summit: Lessening Our Ecological Footprint." *Environmental Health Perspectives* 110 (11): A682–685.

Schneider, Stephen H. 1989. "The Greenhouse Effect: Science and Policy." *Science* 243 (4892): 771–781.

Schot, Johan, and Kurt Fischer. 1993. "Introduction: The Greening of the Industrial Firm." In *Environmental Strategies for Industry: International Perspectives on Research Needs and Policy Implications,* edited by K. Fischer and J. Schot. Washington, DC: Island.

Setlow, Carolyn. 2001. "A Lesson in Pro-Environmental Retailing." *DSN Retailing Today* (August 20): 16.

Shaw, Elizabeth C., and Kali N. Murray. 1999. "Introduction: The Nexus Between

Environmental Justice and Sustainable Development." *Duke Environmental Law and Policy Forum* 9 (2): 147–152.

Shipan, Charles R., and William R. Lowry. 2001. "Environmental Policy and Party Divergence in Congress." *Political Research Quarterly* 54 (2): 245–263.

Sinclair, Darren. 1997. "Self-Regulation Versus Command and Control? Beyond False Dichotomies." *Law and Policy* 19 (4): 529–560.

Sinding, Steven W. 2000. "The Great Population Debates: How Relevant Are They for the 21st Century?" *American Journal of Public Health* 90 (12): 1841–1845.

Siy, Eric, Leo Koziol, and Darcy Rollins. 2001. *The State of the States: Assessing the Capacity of States to Achieve Sustainable Development Through Green Planning.* San Francisco: Resource Renewal Institute.

Skrzycki, Cindy. 2003. "Under Fire, EPA Drops the 'Senior Death Discount.'" *Washington Post* (May 13): 1.

Social Investment Forum. 2003. *2003 Report on Socially Responsible Investing Trends in the United States.* Washington, DC.

Soden, Dennis L., and Brent S. Steel. 1999. "Evaluating the Environmental Presidency." In *The Environmental Presidency,* edited by D. L. Soden. Albany: State University of New York Press.

Speer, Tibbett L. 1997. "Growing the Green Market." *American Demographics* 19 (8): 45–49.

Speir, Jerry. 2001. "EMSs and Tiered Regulation: Getting the Deal Right." In *Regulation from the Inside: Can Environmental Management Systems Achieve Policy Goals?* edited by C. Coglianese and J. Nash. Washington, DC: Resources for the Future.

Spence, Laura J., Ronald Jeurissen, and Robert Rutherfoord. 2000. "Small Business and the Environment in the UK and the Netherlands: Toward Stakeholder Cooperation." *Business Ethics Quarterly* 10 (4): 945–965.

Speth, James Gustave. 2003. "Perspectives on the Johannesburg Summit." *Environment* 45 (1): 24–29.

Sprinz, Detlef, and Tapani Vaahtoranta. 1994. "The Interest-Based Explanation of International Environmental Policy." *International Organization* 48 (1): 77–105.

Starkey, Richard. 1996. "The Standardization of Environmental Management Systems." In *Corporate Environmental Management: Systems and Strategies,* edited by R. Welford. London: Earthscan.

Stauber, John C., and Sheldon Rampton. 1996. "Green PR: Silencing Spring." *Environmental Action Magazine* (January 1): 16.

Stavins, Robert N. 2000. "Experience with Market-Based Environmental Policy Instruments." Discussion Paper no. 01-58. Washington, DC: Resources for the Future.

Steinzor, Rena. 2003. "Testimony Before the Subcommittee on Fisheries, Wildlife, and Water of the U.S. Senate Regarding Implementation of the Clean Water Act." Washington, DC: Center for Progressive Regulation.

Stewart, Richard B. 1975. "The Reformation of American Administrative Law." *Harvard Law Review* 88 (8): 1667–1813.

———. 2001. "A New Generation of Environmental Regulation?" *Capital University Law Review* 29: 21–182.

Stigler, George J. 1971. "The Theory of Economic Regulation." *Bell Journal of Economics and Management Science* 2 (1): 3–21.

Stone, Christopher D. 1974. *Should Trees Have Standing? Toward Legal Rights for Natural Objects.* Los Altos, CA: Kaufman.

Sustainable Forestry Board. 2002. *2002–2004 Edition Sustainable Forestry Intiative (SFI) Program.* Washington, DC: American Forest and Paper Association.

Sutherland, Donald. 2000. "Global Reporting Initiative Aims for High Standards." *Environment News Service* (January 19).

Switzer, Jacqueline Vaughn, and Gary Bryner. 1998. *Environmental Politics: Domestic and Global Dimensions.* 2nd ed. New York: St. Martin's.

Sykes, Alan O. 1995. *Product Standards for Internationally Integrated Goods Markets.* Washington, DC: Brookings Institution.

Tarlock, Dan. 2002. "Sixth Annual Lloyd K. Garrison Lecture on Environmental Law: The Future of Environmental 'Rule of Law' Litigation." *Pace Environmental Law Review* 19: 575–610.

Teske, Paul. 2004. *Regulation in the States.* Washington, DC: Brookings Institution.

Teubner, Gunther, Lindsay Farmer, and Declan Murphy, eds. 1994. *Environmental Law and Ecological Responsibility: The Concept and Practice of Ecological Self-Organization.* New York: Wiley.

Thurber, James A. 1991. *Divided Democracy: Cooperation and Conflict Between the President and Congress.* Washington, DC: Congressional Quarterly.

Tibor, Tom, and Ira Feldman. 1997. "Development of ISO 14000." In *Implementing ISO 14000: A Practical, Comprehensive Guide to the ISO 14000 Environmental Management Standards,* edited by T. Tibor and I. Feldman. New York: McGraw-Hill.

Tietenberg, Tom H. 1990. "Economic Instruments for Environmental Regulation." *Oxford Review of Economic Policy* 6 (1): 17–33.

Tobey, James A. 1990. "The Effects of Domestic Environmental Policies on Patterns of World Trade: An Empirical Test." *Kyklos* 43 (2): 191–209.

Tokar, Brian. 1997. *Earth for Sale: Reclaiming Ecology in the Age of Corporate Greenwash.* Boston: South End.

Train, Russell E. 1976. "Statement at a Public Meeting on Chlorofluorocarbons." Washington, DC: Environmental Protection Agency.

Tucker, Neely, and Michael Grunwald. 2002. "U.S. Court Upholds Pollution Standards; Whitman Says EPA Will Support New Air Quality Rules." *Washington Post* (March 27): A1.

UNEP (United Nations Environment Programme). 2000. *Handbook for the International Treaties for the Protection of the Ozone Layer.* 5th ed. Nairobi.

UNEP and WMO (World Meteorological Organization). 2002. *Scientific Assessment of Ozone Depletion: 2002.* Executive summary, prepared by the Scientific Assessment Panel of the Montreal Protocol on Substances That Deplete the Ozone Layer. Geneva.

United Nations Conference on Environment and Development. 1992. *Agenda 21: Report of the United Nations Conference on Environment and Development.* Rio de Janeiro, June 3–14.

United Nations Framework Convention on Climate Change. 2004. *Information on National Greenhouse Gas Inventory Data from Parties Included in Annex I to the Convention for the Period 1990–2002, Including the Status of Reporting.* Executive summary. Bonn.

United Nations World Commission on Environment and Development. 1987. *Our Common Future.* Oxford: Oxford University Press.

Urstadt, Bryant. 2004. "A Four Year Plague." *Harper's* 81 (3): 308.

Uzumeri, Mustafa V. 1997. "ISO 9000 and Other Metastandards: Principles for Management Practices?" *Academy of Management Executive* 11 (1): 21–36.

van Beers, Cees, and Jeroen C. J. M. van den Bergh. 1997. "An Empirical Multi-Country Analysis of the Impact of Environmental Regulations on Foreign Trade Flows." *Kyklos* 50 (1): 29–46.

van Gestel, Rob. 2005. "Self-Regulation and Environmental Law." *Electronic Journal of Comparative Law* 9 (1). http://www.ejcl.org/91/art91-4.html.

van Vliet, Martijn. 1993. "Environmental Regulation of Business: Options and Constraints for Communicative Governance." In *Modern Governance: New Government-Society Interactions,* edited by J. Kooiman. London: Sage.

Victor, David G. 2004. *Climate Change: Debating America's Policy Options.* New York: Council on Foreign Relations.

Victor, David G., and Eugene B. Skolnikoff. 1999. "Translating Intent into Action." *Environment* (March): 16–23.

Vig, Norm J. 1999. "Governing the International Environment." In *The Global Environment: Institutions, Law, and Policy,* edited by N. J. Vig and R. S. Axelrod. Washington, DC: Congressional Quarterly.

———. 2003. "Presidential Leadership and the Environment." In *Environmental Policy: New Directions for the Twenty-First Century,* edited by N. J. Vig and M. E. Kraft. Washington, DC: Congressional Quarterly.

Vinod, Thomas, and Tamara Belt. 1997. "Growth and the Environment: Allies or Foes?" *Journal of Social, Political, and Economic Studies* 22 (Fall): 327–334.

Viscusi, W. Kip, and Ted Gayer. 2002. "Safety at Any Price?" *Regulation* 25 (3): 54–63.

Vitousek, Peter M. 1994. "Beyond Global Warming: Ecology and Global Change." *Ecology Law Quarterly* 75 (7): 1861–1876.

Vogel, David. 1986. *National Styles of Regulation: Environmental Policy in Great Britain and the United States.* Ithaca: Cornell University Press.

———. 1989. *Fluctuating Fortunes: The Political Power of Business in America.* New York: Basic.

———. 1995. *Trading Up: Consumer and Environmental Regulation in a Global Economy.* Cambridge: Harvard University Press.

von Moltke, Konrad, and Onno Kuik. 1997. *Global Product Chains: Northern Consumers, Southern Producers, and Sustainability.* Amsterdam: Institute for Environmental Studies Vrije Universiteit.

Walt, Stephen M. 1998. "International Relations: One World, Many Theories." *Foreign Policy* 110 (Spring): 29–32, 34–46.

Waterman, Richard W., and Kenneth J. Meier. 1998. "Principal-Agent Models: An Expansion?" *Journal of Public Administration Research and Theory* 8 (2): 173–202.

Weaver, R. Kent, and Bert A. Rockman. 1993a. "Assessing the Effects of Institutions." In *Do Institutions Matter? Government Capabilities in the United States and Abroad,* edited by R. K. Weaver and B. A. Rockman. Washington, DC: Brookings Institution.

———, eds. 1993b. *Do Institutions Matter? Government Capabilities in the United States and Abroad.* Washington, DC: Brookings Institution.

Weinberg, Philip. 2003. "Unbarring the Bar of Justice: Standing in Environmental Suits and the Constitution." *Pace Environmental Law Review* 21: 27–52.

Welford, Richard. 1996. "Life Cycle Assessment." In *Corporate Environmental Management: Systems and Strategies,* edited by R. Welford. London: Earthscan.

Wenzler, Mark. 2002. "Cough! New Rules Under the Clean Air Act Throw Up a Smoke Screen to Hide More Pollution." *Legal Times* (September 2): 36.

West, William F., and Andrew W. Barrett. 1996. "Administrative Clearance Under Clinton." *Presidential Studies Quarterly* 26 (Spring): 71–90.

White, Allen L. 1999. "Sustainability and the Accountable Corporation." *Environment* (October 1): 30–43.

White House Task Force on Recycling. 2001. *Greening the Government: A Guide to Implementing Executive Order 13101.* Washington, DC: Executive Office of the President.

Whitford, Andrew B. 2005. "The Pursuit of Political Control by Multiple Principals." *Journal of Politics* 67 (1): 29–49.

Whitman, Christine Todd. 2005. *It's My Party Too: The Battle for the Heart of the GOP and the Future of America.* New York: Penguin.

Williamson, Oliver E. 1985. *Economic Institutions of Capitalism: Firms, Markets, Relational Contracting.* New York: Free Press.

Wilson, Graham K. 1982. "Why Is There No Corporatism in the United States?" In *Patterns of Corporatist Policy-Making,* edited by G. Lehmbruch and P. C. Schmitter. London: Sage.

———. 1990. *Business and Politics: A Comparative Introduction.* 2nd ed. Chatham, NJ: Chatham House.

Wilson, Woodrow. 1887. "The Study of Administration." *Political Science Quarterly* 2: 197–222.

Worsham, Jeff. 1997. *Other People's Money: Policy Change, Congress, and Bank Regulation.* Boulder: Westview.

WTO (World Trade Organization). 2001. "Doha WTO Ministerial 2001: Ministerial Declaration." Geneva.

———. 2004. *Trade and Environment at the WTO: Background Document.* Geneva.

Yandle, Bruce. 1983. "Bootleggers and Baptists: The Education of a Regulatory Economist." *Regulation* 7 (May–June): 12–16.

———. 1999. "Grasping for the Heavens: 3-D Property Rights and the Global Commons." *Duke Environmental Law and Policy Forum* 10: 13–44.

———. 2000. "Public Choice and the Environment." In *Political Environmentalism: Going Behind the Green Curtain,* edited by T. L. Anderson. Stanford: Hoover Institution.

Yandle, Bruce, Madhusudan Bhattarai, and Maya Vijayaraghavan. 2004. "Environmental Kuznets Curves: A Review of Findings, Methods, and Policy Implications." Research study. Bozeman, MT: Property and Environment Research Center.

Zeckhauser, Richard J., and W. Kip Viscusi. 1990. "Risk Within Reason." *Science* 248 (4955): 559–564.

Zosel, Thomas W. 1995. Correspondence of Thomas W. Zosel, Manager, Environmental Initiatives, 3M, to Lisa Friedman, associate general counsel, EPA. August 28.

Index

About the Book

This comprehensive overview of US environmental regulation—from the inception of the EPA through the George W. Bush administration—goes beyond traditional texts to consider alternatives to the existing regulatory regime, as well as the challenges posed by the global nature of environmental issues.

Thoughtful and evenhanded, *Governing the Environment* covers the full range of topics relevant to our understanding of current environmental policy. Clear, concise chapters move from the context of environmental policy to regulatory design, reform efforts, and notable private sector innovations.

In the process, the author argues that we've taken conventional environmental regulation as far as it can go—that we need to look for alternative ways of governing the environment, involving corporations that have expertise in the areas of technology, products, and markets. But, he cautions, there must be a careful integration of private sector initiatives and public regulation.

A notable feature of the text is an examination of the difficulties inherent in managing global environmental problems. Exploring recent efforts toward global environmental governance in the face of competing economic demands, the final chapter considers the ways in which a system of governance might compensate for the lack of effective international regulatory institutions.

Marc Allen Eisner is Henry Merritt Wriston Chair of Public Policy and professor of government at Wesleyan University, where he also serves as a member of the university's multidisciplinary Environmental Studies Certificate Program. He is author of several books, including *Antitrust and the Triumph of Economics, Regulatory Politics in Transition, The State in the American Political Economy,* and *From Warfare State to Welfare State;* and coauthor of *Contemporary Regulatory Policy,* 2nd ed.